ADAPTING BUILDINGS AND CITIES FOR CLIMATE CHANGE

This book is dedicated to
the late Graeme Robertson

No man is an island, entire of itself...
any man's death diminishes me,
because I am involved in mankind;
and therefore never send to know for whom the bell tolls;
it tolls for thee.

John Donne
Meditation XVII
Written in 1624

ADAPTING BUILDINGS AND CITIES FOR CLIMATE CHANGE

A 21st century survival guide

Sue Roaf

David Crichton and Fergus Nicol

AMSTERDAM • BOSTON • HEIDELBERG • LONDON • NEW YORK • OXFORD
PARIS • SAN DIEGO • SAN FRANCISCO • SINGAPORE • SYDNEY • TOKYO
Architectural Press is an imprint of Elsevier

Architectural Press
An imprint of Elsevier
Linacre House, Jordan Hill, Oxford OX2 8DP
30 Corporate Drive, Burlington, MA 01803

First published 2005
Reprinted 2005

British Library Cataloguing in Publication Data
A catalogue record for this book is available from the British Library

Library of Congress Cataloguing in Publication Data
A catalogue record for this book is available from the Library of Congress

ISBN 0 7506 5911 4

For information on all Architectural Press publications
visit our website at www.architecturalpress.com

Working together to grow
libraries in developing countries

www.elsevier.com | www.bookaid.org | www.sabre.org

ELSEVIER   BOOK AID International   Sabre Foundation

Typeset by Newgen Imaging Systems (P) Ltd, Chennai, India
Printed and bound in Italy

CONTENTS

PREFACE

This is a book I have been thinking about writing for over 25 years.
Every study I have worked on, in those intervening years, has been
a stepping-stone towards this publication on the future of architecture. That journey started in the far distant past, in the ancient villages and cities of Iraq, the cradle of civilization where, through
seven years of excavation, we touched the lives of those people
who ate from the pots, played with the toys, drove the chariots
and built the buildings that we uncovered, not decades or centuries,
but millennia ago, on the once fertile plains, once again scarred by
war. The path to this book passed through nomad tents on tribal
roads, and across vast deserts where families, using little more
energy than twigs to cook on, lived in comfort, and in some cases
luxury, in the extreme climates of what we would see only as barren lands.

Climate in those regions, on the fringes of agriculture, has always
been about survival, but the study that first alerted me to the scale
of the potential impacts of climate change on our lives in the more
temperate lands was one, not on buildings in hot deserts, but on
the ice-houses of Britain. Writing on their history in the 1980s, it
became obvious that this ancient technology, forgotten behind the
miracle of refrigeration, had become climatically obsolete as the
world warmed, and that even very small changes in global temperatures, fractions of a degree, could be responsible for the demise
of a great international industry, if those changes cross a critical
thermal threshold, such as the temperature at which ice melts.

The image below shows how central to our very survival the
simple substance ice is, and what a key role it is playing in the
re-ordering of global climates, oceans and landscapes.

By the late 1980s the growing global problems of ozone depletion and climate change were beginning to be talked of more often.
My concern was growing at the unfairness of the reality – that
people in the developing countries are already dying in large numbers because of climate change, whilst it is those in the West

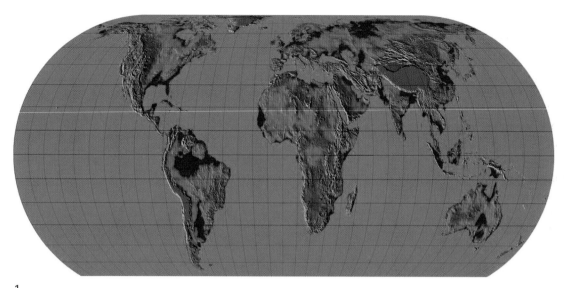

1.

Map of the world showing in red those areas that would be inundated if all the ice caps melted, causing a rise in global sea levels of up to 100 m. (*Source:* Laurence Williams, *An End to Global Warming*, 2002, Pergamon; reproduced with permission)

who are generating the carbon dioxide emissions that are warming the world.

The desire to show that it need not be like this led to the building of the first photovoltaic home in Oxford, in which my family still comfortably resides. This simple building emits only a few hundred kilograms of CO_2 a year instead of five or six thousand and is *more* comfortable than a highly polluting one. We cut down our greenhouse gas emissions to less than 10% of typical emissions with no loss of quality of life. So why isn't everyone doing it? Why are architects building 'glass houses' and windowless plywood 'blobs' instead of the types of solid, resilient, buildings that offer us some hope for survival in the coming decades?

It beats me! But what I do know is that the road that many of us have followed from the Energy Crisis of the 1970s through the growing issues of climate change, fossil fuel depletion and sustainability has led us towards a present, and a future, that is very different from anything that has been before. One can see why many people want to avoid thinking about it – a future where the issue is increasingly not about comfortable concepts like 'sustainability', but about the harsher realities of designing for 'survival'.

If only the global community had acted more firmly in the 1970s when they saw the challenges ahead perhaps we would not now be facing the predicaments around us! The unavoidable truth is that it has been left to our generation alone, of all those that have come before, to face the awesome challenge of redesigning the world to accommodate the new forces of the late fossil fuel age, of dark cities, a world of slowing economic growth, of climate change and an exploding global population.

It is the scale of the catastrophic changing of circumstances around us that makes it difficult to grasp at any heart to the problem. We are still only equipped with the old ways of thinking, that showed us an illusion of a clear path ahead. But many of us who, for years, have been watching, and working so diligently to get a handle on controlling the impacts of late-20th-century development have been surprised by how wrong we got it. We have only been scratching the surface of the problem. In what we once saw as the manageable game of sustainable development, our eyes have been so far off the ball that what follows in this book may be unbelievable, or unpalatable, to many readers. Very few people – remarkable among them being my co-authors David Crichton and Fergus Nicol and the pioneering thinker Edward Mazria[1] – have been able to see beyond the 'business as usual' carrot that draws us, blinkered, on our way.

Few have questioned the horizons, or understood that what we once saw as a single, efficient, road forward to a clean, bright, future has now widened out into a quagmire of complex interrelated forces that urgently require us to think outside the envelope of our own buildings, and above all, to open windows, to embrace a new age of architecture, planning and politics of development. We *can* make a difference, we *can* leave a world fit for our children and grandchildren, but the task is urgent and the task is huge.

Can it be that for decades we have been looking for the warnings in all the wrong places? Because the one thing that is increasingly clear is that the writing is now on the landscape, and the wall.

Sue Roaf

NOTE

1 See http://www.metropolismag.com/html/content_1003/glo/index.html.

ACKNOWLEDGEMENTS

My heartfelt thanks go to my co-authors David Crichton and Fergus Nicol, both of them visionaries in their fields. Also to those who have so generously contributed to the contents of the book – Janet Rudge, Sari Kovats, Fiona Mullins, Aubrey Meyer, Colin Campbell – and all of those who have helped in preparing the contents of this book through thought, word or deed.

For wonderful illustrations I would like to thank: UKCIP, Laurence Williams, Richenda Connell, Jacquelyn Harman, Adrian Arbib, Mark Lynas, Paul Eugene Camp, Aubrey Meyer, Claire Palmer, Fergus Nicol, Jane Matthews, Gavin Kenny, Mary Hancock, David Crichton, Edward Mazria, Rob Wilby, Isaac Meir, Charles Knevitt, Bryan Lynas, Tim Helweg, Rodrigo Leal, John Mardaljevic, Bill Hughes, Colin Campbell, Louis Hellman, Steve Sharples, Cliff Wassman, Janet Rudge, Sari Kovats, Russell C. Schnell, Mark Watham, Alex Hollingsworth, Rosanna Salbashian, Bill Bordass, Catherine Streater, David Infield, Emma Perry and Frances Bergmann.

For helping to make the book happen at Architectural Press I thank: Alison Yates, Catharine Steers, Elaine Leek and Margaret Denley.

We are deeply grateful to the following sponsors for making it possible to have this book in colour – their support has meant a great deal to us. Thank you:

The Ecology Building Society
Friends of the Earth

It should be noted that the particular views expressed in this book are solely those of the authors.

ABOUT THE AUTHORS

Professor Susan Roaf, BA Hons, AADipl, PhD, ARB, FRSA, WCCA, Fellow of the Schumacher Society, Freeman of the City of London

Educated at the University of Manchester, the Architectural Association and Oxford Polytechnic, Professor Roaf completed a Doctorate on the Windcatchers of Yazd, in 1989 after some ten years spent in the Middle East, living in the Desert city of Yazd, with the Beiranvand Tribe in Luristan and excavating for 7 years in Iraq with her husband. Her first book was on the ice-houses of Britain, followed by books on energy efficient buildings, ecohouse design, benchmarks for sustainable buildings, and climate change. She is currently a Professor of Architecture at Oxford Brookes University and is engaged in research and teaching on subjects as diverse as photovoltaics in buildings to eco-tourism in the North West Frontier Province of Pakistan and the technologies of the ancient world. She is a Liberal Democrat Councillor for Wolvercote Ward in Oxford.

Professor David Crichton, MA, FCII, Chartered Insurance Practitioner

David has many years' experience in underwriting and claims at senior management level in the insurance industry and is a Fellow of the Chartered Insurance Institute. He now works as a research consultant for insurers on climate change impacts and is a Visiting Professor at the Benfield Hazard Research Centre at University College London and also at Middlesex University Flood Hazard Research Centre. He is an Honorary Research Fellow at the University of Dundee. He has spoken at insurance and climate change conferences in four continents and has worked with the UN and NATO, as well as with many governments. He is based in Scotland where he has advised more than 20 local authority planning and building control departments on flood insurance issues and he is a member of the Research Committee of the Scottish Building Standards Advisory Committee.

Affiliations:

Benfield Hazard Research Centre, University College London

This is the largest natural hazard academic research centre in Europe, with specialists in all forms of natural disasters. Some of David's recent publications on flood insurance in Britain can be downloaded free from their website at www.benfieldhrc.org.

Middlesex University Flood Hazard Research Centre, London

This is the largest flood hazard research centre in the UK.

University of Dundee

This is arguably the leading centre of expertise in hydrology and flooding in Scotland and has close links with the insurance industry. It is the home of the British Hydrological Society flood events database and the home of the UK National Flood Insurance Claims Database.

Professor Fergus Nicol, BSc

In the sixties and early seventies Fergus Nicol researched building physics and human thermal comfort at the Building Research Establishment and the Human Physiology Unit of the Medical Research Council. He also taught in the Schools of Architecture at the University of Science and Technology in Kumasi Ghana and the Architectural Association in London. After a period at Bookmarks bookshop he returned to teaching and research in 1992.

Fergus is best known for his work in the science of human thermal comfort where he has developed, with Professor Michael Humphreys, the 'adaptive' approach to thermal comfort. He has run a number of projects over the last 10 years funded by the EPSRC and other funding agencies including the DETR, the DfID and a major EU project Smart Controls and Thermal Comfort (SCATS). He works at Oxford Brookes and London Metropolitan Universities. At both Fergus was responsible for developing multi-disciplinary Masters courses in energy efficient and sustainable buildings. Fergus was recently awarded professorships by both universities and is Deputy Director of the Low Energy Architecture Research Unit (LEARN) in the London Metropolitan University.

Fergus is a founder member of the UK thermal comfort Interest Group and is a member of UK and European consultative committees providing advice on comfort issues in building ventilation, and, with Michael Humphreys, is rewriting the new *CIBSE Guide A* section on thermal comfort. He was responsible for the international conference 'Moving comfort standards into the 21st Century' in Windsor, UK in April 2001 attended by most of the international experts in thermal comfort and thermal comfort standards. In October 2002 he co-chaired a conference in Jakarta, Indonesia entitled 'Building research and the sustainability of the built environment in the Tropics'.

1 CLIMATE CHANGE: THE BATTLE BEGINS

WAR IS ALREADY UPON US

The war against climate change pitches mankind against a global threat that vastly eclipses that of terrorism,[1] in battles that have already claimed the lives of hundreds of thousands of ordinary men and women from every continent. Climate change has led us into an era in which war and conflict are endemic,[2] the widespread extinction of species approaches catastrophic proportions,[3] and whole regions and countries will be lost beneath the swelling seas and the expanding deserts of a rapidly warming world. And the really bad news is that 'the world has only one generation, perhaps two, to save itself'.[4]

We all instinctively know, already, that the climate is changing, from the small noticed things like the unseasonable patterns of the flowering of plants, the falling of snow and the growing in strength of the wind and the rain. With this knowledge comes a growing apprehension of danger. Deep down, in quiet moments, we ask ourselves questions that a year or two ago were unthinkable:

- What will I do when the lights do go out?
- Will the house flood next year?
- Will my home get so hot this summer that I won't be able to stay in it?
- How long could I survive in this building without air conditioning?
- Where will we go?
- Will we survive?

This book is written to enable you, the reader, to get a clearer view of the ways in which the climate is changing and how these changes will affect *your* life tomorrow and the day after, in the buildings, settlements and regions in which you live and work.

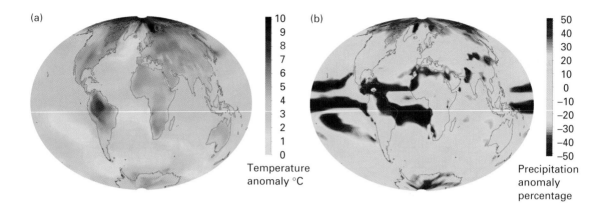

(a) Temperature anomaly °C

(b) Precipitation anomaly percentage

Only by emotionally registering, by consciously taking on board, the scale of the impending global disaster ahead will any of us find the strength to act in time to avert the worst of its impacts.

But not only do we have to act fast, we also have to act *together*. Actions will only be effective if we, all, act together because each of us is 'involved' in the fate of all mankind through the common air that we breathe and the climate we occupy.

As you will see throughout this book, people can apparently be 'familiar' with the excellent science of climate change, and 'know' intellectually the problems that exists, but still fail to engage with them, or act upon that knowledge. We know now that many of the gases we emit from the burning of fossil fuels are altering the climate. Every schoolchild learns, or should learn, how these gases are building up in the upper atmosphere to form an increasingly dense layer that allows solar radiation into the Earth's atmosphere, but as this layer gets denser, it prevents more and more heat from radiating back out into space so warming the lower atmosphere and changing our climate.[6]

The evidence for climate change is growing more alarming each year. The exceptionally hot summer of 2003 warned experts that the pace of this warming is faster than previously envisaged in their worst case scenarios.[7] Yet rather than acting to reduce emissions, many apparently well-meaning and well-informed people appear to act wilfully to make the situation worse in communal acts of 'denial', and nowhere more so than in the built environment. Buildings are responsible for producing over half of all climate change emissions, but year on year, 'modern' buildings become more and more energy-profligate and damaging to all our children's future. Climate change is personal. 'They' are harming 'our' grandchildren.

In London, for instance, where more is known about the urban impacts of climate change than for almost any other city in the world, Labour politicians have heavily promoted the huge

1.1.
Scientists have established that climate change is really happening and can, to an extent, model future climates. Here we see the change in the annual average (a) temperature and (b) precipitation, predicted for the 2080s period, relative to 1961–90, for one climate model, the HadCM3 ensemble-average under an A2 forcing scenario. (*Source: UKCIP02 Scientific Report*,[5] p. 19)

(a)

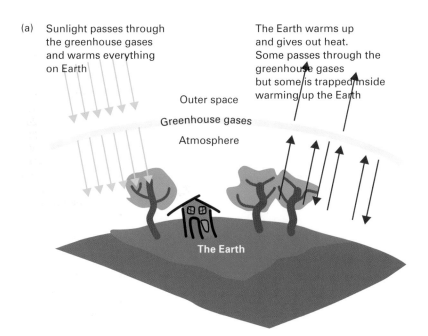

Sunlight passes through the greenhouse gases and warms everything on Earth

The Earth warms up and gives out heat. Some passes through the greenhouse gases but some is trapped inside warming up the Earth

Outer space

Greenhouse gases

Atmosphere

The Earth

(b)

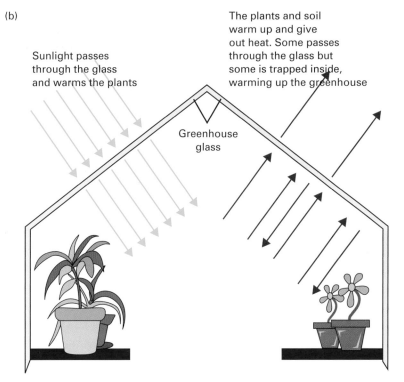

Sunlight passes through the glass and warms the plants

The plants and soil warm up and give out heat. Some passes through the glass but some is trapped inside, warming up the greenhouse

Greenhouse glass

1.2.
The basics of climate change are taught in all British schools and such images of how the greenhouse effect (b) works in relation to the global atmosphere (a) are very familiar to children by the age or 7 or 8. (*Source:* http://www.defra.gov.uk/environment/climatechange/schools/12-16/info/cause.htm)

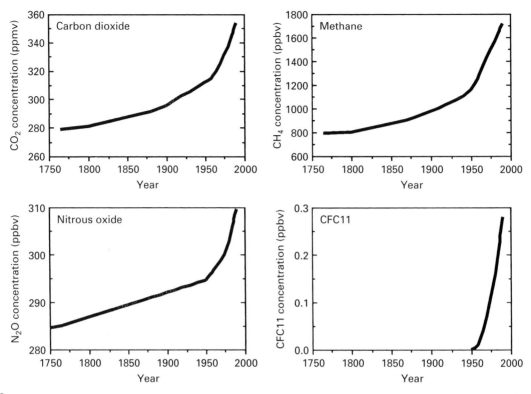

1.3.

In the middle of the 20th century more and more of the world's rapidly growing population bought cars and heated and cooled their buildings, resulting in a rapid increase in concentrations (parts per million/billion by volume) of the major greenhouse gases in the global atmosphere: carbon dioxide (CO_2), nitrous oxide (N_2O), methane (CH_4) and CFC11. (*Source:* Houghton J.T., Jenkins, G.J., Ephraums, J.J (eds) (1990) *Climate Change: The IPCC Scientific Assessment.* Cambridge: Cambridge University Press, p. xvi)

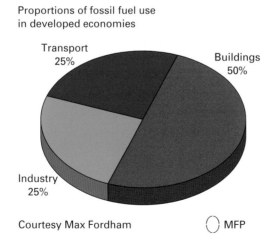

Proportions of fossil fuel use in developed economies

Transport 25%

Buildings 50%

Industry 25%

Courtesy Max Fordham   ◯ MFP

1.4.

Graph showing the relatively large impacts of buildings in the developed world in terms of their emissions of climate change greenhouse gases. (*Source:* MAX Fordham and Partners) developments of the Thames Gateway area, east of the capital, on the coastal flood plains of the River Thames which have periodically flooded throughout history, well before rising sea levels and stronger storm surges increased the risk of loss of life and property to the seas here. Leading architects have even suggested that proposed settlement densities are too low, even when they must 'know' of the risks of putting buildings and people in such locations. Are such architects going to live there themselves? How much do such architects and developers really 'know'?

US President George W. Bush has repeatedly refused to acknowledge that climate change is happening at all, to the extent that by the end of 2003 there were 12 US states suing the US Environmental Protection Agency because of the failure of the US government to take action against climate change. And yet the US administration 'knows' of the dangers of climate change to their own 'homeland' because a Pentagon Report in 2003 told them of the endemic war and conflict the world would face as a result of it.[2] But perhaps Bush reasoned that action on climate change would not be a vote-winner, so how important could it be? How much did the American president actually 'know' and when?

The Australian government continues to be oblivious to the pleas for shelter of the islanders of Tuvalu, where the whole island is more frequently being covered completely by the rising sea every year; and, with impending disaster so close to their own doorsteps, the Australians are refusing not only to give the islanders a refuge but also to consider cut-backs in their own greenhouse gas emissions, on this, the most vulnerable continent on the planet to the impacts of the warming climate. But, perhaps it is too difficult to connect the idea of gas emissions to environmental impacts in remote islands, and it could be understandable that the Australian people feel no sense of responsibility for the plight of the people of Tuvalu. But how much do the Australian people 'know' about the plight of their own sunburnt country in a changing climate?

Should the word 'know' here be replaced, perhaps, with 'care'?

No wonder that so many people today feel that 'it's a mad world', but why? Surely we are a rational species? Perhaps it all has to do with the actual process of changing, the extent and speed of the required changes, and the costs and risks of acting, or not acting, to make those changes happen.

J.K. Galbraith noted in 1958 that 'conventional wisdom' generally makes people indisposed to change their minds and reminds readers of John Maynard Keynes' most famous saying:[8]

Conventional wisdom protects the continuity in social thought and action. But there are also grave drawbacks and even dangers in a system of thought which by its very nature and design avoids accommodation to circumstances until change is dramatically forced upon it . . . the rule of ideas is only powerful in a world that does not change. Ideas are inherently conservative. They yield not to attack of other ideas but to the massive onslaught of circumstances with which they cannot contend.

We are faced now with the massive onslaught of the circumstances of climate change. This book describes some of those circumstances in relation to buildings, settlements and lifestyles of this, and future decades. As you read on it will become clearer how very difficult, if not impossible, we will find it to contend with the impacts of climate change, to meet head on the challenges of changing 'social thought and action', and to re-direct the super-tanker of conventional wisdom.

That is why you, the reader, are important, and why this book has been written to make you 'disposed to change your mind', and in turn change the minds of those in your circle of influence, and those in theirs, and so on until the ripple grows to be a tidal wave of change in the attitudes of our society. And though none of us wants it, and we may wish that we lived in different times, it is the responsibility of each and every one of our generation, and ours alone in the whole history of human kind, to take up arms in this battle for our very survival.

But why has it taken us so long to act? The Climate War is already upon us. How did it come to this?

THE ENEMY WAS SIGHTED LONG AGO

The possibility that the climate could be changing was first identified as far back as the 1960s, and the battle against climate change, and its main contributory gas, CO_2, began.

Physical measurements of global CO_2 emissions have been taken since the 1950s.[9] The Mauna Loa atmospheric CO_2 measurements constitute the longest continuous record of atmospheric CO_2 concentrations available in the world. The Mauna Loa site, on the island of Hawaii, is considered one of the most favourable locations for measuring undisturbed air because possible local influences of vegetation or human activities on atmospheric CO_2 concentrations are minimal and any influences from volcanic vents may be excluded from the records.

The methods and equipment used to obtain these measurements have remained essentially unchanged during the 50-year monitoring programme. Because of the favourable site location, continuous monitoring, and careful selection and scrutiny of the data, the Mauna Loa record is considered to be a precise record and a reliable indicator of the regional trend in the concentrations

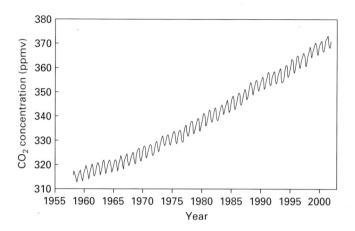

1.5.
The Mauna Loa carbon dioxide record, 1958–2002. (*Source:* Climate Monitoring and Diagnostics Laboratory of the US National Oceanic and Atmospheric Administration, Mauna Loa, Hawaii)

of atmospheric CO_2 in the middle layers of the troposphere. The record shows an 18% increase in the mean annual concentration, from 315.98 parts per million by volume (ppmv) of dry air in 1959 to 372.95 ppmv in 2002. The 1997–98 increase in the annual growth rate of 2.87 ppmv represents the largest single yearly jump since the Mauna Loa record began in 1958.

Such data are used to inform and validate the computer models of the climate[10] which have been used to depict and predict former, current and future climates right down to a resolution of fifty, and now even five, kilometre squares.[11] Such models have provided sufficiently credible evidence, where, for instance, predicted temperatures resemble closely temperatures experienced, for the virtually universal consensus amongst internationally respected scientists and meteorologists that increasing atmospheric concentrations of carbon dioxide, and other gases, with significant absorptivity in the far infra-red, 'the greenhouse gases', have already led to significant changes in the climate of the world with far-reaching implications for everyone on this planet.[12]

It was the scientists who charted, and modelled, the first manifestations of the enemy that threatens our species, but issues such as the changing climate, the loss of biodiversity, terrestrial and atmospheric pollution, and resource depletion, are only the standards of the enemy, caught flying in the wind. What the intellectuals, economists and politicians did was to identify the real enemy in our ecosystem – ourselves.

THE WARNING IS SOUNDED

The global environmental trumpet was sounded for the first time, warning of the enormity of the problems we face, at the first general meeting of the Club of Rome in 1970. The meeting was convened to discuss the state of the world and the development of a computer model of world '*problematique*', to include issues with global dimensions such as population, resources and environment.[13]

In 1970 and 1971, the first large-scale modelling studies of global environmental conditions were actually created, both prepared as input to the 1972 UN Conference on the Human Environment, and both noting the possibility of 'inadvertent climate modification'. The Study of Critical Environmental Problems (SCEP) focused on pollution-induced 'changes in climate, ocean ecology, or in large terrestrial ecosystems'. It cited the global climate models as 'indispensable' in the study of possible anthropogenic climate change.

In 1971 the influential *Study of Man's Impact on the Climate* (SMIC)[14] also endorsed the climate models. Both SCEP and SMIC recommended a major initiative in global data collection, new international measurement standards for environmental data, and the integration of existing programs to form a global monitoring network. These reports are widely cited as the originators of public policy interest in anthropogenic climate change and all these early studies predict 'overshoot and collapse'.

By the time that Edward Goldsmith and four colleagues published their seminal book *A Blueprint for Survival*[15] in 1972, climate change had been woven into the fabric of wider environmental concerns, even by non-experts in the climate field, such as these authors. The book contained a general plea for the application of ecological common sense in the face of mounting evidence of the approaching global environmental crisis.

The Blueprint demanded a radical change in our approach to the environment, necessary if we are indeed to avoid 'undermining the very foundations of survival' for our species and the planet, citing the rise in global population, the increase in per capita consumption, disruption to ecosystems and depletion of resources at a rate that was not supportable. These trends, they estimated, would inevitably lead to a collapse in society if nothing was done about it. They, interestingly, foretold that politicians would tend to act to exacerbate the problems rather than act to solve them:

At times of great distress and social chaos, it is more than probable that governments will fall into the hands of reckless and unscrupulous elements, who will not hesitate to threaten neighbouring governments with attack, if they need to wrest from them a larger share of the world's vanishing resources.[16]

The book was, however, largely concerned with the impacts of over-exploitation of the Earth's resources, the underlying problem that lies at the very root of our dilemma today. It provides excellent benchmarks against which we can measure the extent to which our species has effectively degraded the natural capital of our planet and polluted its ecosystems. But the authors also mention, in a couple of paragraphs, the potential for CO_2 emissions to lead to significant climate change:

The CO_2 content of the atmosphere is increasing at a rate of 0.2 per cent per year since 1958. One can project, on the basis of these trends, an 18 per cent increase by the year 2000, i.e. from 320 ppmm to 379 ppmm. SCEP considers that this might increase temperature of the earth by 0.5 °C. A doubling of CO_2 might increase mean annual surface temperatures by 2 °C.

They were subsequently proved to be very close to the actual recorded warming between 1947 and 1997 of between 0.25 and 0.5 °C.

In the early 1970s, several other large-scale atmospheric issues came to the attention of the general public. Notable among these were acid rain, upper-atmospheric pollution problems raised by supersonic transport and stratospheric ozone depletion. What is so difficult to grapple with is the issue of who exactly is the invisible enemy in this war, where are they, who owns the problem and how does one fight against air?

FIRST ENCOUNTERS

While the scientists of the world have long been wrestling with the theoretical problem of climate change and resource depletion, for the general public the first of the 'environmental shocks' that brought home the reality that the 20th century dreams of infinite cheap energy and limitless resources were unrealistic was the Energy Crisis of the mid-1970s. With it came the dawning realization that oil, the magic energy source from which the wealth and enjoyment of nations was built, of which every barrel can do the same 'work' as 540 man hours of effort,[17] would one day run out. Futurologists then claimed we only had 30 years of oil left, a prediction that has proved to be, perhaps, less than half right, but globally, people started counting the barrels, and comparing them to the available reserves, and understandably, investing in renewable energy programmes.

The first public blow had been struck; mankind was perceived to be vulnerable and, by now, officially engaged in a battle, not against the air, but against their own fossil fuel dependency and time, two equally powerful adversaries. And the richest nations, ironically, became the most vulnerable.

THE WEAPONS ARE HONED

In 1971 SMIC had recommended that a major initiative in global data collection, new international measurement standards for environmental data, and the integration of existing programs to form a global monitoring network should be developed. The ozone challenge provided the perfect opportunity to see how effectively mankind, communally, could respond to what appeared to be a rapidly developing, global, catastrophe.

Ground-based measurements of ozone were first started in 1956, at Halley Bay, Antarctica. Satellite measurements of ozone started in the early 1970s, but the first comprehensive worldwide measurements started in 1978 with the Nimbus-7 satellite. In addition to the physical measurements, in 1974 M.J. Molina and F.S. Rowland published a laboratory study[18] demonstrating the ability of CFCs to catalytically break down ozone in the presence of high frequency UV light. Further studies estimated that the ozone layer would be depleted by CFCs by about 7% within 60 years.

Based on the recommendations of such studies, the United States banned CFCs in aerosol sprays in 1978, showing a level of real leadership at this stage, that spoke of the courage of the then US administration. Slowly, various nations agreed to ban CFCs in aerosols but industry fought the banning of valuable CFCs in other applications. A large shock was needed to motivate the world to get serious about phasing out CFCs and that shock came in a 1985 field study by Farman, Gardiner and Shanklin[19] that summarized data that had been collected by the British Antarctic Survey showing that ozone levels had dropped to 10% below the normal January levels for Antarctica.

The severity, and rate, of the global ozone depletion spurred the United Nations to sponsor a resolution called the Montreal Protocol that was originally signed in 1987, based on negotiations started between European-Scandinavian countries and the United States over CFCs in aerosol sprays in 1983. The protocol went through a series of revisions, each one named after the city where the revision committee met, as new information from science and industry has become available. The meeting in Copenhagen in November 1992 laid down the most stringent phase-out schedule of CFCs for the world to date; and was signed by over 100 nations representing 95% of the world's current CFC consumption. Trade sanctions on CFCs, halocarbons and products containing them, were imposed as of April 1993 on nations not signing the protocol, and in May 1993 this ban was extended to the export of halocarbon solvents such as methyl chloride and carbon tetrachloride. This protocol laid out a schedule for the phase-out of CFCs and related halocarbons by the year 2030. An additional impact of the protocol was to mandate the sharing of technology between countries in order to speed the replacement and recycling of CFCs.

In 1988, Sweden was the first country to legislate the complete phase-out of CFCs, with a scheduled phase-out in all new goods by 1994. In March 1989 environmental ministers of the EEC announced a total phase-out of CFCs in Europe by the year 2000.[20] What the ozone problem demonstrated, to the world, is that when faced with a challenge as large as that of the stratospheric ozone problem, the global community has the science, the strategy, the will and the fiscal, legal and statutory mechanisms to contain that problem. It provided a precedent study for the larger challenge of containing climate change. It does offer some hope that we can act communally, to maximize our chances of survival.

On 5 August 2003, ozone values over Antarctica[21] were already below 200 DU or Dobson Units,[22] with an ozone hole affecting most of the continent, showing an unprecedented spread of the hole. Temperatures in the ozone layer were low enough for polar stratospheric clouds to have formed over the continent, further deepening the hole.

THE COUNCIL OF WAR MEETS[23]

By the mid 1980s, the simulated predictions of the scientists on the warming climate began to demonstrate a close approximation to what was actually happening in the measured record, with clear evidence of increasing temperatures and the frequency and intensity of extreme weather events. The sheer scale of the problems humanity, and the planet, might face if, indeed, the climate was changing more than its natural variability would allow, began to manifest themselves, in the dollars spent in insurance payouts on

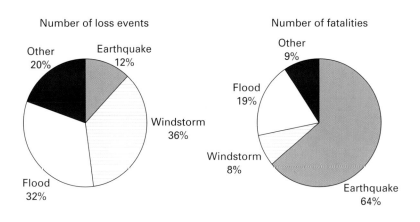

1.6.
Related number of insurance loss events and related fatalities by event types and number of fatalities in 2001. (*Source:* Munich Re, *Topics: Annual Review of Natural Catastrophes 2001*; for the 2002 review see: http://www.munichre.com/pdf/topics_2002_e.pdf) Such figures underestimate climate-related deaths, as reported by other sources.

climate events, the numbers killed in climate-related events and the movement of species and deserts across the face of the globe.

In 1988, at the behest of national governments from around the world, the United Nations Environment Programme and the World Meteorological Organization, by now the 'War Council' leaders, established the Intergovernmental Panel on Climate Change (IPCC),[24] consisting of hundreds of leading scientists and experts on global warming. The Panel was asked to assess the state of scientific knowledge concerning climate change, evaluate its potential environmental and socio-economic impacts, and formulate realistic strategies to deal with the problem.

Two years later, in 1990, the IPCC published a report concluding that the growing accumulation of human-made greenhouse gases in the atmosphere would 'enhance the greenhouse effect, resulting, on average, in an additional warming of the Earth's surface' by the next century, with continued temperature increases thereafter unless measures were adopted to limit the emissions of these gases. In 1992, at the Earth Summit in Rio de Janeiro, the United Nations Framework Convention on Climate Change (UNFCCC)[25] was adopted. The treaty called for industrialized countries to take the first step to prevent 'dangerous anthropogenic interference' with the climate by voluntarily reducing their emissions to 1990 levels by the year 2000. These voluntary measures were not effective, however, and the majority of the nations around the world are now emitting more greenhouse gases than ever before.

Since Rio, there have been nine follow-up COP meetings (Conference of Parties) to try to establish agreements on exactly how emissions and impacts are going to be measured, and how to manage and programme the targets and tools used in the negotiations. On 11 December 1997, at the conclusion of COP-3 in Kyoto, Japan, more than 150 nations adopted the Kyoto Protocol. This unprecedented treaty committed industrialized nations to make legally binding reductions in emissions of six greenhouse gases:

- carbon dioxide
- methane
- nitrous oxide
- hydrofluorocarbons (HFCs)
- perfluorocarbons (PFCs)
- sulphur hexafluoride (SF6)

The called-for reductions varied from country to country, but would cut emissions by an average of about 5% below 1990 levels by the period 2008–12. The United States agreed to reductions of 7%, Japan to reductions of 6% and the members of the European Union to joint reductions of 8%. Key to the US agreement to such a relatively ambitious target was a concurrent agreement that a system of emissions trading among industrialized countries be established, by which nations with binding limits could buy and sell, among themselves, the right to release greenhouse gases.

Much has happened since then, but by 12 August 2003, 84 Parties had signed, including Canada, and 113 Parties have ratified or acceded to the Kyoto Protocol.[26] In December 2003, COP9 was held in Milan, to discuss the tricky issue of carbon sinks and emissions trading, and how to incorporate them in the global targets for the Protocol, an increasingly central issue as many countries attempt to avoid the need to make deep cuts in their own

Box 1.1 Carbon trading (*by Fiona Mullins*)

The United Nations Framework Convention on Climate Change (UNFCCC),[i] the Kyoto Protocol and emerging greenhouse gas emissions trading schemes are based on calculations of tonnages of each greenhouse gas (CO_2, CH_4, N_2O, HFCs, PFCs, SF_6). National greenhouse gas inventories of emissions are calculated and reported for UNFCCC compliance (and for future compliance with the Kyoto Protocol if it enters into force). The inventories are reported both in the tonnages of the actual gases (CO_2, CH_4, N_2O, HFCs, PFCs, SF_6) and also aggregated as a total CO_2 equivalent number. Each metric tonne of non-CO_2 gas is converted to CO_2 equivalents using a global warming potential number.

Greenhouse gas quantities are normally expressed in CO_2 equivalent units (CO_2e). Because each gas has a different impact on global warming, each non CO_2 gas is multiplied by a Global Warming Potential (GWP) which reflects its impact relative to CO_2. The input data to this calculation are the tonnages emitted of each greenhouse gas, but the totals are reported in tonnes of CO_2 equivalent. For example each tonne of CH_4 is equivalent to 21 times a tonne of CO_2 because that is the standard metric used to approximate the effect of a tonne of CH_4 in the atmosphere compared to a tonne of CO_2 over a 100 year timeframe.

Emissions trading schemes for greenhouse gases use this same calculation methodology. For the UK emissions trading scheme, all greenhouse gases are potentially included, with some companies bringing N_2O and HFCs into the scheme as well as CO_2. The non-CO_2 units are translated into CO_2 equivalents for reporting and compliance purposes. For the EU emissions trading scheme, only CO_2 emissions are included in the first phase (2005–08) so the only relevant unit is metric tonnes of CO_2. Other gases may be added later as monitoring of them improves.

[i] See http://unfccc.int/index.html.

greenhouse gas emission inventories by investing in cheap 'carbon sinks' abroad.

AGENDA 21: THE ARMY IS FORMED

The world has responded to the global environmental challenges it faces diligently, it has put the necessary science and intelligence in place to understand the problem and it has developed the programmes to tackle the identified challenges. It has also built up the armies needed to fight the war with an implementation framework designed to effect the necessary changes and, importantly, to build the capacity individuals and communities around the world need to make sure those changes happen. This process started at Rio.

In 1992, the Earth Summit in Rio de Janeiro, properly titled the 'United Nations Conference of Development and the Environment', was profoundly influential. Twenty years after the first global environmental conference in 1972 in Sweden, the United Nations sought to help governments rethink economic development and find ways to halt the destruction of irreplaceable natural resources and pollution of the planet.[27] One hundred and eight heads of state were represented and the documents it produced included the Rio Declaration on Environment and Development, Agenda 21, the Framework Convention on Climate Change, and the Convention on Biological Diversity. Although these documents have not all achieved universal ratification, they have served as blueprints for the implementation of important sustainable development initiatives.

The Summit's message – that nothing less than a transformation of our attitudes and behaviour would bring about the necessary changes (harking back to Goldsmith's Blueprint of 1972) – was transmitted by almost 10 000 on-site journalists and heard by millions around the world. The message reflected the complexity of the problems faced. Governments recognized the need to redirect international and national programmes and policies, in light of a 'grand survival plan' to ensure that all economic decisions fully took into account the environmental impacts of their actions, establishing for the first time in the context of international law, acceptance of 'the polluter pays principal'. The Rio Declaration set forth 27 universally applicable principles of sustainable development within which important themes were:

- Patterns of production: particularly the production of toxic components, such as lead in gasoline, or poisonous waste, many of which are major contributors to greenhouse gas emissions.
- Alternative sources of energy: to replace the use of fossil fuels which are linked to global climate change.

- A new reliance on public transportation systems: emphasized in order to reduce vehicle emissions, congestion in cities and the health problems caused by polluted air and smog. Transport emissions are a major contributor to greenhouse gas emissions.
- The growing scarcity of water: a major issue which is linked to a warmer climate as well as to increasing population and pollution.

The two-week Earth Summit in Rio was the climax of a sophisticated process, begun in December 1989, of planning, education and negotiations among all member states of the United Nations, leading to the adoption of Agenda 21, a wide-ranging blueprint for action to achieve sustainable development worldwide. Although Agenda 21 had been weakened by compromise and negotiation, it was still the most comprehensive and potentially effective programme of action ever sanctioned by the international community.

Much of the success of Agenda 21 has been derived from the training on environmental issues, instilled within its delivery, to the army of workers it has enlisted in the war on environmental degradation and climate change, from local council employees to heads of state. These forces have been armed, through the Agenda 21 process, with the units and measures, tools and methods, indicators and benchmarks that enable the most ordinary of people to be part of the most extraordinary monitoring project ever seen, the measuring of the rates and extent of the degradation of the planet on which we depend for our very survival. For, only by measuring the rates and extent of that degradation has it been possible to understand the risks we actually do face, and develop strategies to mitigate and avert them.

If one, simplistically, thinks of the climate change issue in terms of a war, then in overall command is the UN and its related

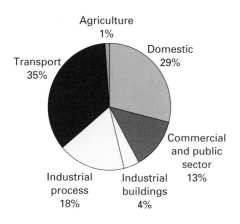

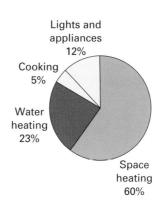

1.7.
Total UK delivered energy consumption by sector (*left*) and carbon emissions from building by source (*right*). (*Source:* Pout, C.H., MacKenzie, F. and Bettle, R. (2002) *Carbon Dioxide Emission from Non-domestic Buildings: 2000 and Beyond.* Watford: Building Research Establishment and Department for Environment, Food and Rural Affairs, p.10)

organizations. Beneath it are the services represented by global treaties, gathered under banners such as Climate Change, Health, Poverty and Biodiversity, within which the laws, regulations and guidelines targeted at specific aspects of the global problem are developed. The IPCC and the WHO (World Health Organization) are definitely embedded in the Intelligence Unit at HQ, while Agenda 21 is responsible for the marshalling and training of the massed ranks of the forces. Nations act rather like battalion leaders commanding significant forces, under sectoral units such as transport, the environment and education. It is perhaps possible to compare other big players such as the World Trade Organization to parallel armies, acting, or not as the case may be, alongside the UN in its fight against climate change.

Within any army there are rogue commanders and infiltrators of the opposing forces who, for reasons of ignorance, convenience, malice or personal profit, attempt to impede the progress of the forces,[28] but no doubt, as the risks escalate, any restraint with which such counter forces are dealt will decrease as the gloves come off. Internal fighting will break out and the obvious growing tensions between lobby groups will flare up. A case in point are the interests of the mining and agricultural sectors of Australia where the dominant coal industry has been able to protect their group interests, the selling of coal, against the weaker farmers' lobby who stand to lose everything as the great 'sunburnt country' gets browner.

Similarly, in the United States the oil lobby funds much government thinking on environmental issues while the farmers of the Mid-West who are slowly losing their lands to the droughts, floods and hurricanes, currently find it less easy to get a fair hearing at the top table in Washington. It is now happening that such minorities are turning to the law for recompense, just as those who were harmed by the knowing and malicious actions of the tobacco barons and the asbestos industry have recently won such major class actions in America.[29] It is certainly the case that in many places on the earth the water wars between nations and interest groups have begun, and the parties are also resorting to law to get justice in the face of environmental disputes.[30]

THE BATTLE RAGES

The battle, on many fronts, is getting more and more heated as the climate warms. The world is hotter now than it has been at any time in the past 2000 years. A recent study reconstructing the Earth's climate over the past 200 years has shown that at no time has it been warmer than the present and that from 1980 onwards

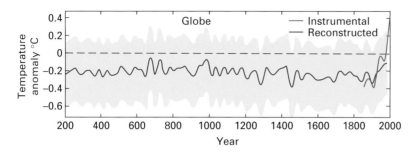

1.8.
Reconstructed global temperature anomaly (based on 1961–90 instrumental reference period), adapted from Mann and Jones[31])

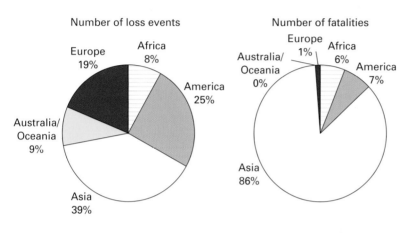

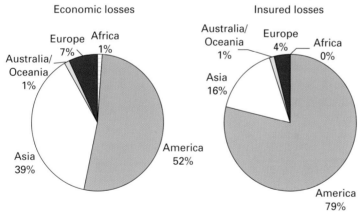

1.9.
Payouts by the insurance industry for natural disasters by geographical region. (*Source:* Munich Re, *Topics: Annual Review of Natural Catastrophes 2001*, see: http://www.munichre.com/pdf/topics_2002_e.pdf)

is clearly the warmest period in the past 200 years,[31] with 2003 becoming the third hottest year on record.

The increase in the climate change impact on the economy is well reflected in the magnitude and related costs for extreme climate events – up to 80% of all payouts by value – to the international insurance industry.[32]

In July 2003 Sir John Houghton, former Chairman of the International Panel on Climate Change, warned the British public, in an article in the *Guardian* newspaper, that global warming was now a real Weapon of Mass Destruction,[33] wielded by man himself:

The World Meteorological Organisation warned in July 2003 that extreme weather events already seemed to be becoming more frequent as a result [of global warming]. The US mainland was struck by 562 tornados in May (which incidentally saw the highest land temperatures globally since records began in 1880), killing 41 people. The developing world is the hardest hit: extremes of climate tend to be more intense at low latitudes and poorer countries are less able to cope with disasters. Pre-monsoon temperatures in India reached a blistering 49 °C (120 °F)–50 °C (9 °F) above normal. Once this killer heat wave began to abate 1500 people were dead. While none can ascribe a single weather event to climate change with any degree of scientific certainty, higher maximum temperatures are one of the most predictable impacts of accelerated global warming ...

TARGET LOCK-ON IS PROVING DIFFICULT

It is unlikely that the Kyoto Protocol's target of cutting the developed world's emissions by 5% from their 1990 levels by 2012 will be met. COP9 delegates in Milan in December 2003 were informed that, according to the latest projections, rather than approaching the target of 5% reductions by 2010 the greenhouse gas emissions from industrialized nations could have risen 17% by 2010 compared with 1990.[34]

The main policy item on the agenda in Milan was how the Protocol accounts for forestry. The Protocol's Clean Development Mechanism allows developed nations to invest in clean technologies in developing countries and offset the resulting emissions reductions against their own targets.

Countries are still arguing over the criteria for including forestry projects in this equation, and how to measure their effects. Many non-governmental organizations are uneasy about the importance of 'carbon sinks' in the overall balance, because it is an increasingly widely held belief that trees are temporary, and should not be on a par with reduced emissions; that there is no long-term way of guaranteeing that carbon stays locked up in a tree and sink projects are not a viable alternative to emission cuts,[35] regardless of the obvious convenience of being able to sponsor cheap planting projects at home and in the developing world rather than tackling the very pressing problems of how to reduce emissions at home. Wealth has always been traditionally associated with high energy consumption: the wealthier a country the more they consume.

In December 2003 the European Commission announced that 13 of the 15 EU member countries were not on target to meet their 1997 Kyoto emissions reductions targets of 8% on 1990 levels by

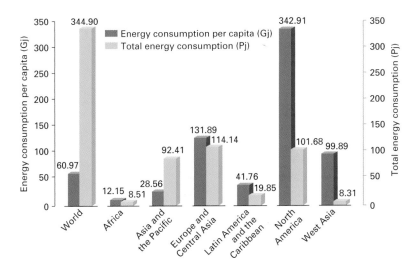

1.10.
Total and per capita energy consumption 1995 by region. (*Source:* http://www.unep.org/geo2000/english/figures.htm)

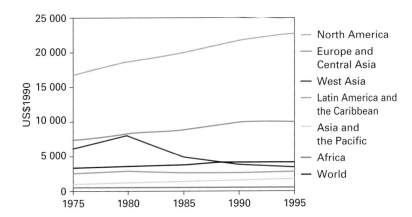

1.11.
Gross Domestic Product per capita 1995 by region. One of the problems faced is that the wealth of nations is directly related to their emissions in the tradition analyses of the trends in the 20th century economy. This will change radically with the new predicted clean economies of the 21st century in which high emissions per capita will be a sign of poverty. (*Source:* http://www.unep.org/geo2000/english/figures.htm)

2010. Only Sweden (by 3.3%) and Britain (by 1.4%) are set to meet the targets. As a whole the EU would only reduce the emissions by 0.5% with existing policies. Spain will undershoot the target by 33.3% and Ireland by 26.8%. Carbon dioxide emissions from cars and trucks in Europe were the main culprit and continued to rise.[36] The United States continues to stonewall. Russia has been sitting on the fence, and if they failed to ratify the convention, it would have failed to become valid.

The Kyoto targets appear to have got bogged down in, at times, obstructive, negotiations that are effectively reducing their potential value in controlling climate change. As the impacts of the warming world, manifested in continued rise in extreme weather events, become increasingly apparent, more attention is being given to a potentially more radical approach to carbon emission reductions, that of 'Contraction and Convergence' (C&C), which has recently

Box 1.2 Ratification of the Kyoto Protocol

To enter into force, the Protocol must be ratified by 55 Parties to the UNFCCC, including Annex I Parties representing at least 55% of the total carbon dioxide emissions for 1990 (http://unfccc.int/resource/docs/convkp/kpeng.html). As of November 2003, 120 Parties had signed the Kyoto Protocol and 84 had either ratified or acceded to the Protocol, collectively representing a commitment to a 44.2% reduction in global carbon dioxide emissions; 10.8% shy of the level required for the Protocol to take effect. The United States signed the Protocol on 11 December 1997 but has failed to ratify it. The US national commitment alone would account for a 36.1% reduction in global carbon dioxide emissions.[i]

[i] For the latest details of who is in and who is out of Kyoto see http://unfccc.int/resource/kpstats.pdf and http://unfccc.int/resource/kpthermo.html.

been described as looking increasingly like 'the only game in town'.[37] C&C is all about reducing the total global output of greenhouse gases, while gradually reducing national emissions to targets based on population. It would mean cutting total global emissions from an average of one tonne of carbon per person to 0.3 tonnes per person over time, and it has the potential to smooth over the political and economic cracks that are threatening to tear down the Kyoto Protocol.

The convergence figures represent what it is estimated to be the carbon emissions reductions needed to stabilize climate change. The discrepancy between the reality of what we emit and what

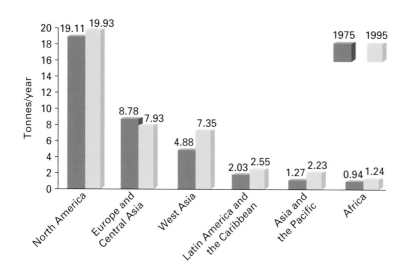

1.12.
CO_2 emissions per capita for the different regions of the world in 1975 and 1995 demonstrating how large the gap is between different countries and the scale of the challenges we face in trying to establish protocols for the equitable emissions of carbon dioxide. (*Source:* http://www.unep.org/geo2000/english/figures.htm)

is required is being faced up to by some governments and the EU. On 12 August 2003 the European Commission unveiled tough proposals to cut emissions of particular potent greenhouse gases by a quarter before 2010, in the fight against global warming.[38] A start at least.

Box 1.3 Contraction and convergence (*by Aubrey Meyer*)

ESSENTIAL PROPOSITION OF C&C

The C&C model[i] formalizes the objective and principles of the UNFCCC. It first proposes a reviewable global greenhouse gas (ghg) emissions 'contraction budget' targeted at a safe and stable future level for atmospheric ghg concentrations.

The internationally tradable shares in this budget are then agreed on the basis of 'convergence' from now, where shares are broadly proportional to income, to a target date in the budget timeline, after which they remain proportional to an agreed base year of global population. Recognizing that the bigger the budget, the greater the risks, and that decarbonization is further enhanced if revenue from emission trading is re-invested in zero emissions techniques. This reduces the randomness that has dogged negotiations since 1992 over future emissions commitments/entitlements, as it resolves the conflict between the GDP-led approaches and those emphasizing responsibility for the historic build-up of atmospheric concentrations.

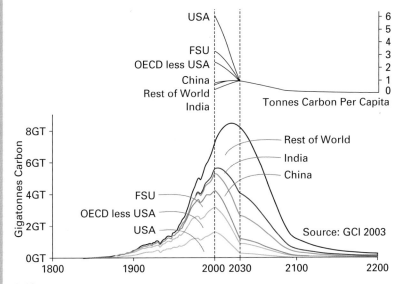

1.13.
Global (6 regions as shown) carbon 'contraction' 2000–2100 for 450 ppmv atmospheric concentration with 'convergence' to equal per capita shares globally by 2030. (*Source:* Aubrey Meyer; see C&C demonstration at http://www.gci.org.uk/images/ CC_Demo(pc).exe and see C&C imagery at: http://www.gci.org.uk/images/C&C_Bubbles.pdf)

CONTRACTION

On the basis of precaution, and guided by the scientific advice of the IPCC, all governments or regional groupings of governments jointly and severally agree to observe such an atmospheric target. With this it is possible to calculate the total diminishing amount of greenhouse gases that the world can emit for each year in the coming century. Whatever the rate chosen, C&C views this event as a whole as 'Contraction'.[ii]

CONVERGENCE

On the basis of equity, convergence means that each year's ration of this global emissions budget can be shared so that each country, or group of countries, progressively converges on the same allocation per inhabitant by an agreed date, for example by 2030. This recognizes the principle of globally equal rights per capita to the 'global commons' of the atmosphere, but achieved by smooth transition.[iii] Where countries or groups do have a diversity of natural endowments, C&C acknowledges this too by embracing, for example, the European Union, which operates as a unit at the international level whilst creating its own convergence arrangements.

EMISSIONS PERMIT TRADING

Only emissions in excess of the total of permits created under C&C are not permitted ('hot-air'). Countries unable to manage within their agreed shares would, subject to the above and appropriate rules, be able to buy the unused parts of the allocations of other countries or regions. Sales of unused allocations would give low per capita emitting countries the income to fund sustainable development in zero-emission ways. High per capita emitting countries gain a mechanism to mitigate the premature retirement of their carbon capital stock whilst also benefiting from the export markets for renewable technologies this restructuring would create. All countries therefore benefit from more rapidly avoided global damages.

SUSTAINABLE GROWTH

Climate change increasingly augurs potentially catastrophic losses. C&C mitigates this by integrating the key features of global diplomacy and development necessary for long-term prosperity and security. C&C synthesizes the objective and principles of the UNFCCC in a constitutional rather than a stochastic manner, so that the necessary foundation for the transition to a new growth and prosperity is specifically guided by this agreement to the zero carbon energy technologies that make this prosperity with security possible.

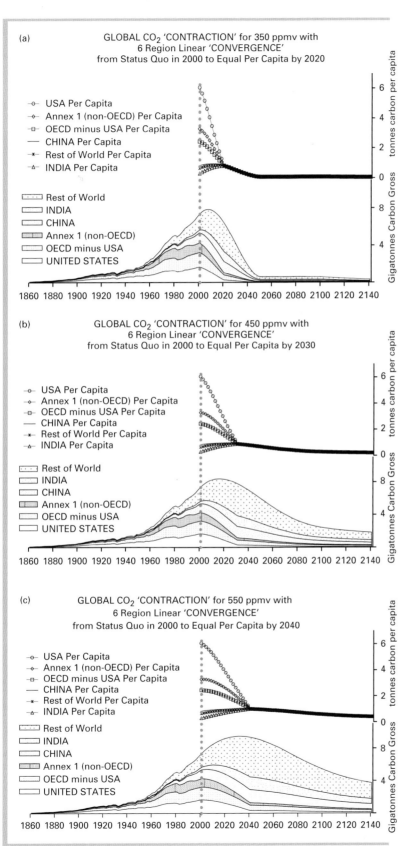

1.14.

C&C diagrams demonstrating the required emissions modification to stabilize the global carbon dioxide concentrations at (a) 350 ppm by 2020; (b) 450 ppm by 2030; and (c) 550 ppm by 2040. (*Source:* Aubrey Meyer)

ⁱ CCOptions will calculate any rates of contraction and convergence for all countries' CO_2.

ⁱⁱ The example chosen shows global CO_2 emissions reduced to 40% of 1990 output value by 2100 giving a stable atmospheric concentration of 450 parts per million of CO_2 by 2100. Other contraction 'shapes' are possible for the same concentration outcome. Different rates of contraction are possible leading to different concentration outcomes but damages from climate change increase proportional to delay.

ⁱⁱⁱ The example shows global pre-distribution of contraction through linear convergence so shares are proportional to international populations by 2050 with figures for population growth frozen from 2050 forwards. Different rates of convergence are possible and different dates of freezing population are possible. Both of these affect the pre-distribution of the tradable emissions entitlements.

FIGHTING IN THE RANKS

Resistance to changing our own ways of life is enormous and is fought on many fronts. One of President George W. Bush's first actions when he came to power was to withdraw the United States from the Kyoto treaty. Despite the States being one of the most vulnerable continents to extreme weather damage, the issues of global warming have been, by and large, presented to the American people as 'not an issue'. In October 2003 the US Senate rejected a plan, by 55 votes to 43, to curb carbon dioxide emissions from industry. The Bill, sponsored by John McCain (Republican) and Joe Liberman (Democrat), would have required industrial plants, not vehicles, to cut back emissions of carbon dioxide and other greenhouse gas emissions to 2000 levels by 2010. Larry Craig, the Idaho senator, said there was no need for a 'massive new regulatory process' for industrial carbon dioxide. 'It is not a pollutant. It does not represent a direct threat to public health.' The White House opposes the Bill as it requires 'deep cuts in fossil fuel use' to meet an 'arbitrary goal', and would drive up energy bills and pump prices.[39]

The growing gulf between European and American policies towards the environment was highlighted when Margot Wallstrom, the EU Environment Commissioner, while on a visit to London in late October 2003 and without provocation lambasted the Americans for pressuring Russia not to sign the Kyoto Protocol, the US Marine Administration for sending polluted boats to the UK to be broken up and US companies involved in GM crops for trying to lie to the European consumer. The Natural Resources Defence Council (NRDC), a leading US environmental organization counted more than 100 anti-environment actions taken by the US

Numbers of disasters

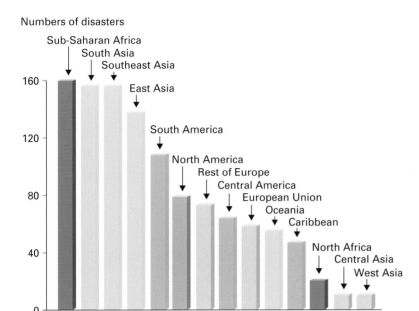

1.15.
The number of climate-related disasters experienced per continent 1993–97. (*Source:* http://www.unep.org/geo2000/english/figures.htm)

government in 2002 alone. A number of reasons for this have been suggested, including:[40]

- The US voter is typically not concerned about environmental issues (and is very ill informed about them).
- Right wing lobbies, such as industry associations and ideological think-tanks, play a significant role in influencing policy, greater than in Europe.
- The gulf between the United States and the EU on these matters has widened even further as a result of the current US administration downgrading transatlantic relationships and consequentially devaluing 'European' concerns.

The United States, which has known, in depth, about the problems and science of climate change for over 40 years and was the first nation in the world to sign the 1992 United Nation Climate Change Convention, has, with its blocking tactics over Kyoto, managed to prevent the world from 'locking-on' to clear and achievable targets that may provide the direct strike at the problem we need to survive, and meanwhile the problem grows in strength daily.

IS THE BATTLE LOST ALREADY?

What is clear now is that this war is the great war of our time, and perhaps of all time. We must act firmly and effectively in the face of the incontrovertible evidence[41] before us to fight it.

We cannot trust to governments alone, or corporations, or councils to do what is necessary. There is no magic technical or surgical solution in this old-fashioned war. There is a crucial role in the front line of this battle for every man, woman and child on the planet.[42]

There are some basic rules in this war. Rule number one is that: From those who have the most, the most must be expected. Equality and proportionality are the two key guiding principals that will help us survive through the 21st century. And because buildings use more energy than any other single sector in the developed world, then it is from the building sector that the greatest cuts have been predicted as possible, and must be forthcoming. They use more energy than any other sector – they must make the biggest cuts.

This book shows that it may be possible to effect the 'radical change in our approach to the environment' called for by Goldsmith in 1972 and the authors of Agenda 21, 20 years later. These changes will cost real money, and cause real pain, but any war does. By March 2004 over 110 billion dollars have already been spent by the United States alone on invading the single country of Iraq.[43] How much are we willing to spend on saving the world? It is money we have to spend, and pain we have to shoulder, because it is increasingly looking as if radical change, like contraction and convergence, is 'the only game in town', if we intend to survive on this planet.

So how long do we have to wait for answers to the key questions of the next two decades of the 21st century:

- Will that radical change happen?
- Can we adapt our buildings and cities to survive through the 21st century?
- Are we already too late?

NOTES AND REFERENCES

1   In January 2004 Sir David King, the Chief Scientific Adviser to the UK Prime Minister, made an address to the House of Lords in which he clearly stated that climate change was now a greater threat to humanity than terrorism. See http://news.bbc.co.uk/1/hi/sci/tech/3381425.stm.

2   On 22 February 2004 Mark Townsend and Paul Harris of the *Observer* published an article, on page 3, on a secret report produced by eminent scientists for the Pentagon which made chilling reading and warned of the very imminent threat of climate change that would ensure that 'disruption and conflict

will be endemic features of life'. See http://observer.guardian. co.uk/international/story/0,6903,1153514,00.html.

3 A British study covering 40 years of comprehensive evidence reported that butterflies, birds and plants are in decline for around 70%, 54% and 28% of species respectively. The study, published in the US journal *Science* on 19 March 2004, was said by Jeremy Thomas of the UK Natural Environment Research Council to add 'enormous strength to the hypothesis that the world is approaching its sixth major extinction event'. He pointed out that the other events were cosmic, coming from outer space, while this event appears to come from within, from our own species that 'through its over-exploitation and its wastes, it eats, destroys, or poisons the others'. See Tim Radford's article on 'The Decline of Species', on page 1 of the *Guardian*, 19 March 2004.

4 Worldwatch Institute, State of the World Report 2003, see http://www.worldwatch.org/pubs/sow/2003/.

5 Hulme, M., Jenkins, G., Lu, X., Turnpenny, J., Mitchell, T., Jones, R., Lowe, J., Murphy, J., Hassell, D., Boorman, P., McDonald, R. and Hill, S. (2002) *Climate Change Scenarios for the United Kingdom: The UKCIP02 Scientific Report, Appendix 2* published in conjunction with UKCIP, the Hadley Centre and the Climate Research Unit in the School of Environmental Science at the University of East Anglia, by the Tyndall Centre, Norwich.

6 For a full introduction into the process of climate change see http://climatechange.unep.net/.

7 For the global weather warning that extreme weather events are on the increase from the Secretary of the World Meteorological Organization on 3 July 2003, see http://www. unic.org.in/News/2003/pr/pr111.html and http://www.guardian. co.uk/comment/story/o,3604,1007042,00.html.

8 Galbraith, J.K. (1999) *The Affluent Society* (1st edition 1958). Canada: Penguin Books, p. 17.

9 For more information see the Mauna Loa Solar Observatory site on mlso.hao.ucar.edu/. Another good site is http://cdiac.esd. ornl.gov/trends/co2/sio-mlo.htm.

10 As early as 1965, three groups, all in the United States, had established ongoing efforts in general circulation modelling of the climate: Geophysical Fluid Dynamics Laboratory; UCLA Department of Meteorology; National Center for Atmospheric Research. Among the important Climate Circulation Modelling groups established in 1965–75, two were in the United States, a country that has been aware, longer than any other, of the

significance of climate change. These three were the RAND Corporation (Santa Monica, CA); Goddard Institute for Space Studies (New York, NY); and the Australian Numerical Meteorological Research Centre (Melbourne, Australia). For a fuller history of climate modelling see: http://www.aip.org/history/sloan/gcm/1965_75.html.

11 The current climate models, building on the works of such earlier researchers, now use the commonly accepted 'general circulation models' (GCMs) or AGCMs ('atmospheric general circulation models'). These are complex models of the Earth's atmosphere and are time-consuming and expensive to run, usually funded by national governments. Early GCM scenarios were based on a doubling of the pre-industrial equivalent CO_2 concentration in the atmosphere. The models were run until a new equilibrium state was reached corresponding to this increased concentration of CO_2.

    In the 1990s GCMs began to incorporated sub-models of the oceans, variously referred to as 'coupled ocean-atmosphere models' or CGCMs. Because the dynamics of climate change is dominated by the effect of the oceans, these models allow transient (time-dependent) simulations of the future climate to be made. Year on year these models are becoming more sophisticated and can now incorporate the impacts of aerosols in the atmosphere, and climate feed-back, to a resolution of fifty, down to even five, kilometre squares. For an explanation of the models used recently by the UK Climate Impacts programme see http://www.ukcip.org.uk/scenarios/pdfs/UKCIP02TechRep/Cover.pdf.

12 http://www.ipcc.ch/.

13 Meadows, D.H. (1972) *The Limits to Growth; A Report for the Club of Rome's Project on the Predicament of Mankind.* London: St Martins Press.

14 Washington, W.W. (1971) *Study of Man's Impact on the Climate (SMIC).* Cambridge, MA: MIT Press.

15 Goldsmith, E., Allen, R., Allenby, M., Davull, J. and Lawrence, S. (1972) *A Blueprint for Survival.* London: Tom Stacy.

16 Goldsmith *et al.*, *A Blueprint for Survival*, p. 27.

17 Roaf, S. (2004) *Closing the Loop.* London: RIBA Publications.

18 Molina, M.J. and Rowland, F.S. (1974) Stratospheric sink for chlorofluoromethanes-chlorine atom catalysed destruction of ozone. *Nature*, 249, 810.

19 Farman, J., Gardiner, B. and Shanklin, J. (1985) Large losses of total ozone in Antarctica reveal seasonal ClOx/NOx interaction. *Nature*, 315, 207–10.

20 https://www.nas.nasa.gov/About/Education/Ozone/history.html.

21 http://www.theozonehole.com/ozonehole2003.htm.

22 The Dobson Unit: one Dobson Unit (DU) is defined to be 0.01 mm thickness at STP (standard temperature and pressure). Ozone layer thickness is expressed in terms of Dobson Units, which measure what its physical thickness would be if compressed in the earth's atmosphere. In those terms, it is very thin indeed. A normal range is 300–500 Dobson Units, which translates to an eighth of an inch – two stacked penny coins. In space, it is best not to envision the ozone layer as a distinct, measurable band. Instead, think of it in terms of parts per million concentrations in the stratosphere (the layer 6 to 30 miles above the Earth's surface). Such units, measurements, the targets they enable us to set are the basic weapons of our war on climate change. The unit is named after G.M.B. Dobson, one of the first scientists to investigate atmospheric ozone.

  This DU description was written by The Ozone Hole Organization and 'A Riddle inside a Conundrum within a Parable surrounded by an Enigma, and Up A Tree Again Productions'. For full details of their research, Dobson Units and current maps of the ozone hole see: http://www.theozonehole.com).

23 This section was written using some parts of the article by Leonie Haimson in *Grist* magazine on the Agenda 21 summit. See http://www.gristmagazine.com/heatbeat/inshorta.asp.

24 For a complete explanation of the processes of climate change and the related publications of the International Panel on Climate Change, modelling techniques and legislation see www.ipcc.ch/ and for a potted and well informed history see http://www.doc.mmu.ac.uk/aric/eae/Global_Warming/global_warming.html.

25 For a full state of play on the climate conventions see http://unfccc.int/index.html.

26 For a full list of parties signed up to the treaty see http://unfccc.int/resource/convkp.html.

27 http://www.un.org/esa/sustdev/documents/agenda21/index.htm. For a full list of the current Agenda 21 Action Programmes see http://www.unep.org/Documents/Default.asp?DocumentID=52.

28 See the very interesting website for The European Business Council for a Sustainable Energy Future on http://www.e5.org for a run-down of the COP9 awards in Milan. There was some very hard horse trading at COP9 as governments sought to defend the interests of their own voters. See, for instance, a

run-down of the 'Fossil-of-the-day Award', awarded during the COP9 talks, given each day to countries that block progress at the United Nations Climate Change Negotiations. Saudi Arabia, the United States, Canada, Australia and New Zealand all figure in these awards with the US, a country that has not even signed up to the treaty, winning hands down. The current concern is that Russia will not sign the Treaty, but is thought to be using the negotiations as a lever to improve its position in negotiations on parallel international agreements. See http://www.e5.org/modules.php?op=modload&name=News& file=article&sid=408.

29 A report compiled in 2002 by international law firm Baker and McKenzie warned that people are increasingly looking to lay blame for climate change costs and impacts and the main possible legal actions are either of a government suing a government, or an individual or an environmental organization suing a company for failing to do something, or alternatively, as we are now seeing in the United States, for governments or individuals suing the regulatory authorities for failing to deal with greenhouse emissions (http://www.abc.net.au/am/content/ 2003/s979176.htm). The cases in the United States involve a group of environmental groups, joined by three American cities, suing the US export credit agencies for funding fossil fuel projects. Another group is suing the Environmental Protection Agency for a lack of action. Ironically it may be those companies who have publicly taken an anti-climate change line that are most vulnerable because their actions may be proved to have been in bad faith. For a good discussion on this trend see http://www.legalaffairs.org/issues/September-October-2002/ review_appelbaum_sepoct2002.html. For a range of related issues raised see also http://earthscience.surfwax.com/files/ Global_Warming.html and http://www.iisd.ca/climate-l/Climate-L_ News_17.html.

30 People have long talked of the impending 'water wars', covered in Chapter 6 of this book, but they are already happening. Civil unrest within countries, and between countries and different interest groups on the subject of water is an already chronic problem in many part of the world, and long chronicled. See, for instance, Gleick, P. (ed.) (1993) *Water in Crisis: A Guide to the World's Freshwater Resources.* Oxford: Oxford University Press.

31 Mann, M.E. and Jones, P.D. (2003) Global surface temperatures over the past two millennia. *Geophysical Research Letters*, 30: 10.1029/2003GL017814.

32   http://www.zoca.com/swallowtail/articles/climate.html.

33   Michael Meacher, *Guardian*, 28 July 2003, p. 14.

34   http://unfccc.int/cop9/index.html.

35   http://www.nature.com/nsu/031124/031124-14.html. See also note 29 above and the concerns about trading in 'bad faith'.

36   *Guardian*, 3 December 2003, p. 13.

37   For full details of C&C see the excellent website of the Global Commons Institute on http://www.gci.org.uk/contconv/cc.html.

38   *Guardian*, 12 August 2003, p. 3.

39   *Guardian*, 31 October 2003, p. 16.

40   *Guardian*, 31 October 2003, p. 16.

41   The need to be sceptical about the sceptics is clear from high profile examples such as that of Bjorn Lomborg, who in his book *The Sceptical Environmentalist* (Cambridge University Press, 2001), wrote what was perhaps the most thorough attempt to date at debunking concerns of environmentalists, but was robustly lambasted by the academic establishment. See http://www.gristmagazine.com/books/lomborg121201.asp, http://www.mylinkspage.com/lomborg.html). There also exists, predominantly in the United States but elsewhere also, including the UK, an ostensibly un-venal array of 'greenhouse sceptics' who derive much of their funding from the fossil fuel industry and make it their business to energetically refute the science of climate change. A quick trawl through an Internet search engine will demonstrate how effective they are in getting their messages across, although their writings are often taken with more than a pinch of salt by many respected scientists, as is noted on such websites as http://www.kwikpower.com/AREAS/GC/gc04.htm, which mentions a number of such 'sceptics' funded by the ExxonMobil Corporation, including Fred Singer, Patrick Michaels, Robert Balling and Sherwood Idso.

42   This need for everyone to engage in the battle against climate change was clearly stated by UN Secretary-General Kofi Annan when delivering the commencement address to the Fletcher School of Law and Diplomacy in Medford, Massachusetts, USA, on 21 May 2003. Annan noted that the United States, which produced the most greenhouse gases largely because it was the world's most successful economy, must 'join in reducing emissions and in the broader quest for energy efficiency and conservation'. Warning of the 'very real danger' that gains in combating climate change could be lost, he painted a picture of melting polar icecaps threatening coastal areas, extreme

weather causing billion-dollar calamities, and a 'warmer and wetter' world in which infectious diseases spread more easily. 'This is not some distant, worst-case scenario', he cautioned. 'It is tomorrow's forecast.' Looking on the positive side, Mr Annan said the battle against climate change could provide an opportunity to reinvigorate the fight against poverty, inspire changes in corporate and consumer habits, and 'shape globalization so that the environment does not become one of its prime casualties'. 'Today, though we have the human and material resources to win the fight against climate change, the time for a well-planned transition to sustainable development is running out', Mr Annan told the Fletcher School graduates, adding 'unless, that is, you do your part'. http://www.solcomhouse.com/annan.htm.

43 See http://costofwar.com/ for an ongoing running total of the costs of the Iraq war to the USA.

2 THE EVOLUTION OF BUILDINGS

Buildings are our third skin. As our ancestors moved north from the steppes of temperate Africa, hundreds of thousands of years ago, not only did they have to don warmer clothes but they also had to build stronger buildings that would protect them from the heat of the deserts and the cold of the northern climes.

SUSTAINABLE SETTLEMENTS

REGIONALLY APPROPRIATE BUILDINGS

2.1.
Vernacular buildings have evolved over time to make the best use of local materials and conditions to provide adequate, and often luxurious, shelter for populations inhabiting even the most extreme climates of the world. (*Source:* Sue Roaf, digitally produced by Claire Palmer)

The result of this great migration of mankind is an extraordinary diversity of dwellings, built of local materials and shaped to suit local climates, landscapes, and societies.

What did not change, on those migrations, is the underlying human metabolism. People in every society have the same physiology and core temperature of around 37.5 °C, and the same adaptive mechanisms to keep their bodies at this core temperature in even the most extreme climates. What did change were the skins, body forms and behaviour of moving tribes. In hot climates people evolved with darker skins that could regulate the production of vitamin D in high levels of ultra-violet (UV) light. In the north lands with lower levels of UV in the incoming radiation populations selectively developed lighter skin, hair and eye colours.[1] Body forms also changed over time as local populations grew taller and thinner in hot climates, with high surface area : body volume ratios so they could lose heat rapidly in the higher temperatures. In cold climates shorter, fatter people had a lower surface : volume ratio so they could conserve heat more easily.

But in order to survive in temperatures from over 50 °C in the lower attitudes to −50 °C below freezing in the Arctic Circle other factors had to come into play including:

- the wearing of more or less, thinner and thicker, clothes (the second skin);
- the design of buildings (the third skin);
- behavioural adaptations, like changing posture, activity levels and choosing the most comfortable space to occupy, by moving around rooms and buildings and landscapes; and then of course the use of energy from the burning of fossil fuels or the careful use of stored energy in heat or cold stores.

Until recent decades the only energy available to most families in most societies was what they could find, mine, collect and carry home, be it dung, coal, wood, peat, water or ice. These stored sources of energy provided, either passively, or actively through

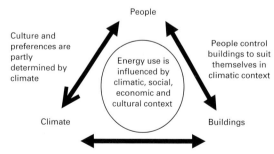

People

Culture and preferences are partly determined by climate

Energy use is influenced by climatic, social, economic and cultural context

People control buildings to suit themselves in climatic context

Climate

Buildings

Building ameliorates climate within traditionally occupied settlements to suit occupants and provide comfort within cultural norms

2.2.
The traditional three-way interaction between climate, people and buildings that dictates our energy needs. (*Source:* Fergus Nicol)

burning, the extra heating, or cooling, of occupied spaces that enabled settlements to be built in ever-more extreme climates. Added to the survival challenges that the increasingly extreme climate posed was the fact that it changed. The climate always has changed.

The last Ice Age occurred only just over ten thousand years ago, when the global temperature was around three degrees centigrade colder than today. Three degrees seems like a very small change, to have such dramatic consequences on the global climate. After all, northern Europe, was largely covered by ice caps then, and humans mostly lived in the lower temperate and equatorial regions of the world, in caves or in transient shelters that have left no archaeological record.

The earliest excavated settlements with buildings were built after this last Ice Age, and were found in the Zagros mountains in Luristan,

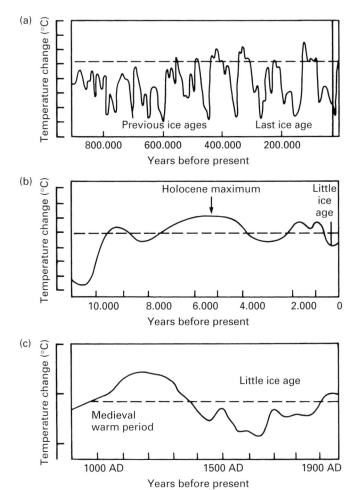

2.3.
Schematic diagrams of global temperature variations over the last (a) 1 000 000, (b) 10 000 and (c) 1000 years. (*Source:* Houghton J.T., Jenkins, G.J., Ephraums, J.J (eds) (1990) *Climate Change: The IPCC Scientific Assessment.* Cambridge: Cambridge University Press, p. 202)

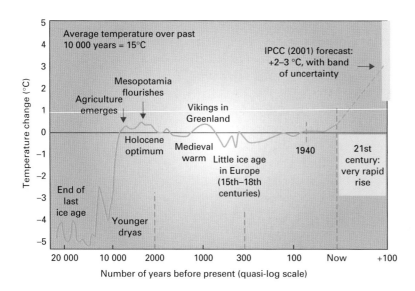

2.4.
Human societies have had long experience of naturally occurring climatic vicissitudes. The ancient Egyptians, Mesopotamians, Mayans and European populations (during the four centuries of the Little Ice Age) were all affected by nature's great climatic cycles. More acutely, disasters and disease outbreaks have occurred, often in response to the extremes of regional climatic cycles, such as the El Niño Southern Oscillation cycle. (*Source:* http://www. who.int/globalchange/climate/ summary/en/)

Western Iran, where at Gange Dareh, a settlement of small, oval mud brick houses was carbon dated to around 7200 BC.

Since then, great cities and civilizations have risen and fallen on many continents, leaving little trace of their original glory, invisible beneath the feet of passing generations.[2] All of these great civilizations were affected by the changing climates, and some, like the Mayans, may have disappeared because of years of droughts, or floods, in their heartlands.

A widespread strategy for surviving in extreme climates is to move to different areas at times of the year when they are comfortable, and leave them when they are not – to migrate.

SEASONAL MIGRATION – NOMADS

The basic reason for having buildings at all is to provide shelter against the climate. It is extraordinary how little of a building can suffice to provide adequate shelter in even the most arduous of climates. The tent, for instance, is used to house people from the deserts of Saudi Arabia to the tundra regions of the Arctic Circle. In fact most areas in these regions are uninhabitable – cold or hot – at particular times of the year when the tribes are elsewhere. Nomadic peoples often occupy peripheral lands that would not traditionally support communities all year around. Their secret is to travel in search of the heat, coolth and food they require to survive, a strategy also employed by the British upper classes who spent the summer in the country and the winter in towns in the 18th and 19th centuries, and in the early 20th century, winters in Nice or Capri.

The Beiranvand tribe of the Zagros Mountains, where permanent settlements perhaps began, are a case in point. The tribe
migrates in spring from the hot plains of Mesopotamia near Dizful
some hundred miles up into the cooler mountain plateau north of
Khorramabad where the wheat they have sewn earlier will be ripen-
ing and the summer can be spent in cool comfort, weaving and
celebrating weddings. This same mountain bowl could be metres
deep in snow in winter, by which time the tribe will be safely back
in their warm winter quarters on the low plains.[3]

2.5.
The Beiranvand tribe on
migration through the Zagros
Mountains in spring, carrying
their worldly goods on the backs
of the pack animals, moving from
the hot Mesopotamian Plains to
their cool high summer camp in
the Zagros Mountains. (*Source:*
Sue Roaf)

2.6.
The simple black tents that serve
to keep the tribe warm in the
winter snow and cool in the
blistering summer heat. (*Source:*
Sue Roaf)

SPRING	AUTUMN	TEMPERATURE	CAMP
AUG		2080m.asl PISH-E KUH	SUMMER GARVESELLA CAMP
JULY		36/20 37/19	
JUNE		37/21 38/20	
		35/15 36/15	TADJEREH
MAY		30/14 30/14 KHORAMABAD	
		29/15 30/14	ANGUZ
APRIL		24/13 25/12	DADABAD
MARCH		25/13 26/8	
	SEPT	35/16 34/15	TRIBAL ROAD
		BADLANDS OF BALAGARIVEH	I L R A H
OCT		34/18 35/17	
NOV		25/13 26/12 PUSHT-E KUH	
DEC		22/9 20/7 500m.asl	DELFIN WINTER CAMP
JAN		22/12 20/10 DIZFUL	
FEB		24/13 22/11	
		PLAINS OF KHUZISTAN	

2.7.
Diagram showing estimated temperatures inside and outside the Beiranvand tents at different months, in the different locations, on the two hundred mile annual migration along the '*il rah*', the tribal road. (*Source:* Sue Roaf, digitalized by Claire Palmer)

The tent, or 'third skin', that divides the tribe from the elements is woven from black goat's wool. With the additional help of the clothes worn, quilted blankets and a small fire, the tent will be occupied in temperatures that range from below zero and up to the high forties centigrade. One tribal leader boasted that their tribe had a wonderful life because they were warm in winter and cool in summer when they drank iced water from their springs, while the town dwellers were cold in winter and hot in summer when they drank only warm water, which offered little or no relief from the heat.

In colder regions such as Mongolia or Central Asia, the Yurt or the Gher are tents made of much thicker materials, of beaten sheep's or goat's wool felt that is better able to withstand the biting wind and driving snow of those regions. The Sani live in animal skin tents. The form of their tents is also more compact, minimizing the surface area of the tent and so reducing heat loss from it. In colder regions tribal people also rely more on their second skin, clothes, for the extra warmth they need in winter. The Sani people of the Arctic not only occupy relatively small dwellings, rather of the proportion of the ice-built igloo, in which there is simply less air to heat, but like the Inuit, they wear full skin body suits lined with fur, even in the tent at night in mid-winter.[4]

The form of a tent is also eminently adaptable so that it can be closed down in winter to provide a snug, smaller, more windproof environment while in summer it can be expanded to provide little more than a well-ventilated shade awning. With tents, the actual form of the tent, the material and performance of its construction and the way in which it is used and adapted over a year are all indicators of the extent to which the people in a season and a region need to increase or decrease the difference between the indoor and outdoor climate. The more extreme the climate, the better the tent must be at keeping it out.

Adapting to new ecological niches in times of threat

The Beiranvand tribe has, over the past 70 years or so, been diversifying into a range of new 'ecological niches', as part of the settled populations of villages, towns and cities. This is part of a tribal strategy for survival in the face of a range of major changes in their habitat and society,[5] including those wrought by climate change and war.

INTRA-MURAL MIGRATION BY SETTLED POPULATIONS

In permanent settlements people do not have the choice to move to more comfortable climates, but they can practise a different form of migration, as they move around their own homes. Not far from Luristan, in the great desert cities of central Iran such as Yazd, are some of the most sophisticated of all the passively designed homes in the world. An important element of the way the local populations could adapt to the extremely hot summer climate, and extremely cold winter climate, is to migrate, intra-murally, within the four walls of the dwelling.

   Annually, the family migrates horizontally around a courtyard. In winter the family will spend most of the day and night in a south-facing glazed winter room overlooking a warm sheltered courtyard. In summer, the living room shifts to the north-facing end of the court where no direct sunlight enters the living areas during the day and cross ventilation may be provided by a windcatcher across the high shaded summer room.

Buildings are climatically coupled to the earth and the air

Diurnally the family migrates from the deep cool basements, where they eat and rest in the hot afternoon. In the mornings and the evenings they sit in the fresh shaded courtyard and at night they climb onto the roof to sleep beneath the stars.[6]

(a)

(b)

2.8.

(a) Axonometric showing the variation in temperatures around a Yazdi house, Iran, demonstrating the advantages of intra-mural migration in achieving a comfortable indoor environment on a hot summer afternoon. 1. Roof, where the family sleeps at night; 2. talar – summer room; 3. basement room with pool for summer afternoons; 4. windcatcher; 5. hot west-facing wall with no rooms; 6. living room; 7. guest courtyard; 8. store; 9. well; 10. water tank; 11. kitchen; 12. stable; 13. ganat – underground canal; 14. trellis; 15. garden pond; 16. deep basement for mid-summer afternoons. (*Source:* Sue Roaf in *Living with the Desert*[7]) (b) Windcatchers on the skyline of Yazd. (*Source:* Sue Roaf)

The rooms on the roof are much more closely coupled to the fluctuating temperatures of the sky while those sunk into the ground are coupled in temperature to the stable earth temperature, with a far lower rate of change, responding to the changes in seasonal mean temperatures rather than the minute to minute temperature changes that can be experienced in the open rooms of the roof of the Havelli in India, for example (Figure 2.10).

Some basements in traditional Asian houses can be as much as 9 m below ground level, providing a stable cool climate even when temperatures soar above 50 °C in heat waves. Some believe that as the temperature changes our best means of survival in extreme climates will be to migrate further and further underground as the challenge of controlling high energy use in hot climates begins to bite.[8]

HEATING AND COOLING BUILDINGS PASSIVELY

The mud brick houses of Yazd, some of which are over 600 years old, have on their roofs a very obvious sign of their great skills at

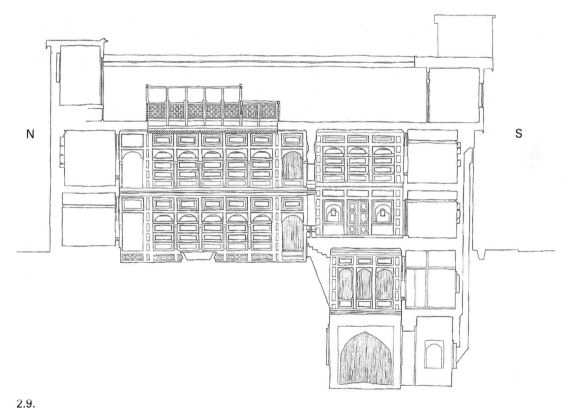

N   S

2.9.
The 9 m deep double basement of the Sethi House in Peshawar, North West Frontier Province, Pakistan, showing the narrow ventilation shaft in the rear wall to stimulate ventilation of the space. (*Source:* Drawn by student on the Masters course in Sustainable Building, Oxford Brookes University)

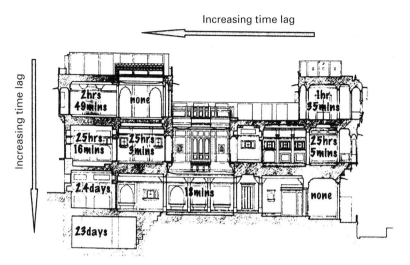

2.10.
The time required for indoor room temperatures to respond to outdoor temperature changes varies enormously according to the extent to which the room is coupled to the earth or the sky temperature. (*Source:* Jane Matthews)

climatic design, in the form of the windcatchers that crown many of their settlements. In the densely inhabited towns and villages of this desert region these towers reach up above the roofs of buildings to catch the faster flowing upper air stream and channel it down to ventilate and cool the rooms below and their occupants. This they do, not only convectively by passing cooler air over the skins of building occupants, but also using radiant coolth. By taking the cold night air, and passing it over the heavy mud-brick walls of the rooms below, the warmth collected in those walls during the day is drawn out and dumped back to the sky, making the rooms below the windcatcher cooler during the day than the outdoor air temperature. In winter the free energy of the sun enters through the glass in the french doors of the south-facing winter room and is trapped inside, unable to escape the closed space, and this heat is stored in the massive mud-brick walls of the room, that re-radiate this free heat back into the room all through the night providing a remarkably steady indoor temperature. This collecting, storing and dumping of energy, heat, by the structure of the building itself is done 'passively' requiring no 'active' input of energy by building users at all.

TRANSPORTING STORED ENERGY – ICE-HOUSES

If it became too hot in summer, even in the basement in Yazd, then a boy could be sent out to get the family an ice-cream or iced sherbet, made with ice from one of the great ice-houses of the city. Just as heat and coolth is stored in the earth and the fabric of buildings, so it can be stored in ice, for years. A very well kept secret today is that, since the dawn of recorded history, we have been able to store the cold of the winter months to re-use it in the heat of summer in the form of ice. Our forefathers cooled their drinks, food, brows and rooms, by cutting the ice off ponds and rivers, or scraping it from mountain sides, in winter and storing it in underground ice-houses through the spring. The ice-houses were opened on the 'salad days' of summer to provide ice for the kitchen, the invalid, the ambassador's salon, the greenhouse and the dining table.[7]

Let them unseal the ice of Qatara. The Goddess, you and [your sister] Belassunna drink regularly, and make sure the ice is guarded[9]

wrote a provincial Governor of Northern Assyria in a letter to his wife, Iltani, in 1800 BC. This, the first written record we have of the storage of ice in an ice-house, comes to us from nearly four thousand years ago from the Plains of Northern Iraq.

Ice-houses were built on every continent on the planet, except Australia, and were used extensively by the Greeks, Romans, Chinese and even the Latin Americans. Ice was cut from the Andes and lowered on ropes by Indians who then transported it some 90 miles on mule back at a brisk trot (where roads permitted) to Lima, a city that used between 50–55 cwt a day (a hundredweight being about 2.5 metric tonnes). Tschudi, travelling in 1840[10] claimed that the trade was so important that its interruption might 'excite popular ferment' and consequently 'in all revolutions' care was taken to avoid commandeering the mules used in the transport of ice.

Right up until the 1980s there are reports of natural ice being stored in winter for use in the 'salad days' of summer. Ice pits in the Kurdish mountains of Northern Mesopotamia were still being filled in the 1980s, apparently because certain local tribal chiefs prefer to drink their Johnny Walker Black Label whisky with natural ice as it was said to improve its taste. If only the British troops in Iraq had known they might have been able to fly in Kurdish ice to cool their tents and the citizens of Basra in the scorching summer of 2003 when the inhabitants of that beleaguered city had no electricity to cool their homes in temperatures over 50 °C, and rioting broke out in the streets, demonstrating, again, the political importance of coolth.

Perhaps we will see a re-emergence of the global ice trade, one of the most remarkable in history, which resulted, in large part, from the simple invention in 1827 on Lake Wenham near Boston, Massachusetts, of the ice-plough by Nathaniel Wyeth. The plough was drawn behind horses and enabled large quantities of blocks of clear, pure ice to be cut from the lakes, stored in huge above-ground ice-sheds and then transported by train to the coast where they were loaded onto wooden sailing barques and transported to

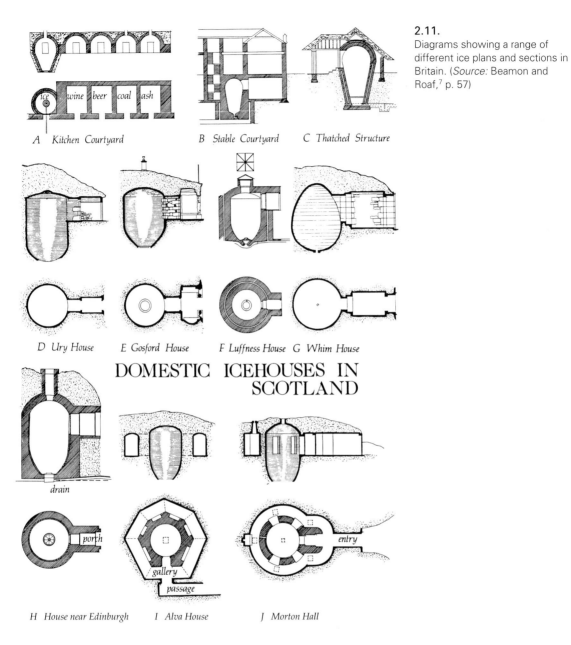

2.11.
Diagrams showing a range of
different ice plans and sections in
Britain. (*Source:* Beamon and
Roaf,[7] p. 57)

A   *Kitchen Courtyard*   B   *Stable Courtyard*   C   *Thatched Structure*

ice   wine   beer   coal   ash

D *Ury House*   E *Gosford House*   F *Luffness House* G *Whim House*

DOMESTIC ICEHOUSES IN SCOTLAND

drain

porch   *gallery*   *entry*

passage

H *House near Edinburgh*   I *Alva House*   J *Morton Hall*

Latin American, Europe, India and as far as China, where ice allegedly was sold for the price of its weight in silver.

Imported ice became most popular in Britain in the 1840s and the last delivery of imported ice to the Royal ice-houses was as late as 1936. Originally from Lake Wenham, this 'arctic crystal' was widely used in Britain where those selling it boasted that they could get a delivery of Wenham ice to any house in Britain within 24 hours. It was gradually replaced by 'Wenham' ice from Norway, from where over 300 000 tons a year were imported by the 1890s. The reason why it was preferred to British ice was that it was

2.12.
Ice harvesting in 1845 at
Rockland Lake, New York State,
USA, by the Knickerboker Ice Co.
(*Source:* Library of Congress,
Washington)

clear and clean whereas the British ice was often pellucid and
polluted.

The end of the ice-houses of Britain

Three factors are cited as being responsible for end of the ice-
houses, and the ice trade, in Britain:

1 World War I took the young men who harvested the ice off
   the land, and made the seas dangerous for those shipping it.
2 The increasing use of the refrigerator obviated the need for the
   laborious process of ice collection and storage.
3 The third reason for the demise of the ice-house was much
   less obvious. It was because the climate had changed. By the
   end of the nineteenth century the mean global temperature
   was rising steadily, heralding the end of the 'Little Ice Age'.

Four periods stand out in the recent history of world climates, as
shown in Figure 2.3:

* A warm post-glacial period reaching a peak 5000–3000 BC; a
   colder epoch culminating in 900–450 BC.
* A warm period around 100–1200, during the early part of which
   the Romans established extensive vineyards in Britain.
* The 'Little Ice Age' when the British climate was considerable
   colder between 1480 and 1850. It was during this period that
   the ice-houses of Britain flourished. In the 16th century the
   Thames froze over on four recorded occasions, in the 17th century eight times, in the 18th century six times and in the 19th

century four times. The last great freeze in Britain was 1878–79, when the Thames and other rivers froze over twice, much to the delight of many as the freezing of the river heralded the great ice fairs where bonfires were light on the river and the Gentlemen of Berwick on Tweed would traditionally celebrate by dining in a great tent on the river.

• The current warm period in which the global temperature has been increasing since around 1870.

The significant thermal factor for the ice-house was that although the mean increase in global temperature was relatively small, only c.0.6 °C between 1860 and 1990, this increase in temperature meant that there were no longer, over time, sufficient cold winters in Britain to regularly stock its ice-houses. So the key factor here for a particular 'thermal' technology is not how much warmer it gets, but whether the increase in temperature experienced crosses a critical threshold of performance for that particular technology.

THE IMPORTANCE OF THERMAL THRESHOLDS FOR THE SURVIVAL OF THERMAL TECHNOLOGIES

Because of climate change, the ice-house is now a climatically obsolete technology in Britain. Is this important lesson applicable to other forms of traditional buildings and technologies? What happens to a traditional house type that becomes climatically 'obsolete'?

Let us investigate this a little further, because if thermal thresholds are important in the performance of, for instance, housing, will a warming climate in already extremely hot regions push indoor temperatures over thresholds of acceptability, and if so, what will be the consequences of that?

We saw this in Basra in the summer of 2003 when the buildings were too hot to occupy and riots broke out. We saw this in the summer of 2003 in France when some 15 000 people died unnecessarily because their buildings could no longer provide adequate protection from the summer heat, and an angry public caused the resignation of at least one minister in the government. What happens if whole regions become regularly too hot to occupy?

Windcatchers – a litmus paper technology

The windcatchers' function is to passively provide comfort in extremely hot desert regions. Many different forms of windcatcher are found in the Middle East. They work basically in three ways:

1 They ventilate basements to remove smells from a heavily used area with few or no windows. In Baghdad where the air

temperature in summer gets up to 50 °C and is too hot to provide 'cooling', windcatchers provide a source of conditioned, fresh air by passing it through high narrow shafts before entering the basement.

2   They cool people by convective cooling where the air temperature is below skin temperature at around 35 °C, and evaporative cooling at higher temperatures where the humidity is not too high.

3   They cool the internal structure of the house, the walls and floors at night removing heat from the building, making it cooler internally during the day.

In the Yazd region, studied in the 1970s, the air temperatures on summer afternoons were over 45 °C outside and 38 °C in the ground floor rooms. Being downwind of orchards, groves and fields can reduce the mean outdoor air temperature by two to five degrees centigrade, and the towers here faced into the wind. Where the house was at the edge of the hot open desert the windcatchers faced away from the unpleasant wind and were used to draw the cooler air from the courtyard with its trees and planting through the summer rooms to exhaust it from the top of the tower. Small changes in the design of the building can have a large impact on its occupiability, even though only small temperature differences have resulted from the changes. This is because these change cross a critical threshold of performance for the occupants.

Below skin temperature (c.32–35 °C) a person can be cooled by convection; above it, they cannot because the ambient air is then heating the body not cooling it. Above this temperature the body can only be cooled by evaporation of sweat off the skin, which is why hot dry climates are more comfortable than hot wet ones because it is easy to lose moisture to the air when it is not saturated. So skin temperature represents a critical temperature range, or threshold.

Many of the villages of the Dasht-e-Kavir, the Great Central Desert, have no cool basements to resort to on the hottest afternoons and measured summer living room temperatures were up above 40 °C in the 1970s, the upper end of physiological limits of survivability in this region.

With climate change, even relatively small increases in *mean* global or regional temperatures will push *absolute* maximum temperatures indoors up towards 50 °C, and over the thermal threshold of habitable room temperatures. People will die, even those adapted to living in very high ambient temperatures.

If we look at the predicted mean global temperature increases over the next fifty to a hundred years we can see predicted mean

2.13.
From the melting mountains of
Europe to the shores of the rising
seas climate change will require
us to adapt our buildings.
(*Source*: Associated Press)

regional temperature increases in Central Iran reaching 4–8 °C. In
this case one would be tempted to postulate that the traditional
houses of the region will cease to be occupiable at all without air
conditioning. Such rural populations cannot afford air conditioning,
and will have only one option, to migrate to other habitats, that
is, to change their ecological niches, to areas where either:

1 they do not need air conditioning to survive, or
2 they can work to earn enough money to afford the air conditioning they need to survive.

BUT BUILDINGS CAN EVOLVE:
A CASE STUDY OF NAPLES

But surely buildings can be made to perform better passively in
such a way that will enable people to stay in their regions even
if it does get hotter? We looked for the answer to this question
in the buildings of the Naples region, looking at the evolution of
buildings over two millennia to see if they really did evolve to perform better in the bay area, famous for its architecture.[11]

The Mediterranean, like the Gulf, is a region that will be badly
affected by climate change (see Chapter 10, Figure 10.4, which
shows areas of Greece, Italy and Spain particularly affected by
increases in summer temperatures by 2050). For this reason
we investigated the palette of environmental strategies used in
cooling a range of buildings through time in the region of Naples.

These included the 1st century AD Casa Julio Polibio in Pompeii, the 16th century Pallazzo Gravina in Naples, the 18th century Villa Campolietto in Herculaneum, the 20th century modern movement icon building of Villa Mala Parte on Capri, a 1950s vernacular villa on Capri and the 1980s 'bioclimatic' building of the Instituto Motori in Naples. What we found was that the simple Roman building evolved, over the following two millennia, into extremely sophisticated and efficient passive building types, but surprisingly the most sophisticated was that of the Baroque period in the late 18th century, since when passive design skills appear to be on the decline.

Villa Julio Polibio

The Villa Julio Polibio, Pompeii, was destroyed in 73 AD with the eruption of Mount Vesuvius. The house was built in several phases with four rows of rooms, around three courtyards: the semi-roofed impluvium, the kitchen court and the garden courtyard. The ground floor rooms were very open to these courts, while the first floor rooms were more sheltered from them.

The most southerly rows, right on the street, have seven small rooms around two larger double height spaces with a stair leading up to a bank of rooms with south-facing windows onto the road. The passive solar gain here is far higher than in the rest of the house and these rooms onto the road would have been warmest in winter.

The second bank is centred around an open kitchen courtyard with central pool and a double height atrium open at the apex with an impluvium, or pool room beneath to catch the rain. This pool was on a direct axis from the street to the inner garden, which could be left open for effective cross ventilation over the surface of the pool to encourage evaporative cooling of the adjacent spaces. There is a second floor across this bank and in summer the upper rooms would have contained much of the incoming heat gain leaving the rooms below to remain cool. The kitchen is on the west side of the building and would have been hotter in summer than the eastern atrium. The coolest rooms in the house were ground floor rooms facing north onto the garden.

The third bank includes the garden and a colonnaded walkway around it to the north, east and west. Note that the main route through the house is to the east of the building and not the west. A good climatic reason for this would be that in designing it this way the walls of the courtyard rooms are never heated and in particular the very hot western sun never touches and heats up the

(a)

2.14.
View (a), plan (b) and temperature readings taken in March 1996 (c) for the Villa Julio Polibio in Pompeii. (*Source:* Sue Roaf and Mary Hancock)

(b)

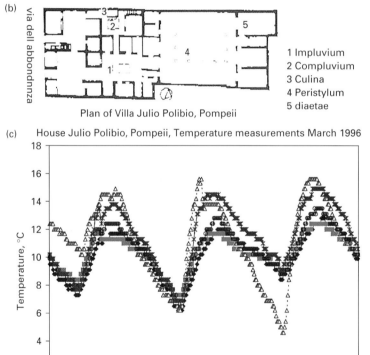

via dell abbondnnza

Plan of Villa Julio Polibio, Pompeii

1 Impluvium
2 Compluvium
3 Culina
4 Peristylum
5 diaetae

(c) House Julio Polibio, Pompeii, Temperature measurements March 1996

Temperature, °C

—◆— Kitchen court
—■— Pomp 1, Diaetae, living room overlooking garden
—△— Pomp 2, peristylum (garden)
—○— Pomp 3, Impluvium, larger rainwater collection area
—✳— Pompeii 4, front room, first floor

eastern wall. Plants may not have survived so well on an eastern wall as the western wall due to the additional heat contained in the afternoon sun. The garden was well planted with six trees, including a fig, and a row of ornamental bushes against the west wall. The trees would have almost entirely shaded the courtyard lending coolth to the house.

The openness of the ground floor rooms and the high thermal mass of the thick masonry walls would keep the temperature in many of the rooms at the mean temperature between maximum and minimum external air temperature. In the very hottest times of the year they may well have splashed water on the floors of the more open spaces to cool them evaporatively and retreated into a ground floor north-facing room and closed the door or hung curtains up to keep out the heat of the daytime air temperatures while they took their afternoon nap. It is probable that the family migrated around the house using different rooms at different times of year and day to select the optimum temperatures available in the house. Human behaviour plays a large part in adapting buildings to make them comfortable throughout the year. It should be noted that in every room there was typically found a single small clay or brass oil lamp showing that lighting levels after dark were very low. It suggests that the custom was for many to go to bed when it got dark. Only in the shrine, atrium and the north-easterly living room was there more than one lamp.

Pallazzo Gravina

Pallazzo Gravina is a courtyard-style renaissance palace dating to the mid 17th century with introverted planning. In the building the resident family were separated from their servants in a system of complex vertical and horizontal planning in which three zones can be identified.

The double-height ground floor includes stables, guards and storage rooms and steps down to cellars. The colonnaded walkway lends shade to the lower walls of the building and floor of part of the court. A single tree in the court harks back to former gardens. The piano nobile, or first floor, is where the family had its living and dining areas and bedrooms and its grandeur is emphasized in the elevations. The second floor housed the staff and more family and the top floor housed store rooms and servants linked to the ground floor by a separate stairwell not used by the family.

The whole building is constructed of tufa, or volcanic stone, which is highly aerated and provides excellent insulation and thermal mass. There are five key climatic strategies used in the building. Massive

2.15.
View of the Pallazzo Gravina.
(*Source:* Sue Roaf)

walls create inter-seasonal heat and coolth stores. Windowed gal-
leria provide a thermal buffer for the family living rooms from the
direct penetration of sun and hot air when closed in mid-summer
into the family living room complexes but enabled them to be noc-
turnally ventilated. Windows were carefully sized to prevent excessive solar gain. A complex ventilation system dependent on two
stack systems in the staircases created the churn to drive cross
ventilation in the interconnected chambers, particularly in the main
north-facing summer rooms on the south of the building facing the
street. In winter the double-depth winter living rooms are not so
connected. The stack would have drawn cool air from the colonnaded and planted courtyard below during the day being driven by
temperature difference up through the stack and at night this churn
would have been enhanced by the warmer air rising from the courtyard floor.

Villa Campolietto

Started in 1755 by Mario Gioffredo this extraordinary building was
finished in 1775 by Luigi Vanvitelli and his son Carlo. This Vitruvian
Baroque villa in Herculaneum is laid out in a square with the four
corner blocks of apartments divided on the piano nobile, on the
third floor, by a huge cross axis of double-height rooms capped by
a large raised rotunda in the centre with windows on four sides
creating a venturi tower. Beneath the ground floor are two further
basement levels including water cisterns and an ice storage room.

(a)

2.16.
Villa Campolietto. (a) View and (b) internal temperature readings taken in March 1996. (*Source:* Sue Roaf and Mary Hancock)

(b)

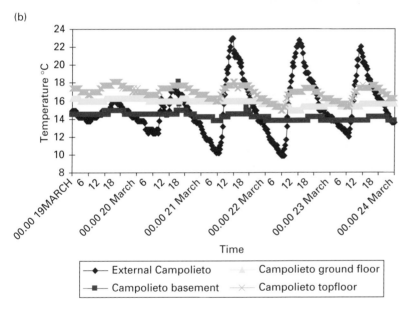

This villa has far larger windows than the previous buildings and the family quarters include south-, west- and north-facing living and dining rooms and bedrooms on the north of the building. The walls are massive, providing inter-seasonal heat and coolth storage capacity, with a plastered tufa construction. Daylight levels are high in the living areas and for summer cooling the ventilation system would have created perfect thermal comfort. The house is situated some half a mile from the sea on a flank of Mount Vesuvius in an elevated position to catch the cool on-shore winds.

The genius of this building is its ventilation systems. In warm weather the whole building could be opened up to catch the wind. In very hot weather the external doors and windows could be shut and the venturi tower of the rotunda above the stairway would draw cooler air up from the basements through the transverse ventilation system. In extreme heat ice from the ice store could have been brought up in boxes to cool individual rooms. In conditions of dire heat basements living areas would have remained cool but we have evidence now of their use in summer. It should also be noted that the gardens have been landscaped to enhance coolth with the use of shade, ponds, fountains and a sunken date grove.

Each corner block has its own independent cross, transverse and stack-driven systems based around vertical stairways with venturi towers above each. These operate independently of the main rooms of the piano nobile of which the three main rooms, the drawing room, the dining room and the music room, have double-height ceilings with a buffer void above to prevent direct penetration of heat into them via the roof. The villa also includes a hidden system of ducts, vents and grills drawing cool air into rooms and expelling warm air from them. The success of the ventilation is that the shore-side location precluded the need for lateral buffering of spaces against the heat, as we found in the previous two buildings. This strongly suggests the movement around the building at different times of day. The southerly drawing room would probably not have been used in mid afternoon on the hottest days but could have been cooled in early evening by opening it to sea breezes.

The importance of thermal mass, or heavy-weight materials in buildings, increases in 'passive cooling systems', in which the design of the building itself, rather than the machines in it, are used to create acceptable internal climates. In a well-designed, heavy-weight building the indoor temperature can track the mean of the outdoor maximum and minimum air temperatures, levelling the diurnal, and even the monthly, swings in temperature to provide safer indoor climates in extreme weather.[12]

Villa Mala Parte

Built in the 1930s on a rock jutting out into the sea from the southern coast of Capri Island, this building is vertically zoned. The ground floor comprises kitchens and store rooms. The first floor has

(a)

(b)

2.17.
Exterior (a) and interior (b) views of Villa Mala Parte, Capri. (*Source:* Sue Roaf)

bedrooms and servants' quarters and the second floor houses the living and dining rooms and the main living apartment. The construction is fairly massive, with 600 mm wide walls of brick. The roof is of uninsulated concrete so potentially forming a heat source. In the lower rooms the central corridor restricts the effectiveness of the cross ventilation and the rooms have limited window openings so preventing excessive solar gain. These remain cool. The upper floor has large unshaded areas of glass windows, which lead to high solar gain levels in summer. They slide open to provide direct cross ventilation but not easily and the very exposed site means that winds can get very strong around the house. This means that on sunny afternoons with a strong cold wind the comfort levels of occupants on this floor would be interesting to record. High level open vents just under the concrete ceiling were designed, presumably, to remove heat from and ventilate the room in such conditions. In fact the building owner's favourite room was the first floor east-facing study with a Kakkleoven for winter warmth and he preferred a first floor bedroom to sleeping in the main bedroom apartment. The windows whistle apparently.

Villa Ranzo

Built by the Ranzo family in the mid 1950, this is a typical neo-vernacular villa on Capri. It is located on the cool side of Capri in the shade of the central landmass so in summer it is cool but in winter the building becomes very cold. The basement rooms are stores and servants' quarters, the first floor the living and kitchen area and the top floor has five bedrooms and four bathrooms. Direct cross ventilation and lateral ventilation via windows and french doors is used in all main rooms and on the west-facing walls a veranda at first floor shades ground floor rooms. The walls are of massive stone and render construction, and the roof is of concrete. The stairwell provides an effective stack moving air between floors.

Instituto Motori

Completed in 1992 the modern headquarters of this research institute is a well-publicized modern bioclimatic building. Covering over 6900 m^2 and housing a range of functions including offices, library, conference hall, café, museum and laboratories, the building is rectangular on a northeast to southwest axis. The basement level has a store and conference hall, and the first, second and third floors consist of offices and laboratories opening off a central hall open in the centre for three floors and above which is the museum

2.18.
View of Villa Ranzo, Capri.
(*Source:* Sue Roaf)

2.19.
View of Instituto Motori, Naples.
(*Source:* Sue Roaf)

on the roof. The flanking offices block off light from the central circulation zone and we found all labs and offices typically had their doors shut. The windows of the building are 'smart', being reversible so that the timber louvres can be put on the outside of the building, but many were broken and their ventilation value in a closed office was limited. The lightweight structure holds little thermal storage potential and provides poor insulation against the heat and cold. All thermal storage capacity would be held in the concrete floors, which were fairly universally carpeted, so reducing their effectiveness. There are no thermal buffering zones against the heat either horizontally or vertically and no apparent zoning of activities according to location in the building in relation to its micro climate.

Buildings of Naples: summary

Table 2.1 demonstrates that, despite the best intentions of the designers, the modern 'bioclimatic' building has the fewest adaptive passive opportunities for modifying indoor climate, followed by the Modern Movement icon building of the Villa Mala Parte. The traditional buildings employed a wide range of effective adaptive strategies to raise or lower indoor temperatures without using fossil fuel energy. The temperature graphs in Figures 2.14 and 2.16 show that while the indoor climate in the Roman house tracked the outdoor climate, in the Rococo Baroque Villa of Campolietto built in the 18th century the indoor climate, using a wide range of passive techniques, could, in places, be de-coupled from the outdoor climate, potentially providing a cool environment even in the scorching heat of the future.

All new office buildings in the Naples region are now air-conditioned in a climate that was once considered 'perfect'. Air-conditioned buildings traditionally have only two adaptive opportunities to ameliorate the heat: (a) shut the internal blinds (the heat is already in the building and cannot escape once the radiation has entered through the glass) and (b) adjust the air conditioning.

THE ADAPTABILITY OF BUILDINGS

How much of a challenge will climate change be to us? Surely we can adapt to the changes ahead with better buildings and technologies?

That humans are adaptable we know. They have settled in flimsy tents from the ice lands of the Arctic to the sand lands of the Equator. They can live without machines in climates from 50 °C below to 50 °C above freezing point.

Table 2.1. Range of adaptive opportunities available to building users to ameliorate their own internal climate using passive and active systems

DESIGN STRATEGY	1	2	3	4	5	6
Cold site					1	
Cool site				1		
Solar orientation	1	1	1			
Sea breezes			1	1	1	
Summer use only			1		1	
Morning/afternoon use	1	1	1		1	
Summer/winter rooms	1	1	1			
Horizontal buffer zones	1	1	1		1	
Vertical buffer zones	1	1	1			
Verandahs/colonnades	1	1	1		1	
Planting	1	1	1		1	
Pools/evaporation	1		1			
Earth Sheltering		1	1	1	1	1
Thermal mass	1	1	1	1	1	
Interseasonal storage		1	1		1	
Basement coolth use		1	1	1	1	
Hypercausts	1					
Shaded from West sun	1				1	
Cross ventilation	1	1	1		1	
Stack cooling		1	1			
Lateral ventilation	1	1	1		1	
Venturi ventilation			1			
Ventilation ducts			1	1		
Door ventilation control	1	1	1		1	
Stack warming	1	1	1			
Insulated roof			1			1
False ceiling insulation			1			1
External shade	1				1	1
High rooms	1	1	1		1	
Small windows	1	1				1
Smart windows						1
Shutters					1	1
Low energy lighting	1	1	1			1
Rainwater storage	1	1	1		1	1
Ice for cooling			1			
	20	20	27	6	19	9

LIST OF THE PASSIVE STRATEGIES
1 – Pompeii, *2* – Gravina, *3* – Campolietto,
4 – Mala Parte, *5* – Ranzo, *6* – Motori.

Source: Roaf, S. and Handcock, M. (1998) Future-proofing buildings against climate change using traditional buildings technologies in the Mediterranean region. *Proceedings of the Eurosolar Conference*, PortoRos, Slovenia.

That buildings are adaptable we also know, and that people can live in the same tent, perhaps not comfortably, at the extremes is sure. But there is a fixed range of temperatures within which a building type will give adequate protection in extreme weather, flanked by thermal thresholds beyond which survival in them may not be assured. We also know that with clever design, building types can be modified and improved in one area to be safe in a significantly wider range of temperatures, as we saw in the Roman and the Baroque buildings of Naples. But there are climate thresholds beyond which buildings cease to be safe to occupy, with the vulnerability of the occupant depending on the form and fabric of the buildings, and the degree of its exposure to extreme climates.

The risk of not surviving in a particular building type and region will be largely dependent on the nature of that building and on how much the climate changes. Both are crucial in the challenge of designing buildings today in which people can be comfortable in 50 years' time.

NOTES AND REFERENCES

1   For a good simple outline of adaptive human responses see http://www.bio.usyd.edu.au/summer/Human/HA_lectures/HA_lect/LECTURE2.pdf.

2   For a good source book on the evolution of the early settlements and empires in Mesopotamia, the cradle of civilization, see Roaf, M. (1990) *Cultural Atlas of Mesopotamia.* Oxford: Andromeda.

3   Roaf, S. (1979) A Study of the Architecture of the Black Tents of the Lurs. Technical Thesis for the Architectural Association Part II exam.

4   For the best book available on the vernacular buildings, see Oliver, Paul (ed.) (1997) *Encyclopaedia of Vernacular Architecture of the World*, in 3 volumes. Cambridge: Cambridge University Press.

5   Black-Michaud, J. (1986) *Sheep and Land. The Economics of Power in a Tribal Society.* Cambridge: Cambridge University Press and Paris: Maison des Sciences de l'Homme.

6   Roaf, S. (1989) The Windcatchers of Yazd. PhD thesis, Oxford Polytechnic. For a further outline of the processes involved see Roaf, S., Fuentes, M. and Thomas, S. (2003) *Ecohouse2: A Design Guide.* Oxford: Architectural Press.

7   For a complete history of the ice-houses and ice trade of the world see Beamon, S. and Roaf, S. (1990) *The Ice-Houses*

of Britain. London: Routledge; and for the desert buildings of the Central Persian Desert see Beazley, E. and Harverson, M. (eds) (1982) *Living with the Desert*. Warminster: Aris and Philips.

8   Two excellent papers that touch on this challenge for Kuwait are: Al-Temeemi, A. and Harris, D. (2004) A guideline for assessing the suitability of earth-sheltered mass-housing in hot-arid climates. *Energy and Buildings*, 36, pp. 251–60; and Al-Mumin, A., Khattab, O. and Sridhar, G. (2003) Occupants' behavior and activity patterns influencing the energy consumption in the Kuwaiti residences. *Energy and Buildings*, 35, pp. 549–59.

9   Page, S. (1969) Ice, offerings and deities in the Old Babylonian texts from Tell el-Rimah, Actes de la XV11e. *Rencontre d'Assylriologie*. Brussels, p. 181.

10   Tschudi, J.J. (1847) *Travels in Peru during the years 1838–1842*. London, pp. 136–7.

11   Roaf, S., Haves, P. and Orr, J. (1998) Climate change and passive cooling in Europe. *Proceedings of PLEA Conference*. Lisbon: James & James Science, pp. 463–6.

12   Baruch Givoni, the doyen of passive design, presents thresholds for the operation of different types of such passive cooling systems.

For the following ventilation strategies:

> **comfort ventilation:** ventilation to produce immediate human comfort, mainly during the day
> **nocturnal convective cooling:** ventilation to cool the thermal mass of building during the night in order to improve comfort during the day

the threshold value of the maximum ambient air temperature for the viability of comfort ventilation he gives as 28–32 °C at indoor air speeds of 1.5–2.0 m/s, depending on the comfort requirements. This is based on the observation that the indoor air temperature approaches the outdoor air temperature as the ventilation rate increases. For comparison, the upper limit of the extended ASHRAE comfort zone (see Chapter 5) is 28 °C at 0.8 m/s air speed. In offices, or similar environments, a combination of higher internal loads and restrictive expectations concerning dress would produce a reduction in the threshold that depends on the particular situation but which may amount to several degrees centigrade. Givoni's rule of thumb for nocturnal convective cooling is that the indoor maximum temperature is less than the outdoor maximum temperature by nearly half the diurnal range in outdoor temperature, providing the envelope and internal gains are modest and the thermal capacity is high. Nocturnal convective cooling is applicable if the maximum ambient temperature is too high for comfort ventilation and the diurnal range is sufficiently large to bring the indoor maximum temperature down into the comfort range. For example, if the minimum outdoor temperature is 24 °C, the threshold value of the maximum outdoor temperature is 40 °C if the indoor temperature is not to exceed 32 °C. If building occupants retreat to a deep basement they can occupy a temperature that may be closer to the mean of the annual mean maximum and minimum temperatures providing an even safer temperature in extreme weather.

The indoor temperatures in passive buildings are then determined primarily by the outdoor temperatures, the form and fabric of the building and the way it is used, and it is possible, therefore, to define threshold values for the outdoor temperatures, in relation to what passive systems would be effective in current and future climates for different regions. In buildings where the loads are significant compared to the heat that can be stored in the thermal mass with the available temperature swings, the threshold for viability depends on the loads and the effective thermal mass as well as the outdoor temperatures and may require complex, validated, simulation to predict performance in a range of climates.

See Givoni, B. (1991) Performance and applicability of passive and low-energy cooling systems. *Energy and Buildings*, 17: 177–99 and a range of his other books on the subject. The importance of the 'adaptation' of local populations in such calculations is clarified in Chapter 5 of this present text.

3 RISK, SCENARIOS AND INSURANCE

INTRODUCTION

All of us are placed at risk by climate change. Some of us are at more risk than others, and for some that risk will prove catastrophic. It is fundamentally important to understand the extent of the risk in order to be able to future-proof the lives of individuals against that risk in the face of the changes ahead.[1]

Risk, we believe, is composed of three elements:

1 The **vulnerability** of the person to a risk was dealt with in Chapter 2, where we looked at the idea that the design and fabric of buildings, and the habits of their occupants, enables local populations to survive in a range of diurnal, seasonal or extreme climatic events. But we saw too that people in traditional buildings have the capability of adapting only so far, after which their very survival is threatened. These limits to the adaptational opportunities people have, to some extent define the vulnerability of those people in that place to climate change. For those who live in settlements on the edge of hot deserts, in 'modern' houses with thin walls and roofs, large windows, dependent on air conditioning, they are infinitely more vulnerable

3.1.
The risk triangle. (*Source:* Crichton, D.C. (2001) in *The Implications of Climate Chango for the Insurance Industry*, ed. Dr J. Salt, Building Research Establishment, UK. © D.C. Crichton 2001)

to changes in climate than those in traditional, thick-walled houses with shading and deep basements.

2   The idea of the **exposure** of a person deals with the third element in the triangle of symbiosis that ties man to his ecosystem, the climate. The degree to which any population will be exposed to the exigencies of climate change is related to their geographical location in relation to latitude, land masses and the patterns of climate change. Some areas of the world will experience far faster and more extreme warming, in particular in the high latitudes of the Northern hemisphere and towards the centres of land masses in areas with 'continental' climates. To date the 'exposure' of Britain to swings of temperature has been damped by its island status. The climate of the UK is strongly influenced by the great sea mass and currents of the Atlantic ocean. On the other hand, through its location on the edge of that ocean, the UK is one of the windiest countries in Europe and more exposed than most to storms. Those in Alaska, whose homes are on the melting tundra, and who face some of the most rapid predicted increases in temperature globally, are infinitely more 'exposed' to the risks of large-scale temperature increases than most, regardless of how much change their homes can accommodate.

3   The nature of the **hazard** is perhaps what will do for many of us in the long run. Hazard is a term that is typically described in terms of the size of the risk and the frequency with which it is experienced. How extreme the climate becomes, and how often will it be extreme are significant. If a river floods homes once in a century then those homes are under considerably less risk than homes that flood every year or two. It is on these two measures of hazard that the insurance industry largely bases its insurance premiums.[2] This can be illustrated with a case study. In 1999 Britain experienced one of the strongest storms in recent history. The 'Braer' depression ranged across Scotland for almost three weeks, reaching UK record-breaking lows of 915 millibars (the lowest pressure ever recorded in Europe is 912 millibars and hurricane Andrew that cost the United States 30 billion dollars in 1992 only reached 924 millibars). And yet its cost to the British insurance industry was (relatively) negligible, despite the strength of its *hazard*, for two reasons. First, it tracked across Scotland only, missing most of England, so the *exposure* of the British Isles to it was relatively low. Secondly, in Scotland building standards are higher than in England. Roofs still have to have sarking beneath the roof finishes and are more firmly constructed than required under English regulations so reducing the *vulnerability* of individual buildings exposed to the storm.

It is, however, important to understand all aspects of the risks we face if we are to act effectively to reduce those risks over time.

RISK AND IMPACT

Risks ultimately either do, or do not, translate into damage to an individual, institution, a landscape, country or the planet. Risk is the potential for that damage to occur. The damage may take the form of a wide range of impacts and in chapters within this book on how hot, wet and windy it will get, respectively, and the discussion on the insurance industry below, we will look at not only how much change we are faced with from the climate but also explore the idea of how vulnerable and exposed different peoples, settlements and buildings have been to such climate hazards in the past, to give an idea of how we may be affected by them in the future. Everything is connected in our world, so climate impacts on a landscape will affect, for instance, the insurance industry that in turn impacts on regional development and the future of buildings and cities in such regions. Our understanding of future risk is still informed by past experience of related impacts.

Impact can be calculated thus:

(possible) Hazard × Vulnerability × Exposure = (possible) Impact

SCENARIO PLANNING

Traditionally people measured risk by applying to particular situations the lessons learnt through past experience. Historic events provided adequate experience against which to evaluate future risk. We now believe from the climate models, touched on in Chapter 1, that if current trends continue, the future climate will be very different from that today. But those future trends will be influenced by the actions taken by us today, because much of the increase in global temperatures is known to be strongly driven by 'anthropogenic', or man-made, emissions of climate change gases.

If we are to model future climates we must include the potential influences of our own actions on the trends. The way this is currently done is by using scenarios of what the future may be like, extrapolated from trends in the current climate and social and economic activity. Against these we can measure the potential costs and benefits in the future of continuing with our 'business as usual' approach, or modifying our behaviour.[3]

Scenario planning involves looking at a range of alternative futures, using projections of current trends, and applying different boundary conditions and strategies to case studies. Brainstorming and 'think-tank' techniques are often used to identify 'stepping stones' and 'tripwires', ways in which strategies might fail, and what are the key drivers for change.

Contrasting scenarios can then be 'scripted' and tested out on decision-makers to help them develop more effective policies with which to minimize the impacts of current decisions on future societies.

Scenarios are plausible descriptions of how things may change in the future, built to reflect what is possible, not what is preferred, desirable or undesirable. They are meant to be politically and morally neutral constructs.

The quality of life of future societies in, and around, buildings depends very much on the quality of the decisions we make about the choice of location and technologies for buildings, the form and fabric of the built environment and the lifestyles we adopt in them. The buildings we will live in, in 20 or 50 years' time, will be, by and large, those we occupy or are building today[4] and so our choices, today, must be based on such descriptions of a probable future, because they are the best chance we have of designing buildings that go some way, at least, towards being appropriate for the rapidly changing world.

Three of the most influential scenario sets in Britain are those of the UK Foresight Programme, the Royal Commission on Environmental Pollution and the UK Climate Impacts Programme (UKCIP). For a detailed outline of how these scenarios were derived see the companion website: http://books.elsevier.com/companions/0750659114.

Foresight scenarios

The UK Foresight Programme began in 1993, drawing on the expertise of thousands of people from the UK's leading businesses, universities, government and other institutions.[5] It was designed to identify technical opportunities and social drivers in a changing world and has helped to shape research priorities both in the private and public sector. Thus, for example, it is now standard practice for research organizations seeking funding from UK Government to be requested to identify how their research will fit in with the 'Foresight Scenarios'. In addition, it is known that the UK government Cabinet Office makes use of the Foresight Scenario methodology in formulating strategies and policies.

The scenarios are only two-dimensional, that is they consider only two dimensions of change, namely social values and governance systems. These scenarios were very important in building up a range of possible social and economic descriptions of the future that might arise if certain decisions were taken today and these scenarios have been widely used as the basis for other more complex scenarios.

RCEP 2000

The Royal Commission Report on Environmental Pollution (RCEP),[6] published in June 2000, has proved to be one of the most influential of all scenario sets for the built environment. The report suggested what appeared to be, then, deep cuts necessary in emissions from buildings of 60% by 2050 and 80% by 2100, to contain climate change. These dramatic cuts, only four years down the road from publication, are now taken for granted and used as target values in government emissions reductions programmes. The RCEP scenarios introduce issues of what energy sources are used and the impacts of related choices on future climates.

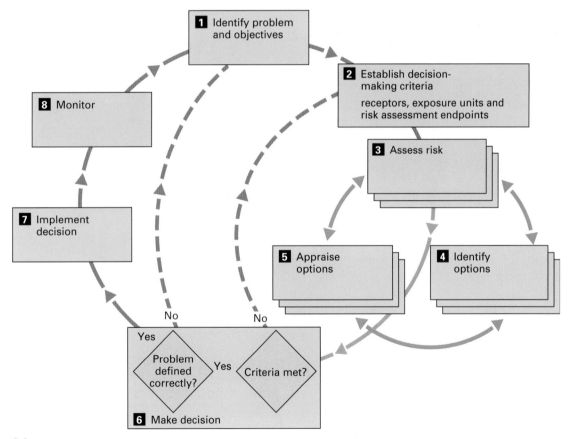

3.2.
Scenarios are essential for risk analysis, where they are used to define the problem and then for the assessment of its associated risks. For every major decision a detailed risk analysis that takes into account the impact on, and from, climate change will be increasingly a requirement. This proposed model for such an analysis is based on the UKCIP report on Climate Adaptation, Risk Uncertainty and Decision-Making. (*Source:* Willows, R.I. and Connell, R.K. (eds) (2003) *UKCIP Technical Report.* Oxford: UKCIP)

The UKCIP02 scenarios: background

These are the scenarios on which are based the following descriptions of future climates in the UK. The UKCIP02 scenarios build on the work of previous scenarios published by UKCIP in 1998, and have been updated to take into account:

- A series of climate modelling experiments completed by the Hadley Centre using their most recently developed models for the UK climate covering four alternative future climates, based on social and economic scenarios, labelled:
  - *Low Emissions*
  - *Medium Low Emissions*
  - *Medium High Emissions*
  - *High Emissions*
- New global emissions scenarios published in 2000 by the IPCC (International Panel on Climate Change).

The UKCIP scenarios provide detailed information on future climates in Britain in relation to different geographical locations in the UK, extremes of weather and rises in sea level. What is presented below are just the headlines of the important UKCIP Summary Report, that fronts a vast amount of scientific research, and thousands of simulation runs, carried out in the UK and abroad in this complex field of trying to predict the future climate.

There is a difference between a *climate scenario* and a *climate change scenario*. The former describe possible future climates rather than *changes* in climate. Climate scenarios usually combine observations about present day climate with estimates of the change in climates, typically using the results from global or regional climate model experiments.

Many of the future changes that will happen over the next 30–40 years have already been determined by historic emissions and because of the inertia in the climate system. We therefore have to adapt to some degree of climate change however much future emissions are reduced.

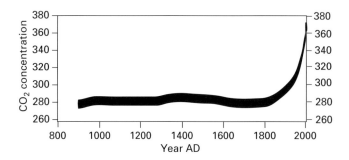

3.3.
Increasing historic concentrations (parts per million) of carbon dioxide in the global atmosphere. The line thickness indicates uncertainty in the concentrations. (*Source:* IPCC, from *UKCIP02 Briefing Report*, summary, p. 5)

The climate of the second half of the 21st century, and beyond, will be increasingly influenced by the volume of the greenhouse gases emitted by human society over the coming decades. By the 2080s, the UKCIP02 scenarios suggest that the atmospheric carbon dioxide concentrations may be between 525 parts per million (ppm) and 810 ppm, as shown in Table 3.1.

In the 1961–90 record, the concentration of carbon dioxide of 334 ppm was significantly greater than the pre-industrial concentration of 280 ppm and by 2000 the atmospheric concentrations of carbon dioxide had reached around 370 ppm. Even if global emissions fall again below today's level, as assumed in the UKCIP02 *Low Emissions* scenario, the future rate of global warming over the present century may be about four times that experienced during the 20th century. If the emissions rate increases to approximately four times today's level, the *High Emissions* scenario, the future warming rate may be about eight times that experienced during the 20th century and such a change in climate will be extremely difficult to adapt to, and will have huge impacts on every person, building, settlement, society and country in the world.

How seriously should we take such predictions?

Temperate Britain has perhaps less to fear than many other countries with more continental climates, while the future scenarios for the USA and Australia,[7] two heavily energy-dependent continents, show a much bleaker picture. There is a vast amount of emerging knowledge on future climates freely available on the Internet[8] and many reputable institutions in countries around the world are working to help develop strategies with which to fight for the future.

We should take such climate change predictions very seriously indeed, and particularly because fears have been expressed that

Table 3.1. Changes in global temperature (°C) and atmospheric carbon dioxide concentration (parts per million or ppm) for the 2080s period (2071–2100 average) for the four UKCIP scenarios. The carbon dioxide concentration in 2001 was about 370 ppm

SRES emissions scenario	UKCIP02 climate change scenario	Increase in global temperature (°C)	Atmospheric CO_2 concentration (ppm)
B1	*Low Emissions*	2.0	525
B2	*Medium Low Emissions*	2.3	562
A2	*Medium High Emissions*	3.3	715
A1FI	*High Emissions*	3.9	810

Source: UKCIP02 Briefing Report,[3] p. 6

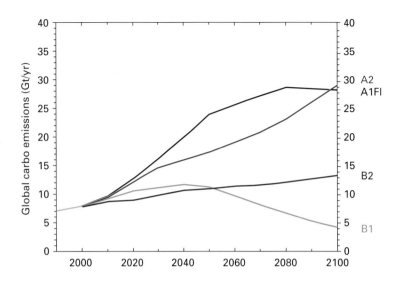

3.4.
Global carbon emissions from 2000 to 2100 for the four chosen SRES emissions scenarios with observed data to 2000. (*Source: UKCIP02 Briefing Report*, p. 6)

the hot summer of 2003, the hottest on record for Europe, is a sign that not only is climate change speeding up but 'the parching heat experience [in the summer of 2003] could be consistent with a worst-case scenario [of global warming] that no one wants to be true'. These are the words of Professor John Schnellnhuber, former scientific adviser to the German government and current head of the Tyndall Centre. He added: 'What we are seeing is absolutely unusual. We know that global warming is proceeding apace, but most of us were thinking that in 20–30 years time we would see hot spells [like this]. But it is happening now.'[9]

THE INSURANCE INDUSTRY

One group that is taking climate change very seriously indeed is the insurance industry, and their deliberations and decisions over the coming years could put millions, who can no longer get insurance for their homes, at the greatest economic risk of their lives.

If the huge (US$1.5 trillion per year) fossil fuel industry is the only industrial lobby that actively engages in the climate battle, it is likely to prevail and progress in addressing the global climate dilemma will continue to stall. Few industries are capable of doing battle with the likes of the fossil fuel lobby. But the insurance industry is. On a worldwide basis, the two are of roughly comparable size – and potential political clout.[10]

As new risks emerge, insurance cover is either provided for them at increased premiums or excluded from existing policies, and the number of uninsurable buildings increases. Insurers in the USA now typically require building owners to take out special policies to cover the mould threat, described as the 'new asbestos' issue for the industry. Although the UK and Australia have not followed the United States in mould exclusion clauses yet, they may well do so over time.[11] Risks in the environment escalate because of changing conditions, building types and materials, chemicals, biological threats and even trends in agriculture.[12]

The insurance industry itself is now at risk in this rapidly changing risk environment. In 2003 the global insurance industry paid out more money over the year than ever before in history, and made record profits! This is because premiums have been rising rapidly and across the board to pre-empt catastrophic payouts that may actually bring the industry to its knees. The fear is that if allowance is made for a £15 billion event, from a terrorist or climate-related event, a £25 billion event will occur. The value of the buildings at the World Trade Center was $1.5 billion a tower but the total costs of the event it is thought will eventually reach $50 billion. The cost of London flooding has been put anywhere between £30 and £80 billion.

The year 2003 was the worst on record for payouts from the industry. Munich Re's annual bulletin[13] was a sobering analysis of natural catastrophes in 2003 and concluded that economic and insured losses continue to increase at a high level. The year 2003 was marked by a series of severe natural hazard events, with the number of fatalities far exceeding the long-term average. It reinforced the fact that in view of the deteriorating risk situation, the insurance industry must continue to act rigorously – for example, by agreeing on limits of liability and risk-adequate premiums.

Highlights of the bulletin included:

- More than 50 000 people were killed in natural catastrophes worldwide, almost five times as many as in the previous year (11 000); such a high number of victims has only been recorded four times since 1980. The heat wave in Europe and the earthquake in Iran each claimed more than 20 000 lives.
- The number of natural catastrophes recorded in 2003 was around 700 and thus at the same level as in the previous year.
- Economic losses rose to over $60 billion (2002: $55 billion). These were mainly the result of tornadoes, heat waves and forest fires – but also severe floods in Asia and Europe.
- Insured losses increased to about $15 billion (previous year: $11.5 billion). The series of tornadoes in the Midwest of the United States in May alone cost insurers more than $3 billion.

The year 2003 was marked not only by natural catastrophes but also by other remarkable events: the power outages in the

United States, the United Kingdom, Denmark and Italy, for example; total losses involving two satellites; numerous terrorist attacks; a major leak of poison gas in China shortly before the end of the year.

Box 3.1 2003 Insurance Industry Payouts Related to Climate

Windstorms:

- Hailstorms hit the US MidWest in April and May: cost insured losses of $5 billion.
- Tornadoes in May in the United States cost over $3 billion (one of the ten most costly storms in insurance history).
- Hurricane Isabel, in the second half of September, swept over the US East Coast and devastated more than 360 000 homes with an economic loss of around $5 billion, of which $1.7 billion was insured.
- Europe suffered comparatively little damage from windstorms, with economic losses of around $1 billion and insured losses of $300 million.

Heat waves:

- Germany alone recorded temperatures from June to August corresponding to a 450-year event in climatological terms. Predictions are that if the atmosphere continues to warm up unchecked, such a heat wave could become a mere twenty-year event by 2020 in large areas of western and central Europe and large parts of the western Mediterranean region.
- Costs: approx. $13 billion, an extremely large amount, but the burden imposed on insurers by, for example, drought-related losses is relatively small because reduced yields in the agricultural sector as a result of dry weather are mostly not yet covered for insurance within the European Union.

Wild fires:

- In Australia, southwest Europe, Canada and the United States fires swept through whole region. In October and November alone, thousands of homes fell victim to the flames in California.
- Costs: $2 billion for the insurance industry, representing almost 60% of the economic losses.

Floods:

- In China, the swollen waters of the Huai and Yangtze flooded 650 000 homes and caused an economic loss of almost $8 billion.
- Southern France was under water in many parts at the beginning of December, when numerous rivers, including the Rhône, flooded their banks after extreme rainfall.
- Costs: insured losses $1 billion and economic losses of around $1.5 billion.

However, the extent of the losses caused by these events was much smaller than that caused by the natural catastrophes and they claimed fewer lives. Munich Re found that while windstorms and severe weather in 2003 accounted for only about a third of the approximately 700 events recorded, they were responsible for 75% of all the insured losses caused by natural catastrophes.

Insurance companies, virtually without exception, are convinced that the increasingly severe weather-related events are linked to changes in climate generating new types of weather risks and threatening greater losses. The insurance industry is preparing itself for increasing risks and losses, but the call is now for 'above all, transparency and a limitation of the risks'. This is not an easy prospect, as it does not just mean putting up premiums and making more profits but also, for instance, informing one home or office block owner in London that they will flood if the Thames Barrier overtops, while the one at the other end of the street will not. Today they are both charged the same rate to insure their office or house, as the risks are spread across the portfolio. Building owners are not informed that they are vulnerable to such events, or for instance dam breakage, or increasingly to litigation from building owners and occupiers on properties that become too uncomfortable in hot weather. The impact on property prices and insurability, when such information does become available in an increasingly 'transparent' market place, could be profound.

The insurance industry – viability

The insurance industry has the skills to provide the assessment, quantification and mapping of risks, prompt disaster recovery, fraud control, avoidance of duplicate administration and the access to international financial resources. It can thus contribute considerably to an efficient risk management system. The insurance industry also provides strong financial incentives for loss prevention and mitigation to their clients and the public, for example by means of deductibles. (United Nations Environment Programme Insurance Industry Initiative paper on the Kyoto Protocol)[14]

The concerns of many insurers are not just about the uncertainties around the increase in the frequency and severity of storms and floods which could cause problems, but also the implications of changing responses and attitudes of governments and corporate clients. The activities of pressure groups and concerns of individual consumers are also very important and will increasingly affect insurers' strategies.

For many years insurers have accepted risks with surprisingly limited information about the natural hazards that impact so much on their claims costs. Increases in the frequency and severity of natural disasters and concerns about the effects of climate change are resulting in a new and healthy dialogue developing between the research community and the insurance industry.

In 1994, a study group set up by the Society of Fellows of the Chartered Insurance Institute published a very significant report entitled 'The Impact of Changing Weather Patterns on Property Insurance'. For the first time, there was a comprehensive analysis of the potential effects of climate change on the UK insurance industry. This study was followed by an update of that report in 2001[15] and by a range of widely available reports from different perspectives.[16] These reports raised questions about whether insurers would be able to continue to provide flood cover in the UK in the light of climate change.

Flood is not the only issue, of course; other perils could cause problems for insurers. In particular, buildings will be vulnerable to storm and subsidence damage and damage caused by driving rain, and research by the Building Research Establishment using insurance claims data has resulted in recommendations that building standards should be reviewed in the light of climate change impacts.[17] Both the Office of the Deputy Prime Minister (ODPM) and the Scottish Executive need to urgently consider and implement changes to building standards as a result.

In June 2000 the Royal Commission Report on Environmental Pollution was published[18] shortly followed by the World Disasters Report 2000 from the International Federation of Red Cross and Red Crescent Societies. Both these reports have re-emphasized the need for action to mitigate climate change and to adapt to its impacts, and will put renewed pressure on governments and insurers to take firm action.

How big is the problem? Average annual insured losses from global natural disasters have increased from $0.6 billion in the 1960s to $9.8 billion in the 1990s (all at 1998 values).[19] Such increases in the costs of natural disasters are not necessarily due to climate change. As Munich Re point out, they are due to a combination of factors such as population growth, rising standards of living, concentration of population in urban areas, settlement in hazardous areas, vulnerability of modern societies and technologies, as well as changes in climate and environment. The point is that in the future, climate change is likely to accelerate the rate of increase in the losses.

Of all the causes listed above, the future impacts of climate change are the hardest to predict. It seems clear now that global mean temperatures are rising and that sea levels will continue to rise, but how will this affect claims experienced? In the UK the experts predict that there will be more droughts and subsidence, but also more coastal flooding in the Southeast and more river and drainage flooding everywhere. While it is not yet clear if there will be more frequent and more severe storms, there is increasing evidence to suggest that storm tracks will move south. This will mean more severe storms in the south of England where construction standards are lower than in the north, where storms have traditionally been more frequent. This will lead to higher damage levels and claims problems for insurers.[20]

In the past, historic claims experienced were a good measure for predicting future risk. The increases in numbers and costs of natural disasters indicate the need for a new approach to underwriting. Insurers are therefore investing heavily in geographic information systems, detailed databases, and sophisticated modelling techniques to fine tune their underwriting.

In addition to traditional risk management skills, insurers will increasingly find the need to work with academia and government, and this process has already started. Insurers are uniquely placed to contribute to society's efforts to reduce the impact of natural

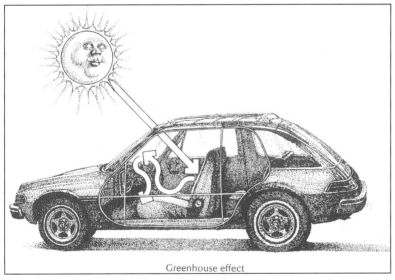

Greenhouse effect

3.5.
Imagine being in a metal car with the windows shut on a hot day, with no air conditioning and not being able to park in the shade! Edward Mazria's diagram shows how passive solar heating works as well as the greenhouse effect, because, as with glass, the re-radiated heat cannot pass back out through the upper atmosphere which is why the world is warming. Being stuck in a glass and steel building with no opening windows would be rather like that when the electricity fails – impossible to occupy. And yet insurers demand the same premiums for such offices as they would for low, naturally ventilated, well-shaded buildings, if they are in the same post code area. As the world warms anomalies like this in premiums will be questioned. *(Source:* Edward Mazria (1979) *The Passive Solar Energy Book.* Emmaus, PA: Rodale Press)

disasters, but they will have to learn new skills if their contribution is to be effective. Insurers will need to continue to work to improve their understanding of science and the built environment. They need to measure and manage their exposures, and reduce the vulnerability of the assets they insure if they are to be able to continue to write business at the premium levels people are prepared to pay. The issue of availability and affordability of insurance will become much more important, with possible threats of government intervention should an 'insurance underclass' develop.

If the climate is changing as rapidly as some of the latest scenarios suggest, it could present one of the biggest potential threats faced by insurers over the next 20 years and beyond. It could also present some of the biggest opportunities. Not just new business opportunities, but opportunities for a new spirit of dialogue and cooperation between insurers, governments and the research community.

As public concern about greenhouse gas emissions and polluting industries increases, so insurers can expect pressure groups to demand that insurers use their power in the stock market to influence the policies of the companies they invest in. After all, the insurance industry, especially its pension funds business, controls some 30% of all the stocks and equities in the world's stock exchanges. The United Nations Environment Programme's Insurance Industry Initiative is an imaginative way for insurers around the world to work together and to demonstrate their commitment to corporate responsibility.

The UK is changing rapidly and over the next 20 years there will be major demographic, social and economic changes. Government and business are increasingly turning to scenario planning to develop their long-term strategies.

The insurer can reduce the risk of flood claims by reducing the number of flood plain properties it insures. It is estimated that in England and Wales, there are some 1.3 million homes in flood plains. This is not surprising, given the tendency to want to build near river crossings, or along transport corridors, such as river valleys. What should be of great concern to insurers is that this number is still increasing, despite improved knowledge of the hazard. The reason lies in the way the planning systems operate.

The UK Environment Transport and Regional Affairs Select Committee on Climate Change, in their report published in March 2000, stated that 'there is evidence that climate change concerns have not been fully incorporated into current planning practices' (section 8.8) and further stated:

We urge the Government to continue researching the impacts of climate change and to use this to develop a strategy for adaptation. We note the start made on this in the Draft Programme. If future costs are to be minimized, it is critical that changes are made in some policy areas, for example land use planning in coastal areas and flood plains.

Managing risk

To reduce the risk, it is only necessary to reduce one of the sides of the risk triangle (Figure 3.1), but it is obviously better to try to reduce all three. Dr A. Dlugolecki has developed what he calls an 'Integrated Property Damage System'[21] in which he shows that as the risk increases, insurers move from a 'passive system' of simply paying for the damage. First, they progress to a 'reactive' system and then evolve into a 'planning' system. In other words, as the risk increases, insurers begin to act collectively to feed back information to the other components of the economic system, and if the risk becomes severe enough, insurers will insist on risk mitigation or will reduce their exposure.

There are clear signs that the UK market is beginning to move from a passive system to a reactive system, with UK insurers starting to work together to collect information and commission research. In the United States, however, largely as a result of Hurricane Andrew

3.6.
The Pompidou Centre in Paris was designed by Renzo Piano, Richard Rogers and Gianfranco Franchini for a design competition in 1970. Construction started in 1972, cost 993 million francs, and the building was opened in 1977. Nineteen years later in 1996 the building closed for four years for a total refurbishment, for which the final bill was a further 576 million francs (one pound sterling is worth 9.44 francs at early 2004 exchange rates) (see: www.centrepompidou.fr). Offices pay the same insurance premiums regardless of their day to day maintenance or long-term refurbishment requirements. (*Source:* Sue Roaf)

in 1992, the industry is already beginning to move into a 'planning' system.

Not all risks are insurable, of course, and risk aversion is one of the main driving forces for disaster mitigation, and one of the main hindrances for investment.[22] If insurers are not prepared to accept the risk of, say, a new factory to be built in a flood plain, then the developer is unlikely to proceed.

Will the insurance industry be able to weather the storms ahead? Will it have enough capacity for the claims costs that could arise? The answer is almost certainly 'yes', at least for the time being. If anything, the insurance industry has recently been suffering from too much capacity, and during the late 1990s this kept premiums low; not only insurers but reinsurers were cutting premiums for some years. This was happening around the world; premium rates were going down while exposure values were going up. This is nothing new for insurers who are used to 'the underwriting cycle' – in times of profit, capital is attracted into the industry, capacity increases and, according to the laws of supply and demand, price falls until losses result in a reduction of capacity as weaker insurers drop out. The influx of capital was restricted to some extent by the barriers to entry in the insurance industry created by regulations such as the need for government authorization and a good solvency margin.

There are four major differences now:

1 There has been a general move towards deregulation of rates, especially in Japan and continental Europe, which has led to strong price competition.
2 The growth of the securitization market in the 1990s makes it easier for capital to flow into the market if the returns are good enough. This means that as soon as premiums start to rise, capital immediately starts flowing into insurance bonds, thus driving premiums down again.
3 Previous cycles have been against the background of continuous growth in demand for insurance as society becomes wealthier. In the 1990s, multinational corporations have increasingly decided not to insure at all because for them it is just 'pound swapping' over time, and the exchange rate is not favourable.
4 Last, but certainly not least, in the past, strong insurers could ride out bad times by realizing capital gains on investments, thanks to a healthy stock market. The stock market is anything but healthy at present, and there is no longer the cushion of investment profits.

Catastrophes are normally good for insurance business; they result in increased demand for insurance and make it easier for insurers to carry rate increases. Capacity has not been a problem right up to quite recently. The market was confident even in 1999 that the combination of another Northridge earthquake, another Hurricane Andrew and another 1987 style stock market crash would still not wipe out over-capacity in the industry.[23] Since then we have had the terrorism attack on the World Trade Center and confidence has taken a nosedive.

CONCLUSIONS

It is certainly clear that a new era of insurance is starting. In an important paper published by the Royal Geographical Society, Professor Clark has pointed out that insurance can have an important role to play in managing flood risks.[24] It offers much needed support to accelerate economic and social recovery following a disaster, but with pricing policies or restrictions on availability of cover, could discourage new development in flood plains. As insurers obtain access to better data, so the uncertainty of the identification of high hazard areas reduces and these areas become less insurable. Clark supports a closer relationship between insurers and planners, and refers favourably to the Scottish planning system where an insurance expert is consulted by the planning authorities on land use strategies.

In the long run, the price of insurance should reflect the degree of risk. If insurers are unsuccessful in managing risk through controlling exposure and vulnerability, rising hazard will mean increased risk, which means increased pricing or less cover. At a micro level, insurers will become increasingly selective, using GIS technology and stiffer price discrimination based on differences in exposure and vulnerability. For example: lower 'premium' incentives for buildings built to higher standards and inspected at each stage of construction; higher premiums for buildings that are more vulnerable to terrorist attack being 'target' buildings by dint of their form, location or construction; higher premiums for climate-vulnerable buildings that are more exposed to wind, flood and excessive heat gain from solar radiation, such as those that rise above the urban 'canopy' of a city, are located on the flood plain or that are over-glazed.

The irregularity of extreme events makes it hard to assess the probability of loss for any one year, and if the frequency is changing then traditional actuarial methods may be of little help. In such a situation, there will be pressures for a conservative approach to underwriting; the 'when in doubt, throw it out' syndrome will become more common for high hazard, high exposure or high vulnerability cases. On the other hand, if the industry takes this approach too far, there will be social and political pressures and the ultimate threat of nationalization. The behaviour of the insurance industry over the coming years will provide a litmus paper for us all, of the rate of growth of the climate change hazard.

We are all at risk from the impacts of the changing climate. Our *vulnerability* to it will depend on the infrastructure of our lives, the buildings we live in and the investments we make. Our *exposure* to that risk will depend on where that infrastructure is in relation to the hazards perpetrated on us by the changing climate. In order to judiciously plan to minimize risk to ourselves we need to know more about the scale of the climate *hazard* that may affect us, and it is those hazards that are explained in the following chapters.

NOTES AND REFERENCES

1   There are many different definitions of what risk is and for a fuller discussion of climate change and risk see http://www.ukcip. org.uk/risk_uncert/main_risk_uncert.htm/.

2   See Crichton, D.C. (2001) *The Implications of Climate Change for the Insurance Industry* (ed. J. Salt). Watford: Building Research Establishment.

3   For a full outline of the UK Climate Impacts Programme (UKCIP) work on current and future climates see http://www.ukcip. org.uk/publications/pub.html including: Hulme, M.J., Turnpenny, J. and Jenkins, G. (2002) *Climate Change Scenarios for the United Kingdom: The UKCIP02 Briefing Report.* Published in conjunction with UKCIP, the Hadley Centre and the Climate Research Unit in the School of Environmental Science at the University of East Anglia, by the Tyndall Centre, Norwich; Hulme, M., Jenkins, G., Lu, X., Turnpenny, J., Mitchell, T., Jones, R., Lowe, J., Murphy, J., Hassell, D., Boorman, P., McDonald, R. and Hill, S. (2002) *Climate Change Scenarios for the United Kingdom: The UKCIP02 Scientific Report, Appendix 2* published in conjunction with UKCIP, the Hadley Centre and the Climate Research Unit in the School of Environmental Science at the University of East Anglia, by the Tyndall Centre, Norwich.

For information concerning local climate impacts contact the Hadley Centre on www.meto.gov.uk/research/hadleycentre or for detailed information on flood risks contact The Environment Agency on http://www.environment-agency.gov.uk/contactus/? lang = _e. For data sets for future climates for use in building performance simulations, contact the Chartered Institute of Building Service Engineers and ask to be put in contact with their climate data group or via: http://www.cibse.org.

4   http://www.ukcip.org.uk/scenarios/index.html.

5   Details of Foresight can be obtained from http://www.foresight. gov.uk/.

6   RCEP (2000) *Energy – the Changing Climate: Summary of the Royal Commission on Environmental Pollution's Report*. London: HMSO. A full copy of the report can be downloaded from: http://www.rcep.org.uk/energy.html.

7   See http://www.cru.uea.ac.uk/~mikeh/research/usa.pdf and http://www.cru.uea.ac.uk/~mikeh/research/australia.pdf, respectively.

8   Good starting points for researching future climates are the sites of the International Panel on Climate Change (IPCC) on http://www.ipcc.ch/ and related sites: ftp://ftp.ecn.nl/pub/bs/OpenProcess/gridded_emissions/ and http://sres.ciesin.org/ and http://www.grida.no/climate/ipcc/emission/index.htm. For a full outline of the limits to future emissions set under International Treaties see the site of the United Nations Framework Convention on Climate Change since its inception: http://unfccc.int/. The UK government climate change research is co-ordinated by the Hadley Centre on: www.meto.gov.uk/research/hadleycentre. A full UK greenhouse gas inventory 1990–2000 is available at: www.aeat.co.uk/netcen/airqual/reports/ghg/ghg3.html. And an excellent introductory site is that of the Climate Research Unit of the University of East Anglia on: http://www.cru.uea.ac.uk/.

9   http://www.greenpeace.org.au/features/features_details.html?site_id=45&news_id=1147.

10 www.aag.org/HDGC/www/hazards/supporting/supmat2-4.doc.

11 http://www.aar.com.au/pubs/prod/recall2mar03.htm#Insur.

12 *Guardian*, 8 October 2003, p. 6.

13 http://www.munichre.com.

14 Knoepfel, I., Salt, J. Bode, A. and Jacobi, W. (1999) *The Kyoto Protocol and Beyond: Potential Implications for the Insurance Industry*. UNEP Insurance Industry Initiative for the Environment.

15 Dlugolecki, A., Agnew, M., Cooper, M., Crichton, D., Kelly, N., Loster, T., Radevsky, R., Salt, J., Viner, D., Walden, J. and Walker, T. (2001) *Climate Change and Insurance*. London: Chartered Insurance Institute Research Report (available on www.cii.co.uk).

16 See Crichton, D. (2003) *Flood Risk and Insurance in England and Wales: Are There Lessons to be Learnt from Scotland?* Technical Paper Number 1, Benfield Hazard Research Centre, University College London. A range of other papers is available for free downloading from: www.benfieldhrc.org/SiteRoot/activities/tech_papers/flood_report.pdf. See also RICS Working Party (2001) *Flooding: Issues of Concern to Chartered Surveyors*. London: RICS.

17 See Building Research Establishment (BRE) (2003) *Assessment of the Cost and Effect on Future Claims of Installing Flood*

Damage Resistant Measures. Commissioned and published by the Association of British Insurers, London, May 2003. Available from http://www.abi.org.uk/Display/File/78/Flood_Resistance_report.pdf. See also Scottish Executive (2002) *Improving Building Standards: Proposals*. Edinburgh: Scottish Executive (available from www.scotland.gov.uk).

18 http://www.rcep.org.uk/energy.html.

19 http://www.munichre.com. See Munich Re, *Topics 2000,* Published January 2000.

20 See Crichton, D. (1998) Flood Appraisal Groups, NPPG 7, and Insurance, in Faichney, D. and Cranston, M. (eds), *Proceedings of the 'Flood Issues in Scotland' Seminar* held in Perth in December 1998. Scottish Environment Protection Agency, Stirling, Scotland, pp. 37–40; and see Crichton, D. (1999) UK Climate Change Programme. UK Insurance Industry. Minutes of Evidence to the Select Committee on Environment, Transport and Regional Affairs. 25 March 1999 (http://www.publications.parliament.uk/pa/cm199899/cmselect/cmenvtra/171/9832410.htm); also Davis, I., personal communication; and Crichton, D. (2003). 'Floods, who should pay? Lessons for Central Europe.' Proceedings of a conference on 7 March 2003 on European Flood Risk, Benfield Greig Hazard Research Centre at University College London.

21 Dlugolecki, A. (1998) 'Overview of Insurance System re Extreme Events', paper presented at the IPCC Workshop in Toronto, Canada, April/May 1998.

22 Kok, M., Vrijling, J., Van Gelder, P. and Vogelsang, M. (2002) Risk of flooding and insurance in The Netherlands, in *Flood Defence 2002* (Proceedings of the 2nd International Symposium on Flood Defence), eds Baosheng Wu *et al*. New York: Science Press.

23 *The Economist*, 16 January 1999.

24 Clark, M. (1998) Flood Insurance as a Management Strategy for UK Coastal Resilience, *The Geographical Journal*, 164, no 3, pp. 333–43.

4 HOW HOT WILL IT GET?

On 16 December 2003 the World Meteorological Office in Geneva issued a press release stating that 2003 was the third warmest year on record globally.[1] The warmest year on record remains 1998, when the global surface temperature hit +0.55 °C (+0.99 °F) above the 1961–90 annual average. The second warmest year was 2002, when the global surface temperature was +0.48 °C (+0.864 °F) above the 1961–90 baseline. The global surface temperature for 2003 was around +0.45 °C (+0.81 °F) above the 1961–90 annual average.

The press release catalogued a wide range of climate events that are related to this warming world. It highlighted the fact that Europe experienced the hottest summer on record during June, July and August 2003, when temperatures across parts of Europe were consistently 5 °C (9 °F) warmer than average for several months. Nationwide seasonal temperatures were warmest on record in Germany, Switzerland, France and Spain. At many European locations, temperatures rose above 40 °C (104 °F).

In France, Italy, The Netherlands, Portugal, the United Kingdom and Spain, over 30 000 additional deaths were attributed to the heat. The death toll in England and Wales caused by record temperatures in August was as high as 900.[2] The death toll in France from the August 2003 two week heat wave was estimated at 11 435 more people than usual in late August,[3] but rose to over 15 000 in later counts. The subject of why people die at high and low temperatures is covered in depth in the following chapter on thermal comfort.

But heat has many strange health impacts, and perhaps the strangest victim of the 2003 heat wave was the Manchester solicitor who drove 250 miles from London to his home with his air conditioning on maximum and directed at his midge-bitten foot. After his toes went numb and one started to go black a doctor

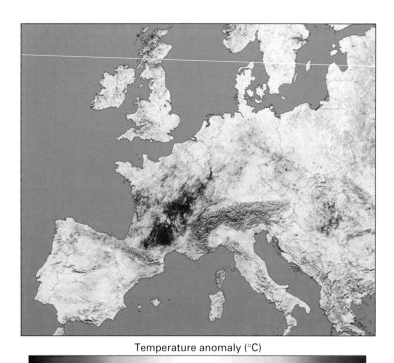

Temperature anomaly (°C)

-10   -5   0   5   10

4.1.
Image showing the differences in daytime land surface temperatures between July 2001 and July 2003 compiled by data collected by the Moderate Resolution Imaging Spectroradiometer (MODIS) on NASA's Terra satellite.
(*Source:* Reto Stockli and Robert Simmon, NASA Earth Observatory Team, based upon data provided by the MODIS Land Science team)

diagnosed frost bite.[4] Death by air conditioning has been recorded before for an aboriginal woman in Queensland who was hospitalized in a ward with air conditioning and went into cold shock because she could not physiologically cope with the relatively low temperatures in the ward. At the other end of such 'cooling' systems people have also been known to faint when passing the outlets of air conditioning systems on a street in the heat.

HOW HOT WILL IT GET IN TEMPERATE BRITAIN?

According to publications by the UK Climate Impacts Programme (UKCIP) average annual temperatures across the UK may rise between 2 and 3.5 °C by the 2080s, depending on the scenario. In general there will be greater warming in the Southeast than the Northwest and there may be more warming in summer and autumn than in winter and spring, a prediction that seems to have been leant credence by the hot summer and warm autumn of 2003.[5]

Under the *High Emissions* scenario, the Southeast may be up to an astonishing 5 °C warmer in the summer by the 2080s. During the last Ice Age, only 10 000 years ago, temperatures were only just over 3 °C colder than today so who knows what such predictions for

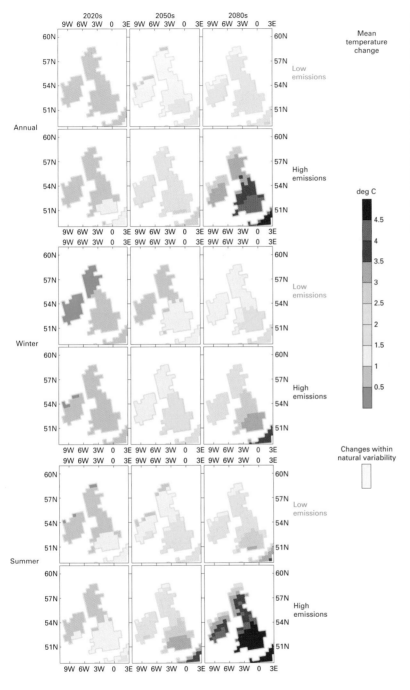

4.2.
Changes in average annual, winter and summer temperature for the 2020s, 2050s and 2080s for the *Low Emissions* and *High Emissions* scenarios showing that the Southeast of England will get very hot indeed by 2080 under *Low* and *High* scenarios. (*Source:* UKCIP02 Climate Change Scenarios, funded by DEFRA, produced by Tyndall and Hadley Centres for UKCIP) For a review of how such scenarios are developed see http://books.elsevier.com/companions/0750659114.

future climates hold in store for our children and grandchildren in terms of actual climate extremes.

These are average figures and the mean maximum temperatures will be far higher. Figure 4.3 shows four different localities, representing four different climatic regions in the UK, and the graphs

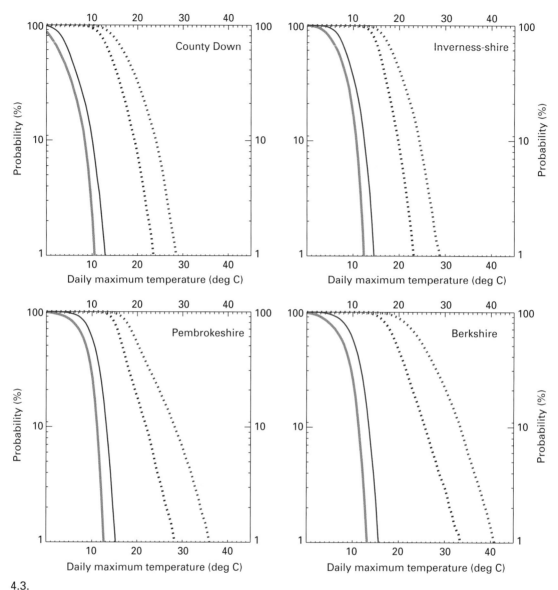

4.3.
The probability of a given daily maximum temperature in summer (*dashed*) and winter (*solid*) being exceeded on any given day. Dark grey = present climate; red = the *Medium High Emissions* scenario for the 2080s. This shows that in Berkshire even temperatures of 40 °C may be exceeded by 2080 under the *Medium High* scenario. (*Source:* UKCIP02 Climate Change Scenarios, funded by DEFRA, produced by Tyndall and Hadley Centres for UKCIP)

show that on any given day, the daily maximum temperature will exceed a certain value. For example, the Berkshire graph shows that, under the *Medium High Emissions* scenario, there is around a 5% probability that, in the 2080s, the area will experience a summer maximum temperature of above 35 °C and a 1% probability that it will go over 40 °C. These maximum temperatures are simulated by

Table 4.1. More and more years will be extremely hot over time. The table shows the percentage of years experiencing various extreme seasonal anomalies across central England and Wales for the *Medium High Emissions* scenario, with the anomalies shown relative to the average 1961–90 climate

	Anomaly	2020s	2050s	2080s
Mean temperature				
A hot '1995-type' August	3.4 °C warmer	1	20	63
A warm '1999-type' year	1.2 °C warmer	28	73	100
Precipitation				
A dry '1995-type' summer	37% drier	10	29	50
A wet '1994/95-type' winter	66% wetter	1	3	7

Source: UKCIP02 Briefing Report,[5] p. 10

the model for areas of 50 × 50 km in size. They are again lower than temperatures that would be actually measured at a specific site.

The frequency of extreme hot spells will also increase, as shown in Table 4.1.

One clear pattern that has emerged is that the temperatures at night over many land areas are increasing at about twice the rate of daytime temperatures, and as one reads through this book many designers will be flagging design-related issues. So, for example, warmer nights means that special care will have to be given to the environmental conditions in bedrooms. Another design problem relates to west-facing rooms with windows facing the low western sun when the ambient temperatures are at their highest in the afternoon so combining incoming sum with higher air temperatures.

A further consideration, that will considerably worsen future climates, particularly in London, is that of the Urban Heat Island effect[6] that makes the centres of heavily built-up areas warmer than their hinterlands. Heat Islands are very much influenced by:

- The amount of building there is in a neighbourhood. This influences how much heat they can store in a day, week, month or season. It represents the thermal capacity of the area, rather like having more bricks in a storage radiator.
- How good a heat exchanger individual buildings are. Buildings like the Barbican development in London make perfect exchangers, sticking up into the air with lots of fins and concrete balconies to absorb heat and lose it.
- The absorbtivity or reflectivity of buildings, which influences how much heat they take in and how much they reflect back to the sky or the building opposite.
- The streetscape and how easy it is to dissipate the heat from the city by wind. If all the streets are linked to roads that channel

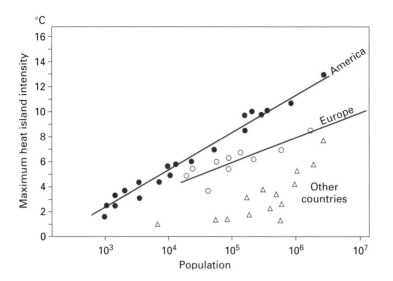

4.4.
Comparison of the strength of the Heat Island effect between American and European cities showing that the high rise, highly serviced buildings of North America generate significantly higher Heat Island temperatures than lower denser European cities. (*Source:* Littlefair, P. *et al.* (2000) Solar access, passive cooling and microclimate in the city: the Polis Project. *ACTES Proceedings*, Lyon, France, pp. 983–8)

the constant sea breezes, as in Naples, then heat can be regularly flushed out of the city. If the main streets impede the natural flows of air, then heat will be trapped in the city.

• How densely the area is populated. More people, each producing around 50 to 100 watts of heat, also means more machines and cars that give out heat.

The increases in temperature vary from region to region, but in cities such as Athens it can be between 8 and 13 °C warmer inside than outside the city. For London, in the centre of the city it can be as much as 8 °C warmer than the surrounding countryside. The Heat Island is highly changeable, most pronounced at night and weakening with increasing wind speed and distance from the city centre; the location of the thermal maximum of the Heat Island shifts with slight changes in wind direction. The number of nights with intense Heat Islands (greater than 4 °C warmer than the surrounding countryside) has been climbing steadily since the 1950s.

The Heat Island effect may be influenced by the amount of cloud in the sky and simulations suggest large decreases in summer cloud cover over the whole of the UK, but especially in the south. Reductions in cloud cover under the *Low Emissions* scenarios are around 10% by 2080, but as large as 25% or more under the *High Emissions* scenarios, which will make solar energy technologies more viable but also may exacerbate the Heat Island effect.

Cloud cover increases slightly in winter, by no more that 2–3%, over the whole country. Autumn and spring become sunnier, particularly in the Southeast. In summer, solar radiation increases by 10, 20 and even 30 Wm^{-2} over southern England, consistent with rainfall predictions and the increase in the predicted diurnal range

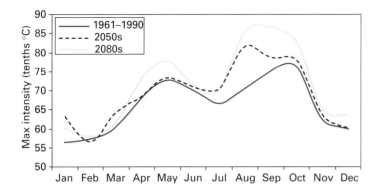

4.5.
The Heat Island effect in London, showing that the increase in night time temperature exceeds that in the day. (*Source:* R.L. Wilby, The Environment Agency)

of the temperature. This was apparent in the summer of 2003 where the mean Central England Temperature (CET) was 17.3 °C over the summer, making it the fourth warmest summer period on record. But the record for the highest maximum temperature ever recorded in the UK was broken on 10 August 2003 when 38.5 °C (over 100 °F) was recorded at Brogdale, near Faversham in Kent. The CET between March and August was also the warmest March to August ever on record, at 1.73 °C above the long-term average.

Nights will warm more than days during the winter, and days warm more than nights during summer. It will stay warmer longer in summer, with up to 3–4 °C night time warming experienced, with a temperature that would now occur at 7.00 pm occurring at 11.00 pm under the *High Emissions* scenario.

The temperature of the Heat Island experienced in London will also be influenced by wind speeds, a factor that is influenced by pressure gradients across the country. The largest average wind speeds predicted, in the London's Warming Technical Report, occur along the coast, where between 4% and 10% increases in the average may be experienced in winter, but with smaller increases in summer. This is one of the more difficult factors to predict using current models.

WHAT WILL THE EFFECT OF THIS BE?

The wide range of impacts outlined below is to give you an indication of the variety and the extent of the influence of climate change on the lives of individuals in their own homes, around the world. Many of the issues raised link to points in other chapters and demonstrate the interconnectivity of the buildings we live in, the metabolism of the planet at large and the social, political and economic environments we inhabit.

Heat discomfort can interrupt work

Although Britain was not the most exposed country in Europe to the August 2003 heat wave, time is money, and even in temperate London businesses will have to increasingly look to reduce their *vulnerability* to high temperatures in the workplace if such summers become commonplace. Offices that are vulnerable to high temperatures, such as highly glazed buildings, suffered very badly in the heat wave of August 2003 and the Trade Union Congress (TUC), in response to wide-scale 2003 heat discomfort, called for legal maximum temperatures for workplaces.

Current legislation sets a minimum temperature below which no one should have to work, at 16 °C or, where severe physical work is required, 13 °C. The TUC suggested a maximum working temperature of 30 °C, or 27 °C for those doing strenuous work. In London in 2003, even in more traditional offices temperatures were exceeding these limits. It was also suggested that more breaks and a more relaxed dress code would help considerably. Chapter 5 argues that humans actually adapt to a far wider range of temperatures in warmer countries and so over time these limits will widen.

One employment lawyer suggested that employers should think twice before sacking staff who walk out of their workplace because of the heat, as they may find themselves accused of unfair dismissal. Workers can protect their work conditions by local negotiation covering the provision of air-cooling systems, shading for windows and an adequate supply of drinkable water.[7]

Problems of poor internal climates are exacerbated by poor climatic design of buildings and their services. This was emphasized by all the staff of the refurbished HM Treasury building in London (July 2003), who were sent home after lunch because the building was simply too hot to occupy. It is unclear if this was the fault of the designer of the refurbishment, the service engineers or the construction firm that did not properly commission the air conditioning system, but as temperatures increase designers will have to learn how to design and manage to avoid such over-heating.[8] The need to put the building occupiers back into the equation of what makes an adequate building has made people more interested in the process of *post occupancy evaluation* of building performance to ensure that lessons are properly learnt from such failures.[9]

Heat and health

A study by scientists at the World Health Organization in 2003, found that 160 000 people die every year from side-effects of global warming, such as increased rates of death resulting from a range of causes from malaria to malnutrition, predicting that the number would double by 2020. Diseases spread by animals such as rats and insects are more common in warmer climates and issues such as the increasing scarcity of clean water with hotter dryer climates will also play a major part in increasing deaths from illness and malnutrition. In addition, the combination of increasing warmth and more standing water resulting from storms creates conditions conducive to epidemics, such as those of malaria, by providing breeding grounds for the insects and speeding up the life cycle as a result of the warmer conditions.[10]

Climate change will introduce three different types of health impact:

- **Direct impacts** through death and injury from heat waves, storms, floods and drought.
- **Indirect impacts** through the occurrence of health conditions exacerbated by changing weather conditions, e.g. respiratory diseases exacerbated by atmospheric pollution, or ensuing outbreaks of disease, such as typhoid, cholera etc., related to climate events such as floods etc.
- **Migratory impacts** resulting from the movement of sources of infection resulting from the diaspora of diseases via various carriers with warming climates, e.g. malaria and trypanosoma.

The direct health impacts of climate change we see all around us on a regular basis, including deaths resulting from fires, floods and drought.

Heat and cold stress are the main direct causes of death from extremes of temperature and they are dealt with in Chapter 5 on the human thermal response and Chapter 13 on energy and fuel security issues.

The importance of shade for health

We can also see indirect impacts around us in the news as the changing climate begins to impact on our lives and deaths. The increasing strength of solar radiation is also affecting even 'rainy' Britain. In September 2003 the UK government issued a warning to local authorities to remove sunbeds from every leisure centre in the country amid accusations that they are profiting from treatments that endanger the health of the public. Members of the Chartered Institute of Environmental Health, many of whom work for local councils, raised the alarm because they believe that sunbeds are contributing to the rise of the incidence of skin cancer. Research published by the *Journal of the National Cancer Institute* in 2002 shows a strong link between tanning lamps and skin cancer. They called, in their 2003 annual conference, for the inclusion of 'shade provision' to become a requirement for all big planning developments. School playgrounds would be required to provide children and teachers with shaded areas.[11]

Surprisingly, skin cancer is actually a major problem in the UK and exposure to ultra-violet rays and direct strong sunlight increases the risk of contracting skin cancer, by damaging the immune system and causing premature ageing of the skin. Skin cancer is now the second most common form of cancer in the UK. There are 40 000 cases a year and the number of new cases annually rose by more than 90% in the 15 years between 1974 and 1989. Three-quarters of these result from malignant melanoma. Most skin cancers are not life-threatening but must be promptly removed surgically to avoid serious problems.

There are no published statistics available on how many melanomas are linked to travel abroad, tanning lamps or are contracted due to exposure to the sun in the UK. Here again the combination of factors may place a crucial part, for instance holidays in Spain, tanning at the health club, gardening in summer and over-exposure to direct sun in the workplace. In highly glazed buildings care should be taken to ensure staff are not sitting in direct sun during their working day.

Insect infestations impact on our buildings

Insect populations can explode in certain conditions, including particular temperature bands. The smallest of animals can cause severe impacts. When such infestations strike they spread very rapidly; when sudden oak death spread from Oregon and California to Britain, it spread to more than 280 sites within months in England.[12] The same is true of moulds and fungi, which can have a devastating effect on people and buildings, as can termites, spreading north from Devon even now with the warming weather, and mosquitoes that are now found in parts of Kent. So such infestations may well affect our health, timber sources and the structures of our buildings.

The SARS effect

It is the often combination of conditions that really makes for great epidemics, as many found out on the troop ships in the First and Second World Wars when thousands of weak and injured soldiers were crowded together in hot ships providing ideal breeding grounds for a range of potent killers ranging from typhoid and cholera to the impressively lethal stomach bugs.

In late October 2003, 430 people were stuck down with a chronic stomach complaint caused by the norovirus, or Norwalk-like virus

(NLV), on the cruise ship *Aurora* carrying 18 000 passengers and 800 crew. There was talk at that time of a £2.5 million claim against P&O, who operated the ocean liner, by some 250 of the infected passengers. Greece refused to let the liner dock in their waters to take onboard provisions and medical assistance. NLV is the most common cause of stomach complaints in the UK, where 600 000 to 1 million people suffer from it every year, particularly in schools and hospitals and where people are confined in close quarters. Similar viruses have disrupted other cruises.

Similarly, the incidences of Severe Acute Respiratory Syndrome (SARS), caught first from chickens, were concentrated in areas of high density occupation, in hotels and high rise housing estates in Hong Kong. SARS is caused by a coronavirus, a relative of the common cold, and was responsible for over 400 infections and 200 deaths in Southeast Asia and Canada in 2003. It spreads very rapidly and across large distances thanks to air travel, and is thought to spread primarily on droplets of water, through coughing and sneezing. Evidence from a large cluster of cases on a single housing estate in Hong Kong suggests that it can be spread in buildings, and in outdoor locations. Prevention measures for its transmission included the wearing of face masks and the thorough washing of hands.[13] With both the norovirus and the coronavirus the higher density of a population in one area will significantly increase the risks of infection of that population in that area.

The outbreak of SARS had a major impact on eastern markets in 2002. Economists cut the GDP forecast for Hong Kong alone by 2.5% in the wake of the outbreak,[14] while some estimate that the total costs may rise into billions rather than millions of dollars as travellers simply did not want to visit the infected regions. Travel insurers placed an exclusion zone on policies covering Canada, Hong Kong and China and warned people they would not be covered if they caught the infection.[15]

Such outbreaks, on land or sea, demonstrate the potentially huge and growing risks to life and economic welfare arising from densely populated buildings and cities, in combination with rising temperatures.

Air pollution

Air pollution is already a growing health problem in many cities, including London, largely because of rising traffic levels, and will get worse in large urban areas under conditions of climate change. Recent studies show that relatively small rises in urban air pollution can trigger an increased number of potentially fatal heart attacks in people with vulnerable arteries.

During heat waves air quality reduces, and on 7 August 2003 the UK government issued an official heath warning to asthmatics and the elderly, stating that air pollution in London had risen to the highest level for a decade as record temperatures were recorded in the capital. Air-quality monitors in Enfield recorded pollution levels of 131 parts per billion (ppb), almost three times the safe limit set by the World Health Organization, as temperatures soared over 35 °C.

Air quality in the UK in 2003 was the worst ever recorded, with the worst place in Britain for air pollution being a stretch of London's Marylebone Road, between Baker Street station and the Madame Tussaud's exhibition, which exceeded pollution guideline levels 48 times in the first three months of 2003 and 11 times in 2002.[16]

Ozone levels also soared to 80–100 ppb in London at that time, while the highest levels ever recorded in Britain were 250 ppb in Harwell, Oxfordshire in 1976 before strict EU laws restricting vehicle emissions were introduced.[17] However, there has been a gradual rise in the background levels of ozone in Europe since 1940. Government studies show that around 1600 people with breathlessness problems die prematurely every year due to high levels of air pollution and a further 1500, mostly asthma suffers, are admitted to hospital because their symptoms become worse during periods of poor air quality.[18]

An increasingly significant factor in the past few years, particularly in Southeast Asia, has been the contribution to urban air pollution of smoke from large fires experienced in countries around the globe, exacerbated by heat wave conditions.

Predicted future increases in the number and intensity of hot anticyclonic weather events in summer will favour the creation of more temperature inversions trapping pollutants in the near-surface layer of the atmosphere. It is estimated that a 1 degree centigrade rise in summer air temperatures will result in a 14% increase in surface ozone concentrations in London.[19]

But the warming cocktail of atmospheric pollutants is being – incredibly – added to by the decisions of politicians who seem hell bent on worsening the already severe pollution problems we face. In August 2003, it was announced that, in the drive to meet the ever-increasing demand in America for energy, around 50% of which goes to power buildings, the Bush Administration plans to open a huge loophole in America's air pollution laws allowing an estimated 17 000 outdated power stations and factories to increase their carbon emissions with immunity. Critics of the draft regulations unveiled by the US Environmental Protection Agency claimed they amounted to the death knell for the Clean Air Act, the centrepiece of US Environmental Regulations. The proposed new Regulations were being challenged by 13 states, including New York, but if adopted would provide a multi-million dollar victory for US energy corporations. Many of the objectors are particularly concerned about the health impacts of this loophole on the cities and populations in the vicinity of such plants.[20]

In Britain the Labour government has been very open about its desire to promote the interest of the aviation industry, with well-publicized plans for three major new airport developments over the next decade, at the expense of the well-being of ordinary citizens, particularly in Southeast England.[21] Cheap air travel has a bread and circuses ring to it that appeals to politicians seeking re-election, but all political parties have possibly underestimated the intelligence of the local voters and their levels of knowledge on the issues involved. A major concern of people who live near runways, after noise, are the serious health consequences of poor air quality resulting from increased plane activity overhead.

Passenger flights emit more than 8 million tonnes of carbon dioxide every year in the UK, so playing a major part in climate change. This figure is predicted to rise to 19 million tonnes by 2030 if the airline industries are not checked, and ways to do this were the subject of a major review by the Department of Transport in 2003/4.[22]

Fuels burnt in aviation have a wide range of toxic emissions that directly effect human health. Aviation emissions include nitrogen oxide, hydrocarbons, sulphur dioxide, naphthalene, benzene (a known carcinogen), formaldehyde (a suspected carcinogen) and dust particles that harm human health and contribute to global warming. This 'poison circle' can extend for 6 miles around a single runway and run 20 miles downwind. Studies have linked airport pollution to cancer, asthma, liver damage, lung disease, lymphoma, depression, myeloid leukaemia, and tumours.

The size of this problem is emphasized by the fact that today 70% of US residents live within 20 miles of a major airport. In the UK the figures for people living within 30 miles of the four London airports must be fairly similar. Aircraft pollution has been implicated in higher rates of child mortality, premature deaths and cancer deaths in a number of reputable studies.[23]

In the UK air pollution, including that from aircraft and the surface traffic pollution associated with airports, is estimated to kill up to 24 000 people every year and requires medical treatment for thousands more. The health costs of air pollution from the UK aviation sector are estimated at more than £1.3 billion a year.[24] As with vehicular air pollution, the impacts of this pollution will be accelerated with the higher temperatures that are associated with global warming. The traditional view that aviation is a 'sacred cow' and should not be restricted by legislation because it may slow down global economies, is now being questioned, as is the need for more and more airports and air travel, which seems dependent also on oil prices remaining at their current costs.

What is sure is that increasingly warm summers will affect the air quality and in turn the quality of life of millions of citizens in Britain as the weather becomes hotter. Some engineers argue that issues of air quality from transport, industrial and acid rain pollution are a good reason to use air conditioning in buildings, but the most damaging of the fine particulates in air pollution are too small to be removed by air conditioning filters, so invalidating this solution (more of which in Chapter 10 on air conditioning).

Those who are interested in locating sources of air pollution in relation to a particular site in the UK can enter a postcode on the 'What's in your backyard' feature on the Your Environment page of the Environment Agency website; it will also show where pollution is being emitted from industrial sites and landfill sites.[25]

Waste

Increasing temperatures all year round will affect many aspects of our lives. For instance, building, office, household and industrial waste may increasingly become an issue with climate because of:

- greater outdoor odour problems associated with waste disposal due to higher summer temperatures, and
- waste containment problems associated with heavy rains and floods.

Possible need for more frequent waste collection in certain areas due to high summer temperatures and more protection of, and care in selection of, landfill sites may be necessary.

Two hundred thousand homes are close to landfill sites and were thought to be worth, on average £5,500 less because of the nuisance caused by dust, noise, small vermin and water and air pollution caused by the neighbouring rubbish dumps. In the first comprehensive study of the effect of landfill sites on house prices it was found that Scottish homes lost a staggering 41% of their value if they were within a quarter of a mile of a site, while in the East Midlands only a 10% reduction within a quarter of a mile and 8.75% reduction within half a mile were recorded.[26]

Noise

With climate change, a wide range of physical and social adaptations in the population may well affect noise issues in cities. For example, with warmer outdoor temperatures, the growth of the 'café society' may well increase street activity at all times of year in the streets of cities, and sensible pre-planning of open air eating facilities in relation to residential areas is necessary as the warmer evenings may well pre-date the adaptation of populations to higher street noise levels. Thought should also be given to the greater need to open windows in warmer weather and the need to ensure that the noise and pollution impacts of street life and traffic noise do not encourage a move to the climatically unnecessary air conditioning of buildings. The increased need for traffic-free zones in open restaurant areas of a city may become a feature of future inner city planning strategies, to ensure that local office buildings can be naturally ventilated without excessive noise levels. So noise and pollution should be increasingly included as key concerns for urban designers and local councils alike. Even fashionable buildings on sites with high noise and traffic pollution levels are problems, like the £13 million Hammersmith Ark building. It is two decades old, very elegant, with low rents of £32 a square foot, but because of its noisy location on a traffic island, it has proved over those years virtually impossible to rent out.[27]

Fires

Fire hazards are significantly increased with hotter dry seasons, that add to the frequency, and the intensity, of bush and forest fires, creating a greater hazard to life, limb and property. Such fires occur generally in association with extreme dry periods, and strong winds, as was the case with the Great Fire of London in 1666.[28]

Every month from November 1665 to September 1666 was dry. By August 1666, the River Thames at Oxford was reduced to a 'trickle'. The dryness extended to Scotland, at least from May to mid-July. The drought over these two months is noteworthy because it preceded the Great Fire of London, and apparently the east wind, which prevailed during that period, had dried the wooden houses of London until they were like tinder. When the fire started on 12 September, the east wind drove the flames before it, causing great problems with fire fighting and helping the fire to spread rapidly, causing smoke from the fire to reach as far as Oxford.

The prevailing weather was noted as 'hot & dry', and on the first day of the fire John Evelyn noted in his diary, a 'Fierce' eastern wind in a very dry season. It is not clear though whether the wind was caused by the fire, or was there anyway. However, Evelyn did note that there had been a 'long set of fair and warm weather'. On 14 September Evelyn noted: 'The eastern wind still more impetuously driving the flames forward.' On the 15th, he noted that the wind was 'abating', but this may have been due to the fire burning itself out. In any case, this was effectively the end of the Great Fire, and when the rains came on the 19th the fire was quenched and a rainy autumn followed, although Evelyn claimed that smoke could still be seen rising out of the odd basement six months after it ended.

In 2003 alone a number of catastrophic fires occurred around the world, even in Britain:

- April, 2003: In Huddersfield, UK, hundreds of hectares of National Trust moorland were left charred by fires that swept through the tinder dry hills near the city.[29]
- July and August 2003: In Portugal, a national disaster was declared as more than 2300 fire fighters tackled 72 blazes across the country.[30]
- August, 2003: In Canada, 30 000 people had to flee their communities in the Okanagan Mountain Forest Fire, 185 miles east of Vancouver, which had 100 m high flames moving at 30 m a minute across the countryside, leaving at least 200 homes as smouldering rubble in its wake. The fire began to 'crown', moving rapidly from tree top to tree top, and was seen to leap from building to building, some of which exploded in the intense heat. The fire started on 16 August with a lightning strike in the mountains.[31]
- September 2003: On the French Riviera, huge forest fires destroyed over 1000 hectares of woods, following two devastating blazes in July that killed four people, including two Britons, and destroyed more than 18 000 hectares of pine and oak.[32]
- October 2003: The final death toll in the southern Californian fires of October 2003 rose to over 22, including some of the 12 000 fire fighters who battled with the blazes. Estimated damage from the fires, covering over 275 hectares and destroying nearly 3000 homes, could top £1.17 billion. Large fires also raged at the same time in the south of Denver and near Jamestown, Colorado.[33]

The issue of what materials buildings are made of is an important one. In countries such as the United States and Australia, where buildings are typically constructed of timber, or timber-based components, not only is more of the building destroyed during a fire, and the strong winds associated with it, but such buildings add fuel to the fire and intensify the event. Europe is extremely fortunate to have traditional building industries in which buildings have been largely constructed of heavy masonry and are less vulnerable to the catastrophic devastation experienced in many bush and forest fires, where whole suburbs can ignite in fireballs as the timber houses literally explode with the heat. In Britain, the medieval cities were to a far larger extent made of timber-framed construction,

4.6.
Bushfires rage in Victoria,
Australia. (*Source:* Sue Roaf)

which was replaced in London largely by brick buildings after the
Great Fire in 1666.

Biodiversity

Plant and animal species are being lost around the world with rising temperatures at a rate that has alarmed many scientists. Many
plant and animal species are unlikely to survive climate change.
New analyses, published in the journal *Nature* in January 2004,[34]
suggest that 15–37% of a sample of 1103 land plants and animals
would eventually become extinct as a result of climate changes
expected by 2050. For some of these species there will no longer
be anywhere suitable to live. Others will be unable to reach places
where the climate is suitable. The authors of that study claim that
a rapid shift to technologies that do not produce greenhouse gases,
combined with carbon sequestration, could save 15–20% of species
from extinction.

THE RESTRUCTURING OF ECONOMIES IN THE WARMING WORLD

The impacts of biodiversity changes on regional economies

Fishing industries around the world will be highly impacted as river
and ocean waters warm, changing centuries of tradition in their
fishing practices. Every species has a temperature window within
which it thrives and as temperatures change they will migrate to

occupy their 'survival' temperatures. An extra 1 °C in temperature pushed haddock, cod, plaice and lemon sole 200–400 miles north, according to the World Wildlife Fund. There have been more frequent sightings of species such as Hammerhead sharks, trigger fish, sun fish and even red mullet, cuttlefish and black bream in the waters of the Isle of Man. Fishermen in Cornwall may have to start breeding lobsters in captivity to prevent them from being eaten by triggerfish when very young. Scuba divers regularly find octopi along the south coast and Japanese oysters have also started breeding in British waters. These trends may well affect the economic welfare of the fishermen of Britain and the communities they support.[35]

Even more catastrophic is what is predicted will happen to the coral reefs of the world. More than 100 million people around the world depend on reefs for their livelihoods. Corals are very temperature-sensitive and are dying over large areas as ocean waters warm. In the El Niño year of 1998 unusually high temperatures in the India Ocean killed more than 90% of the corals on shallow Indian Ocean reefs and future high temperatures could finish the reefs off completely. Sixteen per cent of all coral reefs globally were calculated to have been destroyed but the worst affected were those in the Indian Ocean. The corals that died were up to 100 years old and would take centuries to recover if sea temperatures stabilized at the current levels. It is predicted that the higher temperatures may be reached every 5 years now and for the latitudes 10 to 15 degrees south, by 2020 all corals species may well be extinct.[36]

The economic costs of such extinctions are enormous. To combat such devastation legislation has just been introduced to make two-thirds of the Great Barrier Reef, off the east coast of Australia, into a protected area under conservation plans announced by the Australian government in December 2002, forming the largest network of protected marine areas in the world. Strong opposition was brought by the Queensland fishing industry where it was estimated that 250 jobs would be lost. Fishing on the reef generates only around £46 million while tourism in the region is worth £1.7 billion.

In May 2003, Hamdallah Zedan, Secretary to the Convention on Biological Diversity,[37] ratified by 187 Nations, said that at the Earth Summit at Johannesburg it had been recognized that our health and our lives depend on biodiversity and that:

The millions of species on earth have evolved complex interactions that allow for their mutual survival. Man has disrupted this at such a rate that nature can no longer adapt. Scientists agree that the incidences of plagues and pandemics will increase as we battle to find ways of controlling these human health challenges.

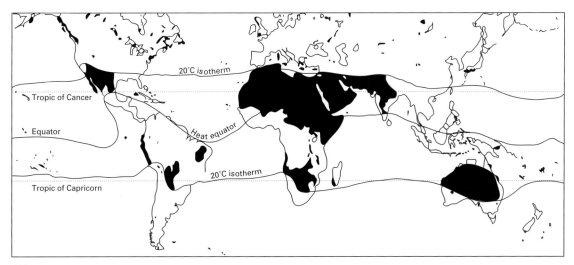

4.7.
Deserts of the world covered 22% of the world's landmass in 1970, and in 2000 this had risen to 33%. (*Source:* Isaac Meir)

Wolves at the gates of the city?

But animals are very ingenious, and even as one ecological niche closes, another may open up. The significance of a range of factors may influence how animals behave in a changing climate. Already we have the phenomenon of wild animals becoming adapted to live in cities, as was clearly outlined in David Baron's book on 'the beast in the garden'.[38] He cites cases of bears moving into New Jersey suburbs, raccoons in Los Angeles and in the UK the urban fox is a common occurrence. The animals are drawn to feed off rubbish bins, a particular problem in the States, where, because of 'urban sprawl', the suburbs are moving into what was wilderness. Animal numbers have risen owing to restrictive laws in some states on the hunting and trapping of a range of larger animals, for instance lynx, bobcats, bears, beavers, foxes, wolves and cougars. There are black bears in the suburbs of Boston for the first time in 200 years and in New Jersey they have multiplied to over an estimated 3300. In December 2003 New Jersey authorized its first bear hunt in 33 years. Coyotes are multiplying too, and their cheek was demonstrated when one ran into the federal building in Seattle, through reception and into the lift! They routinely eat cats and dogs. In Florida the alligator population is growing at an unprecedented rate, helped by people buying up large plots and embracing the wilderness life and feeding the animals. David Baron maintains that the United States (and humans in general, the most pervasive species of all) is engaged in a grand and largely unintentional experiment. The 'range', on which Americans were once so happy to be 'at home', has moved from the plains to the car park at the Mall and shows no sign of withdrawing back to the plains and the mountains.[39]

The death of mountain communities?

As jobs go, so too do the communities they supported. Global warming is already affecting many mountain communities as winter sports are pushed higher and higher up. Fifteen years ago it was possible to guarantee good skiing over Christmas in the Alps, even in the lower resorts. Today this can only be done for sites over 1750 metres or higher, and even then this is not certain. Many ski resorts at lower altitudes face bankruptcy, and increasing environmental impacts are recorded as there is more and more pressure put on providing services at higher altitudes.

A research group from the University of Zurich looked at the situation in relation to predicted future climates and concluded that while today 85% of the 230 resorts in Switzerland are 'snow reliable' (if seven out of ten winters had at least 30–50 cm of snow on at least 100 days between 1 December and 15 August), by 2030 to 2050 this would drop to 63%. If the snow line rises from 1200 to 1800 m one in four resorts in many areas would face ruin, with losses of £925 million a year.

In Austria the snowline is expected to rise 200–300 m by 2030–2050, making many resorts in the central and eastern parts lose their winter industry and in Italy only resorts above 1500 meters can expect reliable falls of snow, that is around half of the winter sports villages. Many such villages are facing major problems already. Many German resorts are also at low altitudes. In Australia an increase of 0.60 °C would hit four of the nine ski resorts and a rise in global temperatures of 3.4 °C, predicted under some scenarios, by 2070 would mean no Australian resort could operate at a profit.

Even the summer climbing industry in the Alps is suffering. For the first time since records began in 1786, the summer 2003 heat wave made the Matterhorn too dangerous to climb. The mountain was closed in August 2003, with its naked slopes covered with heaps of rubble and screed. Two climbers died just trying to get to the restaurant at the start of the climbing routes. The permafrost that holds the mountain peaks together had melted to a depth of 7 feet, making ski lifts and cable cars unstable. The problems became apparent in July 2003, when an enormous rock avalanche hurtled down the mountain's east face, and within two hours another rocked the north face. More than 70 climbers had to be hauled from the mountain, one of the biggest mountaineering rescues in history. The mountain had actually begun to fall apart under their feet. Ice as it warms, but before it melts, may actually be more unstable than when it is turning to water. There is a growing realization that there is going to be a lot more of this type of devastation in mountainous regions as the foundations of the mountains, and their ski lifts and cable cars, become unstable.[40]

Agriculture

Crop belts are moving north, and many English farmers are already growing maize and sunflowers. But high temperatures are also a threat to some forms of farming, as they have resulted in higher than normal deaths at poultry farms that were ill-prepared for heat waves.

The changing climate will alter the face of farming over the planet and agricultural issues, particularly devastating for countries that are suffering from the impacts of creeping deserts as the climate warms, figured largely in the negotiations at Kyoto.[41]

There may also be many benefits for a fortunate country such as the UK as the climate warms. One is the increased production of British wine; in the Campsie Hills, near Glasgow, the Cumbernauld vineyard is thriving and, banking on a good dose of global warming in the area, locals eagerly await the advent of Scottish wine made from Caledonia grapes. Some claim that if the Champagne region of France now overheats and will have to return to making more traditional Bordeaux types of wine, southern England could become the home of sparkling wine.

The geography of wine is set to change dramatically with climate change and those who will suffer worst will be the growers of southern France and Italy who may have to move their grapes to higher elevations or change their grape stock plants. In Scotland grapes such as Muller-Thurgau and Bacchus may do well, while in the southern areas Pinot Noir and Chardonnay grapes may thrive best in the warming climate. Vine growers will have to be very adaptable to survive what climate change is throwing at them.

The growing season for grapes is also extending, with an exceptionally early harvest in 2003. The last time the grape harvest came in so early in France was in 1893, when picking began on 25 August. In Beaujolais it started on 10 August 2003.[42] The yield from this dry year is predicted to be sweeter, drier, less of it and with a superb flavour.

But there are problems for agriculture too. Warmer winters have also allowed aphids to survive in much larger numbers which is forcing growers to spray crops earlier and a new range of insects, wasps and spiders have invaded Britain from across the English Channel.

Gardening

Plants, like humans and other animals, are being influenced by the changing climate. In even the hottest and driest places on the Earth the garden has always been an important climatic design feature, to enhance the enjoyment of life, through the richness of colour and texture, perfumes and appearance, but also a very effective way of providing cooling. The earliest dynasties of Mesopotamia were renowned for their gardens. The Garden of Eden was placed by historians at the confluence of the Tigris and the Euphrates and the poetry of the Sumerians, living over five thousand years ago in that region, lyrically details the beauty of the trees, and plants and flowers enjoyed at the time. Most have also heard of the Hanging Gardens of Babylon and many will have read the rich poetry of the Persians, singing tributes to the beauty of the gardens and their contents with ponds and streams set, in an ordered fashion, in the great walled domains and parks.[43]

On such a great tradition of gardening were built the Roman gardens, as one can see today in Pompeii, where many have been reconstructed from the archaeological evidence garnered from the uncovered city. Vines and fruit trees, woods and flowers and herbs flourish, still reflecting the wall paintings around the houses.[44]

The secret of the success of gardening in some of the hottest places on Earth was to create a micro-climate fed by very selective watering systems and strategies and protected from the barren deserts beyond by high walls that kept out the hot winds and sun and contained the moister micro-climate within: Cold and moist air sinks, and many such gardens contain sunken sections, often covered by a canopy of trees to reduce evaporative transpiration rates and contain the coolth. Perhaps the greatest achievement of any urban gardeners is in the Chinese Desert Oasis city of Turfan, where the main crop of the town, grapes, is also used as an air conditioning system for the whole city where all the pavements and courtyards of houses in the old city are planted with vines that keep out the sun and provide a luxurious micro-climate beneath the vines. Other strategies for gardening in deserts include the planting of only drought-tolerant species,[45] and of minimizing the water loss rates by very careful diurnal and seasonal strategies for planting, watering and harvesting species.[46]

Just as we will rely increasingly on imported wisdom on appropriate building technologies as the climate warms, as traditional approaches to gardening cease to be viable in future climates, with dryer and hotter summers and frost-free winters, many of the lower latitude approaches to garden design and upkeep will have to be incorporated into our strategies for maintaining gardens. Many

4.8.
In the summer of 2003 the American Mid-West suffered from an all time record number of tornadoes, indicating a trend in the increasing frequency of storm events in the region. The frequency and intensity of storms increase as land masses heat up. (*Source:* Extreme Climate Calendar)

of the species in British gardens today may have to be replaced in the future by more drought-tolerant plants.[47]

CONCLUSIONS

Every aspect of the way we live will be affected by climate change. The regions and settlements we live in, the air we breathe, the food we eat, our jobs, our holidays and the buildings we live in. There are a wide range of design challenges we face to accommodate such rapid changes. But one concern must cross our own minds as we see the rate and extent of the warming and note the extent of the changes that may well be wrought on the landscapes and on other species, and that is: Will we ourselves stay comfortable, safe and ultimately survive in the changing climate?

This question is addressed in Chapter 5.

NOTES AND REFERENCES

1 http://www.wmo.ch/web/Press/Press.html.

2 *Guardian*, 27 September 2003, p. 1.

3 *Guardian*, 30 August 2003, p. 19.

4 *Guardian*, 12 August 2003, p. 3.

5 For all related UKCIP reports see http://www.ukcip.org.uk/publications/pub.html, including: Hulme, M. *et al.* (2002) *Climate Change Scenarios for the United Kingdom: The UKCIP02 Briefing*

Report, published in conjunction with UKCIP, the Hadley Centre and the Climate Research Unit in the School of Environmental Science at the University of East Anglia, by the Tyndall Centre, Norwich; Hulme, M. *et al.* (2002) *Climate Change Scenarios for the United Kingdom: The UKCIP02 Scientific Report*, Appendix 2, published in conjunction with UKCIP, the Hadley Centre and the Climate Research Unit in the School of Environmental Science at the University of East Anglia, by the Tyndall Centre, Norwich.

6   There is an increasing amount of work done on the Heat Island effect. Some good references for those interested to start with are: Graves, H., Watkins, R., Westbury, P. and Littlefair, P. (2001) *Cooling Buildings in London*. BR 431. London: CRC Ltd. (see http://www.brebookshop.com); Oke, T.R. (1997) Urban climates and global environmental change, in Thompson, R.D. and Perry, A.H. (eds), *Applied Climatology: Principles and Practice*. London: Routledge, pp. 273–87; and see also *London's Warming: The Impacts of Climate Change on London*, Technical Report, published by the London Climate Change Partnership in November 2003 and available in pdf form, from the UKCIP website on http://www.ukcip.org.uk/publications/pub.html.

7   *Guardian*, Jobs and Money, 9 August 2003, p. 17.

8   *Guardian*, 9 August 2003. For more information on the building design see http://www.betterpublicbuildings.gov.uk/hm_treasury.html.

9   Roaf, S. (2004) *Closing the Loop: Benchmarks for Sustainable Buildings*. London: RIBA Publications.

10 http://www.who.int/globalchange/climate/summary/en/ See also http://www.ukcip.org.uk/publications/pub.html for a pdf version of: Department of Health (2001) *Health Effects of Climate Change in the UK: An expert review for comment*. Leicester: Institute for Environment and Health.

11 There are many concerns about the impact of radiation on the skin, and for a discussion on the subject see http://www.biol.sc.edu/~elygen/Andrea%20Stanley.htm. The World Health Organization sees the establishment of a sun protection programme as a high priority as the young are most vulnerable to skin damage from the sun. See http://www.who.int/uv/publications/en/sunprotschools.pdf.

12 *Guardian*, 29 October 2003, p. 9.

13 *Guardian*, 21 April 2003, p. 3.

14 *Independent on Sunday*, 27 April 2003, p. 11.

15 *Guardian*, 25 April 2003, p. 19.

16 *Independent on Sunday*, 27 April 2003, p. 27.

17 *Guardian*, 19 April 2003, p. 3.

18 *Independent*, 8 August 2003, p. 5.

19 *London's Warming*, The London Climate Change Impacts study, 2002, p. 63 (www.ukcip.org.uk/London/main_London.htm); and particularly badly affected are cities in basin locations such as Sheffield and, surprisingly, Sydney, Australia.

20 *Guardian*, 23 August 2003, p. 1.

21 The UK Government in its White Paper on air transport made a range of recommendations to increase the capacity of UK airports including that two new runways should be built, the first at Stansted airport by 2012 with a second extra runway at Heathrow airport by 2020, providing 'stringent environmental limits' can be met. The paper rules out additional runways at Stansted, Gatwick and Luton and an airport at Cliffe. New runways and/or terminal capacity at Bristol, Birmingham, Edinburgh, Glasgow, Belfast, Cardiff, Manchester, Liverpool John Lennon, Leeds, Bradford and Newcastle airports.

The White Paper contains no evidence that the 'external' health impacts of such decisions have been taken into account during the decisions, as many had hoped for; see http://www.dft.gov.uk/aviation/whitepaper/.

It should be noted that a range of simple strategies could be employed to reduce the unsustainably high levels of air pollution resulting from aviation:

- Taxiing by using two engines instead of four would reduce hydrocarbon emissions by 80% and carbon monoxide emissions by nearly 70%.
- Hyrdrocarbon and other emissions could be further cut by towing aircraft to and from terminals, using fuel vapor recovery procedures, and modifying jet fuel itself (which could reduce nitrogen oxide particulate emissions by 30%).
- Flying 6000 ft lower than their present cruising altitude, airlines could cut the damage caused by vapour trails by 47% – although they would burn 6% more fuel.
- Air traffic control stratagems could cut emissions by a further 10% if planes no longer had to fly 'zig-zag' patterns and were able to avoid queuing for take-off and landing slots (http://www.guardian.co.uk/uk_news/story/0,3604,1098385,0.html).

22 *Observer*, 14 December 2003, p. 4.

23 http://www.earthisland.org/eijournal/new_articles.cfm?articleID=72&journalID=43.

24 http://www.greenparty.org.uk/reports/2001/aviation/aviation-downsides.htm.

25 http://216.31.193.171/asp/1_introduction.asp.

26 *Guardian*, 22 February 2003, p. 10 and *Guardian*, 13 May 2003, p. 15.

27 *Evening Standard*, 19 March 2003, p. 20.

28 There are a number of excellent books on the Great Fire. See H. Clout (ed.) (1999) *The Times History of London.* London: Times Books; Berresford Ellis, P. (1986) *The Great Fire of London: An Illustrated Account.* London: The New English Library; Porter, S. (1996) *The Great Fire of London.* Gloucestershire: Sutton Publishing; and for full accounts of the contemporary diary entries of Samuel Pepys and John Evelyn see: http://www.pepys.info/fire.html.

29 *Guardian*, 15 April 2003, p. 7; see also *Guardian*, 27 April 2003, p. 9.

30 *Guardian*, 5 August 2003, p. 3.

31 *Independent*, 25 August 2003, p. 10.

32 *Guardian*, 1 September 2003, p. 16.

33 *Guardian*, 31 October 2003, p. 16.

34 http://www.nature.com/nature/links/040108/040108-1.html.

35 *Guardian*, 27 August 2003, p. 10.

36 Sheppard, C. (2003) Coral grief. *Nature*, 18 September. For a full text of this paper see: http://www.nature.com/nature/links/030918/030918-8.html.

37 See www.biodiv.org.

38 Baron, D. (2003) *The Beast in the Garden: A Modern Parable of Man and Nature.* W.W. Norton and Company, New York.

39 *Guardian*, 3 December 2003, p. 3. For more on this issue see: www.unep.org.

40 http://www.int-res.com/abstracts/cr/v20/n3/p253-257.html and for the melting Matterhorn story see http://observer.guardian.co.uk/international/story/0,6903,1001674,00.html.

41 http://www.fao.org/NEWS/1997/971201-e.htm. This site outlines some of the concerns recorded at Kyoto. For an excellent site on the impacts of desertification see: http://www.grida.no/climate/ipcc/regional/166.htm.

42 *Guardian*, 17 August 2003, p. 20.

43 Wilber, D.N. (1979) *Persian Gardens and Garden Pavilions*, 2nd edition (1st published 1962). Washington: Dumbarton Oaks.

44 Macdougall, E.B. and Jashmemski, W.F. (1981) *Ancient Roman Gardens*. Washington: Dumbarton Oaks.

45 Cochrane Ali, T. and Brown, J. (1978) *Landscape Design for the Middle East*. London: RIBA Publications.

46 Roaf, S. (1982) *Landscape Gardening Handbook for Iraq*, unpublished textbook prepared for students in the School of Architecture, Mustanseriyeh University, Baghdad.

47 Bisgrove, R. and Hadley, P. (2002) Gardening in the Global Greenhouse: The Impacts of Climate Change on Gardens in the UK. Technical Report, published by the UK Climate Impacts Programme, Oxford (see www.ukcip.org.uk).

5 SAFE AND WARM; EFFECT OF CLIMATE CHANGE ON THERMAL COMFORT AND HEALTH

Fergus Nicol, Janet Rudge and Sari Kovats

We share with other mammals the mechanisms of temperature regulation – shivering, sweating and changing the distribution of blood between the body's peripheral circulation and the deeper organs. But we also use clothing and shelter and burn fuel to warm and cool us. The use of these cultural mechanisms to control our temperature has made it possible for our species to survive in almost all climates, but it has also created new kinds of vulnerability. Our body temperature now depends on the price of clothing or fuel, whether we control our own furnaces or have them set by landlords, whether we work indoors or outdoors, our freedom to avoid or leave places with stressful temperature regimes ... Thus our temperature regime is not a simple consequence of thermal needs but rather a product of social and economic conditions. (R. Levins and R. Lewontin, *The Dialectical Biologist*[1])

INTRODUCTION

This chapter deals with the effects of indoor climate on the comfort and health of building occupants and how this might be altered by climate change. The occupants of any building will respond to the thermal environment at three levels:

- Through unconscious physiological changes – sweating, shivering, muscle tension and changes in the blood flow (more information on thermal physiology is in Box 5.4, page 141).
- Through behavioural responses – consciously through the addition or removal of clothing, or semi-consciously such as changes in posture or moving to a more comfortable spot.
- Using the controls afforded by the building they occupy, some of them without the use of energy – opening windows, drawing

curtains or blinds – others where mechanical building controls are used – fans, heaters or air conditioning.

This chapter starts by looking at the comfort issues: what constitutes a comfortable environment and how we can future-proof buildings against climate change. The chapter then considers the problems related to thermal health in relation to climate change. Climate change is generally characterized as 'warming' and an increase in heat waves and their associated impacts might be expected, such as those experienced during the heat wave in Europe during August 2003. Climate models also suggest that an increasingly cold climate in Western Europe may occur, but in a much longer time frame. We look at the effect this may have in increasing the excess winter illness and even deaths, which are already a feature of health in parts of the world.

THERMAL COMFORT

The role of comfort

There are three reasons why thermal comfort is important to the design of buildings:

- Comfort (and particularly thermal comfort) is an important aspect of user satisfaction.
- The temperature which people try to achieve in their house is an important factor in deciding the amount of energy it will use.
- If a building fails to be comfortable, then the occupants will take actions to make themselves comfortable. These actions will usually involve the use of energy – possibly destroying a carefully constructed low-energy strategy.

The heat balance

In order to stay healthy, we have to keep our internal body temperature at an almost constant 37°C. In order to ensure a constant body temperature the heat produced by the body must, over time, be balanced by the sum total of the heat lost from it. The heat produced (the metabolic rate – generally measured in watts per square metre (Wm^{-2}) of body surface area) is related to a person's activity – the more active the more heat. There are essentially four avenues of heat loss:

- **Convection** – heat loss to (or gain from) the air. This depends on the temperature of the air and on the air velocity next to the body surface (skin or clothes) (see also Box 5.1 on page 139).
- **Radiation** – heat loss direct to (or gain from) surrounding surfaces. This depends on the temperature of the surrounding surfaces (the radiant temperature) (see also Box 5.2 on page 140).

- **Conduction** – heat loss (or gain) direct to surfaces in contact with the body which depends on temperature of the surface. In most cases this is a small contribution to heat loss.
- **Evaporation** – heat loss due to the evaporation of skin moisture. Depends on the amount of water in the air (humidity) and the air velocity next to the body (see also Box 5.3 on page 141).

Heat is also exchanged from the lungs during breathing, this loss is partly convective and party evaporative. The mathematical expression for the balance between heat production and heat loss is one way of calculating the thermal conditions to provide in a building. This is the Heat Balance approach to setting thermal conditions. The basic equation for heat balance is:

$$M - W = Ev + Ra + K + Co + Re + S \ (\text{Wm}^{-2}) \tag{1}$$

Where M = rate of metabolic heat production
W = energy used in doing mechanical work
Ev = Heat loss by evaporation from the skin
Ra = Heat loss through radiation
K = Heat loss by conduction (generally negligible)
Co = Heat loss by convection
Re = Heat loss by respiration (convective and evaporative)
S = Heat stored in the body (= 0 over time)

More detail of the physical processes underlying thermal comfort is given in the appropriate boxes, which touch briefly on the main points. Don McIntyre's excellent book *Indoor Climate*,[2] or Ken Parsons' *Human Thermal Environments*[3] are good starting points for those who want to know more.

Because of the importance of keeping the internal body temperature constant the body has a number of ways of controlling the rate at which heat leaves the body. These actions are referred to as thermoregulation. Such responses as changes of blood supply to the skin to increase or reduce heat loss, or in more extreme cases, sweating in hot conditions or shivering in the cold. See Box 5.4 on page 141 for more detail on thermoregulation.

Thermal comfort is a psychological phenomenon defined by the American Society of Heating, Refrigeration and Air conditioning Engineers (ASHRAE) as 'That state of *mind* which expresses satisfaction with the thermal environment [emphasis added]'. This psychological phenomenon is often taken to be a response to the physical environment and the physiological state of the body, but is almost certainly affected by the attitude of the person to their surroundings and their experience of thermal environment as well as its current state. (See Box 5.5 on page 142 for more detail on psychophysics.)

Conscious ('behavioural') thermoregulation is generally triggered by thermal discomfort. Discomfort is usually the result of a change in the core temperature coupled with information from the thermal sense at the skin that the body risks continued thermal imbalance (e.g. a draught in a cold room). Generally a situation that is moving in a direction to restore thermal balance is considered pleasurable (e.g. a cool breeze on a hot day). Thermal sensation is therefore part of a feedback system to maintain thermal equilibrium, so that a comfortable environment is one where occupants can maintain thermal balance as a dynamic equilibrium. An uncomfortable environment is one in which we cannot prevent discomfort. See below for more information on these behavioural actions.

The complexity of the thermoregulatory processes and their dynamic nature has made them difficult to characterize mathematically. Steady-state formulations for thermal comfort such as that of Fanger[4] have been found to underestimate the extent to which people will naturally adapt to changes in the environment, particularly in variable conditions.[5,6]

Adaptive behaviour as a way of looking at comfort

Field studies and rational indices

One method that has been widely used to investigate the conditions we find comfortable is the field study. This takes a group of subjects who are going about their normal everyday lives and asks them how hot they feel on a scale, such as those shown in Table 5.1 (i.e., their 'comfort vote'). At the same time, the physical environment (temperature, humidity, air movement) is measured. Over a period of time the way in which the subjective responses change can be related to these measured physical conditions.

Table 5.1. Seven point ASHRAE and Bedford scales of thermal sensation. The −3 to +3 scale is generally used for mathematical evaluation of comfort in indices such as Fanger's Predicted Mean Vote (PMV), the 1 to 7 scale is used in survey work, to avoid confusion

ASHRAE descriptive scale	Numerical equivalent		Bedford descriptive scale
Hot	+3	7	Much too hot
Warm	+2	6	Too hot
Slightly warm	+1	5	Comfortably warm
Neutral	0	4	Comfortable, neither warm nor cool
Slightly cool	−1	3	Comfortable and cool
Cool	−2	2	Too cold
Cold	−3	1	Much too cold

Figure 5.1 shows the mean comfort vote of subjects from a number of field surveys plotted against the mean temperature recorded. The rate of change of comfort vote with temperature is much lower from one survey to another than it is within any particular survey.

The reasons for this observation from field surveys have been the subject of considerable speculation and research, most of which has concentrated on the context in which field surveys are conducted. Nicol and Humphreys suggested, in 1973,[7] that this effect could be the result of a feedback between the thermal sensation of subjects and their behaviour and that they consequently 'adapted' to the climatic conditions in which the field study was conducted.

Unlike laboratory experiments, field studies include the effects of all the behaviours of normal subjects during their everyday lives. Some of the behavioural actions are concerned with the thermal environment, and will therefore affect the relationship between thermal comfort and the environment. The adaptive approach seeks to explain the differences between the field measurements and those obtained in the laboratory by looking at the cumulative effect of behaviour in this relationship.

People and indoor climate

The corollary of the effect shown in Figure 5.1 is that in field surveys the temperature that people find comfortable (the 'comfort temperature') is closely related with the mean temperature measured. This was found to be the case in surveys conducted over a wide range of indoor climates, shown in Figure 5.2.[8] The strong relationship between the comfort temperature and the mean temparature measured during the survey is clear.

As an example of how effectively adaptive actions can be used to achieve comfort, Figure 5.3 shows the actual proportion of subjects comfortable among office workers in Pakistan at different indoor temperatures. The data were collected over a period of a year so the comfort temperature was continually changing, as was

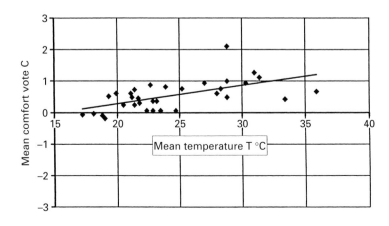

5.1.
A wide range of comfort studies shows that the mean comfort vote is little affected by the mean indoor temperature. Each point represents the mean from a complete study

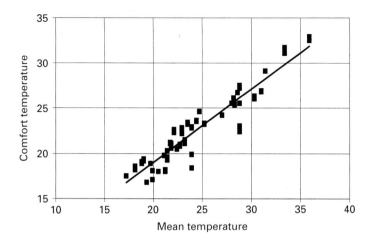

5.2.
The variation of comfort temperature with mean indoor temperature from surveys throughout the world. (*Source:* data presented in Humphreys, 1976[8])

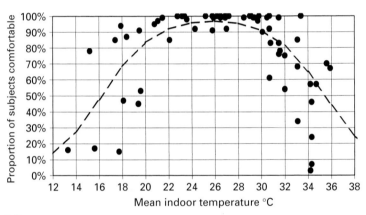

5.3.
Pakistan: the proportion of office workers who were comfortable at different indoor temperatures. Each point on the graph represents the results of one survey of about 20–25 people in a single office. It will be noticed that on many occasions the subjects recorded no discomfort. With a continually changing indoor temperature and comfort temperature Pakistani buildings were found comfortable at temperatures ranging between 20 and 30 °C with no cooling apart from fans. (*Source:* Nicol *et al.*, 1999[9])

the indoor temperature.[9] The major methods these workers had to control their comfort were changing their clothing and using air movement, fans being universally available in Pakistani offices. The curve shows the mean probability of comfort calculated using probit regression. Each point represents the proportion comfortable in a particular city in a particular month. Note that little discomfort is recorded at indoor temperatures between 20 and 30 °C.

Adaptive actions
Interest in the phenomenon outlined above has led to the development of the so-called *adaptive* approach to thermal comfort which attributes the effect to an accumulation of behaviours or other factors which, taken together, are used to ensure comfort.

In a defining paper on the approach, Humphreys and Nicol[10] explained the meaning of adaptive actions (see Box 5.7, page 145).

Box 5.7 shows some of the actions which may be initiated in response to cold or to heat. The lists are intended to be illustrative of an indefinitely large number of conceivable types of action, and are by no means comprehensive. It will be noticed that the lists contain physiological, psychological, social and behavioural items. The lists have in mind the climate and culture of the UK and some items would need modification for other lands.

The set of conceivable adaptive actions in response to warmth or coolth may be classified into five categories:

1 Regulating the rate of internal heat generation.
2 Regulating the rate of body heat loss (see Box 5.6 on page 143 for more detail of the use of clothing).
3 Regulating the thermal environment.
4 Selecting a different thermal environment.
5 Modifying the body's physiological comfort conditions.

Because there are very many conceivable adaptive actions, comfort is likely to be restored by means of a coordinated set of minor actions, rather than by means of a single mode of action. For example, a response to coldness might entail a slight increase in muscle tension, a barely perceptible vasoconstriction, a slightly 'tighter' posture, putting on a sweater and the desire for a cup of coffee. The effect of each might independently be small, but the joint effect can be large, not least because changes in heat flow and changes in thermal insulation are multiplicative in their effect on temperature differential. The more subtle adaptations are unlikely to be captured by questionnaire responses about clothing and activity, and would therefore be 'invisible' to the usually recommended procedures for the evaluation of Predicted Mean Vote (PMV) (Fanger[4]) and Standard Effective Temperature (SET) (Nevins and Gagge[6]).

Adaptation can be regarded as a set of learning processes, and therefore people may be expected to be well adapted to their usual environments. They will feel hot when the environment is hotter than 'usual' and cold when it is colder than 'usual'. The adaptive approach is therefore interested in the study of usual environments. In particular, what environments are 'usual', how does an environment become 'usual', and how does a person move from one 'usual' environment to another? (The heat exchange equation is able to indicate what might be meant by a 'hotter' or a 'colder' environment, but has nothing to say about what might be a 'usual' environment.)

Not all researchers agree on the wide range of adaptive actions outlined by Humphreys and Nicol, and there is generally a feeling that adaptation is concerned with behavioural, more or less conscious actions.

The adaptive principle

The fundamental assumption of the adaptive approach is expressed by the adaptive principle: *If a change occurs such as to produce discomfort, people react in ways which tend to restore their comfort.* This principle applies to field surveys conducted in a wide range of environments and thus legitimizes meta-analyses of comfort surveys such as those of Humphreys,[11] Auliciems and deDear,[12] and deDear and Brager.[6] These meta-analyses have been used to generalize from the results of a number of individual thermal comfort surveys.

By linking people's actions to comfort the adaptive principle links the comfort temperature to the context in which subjects find themselves. The comfort temperature is a result of the interaction between the subjects and the building or other environment they are occupying. The options for people to react will reflect their situation: those with more opportunities to adapt themselves to the environment or the environment to their own requirements will be less likely to suffer discomfort.

The prime contextual variable is the climate. Climate is an overarching influence on the culture and thermal attitudes of any group of people and on the design of the buildings they inhabit. Whilst the basic mechanisms of the human relationship with the thermal environment may not change with climate, there are a number of detailed ways in which people are influenced by the climate they live in and these play a cumulative part in their response to the indoor climate. The second major context of nearly all comfort surveys has been a building, and the nature of the building and its services plays a part in defining the results from the survey. The third context is time. In a variable environment such as will occur in most buildings occupants will respond to changes in the environment. They will do this by taking actions to suit the environment to their liking or by changing themselves (for instance by posture or clothing) to suit the environment. This implies that the comfort temperature is continually changing. The extent of these changes and the rate at which they occur is an important consideration if the conditions for comfort are to be properly specified.

The relationship with outdoor climate

Humphreys (1978)[11] took the indoor comfort temperature determined in a number of surveys conducted world-wide and plotted

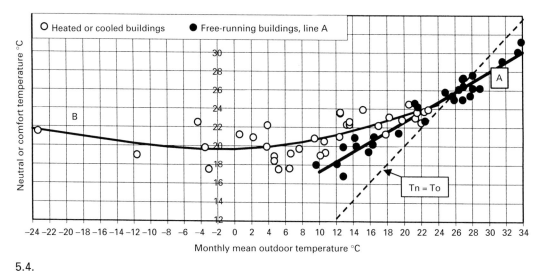

5.4.

The change in comfort temperature with monthly mean outdoor temperature. Each point represents the mean value for one survey (this graph is from Humphreys, 1978[11]). The buildings are divided between those that are climatized at the time of the survey and those that are free-running. Subsequent analysis of the ASHRAE database of comfort surveys[13] showed similar results.

them against the outdoor monthly mean temperature at the time of the survey. The results are shown in Figure 5.4. He found a clear division between people in buildings that were free-running (neither heated nor cooled) at the time of the survey and those in buildings that were climatized (heated or cooled) at the time of the survey. The relationship for the free-running buildings was closely linear. For climatized buildings the relationship is more complex.

The feedback mechanisms create order in the relationship between indoor climate and comfort temperature. In a free-running building the indoor climate is linked by the building to outdoor conditions. When the building is being climatized the relationship changes, because the indoor climate is decoupled from that outdoors.

People in buildings: adaptive opportunities

Buildings differ in a number of ways: in addition to their individual physical form, they differ in their services; in what sort of heating or cooling system is provided and whether it is used; in the possibilities they offer for occupants to control their environment and in the policies of management about whether there is a dress code and so on.

There are other aspects of building services which affect the comfort of occupants. Leaman and Bordass[14] have demonstrated that there is more 'forgiveness' of buildings in which occupants have more access to building controls. By forgiveness they mean that the attitude of the occupants to the building is affected so that they will overlook shortcomings in the thermal environment more readily.

A more robust characterization is that of Baker and Standeven.[15] They identify an 'adaptive opportunity' afforded by a building that will affect the comfort of its occupants. The premise is that the more opportunity occupants have to adapt the environment to their liking the less likely are they to experience thermal stress and the wider will be the range of acceptable conditions (Figure 5.5). Adaptive opportunity is generally interpreted as the *ability* to open a window, draw a blind, use a fan and so on. It must also include dress code working practices and other factors that influence the interaction between occupant and building. Changes in clothing, activity and posture and the promotion of air movement will change the comfort temperature. Other adaptive opportunities will have no direct effect on the comfort temperature, but will allow the occupants to change the indoor climate to suit themselves. Actual adaptive behaviour is an amalgam of these two types of action – changing the conditions to accord with comfort and changing the comfort temperature to accord with prevailing conditions. The range of conditions considered comfortable is affected by the characteristics of the building and the opportunities for individual adaptation by occupants.

In reality it has been found difficult to quantify the adaptive opportunity in terms of the availability of building controls. Nicol and McCartney[16] showed that the mere existence of a control did not mean that it was used, and that merely adding up the number of controls does not therefore give a good measure of the success of a building or its adaptive opportunity. It would seem that as well as

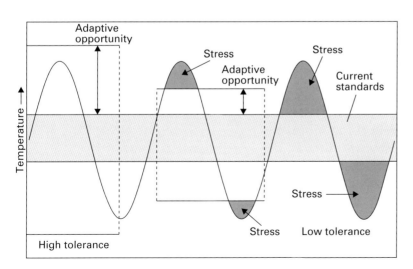

5.5.
Effect of adaptive opportunity: the greater the opportunity to control the environment – or the occupants' requirements – the less likelihood of thermal stress. (*Source:* adapted from Baker and Standeven, 1995[15])

the existence of a control a judgement is needed as to whether it is useful in the particular circumstances. For example, solar shading may be useless on one face of a building, but essential on another. In addition the perceived usefulness of a particular control will change from time to time depending on conditions.[17]

Time as a factor in the specification of comfort temperatures

When people take actions in response to a thermal environment that is causing discomfort these actions take time to accomplish. There are a number of actions that can be taken: some, like opening a window, take little time, while others, such as the change of fashion from winter to summer clothes, take longer. The change is fast enough to keep up with the fluctuations in the weather from season to season but not always quick enough to account for all the changes in the weather.[18] In his comparison between outdoor temperature and the comfort temperature indoors (see Figure 5.4), Humphreys (1978)[11] used records of the monthly mean of the outdoor air temperature as the defining variable. deDear and Brager[6] use the mean of outdoor effective temperature without defining the period over which it has been measured. The weather can change dramatically within a month and both people and the buildings they inhabit change at a rate that will not be reflected by a monthly estimate. Box 5.8 on page 146 suggests a way in which the effects of time can be included in the model of comfort and adaptation.

An adaptive case study – avoiding discomfort in Pakistan and Europe

In the past countries have been assumed to take a path of increasing technological sophistication. In the response to climate change it may be necessary to relearn skills that have fallen into disuse. As fuel prices increase, the ability to adapt to our surroundings is likely to be one of those skills.

A number of studies have been made of thermal comfort in Pakistan,[9] and of the use people make of the thermal controls that are available. Pakistan is a country where the incidence of air conditioning is low, and where a wide range of temperature is found, not only outside but also inside buildings. This is partly because the 'level of technology' is less developed in Pakistan, but crucially it is because the price of fuel is relatively much greater because of the exchange rate for the Rupee against the dollar. Even for relatively well-off Pakistanis the cost of running the air conditioning can be prohibitive.

Five cities were identified in different climatic areas of the country and a study was conducted of office workers who were going about their normal work routine. Surveys of about 100 workers were made in each of the cities on a monthly basis for a period of one year. In addition to subjective responses from the subjects on the Bedford scale (Table 5.1) they were also asked for their preference for a warmer or cooler environment and an estimate of the moisture of their skin. Details were collected of the clothing they were wearing, of their activity and of their use of building controls (windows, fans, lights and heaters). Measurements were made of the globe temperature, the air temperature, the humidity and the air velocity. Outdoor temperatures were collected from local meteorological stations.

From these measurements it is possible, among other things, to relate the extent to which different adaptive actions are taken by the subjects at different temperatures. Two types of adaptive actions are investigated: those that change the comfort temperature of the subject and those that seek to change the environment to suit the subject. Examples of the former are the use of clothing and metabolic rate, and the changes in these are illustrated in Figure 5.6. Also shown are the changes in air velocity and skin moisture. Changes in air velocity will be caused by the use of fans (which are found in all Pakistani offices) and to a lesser extent the opening of windows, but it will have the effect of increasing the temperature which occupants find comfortable. Skin moisture only serves to illustrate the physiological state of the subjects. A graph of discomfort at different values of the indoor temperature at the time of the survey is given in Figure 5.3 above. There is clearly little discomfort between 20 and 30 °C. Most of the changes in clothing and air movement occur in the same range of temperatures.

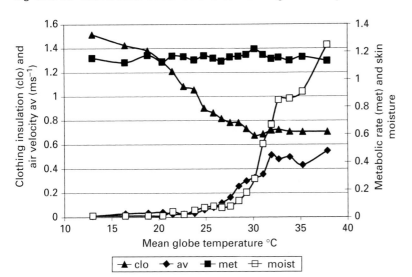

5.6.
Use of adaptive actions to suit the subject comfort temperature to the environment in Pakistan. (*Source:* Fergus Nicol)

A similar pattern occurs in the use of building controls (Figure 5.7). The use of heating ceases when the indoor temperature exceeds 20 °C and fans are all running when the temperature reaches 30 °C. Windows are more likely to be opened as the temperature rises, though at temperatures above 35 °C they are likely to be heating rather than cooling the office and there is some evidence that fewer subjects are opening them at these high temperatures. Lighting is hardly affected by temperature – the use of blinds (which was not recorded) is often to exclude the solar heat and glare at high temperatures. Indoor temperatures are constrained to an 'acceptable zone' of 20–32 °C for about 70% of the time (Figure 5.8).

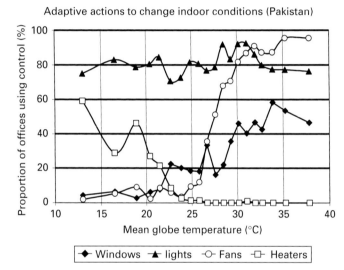

5.7.
Use of various controls to suit the environment to the subject in Pakistan. (*Source:* Fergus Nicol)

5.8.
Distribution of indoor temperatures in Pakistani buildings. Temperatures are largely constrained to the range of 20–32 °C. The curve shows a normal distribution with the same mean and standard deviation. (*Source:* Fergus Nicol)

A similar analysis of the results from the SCATS survey[19] is shown in Figures 5.9 to 5.11. The results given apply only to buildings which were free-running at the time of the survey: many of the buildings were air-conditioned and so the temperature of the building was not in the control of the occupants. Figure 5.11 suggests that there is more discomfort in European buildings but a range of indoor temperature from 19 to 27 °C probably gives rise to little increase in discomfort. Figure 5.12 shows that the indoor temperature remains within these limits for over 80% of the time. Again much of the adaptive action takes place between these limits. The reason for the greater dissatisfaction in Europe is not clear, but

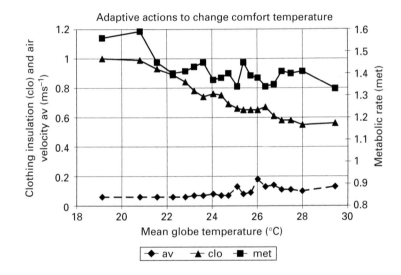

5.9.
Use of adaptive actions to suit the subject comfort temperature to the environment in Europe. (*Source:* Fergus Nicol)

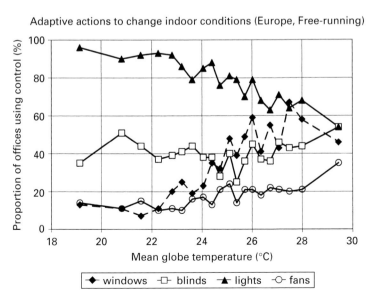

5.10.
Use of various controls to suit the indoor environment to the subject in free-running buildings in Europe. (*Source:* Fergus Nicol)

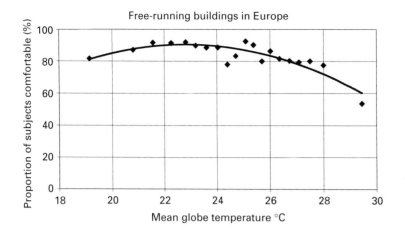

5.11.
Proportion of European subjects comfortable at different temperatures in free-running buildings. Separating the countries gives a higher level of comfort, but over a narrower band of temperatures. (*Source:* Fergus Nicol)

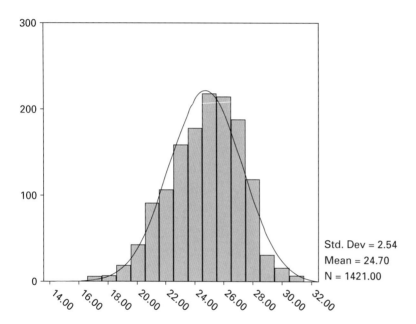

5.12.
Distribution of indoor temperatures in European buildings: the temperatures fit the range of comfort temperatures, falling mostly between 19 and 27 °C. (*Source:* Fergus Nicol)

there are a number of possible reasons, one being the international nature of the European survey population, another the more constrained workforce in Pakistan, where unemployment is high.

HEALTH EFFECTS OF HEAT AND COLD

In the UK it has long been recognized that there are more deaths in winter than in summer. The causes of this excess winter mortality and the parallel increase in winter illness have been the subject of a great deal of research in recent years and we report on this below. The impact of hot weather on human health has gained importance due to the threat of global climate change, and the major heat wave event that occurred throughout Europe in 2003, affecting France, Spain, Portugal and other countries in Western Europe. France was most affected and more than 10 000 excess deaths occurred during the heat wave.[80]

Physiological effects of cold

Most cold-related deaths in the UK appear to be associated with chest and heart illnesses. Between 1992 and 1999, annual numbers of excess winter deaths ranged from 23 000 to 45 000 in England,[81] depending partly on the severity of the winter. Cardiovascular and respiratory diseases are the predominant causes of such deaths in the UK, despite a persisting, widespread assumption that hypothermia (cooling of the body core) is largely responsible.[20] A strong relationship has been shown between changes in external temperature and numbers of deaths from these two major causes.[21] Curwen[22] estimated that a third were attributable to respiratory disease and more than a half to cardiovascular disease (mainly heart attacks and strokes). According to Collins,[23] although numerically more deaths are ascribed to circulatory (cardiovascular) disease, the greatest proportional effect of winter temperatures is on deaths from respiratory disease. Keatinge and Donaldson[24] refer to the time lapses observed between temperature drops and peaks in numbers of deaths, which clearly vary according to the diagnosed cause of death, such that there is a lapse of up to three days for coronary thrombosis and 12 days for respiratory disease. These indicate that the greater part of the seasonal influence is probably due to the direct effect of cold rather than other, indirect, factors, such as reduced vitamin C in the winter diet, for example. As Khaw observes, there are

seasonal changes in environmental and other factors such as air pollution, sunlight exposure, influenza incidence, and diet [that] have variously been implicated in seasonal changes in mortality.[25]

However, she concludes that temperature is the leading candidate.

Collins recently reviewed the long-known association between cold ambient temperatures and respiratory illnesses with reference to the physiological and epidemiological evidence.[23] Although most studies have focused on damp and mouldy living conditions rather than cold house temperatures, here he concentrates on cold indoor conditions, how these relate to dampness and mould and, consequently, with allergic response respiratory conditions. As Collins demonstrates, the effects of ambient temperature on physiological function can be explained in terms of pathology. These effects include asthma attacks, which can be triggered by breathing in cold air, reduced resistance to respiratory infection, and wheeze in children associated with dampness and condensation on cold surfaces, which produces allergenic mould growth. However, it is much harder to demonstrate these effects at the population level, due to the difficulties of obtaining accurate exposure details, measures of environmental factors or determining individual susceptibilities.

Evidence for a relationship between temperature and cardiovascular mortality includes, for example, findings on seasonal variation in blood pressure, which is related independently to both indoor and outdoor temperature, indoor temperature having the stronger impact.[25] If blood pressure is raised, as in response to cold, circulatory conditions can be affected. Collins concludes that it is methodologically very difficult to show a definitive link between home temperatures and specific health outcomes, but that both indoor and outdoor cold temperatures can exacerbate respiratory illnesses in the presence of respiratory pathogens.[26]

Physiological effects of heat

Healthy persons have efficient heat regulatory mechanisms which cope with increases in temperature up to a particular threshold. The body can increase radiant, convective and evaporative heat loss by vasodilatation (enlargement of blood vessels in the skin) and perspiration (Kilbourne[27]). Heat can increase blood viscosity. Healthy volunteers ($n = 8$) exposed to 41 °C for 6 hours experienced elevated platelet counts and increased blood viscosity (Keatinge et al.[27]). Severe perspiration can also lead to a reduction in plasma volume. Increased blood viscosity is considered a plausible physiological mechanism by which heat stress can lead to arterial thrombosis that can further lead to a heart attack or stroke. However, the effect of heat on blood viscosity is less well understood than that of cold.

The increased sweat production in the heat can lead to two types of problems: (i) dehydration and (ii) hyponatremia (caused by drinking large quantities of water with low salt concentrations). A significant proportion of heat stroke cases are due to exercise in hot weather in young healthy people, so-called 'exertional heat stress'.[28,29] For less fit subjects, heat illnesses can occur at low levels of activity, or even in the absence of exercise. Low fitness levels lead to a low cardiovascular reserve and thus to low heat tolerance.[30]

Climate and issues of public health

Excess winter mortality
Excess winter mortality is a particular problem in Britain, where it is thought to be associated with poorly insulated houses, in which

internal temperatures track the external temperature, providing little protection against the cold, and where occupants cannot afford to adequately heat such homes to safe temperatures. Such a combination of circumstances, i.e. energy inefficient homes and low household incomes, is known as *fuel poverty*.

Excess winter mortality is measured as the number of deaths to occur during the winter months (December to March) in excess of the average for the rest of the year. Alternatively, it is measured as a ratio of these figures. This phenomenon is evident in all but equatorial climates and is apparently associated with low temperatures, or the relative seasonal fall in temperature. As Wilkinson *et al.*[31] point out, it is a linear relationship and not simply a step increase in the winter period showing an effect of just the very coldest days, although escalating numbers may reach headlines during cold snaps. Typically, the UK suffers up to three times the ratio of excess winter deaths compared with countries such as Sweden or Germany, where winters are colder but homes are warmer and better insulated. For every 1 °C fall in temperature below 20 °C, mortality increases by between 1 and 2% in the UK.[32]

British householders appear to be less well protected from the cold in their homes than their continental neighbours, although there is some debate over the comparative effect of outdoor and indoor temperatures on excess winter mortality. Curwen[33] and Boardman[34] have shown it to be inversely correlated with outdoor temperatures in Britain, but international differences in seasonal

5.13.
The elderly are some of the most vulnerable in society to extremes of heat and cold. (*Source:* the Help the Aged British Gas partnership)

mortality do not reflect a similar association in accordance with national differences in absolute external temperature levels.[35]

Boardman concludes that the closer relationship between outdoor and indoor temperatures in Britain, because of deficiencies in the building fabric, is key to the higher numbers of excess winter deaths compared with many other countries. The Eurowinter Group in 1997[76] showed that in some European countries with milder winters, indoor temperatures were lower at given outdoor temperatures and bedrooms were less often heated than where cold winters were normally experienced. At the same time, other protective measures against the cold were less prevalent, such as clothing and outdoor activity, which the Eurowinter study also associated with higher winter mortality.

Seasonal patterns of mortality have changed as public health measures, or improved medical care, help to reduce summer epidemics of infection, particularly among infants. As further socio-economic changes take place, the ratio of winter over summer deaths falls off over time, or 'de-seasonality' follows seasonality.[36] Both seasonality and subsequent de-seasonality have developed later in England and Wales than in certain countries with colder winters.

The use of central heating seems to reduce the incidence of winter deaths. Sakamoto-Momiyama[37] suggested that the increased use of central heating in homes is the main reason for the appearance of de-seasonality in many developed countries although Henwood[38] describes the direct evidence as inconclusive. In Britain, where central heating ownership spread later than in countries with very cold winters such as Canada, Norway and Sweden, the pattern of de-seasonality was shown to have followed behind those countries. As Boardman has noted,[35] excess winter mortality is higher in Britain than in these and other countries, like France and Denmark, with more similar winter temperatures to the UK.

Khaw[25] observes that outdoor temperatures are most used in mortality analyses, but that outdoor temperature may be a marker for indoor temperature exposure, because of their close relationship. Indoor temperatures have been observed by some to have an impact, but are not strongly related to latitude:

Scandinavian countries (which tend to have indoor heating and building insulation) have less seasonal variation in mortality than more southern countries such as Portugal and Israel where central heating is not widespread and indoor temperatures may vary more in line with outdoor temperatures throughout the year.[25]

The ability to pay to run the central heating, once it is in the building, would obviously be key to the resultant indoor temperature and its effect on health.

Heat wave events and mortality

Episodes of extreme hot weather have a greater impact on mortality than the number of deaths reported as due to classical heat illness. Short-term peaks in mortality are associated with heat waves. Lower than expected mortality can be seen following heat wave events, indicating that some of the mortality during the heat wave is attributable to deaths brought forward by a matter of days or weeks (short term mortality displacement). A study of a heat wave in Belgium calculated that 15% of the excess mortality was due to deaths brought forward, based on a deficit in deaths in the elderly following the heat wave.[39] A study of 'heat wave' episodes in the Netherlands, using the official weather service definition, estimated excess mortality was in the range of 5–15% for different cause and age groups. The excess was always greater in mortality in the elderly, and from respiratory disease.[40]

Some heat wave events are very severe and can be considered a natural disaster if public services are overwhelmed. The heat wave in July 1987 in Greece was associated with 2000 excess deaths.[41] In France, in 2003, the mortuary service and hospitals were unable to cope with the excess.

The mortality impacts of heat wave events have been estimated using episode analyses. Attributable mortality is estimated by subtracting the 'expected' mortality from the observed mortality during a pre-defined period. The expected mortality is calculated using a variety of measures, including moving averages, and averages from similar time periods in previous years. Estimates are therefore very sensitive to the method used to estimate the 'expected' mortality.[42]

A further difficulty is the lack of standard definition of a heat wave. Many countries do not have local definitions, and it has proved difficult to identify a relative definition for international comparisons. The same temperatures can have different impacts depending on the duration of the event, or the time in the season. Heat waves early in the summer (June/July) are associated with greater impacts on mortality than heat waves of comparable or hotter temperatures in the same population in subsequent months.[43,44]

Vulnerable groups

Vulnerability to cold

Fuel poverty particularly affects the elderly. It is defined as the inability to afford sufficient warmth because of the inefficiency of the building. Older people are especially vulnerable to adverse health effects of cold living conditions. Yet, in the UK, they are often least able to afford sufficient heating and are most likely to live in poorly insulated housing with inefficient heating systems. High numbers of excess winter deaths among those aged over 65 are associated with these factors.

There are known physiological effects of cold on the older population. Pensioners are likely to spend more time at home than others, in which case they are more susceptible to poor thermal conditions, where they occur. The British Geriatrics Society recommends 21 °C as a suitable indoor temperature for older people.[45] Collins[46] has also identified benchmark indoor temperatures for maintaining health: between 18 and 24 °C, there is no risk to healthy, sedentary people; below 16 °C resistance to respiratory infections may be affected; below 12 °C there is increased risk of cardiovascular events, due to raised blood pressure. Hypothermia, or cooling of the body core, is caused by prolonged cold and the risk of this increases below 5 °C.[45] Older people are most at risk because they are generally less mobile than others and, additionally, because with age the body's thermoregulatory system may deteriorate, which affects awareness of temperature extremes. This means that they may not take appropriate avoiding action when the temperature drops. Circulatory disease is exacerbated by 'cold stress', which results from fluctuations in temperature[47] and can arise from moving between warm and cold rooms. However, moving from a cold dwelling to the cold outside produces greater cardiovascular strain than going out from a warm house.[48]

Other groups vulnerable to cold-related illness are the very young and the chronically sick. Children are particularly subject to 'wheeze' in damp conditions, which often occur together with cold. Further cold effects are that low temperatures slow reflexes and affect coordination, especially among older people, and can therefore be the cause of accidents in the home. Apart from the recognized physical effects of cold housing on health, mental health problems can also arise from the compounded stress of living in debilitating cold and damp conditions.

Increasing ownership of central heating has been linked with the declining numbers of excess winter deaths over recent decades, but it has also been suggested that the spread of central heating may not have benefited the most vulnerable groups.[49] After all, central heating ownership does not guarantee that its use can be afforded by householders. Recent research suggests that increased vulnerability to winter death from cardiovascular disease is linked to indoor temperature and thermal efficiency of housing.[50] Other work has shown an association between the lack of central heating and higher risk of dying in winter but identifies the need to explore further the influence of socio-economic factors and other measures of housing quality.[51] Fuel-poor groups in Britain appear to be far more vulnerable to dying from cold in winter than those who can afford to heat their houses properly.

Vulnerability to heat

There are many physiological factors that impair temperature regulation and so can be predisposing factors for clinical heat illness:[52]

- Dehydration due to reduced food and liquid uptake or intestinal problems.
- Use of diuretics or alcohol abuse.
- Use of other drugs affecting the system: stimulants, beta-blockers, anticholinergics, digitalis, barbiturates, especially combined with hypertension, age, fever, recent infections or skin burns.
- Previous heat illness, low fitness, adiposity, fatigue, sleep deprivation, long term high level exercise, and protective clothing.

Age and illness are strong predictors of heat-related illness, as age highly correlates with increasing illness, disability, use of medication and reduced cardiovascular fitness.

Both individual- and population-level studies provide strong and consistent evidence that age is a risk factor for heat- and cold-related mortality. Studies vary, however, at the age at which the vulnerability is shown to increase. Most population-base time series studies show an effect in adult age groups[53] but the effect is larger in over-65s compared to other ages. The elderly in institutions, such as residential care homes, may be vulnerable to heat-related illness and death.[54] An almost two-fold increase in mortality rate was reported in geriatric hospital inpatients (but not other inpatients) during the 1976 heat wave in the UK.[55]

There is currently little evidence for heat effects on mortality in young age groups (under 15 years) in European populations, as the baseline mortality in this age group is very low. There is anecdotal evidence of heat deaths caused by children being left in cars on hot days. Children are more prone to dehydration due to the higher volume of fluid in their bodies compared to an adult. Hospital admissions in children increase on sunny days.[56]

Epidemiological studies have identified several socio-economic risk factors for heat-related mortality:[57]

- Living alone, or not leaving the house at least once per day.
- Housing (e.g. building type, which floor).
- Presence and use of air conditioning in the home or residential institution.

Case control studies following the 1995[58] and 1999[59] heat waves in Chicago both found that the strongest risk factor for dying in a heat wave was living alone.

Impacts of heat waves are greater in urban than in rural populations. Such populations differ in their basic vulnerability to heat (underlying rates of cardiorespiratory disease) and in their exposures (different types of housing, and higher temperatures caused by the urban heat island effect).[60,61] Mapping of heat wave deaths in St Louis (1966) found the highest rates in inner city areas where population density was higher, open spaces were fewer, and where socio-economic status was lower than in surrounding areas.[62,63] Individuals are more vulnerable to heat stress if they are in poorly designed housing, with no access to air conditioning or cooler buildings. These risk factors are more likely to be present in urban than rural areas. During a heat wave, mortality impacts are greater in cities than in the surrounding areas or in the country as a whole. This has been shown in the UK in 1995,[64] in Greece in 1987,[65] and in 1980 in Missouri, USA.[66] However, this does not mean that rural populations are not affected by heat waves.[67] In developing countries, rural populations may be significantly more vulnerable due to inadequate housing, and lack of access to clean water.

It has proved difficult to demonstrate clear socio-economic gradients for heat-related mortality.[66,68] As with winter mortality, vulnerability may be more closely linked to social activity and housing types which are not directly correlated with socio-economic status. Smoyer is therefore correct in concluding that relatively little is known about the types of places where risk from heat waves is high.[69]

The temperature and mortality relationship

The relationship between daily mortality and temperature is generally U-shaped in European populations. That is, there is a

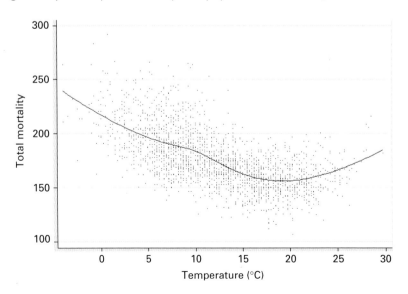

5.14.
Relationship between temperature and daily mortality, Greater London, 1991–96. (*Source:* Sari Kovats)

Table 5.2. Temperature relationships with mortality, for selected causes

Population	% change per 1 °C increase above cut point			Cut point (°C)	Lag (day)	Reference
	All Causes	CVD	Resp.			
Oslo, Norway	0.7 (−0.2, 1.5)	0.8 (−0.4, 0.2)	4.7 (2.2, 7.1)	10	7	Nafstad et al.
London, UK	1.3 (1.0, 1.2)			18	0–1	Pattenden et al.
Netherlands	1.2	1.1	3.1	16.5	1–2	Kunst et al.
Ljubljana, Slovenia	2.2 (1.1, 3.4)			17	0–2	McMichael et al.
Sofia, Bulgaria	2.2 (1.6, 2.9)			18	0–1	Pattenden et al.
Bucharest, Romania	2.8 (2.0, 3.5)			22	0–2	
Madrid, Spain	1.0			20.3	1	Alberdi et al.
Valencia, Spain	3.6 (1.2, 6.0)	2.3 (−1.5, 4.5)	5.7 (−2.9, 8.2)	24	1–2	Ballester et al.
Barcelona, Spain		4.0 (IHD)		25		Saez et al.

Sources:
Alberdi, J.C., Diaz, J., Montero Rubio, J.C. and Miron Perez, I.J. (1998) Daily mortality in Madrid community, 1986–1992: relationship with meteorological variables. *Eur J Epidemiol*, 14, pp. 571–8.
Ballester, D.F., Corella, D., Perez-Hoyos, S., Saez, M. and Hervas, A. (1997) Mortality as a function of temperature. A study in Valencia, Spain, 1991–93. *International Journal of Epidemiology*, 26, pp. 551–61.
Kunst, A.E., Looman, C.W. and Mackenbach, J.P. (1993) Outdoor air temperature and mortality in the Netherlands: a time series analysis. *American Journal of Epidemiology*, 137, pp. 331–41.
Nafstad, P., Skrondal, A. and Bjertness, E. (2001) Mortality and temperature in Oslo, Norway, 1990–95. *European Journal of Epidemiology*, 17, pp. 621–7.
Pattenden, S., Nikiforov, B. and Armstrong, B. (2003) Mortality and temperature in Sofia and London. *Journal of Epidemiology and Community Health*, 57, pp. 628–33.
Saez, M., Sunyer, J., Castellsague, J., Murillo, C. and Anto, J.M. (1995) Relationship between weather temperature and mortality: a time series analysis approach in Barcelona. *International Journal of Epidemiology*, 24, pp. 576–82.

temperature value or range where mortality is lowest, and below this temperature mortality increases (cold effects) and above this 'comfort zone' mortality also increases (heat effects). The majority of studies report a linear relationship above and below a minimum mortality temperature (or range of temperatures (Figure 5.14)).[70] Table 5.2 lists the heat slopes for mortality for selected cause groups in European cities or countries. The effect of temperature on mortality is greater for respiratory and cardiovascular disease than for other causes of death. The warmer the climate, the higher the cut point temperature (though it should be noted that the slope will depend on the choice of cut point).

In the assessment of the short-term effects of extreme episodes (usually extreme weather or high air pollutant exposures) there is the methodological problem of quantifying mortality displacement, or 'harvesting'. A proportion of the 'acute' effect on mortality may be due to the hastening of death in already ill persons by a few days or weeks.

Stressful weather and high levels of air pollutants have independent adverse effects on daily mortality. Few studies have successfully differentiated weather-induced and pollution-induced daily mortality. In studies of heat-related mortality, it can be difficult to separate the effects of exposure to air pollution because it is associated both with daily variations in temperature (exposure) and with daily variations in mortality (outcome). There is some evidence of a physiological synergistic effect between temperature and pollutants.[71,72]

Adaptation: current knowledge

The capacity of humans to adapt to varied climates and environments is considerable. Physiological and behavioural differences between cultures have developed over many millennia as a consequence of exposure to vastly different climatic regimes. The design of vernacular buildings is also sensitive to climate, using a number of techniques to suit the building to the climate, and providing appropriate passive cooling techniques. In many areas the appropriate use of buildings is determined by the local culture. An instance in hot climates is the internal migration from one time of day to another, or from one season to another, between parts of the house that provide more comfortable (less stressful) indoor climates.

Human beings undergo physiological adaptation to warmer climates. Many studies have illustrated this for people moving to hotter countries, and particularly for soldiers or sports persons. The physiological adaptation can take place over a matter of days or weeks. The body responds by increasing the output of sweat and improvement in cardiovascular stability upon heat exposure. Both responses lead to reduced thermal and cardiovascular strain. The rate at which infrastructural changes will take place in response to climate change is likely to be much slower, however.

Buildings as modifiers of temperature

British homes are often poorly built to withstand the cold. The Energy Report for the 1996 English House Condition Survey[73] found that 38% of homes failed to reach the minimum standard needed to safeguard health, according to Collins' benchmark temperature thresholds. In typical winter conditions, over 10% of all homes in England have a living room temperature below 16 °C. When the outside temperature is below freezing, this increases to nearly 18% of all homes, including almost 4% with rooms below 12 °C.[74] The government now acknowledges the link between cold homes and poor health, while the Department of Health recognizes that fuel poverty contributes to inequalities in health status.

Boardman demonstrated the relatively poor domestic building standards required in the UK compared with elsewhere, despite regular increases in demands of regulations concerning insulation and energy efficiency since 1974.[35] The lack of effective insulation is commonplace and many homes in Britain built before the First World War are separated from the elements by a wall only one brick thick. The housing stock is notoriously 'leaky', harking back to an era when homes were heated with open fires that required a good draught to burn well. Air infiltration is rife even in modern homes due to a number of influences, including poor design, methods of construction and quality of workmanship.[75] Boardman describes the problems of heat loss from British housing due to high ventilation rates and the consequent difficulties that arise in attempting to effectively draught-proof older dwellings.

In the rest of Europe the picture is very varied. The Eurowinter Study was a large-scale epidemiological study designed to consider the effect of winter climate and protective behaviour on excess winter mortality.[76] Indoor temperatures were measured across regions and cities in a number of European countries, including Finland, The Netherlands, Germany, England, Italy and Greece. These were taken as one-off readings simultaneously with the administration of questionnaires, which were used to survey heating use, clothing and outdoor excursion behaviour. Among the authors' conclusions were that:

striking differences indoors were higher living room temperatures and more frequent bedroom heating in the colder countries, all at a given level of outdoor cold.[76]

England was found to be nearer the 'warmer' end of the scale in terms of the average outdoor winter temperature (calculated from October to March) and with respect to this conclusion. This was not the case, however, when it was judged by the number of days in the year when the mean daily temperature falls below 18 °C, which indicates the misleading nature of an 'average' temperature when comparing climates.

Consideration of average indoor temperature levels alone, with no reference to daily or other variations, allows no acknowledgement of the possible effect on comfort or health of a changeable climate, such as prevails in the UK. Arguments have been made previously of the health effects of temperature changeability, based on a body of health evidence.[77] The fact that temperatures are changeable means that 'mild' averages disguise the extremes experienced, which, if buildings are energy-inefficient, will be translated into similar indoor conditions. Even so, the Eurowinter Study adds to the accumulation of evidence that indoor temperatures vary across Europe and that in countries with 'mild' winters, buildings tend to offer less protection against the cold than where the winter climate is more extreme.

It is evident that the effect of climate on people and their health is modified – to varying degrees – by the buildings they occupy. In countries with more predictably extreme climates, buildings are generally better equipped to cope with extreme temperatures than those where long periods of cold or heat are not the norm. Thus, insulation and energy efficiency is given higher priority in building regulations for countries like Germany and in Scandinavia. At the same time, it may be that buildings in such countries are traditionally designed to cope with the most uncomfortable seasonal conditions usually experienced, but at the expense of different comfort features required over shorter periods at other times of the year. This would explain the lack of central heating in Southern European countries, where summer conditions are viewed as the priority but indoor temperatures are found to be low during the relatively brief winter season.

In the temperate climate of the UK, where extreme weather conditions are not normally experienced, space and prevention of damp has generally taken priority over insulation in terms of building regulations. It appears that much of the housing stock is poorly insulated and leaky, with inefficient heating systems, so that indoor temperatures closely follow outdoor temperatures, particularly if the occupants are on low incomes and unable to afford sufficient heating for these homes that are hard to heat. Cold and damp conditions frequently occur together, especially where dampness is due to condensation. This occurs on cold surfaces, caused by poorly insulated fabric and lack of sufficient heating or appropriate ventilation.

Buildings that have poor insulation characteristics, or are lightweight, with low thermal capacity, will be as likely to produce uncomfortable indoor temperatures during hot summers as much as in cold winters. If ventilation possibilities through windows are limited, the potential for night cooling during hot weather would also be restricted. It is not likely, therefore, that buildings which, at present, are not well designed to cope with cool winters, will be more able to produce comfortable conditions during the potentially more frequent hot summers.

Health education and warning systems

Education to advise people of appropriate behaviour during hot weather is an essential component of heat-death prevention. Many governments in Europe have issued advice on how to avoid heat-related illness. However, there is evidence that perception of ambient temperature is poorer in the elderly.[78] Therefore, an individual may not recognize that they need to change their behaviour. Further, an understanding of human behaviour during heat events is needed before the most appropriate messages can be developed and targeted. There is a lack of qualitative research on behavioural responses to heat waves and heat wave warnings.

There have been several campaigns at getting people to be warmer in winter. Searches of the published literature found no studies of the effectiveness of heat- or cold-awareness campaigns. Passive warnings for poor air quality, for example, are also largely ignored. The following components are required for an effective heat-health warning system:[82]

- Sufficiently reliable heat wave forecasts for the population of interest.
- Robust understanding in the cause-effect relationships between thermal environment and health.
- Effective response measures to implement within the window of lead time provided by the warning.
- The community in question must be able to provide the needed infrastructure.

A range of methods is used in order to identify situations that adversely affect human health.[79]

Heat early warning systems when accompanied by specific health interventions are generally considered to be effective in reducing deaths during a heat wave.

In the longer term, local authorities and building professionals require education to appreciate the part better building design can play in enabling buildings to remain cool in hot weather. This includes the use of tried and tested techniques as well as the incorporation of modern technological approaches. Schools of architecture and engineering have a responsibility to ensure that such considerations are an essential element in their curricula.

Implications of climate change on buildings and health in the UK

If the likelihood is that winters will be warmer and wetter, while summers will be hotter and drier, then it may be anticipated that the *relative* seasonal temperature differences would not be much altered from those experienced currently. In fact, they could be even greater. It is therefore possible that seasonal mortality variations would still feature in the UK, as they do already in most climates. Although seasonal averages may be warmer, there could be more extreme temperatures and greater variability within seasons, which is also known to have health implications.

Wet buildings are harder to heat. Warmer, wetter winters would evidently present less of a threat in terms of cold temperatures and research to date has not found a relationship between rainfall and excess winter mortality. However, damp reduces the insulating effect of building fabric so, where buildings already have poor insulating qualities, these will be reduced further still by increased rainfall and become more frequently difficult to heat comfortably and affordably. The likelihood of condensation occurrence may also be increased, with possible implications for mould growth and consequent health problems.

CONCLUSIONS

The implications of climate change for comfort and health have been presented. In the case of comfort, building occupants will be increasingly dependent on the opportunities which the social and physical character of the building offer them to adapt to the changes. The effectiveness of these will depend on the ability of occupants to change their behaviour and attitude to the building as the changes occur.

The adaptive principle tells us that people will change themselves and their environment to achieve comfort, but this also assumes that their behaviour is appropriate in the changed circumstances. The tendency to open windows in hot weather, for instance, is only helpful if this has the effect of cooling the building; if the weather outside is very hot this may make things worse.

The temperature at which there is an increased risk of illness due to heat depends on the normal outdoor conditions. This suggests that similar cultural considerations apply to health as to comfort. Countries with a cold climate, such as Scandinavia, have learned to insulate their buildings against the cold. Likewise behaviour in hot climates is more appropriate to the heat. Some of this is related to learning appropriate behaviour (for instance by drinking more water) and some of it is in the provision of appropriate buildings, such as those that take advantage of thermal mass to reduce indoor temperature variability in temperate or desert climates.

For architects there are important lessons to be learned from the scientific analysis of buildings, and in the light of this the study of local vernacular buildings. For national and local authorities the study of buildings and the understanding of the effects of weather patterns in existing climates can give important clues for the provision of warnings and help to communities struggling with unexpected conditions.

The wrong conclusions can also follow – for instance an over-reliance on the provision of mechanical systems to alleviate the more extreme conditions. These can add to the problem of climate change through the excessive use of fossil fuel energy. It is also becoming increasingly clear that the assumption that energy is always available can be misleading when extreme weather puts a strain on energy utilities.

For buildings to provide a safe and comfortable environment in the future they should:

- Provide the means for occupants to regulate the indoor climate.
- Avoid the use of mechanical cooling where possible.
- Avoid the need for large amounts of energy to provide comfortable interiors.

In addition there is a need for:

- Education of building professionals on how to design buildings that meet these needs.
- Education of the public on the ways to avoid heat stress and cold stress in ways that require little energy use.
- The instigation of mechanisms for warning the public and the authorities when dangerous weather episodes are expected.

Box 5.1 Heat loss by convection

We are surrounded by air. When the temperature of the air is lower than skin temperature then we will lose heat from the body by convection. When air temperature is above skin temperature we will gain heat. In cool still conditions air heated by the body will become buoyant when the body heats it. It will then rise up and form a 'plume' above the head and then disperse. Any movement of the air will add to the cooling by helping to strip the warmed air from the body at a greater rate, effectively cooling the air in contact with the body. Air movement is counted relative to the body surface so, for instance, walking will add to the effective air movement. Turbulence in the air stream can also have an effect helping to increase the cooling effect of air movement.

These effects occur whether or not the body is clothed. Where clothing is worn the cooling effect of convection occurs at the clothing surface so instead of the skin temperature it is the temperature of the surface of the clothes which effects the rate of loss of heat.

By insulating the skin the rate of heat loss is reduced. Air movement can also have some impact on the effectiveness of clothing as an insulator: a permeable material allowing the cool air to penetrate further and reduce the garment's effectiveness.

Where the air in contact with the body is hotter than skin temperature all these effects act in the opposite direction to heat the body.

In summary: the cooling (or heating) effect of the air depends on the difference between air temperature and skin (or clothing surface) temperature and on the air movement. The effect of air movement is generally considered to be roughly proportional to the square root of the air velocity.

Box 5.2 Heat loss by radiation

All bodies emit heat at their surface at a rate that is proportional to the fourth power of their absolute temperature (absolute temperature is equal to the centigrade temperature plus 273). At the same time surrounding surfaces are radiating to the body in a similar fashion. So the body loses heat if the surroundings are colder and gains heat if they are hotter. If the surroundings were all at one temperature the situation would be relatively simple. But of course they are not, in any real situation there will be cold windows or hot ceilings, radiators and even the sun. There is not space here to go too far into the details of radiant energy exchange.

The full picture integrates the effect of every part of the surrounding surfaces with every part of the body. The usual simplification is to talk in terms of the 'mean radiant temperature'. This is the temperature of a sphere which would exchange no net radiation with the surroundings. The notion of the mean radiant temperature is very useful. It can be used to assess the cooling or heating effect of the environment.

In a real situation the radiant temperature will vary from point to point in a room and the size of the human body means that it will even vary from point to point on the body. In general a rough estimate of radiant temperature such as the average temperature of the room surfaces is all that can be achieved. The effect of any large surface with a different temperature needs to be taken into account especially as people notice radiant asymmetry (often interpreting it as a 'draught' in the case of a cold surface).

There is only a relatively small temperature range in most buildings. The fourth power law for radiant heat exchange can therefore be approximated so that the radiant heat loss is roughly proportional to the temperature difference between the clothing surface and the radiant temperature.

Box 5.3 Heat loss by evaporation

When water evaporates it extracts a quantity of heat (the latent heat of evaporation) from its surroundings. The evaporation of water from the surface of the skin means much of the latent heat is extracted from the skin and cools it. This cooling effect is very powerful (the evaporation of 1 g/minute is equivalent to 41 W) and is used by the body for cooling when we sweat. It is not the sweating that cools us but the evaporation of sweat from the skin.

After the sweat has been evaporated it must move away from the skin if it is to be successful, in order that more evaporation can occur. The driving force for evaporation is the gradient of the water vapour pressure near the skin surface. The water vapour pressure is that part of the total pressure of the air that is caused by the molecules of water in it. The hotter the air, the more water it is capable of carrying. The maximum driving force is the difference between the vapour pressure at skin temperature and the vapour pressure in the air as a whole.

The heat lost by evaporation from the skin is usually caused by the amount of sweat produced and not the maximum that can be evaporated (this would require the body to be totally wet with sweat). So the sweat glands and not the physical conditions usually govern the heat loss by evaporation. Air movement tends to increase evaporation in much the same way as it increases convection. So the water vapour pressure in the atmosphere and the square root of the air velocity decides the possible heat loss by evaporation.

Box 5.4 Thermal physiology: metabolic heat and the control of deep body temperature

We produce energy by 'burning' food to produce the energy we need to live. Most of this energy takes the form of heat. The body produces this 'metabolic heat' all the time: more is produced when we are active and the more active we are the more heat is produced (see Table 5.3). Heat is transported around the body by the blood. The organs of the body, and particularly the brain, must stay at about 37 °C. The body has mechanisms for controlling the deep body (or core) temperature. If our brain temperature exceeds acceptable limits, the body reacts to restore heat balance.

Table 5.3. Metabolic rate for selected activities

Activity	Wm^{-2}	Met
Reclining	46	0.8
Seated, relaxed	58	1.0
Sedentary activity (office, dwelling school, laboratory)	70	1.2
Standing, light activity (shopping, laboratory, light industry)	93	1.6
Standing, medium activity (shop assistant, domestic work, machine work)	116	2.0
Walking on level:	110	1.9
2 km/h	140	2.4
3 km/h	165	2.8
4 km/h	200	3.4

Source: International Standard 7730. Moderate Thermal Environments: Determination of PMV and PPD Indices and Specification of the Conditions for Thermal Comfort. International Organisation for Standardisation, Geneva, 1994

A drop in core temperature causes vasoconstriction: blood circulation to the surface of the body is reduced, and the temperature of the skin drops cutting the heat loss. A further drop in core temperature leads to increased tension in the muscles and then shivering to increase metabolic heat. A rise in core temperature causes vasodilatation: the blood supply to the periphery is increased, increasing skin temperature and heat loss to the surroundings. A further increase causes sweating to increase heat loss by evaporation.

Box 5.5 Psychophysics: how we feel about the environment

The physiological actions described in Box 5.4 are augmented by the thermal sense in the skin. This adds information about the skin temperature, warning of conditions that might pose a danger. There are two types of skin temperature sensors, one concerned mostly with heat and the other with cold. Our impression of the warmth or cold of our environment arises in part from the skin sensors. It is integrated with the core temperature so that the sensation may be pleasing if the overall effect is likely to restore thermal equilibrium and unpleasant if it works against it. Thus a cold skin sensation will be pleasant when the body is overheated, unpleasant if the core is already cold. The sensation from any particular part of the body will depend on time, location and clothing as well as the temperature of the surroundings.

Psychophysics is the study of the relation between the sensations we experience and the stimuli we receive from the physical world. The relationship between thermal sensation and the thermal environment is hard to model. Psychophysical experiments have concentrated on more defined relationships such as the warmth and cold of surfaces when they are touched. Nevertheless the thinking behind field studies of thermal comfort has been to relate thermal sensation to the stimuli of the thermal environment.

The comfort vote is a method of trying to assign numbers to our thermal sensation. However an ability to say how we feel does not imply a one-to-one relationship between thermal comfort and the physical conditions that cause it. The pleasure given by a thermal stimulus depends not only on the physiological conditions at the time the stimulus is received but also on the social and other conditions prevailing and on the recent thermal experiences of the person concerned. So a particular stimulus can give rise to a range of sensations. We cannot say that a set of conditions will give rise to a particular sensation, only that there is a probability that it will.

Box 5.6 Clothing

Clothing plays a major role in enabling man to survive outside the tropics. Clothing is of particular importance to the adaptive model of thermal comfort. In the physical model of the heat transfer the clothing is assumed to be a uniform layer of insulation between the body and the environment with a single surface temperature. Quite clearly this is an approximate treatment, since the clothing is anything but uniform. The face in particular is generally unprotected and the actual clothing insulation varies from place to place on the body according to the nature of the clothing ensemble. In practice, however, the assumption appears to work quite well, and the overall insulation of the clothing can be expressed as the sum of the contributions from the individual items of clothing being worn, as if they were each spread over the whole of the body surface. In this context the layers of air trapped between multiple layers of clothing and between the clothing and the skin are counted as part of the ensemble.

The insulation of the clothing is generally expressed in 'clo units' where 1 clo $= 0.155$ m^2 kW^{-1}. Tables of clo values for typical ensembles, and for individual clothing items, are given in Table 5.4. There is always a big problem with such descriptive tables: they are culturally defined and a thick suit in one climate might be counted rather thin in another. In addition to acting as insulation against the transfer of dry heat, the clothing has an effect on the heat loss by

Table 5.4. Clothing insulation for selected garments

Garment	I_{cl} (clo)	Garment	I_{cl} (clo)
Underwear		*Shirts – blouses*	
Panties	0.03	Short sleeves	0.15
Underpants with long legs	0.10	Light-weight, long sleeves	0.20
Singlet	0.04	Normal, long sleeves	0.25
T-Shirt	0.09	Flannel shirt, long sleeves	0.30
Shirt with long sleeves	0.12	Light-weight blouse, long sleeves	0.15
Panties and bra	0.03		
		Dresses – skirts	
Trousers		Light skirts (summer)	0.15
Shorts	0.06	Heavy skirt (winter)	0.25
Light-weight	0.20	Light dress, short sleeves	0.20
Normal	0.25	Winter dress, long sleeves	0.40
Flannel	0.28	Boiler suit	0.55
Sweaters			
Sleeveless vest	0.12	*Jackets*	
Thin sweater	0.20	Light summer jacket	0.25
Sweater	0.28	Jacket	0.35
Thick sweater	0.35	Smock	0.30
High-insulative, fibre pelt		*Outdoor clothing*	
Boiler suit	0.90	Coat	0.60
Trousers	0.35	Down coat	0.55
Jacket	0.40	Parka	0.70
Vest	0.20	Fibre-pelt overalls	0.55
Socks		*Shoes and gloves*	
Socks	0.02	Shoes (thin soled)	0.02
Thick, ankle socks	0.05	Shoes (thick soled)	0.04
Thick, long socks	0.10	Boots	0.10
Nylon stockings	0.03	Gloves	0.05

Source: International Standard 7730. Moderate Thermal Environments: Determination of PMV and PPD Indices and Specification of the Conditions for Thermal Comfort. International Organisation for Standardisation, Geneva, 1994

evaporation. It affects evaporative cooling by introducing extra resistance to water vapour depending on its permeability to moisture and it can absorb excess moisture next to the skin. The absorbed moisture is then evaporated from the clothing and not from the skin, so it is not so effective in cooling the skin.

The way clothing works is often more complex than suggested. In some hot dry climates, for instance, the inhabitants wear loose, multiple layered clothing to keep the high environmental temperatures away from the skin, whilst allowing heat loss by evaporation when dry air is pumped through the clothing as the body moves. Another complication in dealing with clothing is that its function is not purely thermal. Our social as well as our thermal needs determine the way we clothe ourselves. Wearing a jacket open or closed can make a significant difference to its thermal characteristics. Chair upholstery may add as much as 0.2–0.4 clo to the standard methods for estimating clothing insulation. The need to specify the value of the clothing insulation and permeability is a source of considerable uncertainty in the heat balance model of human heat exchange.

Box 5.7 Examples of adaptive actions

Some conceivable actions in response to cold:

- Vasoconstriction (reduces blood flow to the surface tissues)
- Increasing muscle tension and shivering (generates more heat in the muscles)
- Curling up or cuddling up (reducing the surface area available for heat loss)
- Increasing the level of activity (generates body heat)
- Adding clothing (reduces the rate of heat loss per unit area)
- Turning up the thermostat or lighting a fire (usually raises the room temperature)
- Finding a warmer spot in the house or going to bed (select a warmer environment)
- Visiting a friend or going to the library (hoping for a warmer environment)
- Complaining to the management (hoping someone else will raise the temperature)
- Insulating the loft or the wall cavities (hoping to raise the indoor temperatures)
- Improving the windows and doors (to raise temperatures/reduce draughts)
- Building a new house (planning to have a warmer room temperature)
- Emigrating (seeking a warmer place long-term)
- Acclimatizing (letting body and mind become more resistant to cold stress)

Some conceivable actions in response to heat:

- Vasodilatation (increases blood flow to surface tissues)
- Sweating (evaporative cooling)

- Adopting an open posture (increases the area available for heat loss)
- Taking off some clothing (increases heat loss)
- Reducing the level of activity (reduces bodily heat production)
- Having a beer (induces sweating, and increases heat loss)
- Drinking a cup of tea (induces sweating, more than compensating for its heat)
- Eating less (reduces body heat production)
- Adopting the siesta routine (matches the activity to the thermal environment)
- Turning on the air-conditioner (lowers the air temperature)
- Switching on a fan (increases air movement, increasing heat loss)
- Opening a window (reduces indoor temperature and increases breeze)
- Finding a cool spot or visiting a friend (hoping for a cooler temperature)
- Going for a swim (selects a cooler environment)
- Building a better building (long-term way of finding a cooler spot)
- Emigrating (long-term way of finding a cooler place)
- Acclimatizing (letting body and mind adjust so that heat is less stressful)

Box 5.8 Characterizing the effect of time on adaptive behaviour

Recent surveys have tried to determine the rate of change of comfort temperature using longitudinal comfort surveys conducted over a period of time.[i, ii, iii] The exponentially weighted running mean of the temperature reflects quite well the time-dependence of the comfort temperature or clothing insulation.

The equation for the exponentially-weighted running mean at time t is:

$$T_{rm(t)} = (1 - \alpha)\{T_{t-1} + \alpha T_{t-2} + \alpha^2 T_{t-3} \cdots\} \tag{1}$$

Where α is a constant such that $1 > \alpha \geq 0$, $T_{rm(t)}$ is the running mean temperature at time t, T_t is the mean temperature for a time t of a series at equal intervals (hours, days etc.), T_{t-n} is the instantaneous temperature at n time-intervals previously. The time interval often used to calculate T_{rm} is a day. The rate at which the effect of any particular temperature dies away depends on α. Equation (1) simplifies to:

$$T_{rm(t)} = (1 - \alpha)T_{od(t-1)} + \alpha \cdot T_{rm(t-1)} \tag{2}$$

Where $T_{od(t-1)}$ and $T_{rm(t-1)}$ are the mean temperature and the running mean temperature for the previous day. Today's running mean can thus be simply calculated from yesterday's mean temperature and yesterday's running mean. The time series gives a running mean temperature that is decreasingly affected by any particular temperature event as time passes. The larger the value of α the more important are the effects of past temperatures.

The aim is then to find the value of α which gives the best correlation of outdoor running mean with the comfort temperature. The correlation of outdoor running mean temperature with comfort temperature rises gradually until α reaches about 0.8 and then starts to decrease. This suggests that though the peak in the correlation with comfort temperature is small, there is a real effect. The correlation with daily mean outdoor temperature T_{od} ($\alpha = 0$) and with the monthly mean of outdoor temperature ($\alpha \cong 0.95$) are both less than the correlation with T_{rm} where $\alpha = 0.8$. A similar effect has been found to apply to clothing insulation.[ii, iii]

[i] McCartney, K.J and Nicol, J.F. (2002) Developing an adaptive control algorithm for Europe: Results of the SCATs project. *Energy and Buildings*, 34 (6), pp. 623–35.

[ii] Morgan, C.A., deDear, R. and Brager, G. (2002) Climate clothing and adaptation in the built environment. Indoor Air 2002: Proceedings of the 9th International Conference on Indoor Air Quality and Climate (ed. H. Levin), Indoor Air 2002, Santa Cruz, USA, vol. 5, pp. 98–103.

[iii] Nicol, F. and Raja, I. (1996) *Thermal Comfort, Time and Posture: Exploratory Studies in the Nature of Adaptive Thermal Comfort.* School of Architecture, Oxford Brookes University.

NOTES AND REFERENCES

1 Levins, R. and Lewontin, R. (1985) *The Dialectical Biologist.* Cambridge, MA: Harvard University Press.

2 McIntyre, D.A. (1980) *Indoor Climate.* Applied Science Publishers.

3 Parsons, K.C. (2003) *Human Thermal Environments*, 2nd edn. Oxford: Blackwell Scientific.

4 Fanger, P.O. (1970) *Thermal Comfort.* Copenhagen: Danish Technical Press.

5 Humphreys, M.A. (1992) Thermal comfort in the context of energy conservation. In S. Roaf and M. Hancock (eds), *Energy Efficient Buildings.* Oxford: Blackwell Scientific.

6 deDear, R.J. and Brager, G.S. (1998) Developing an adaptive model of thermal comfort and preference. *ASHRAE Transactions*, 104 (1), 145–67. See also ASHRAE Standard 55 (2004) *Thermal environment conditions for human occupancy*, American Society of Heating Refrigeration and Air conditioning Engineers, Atlanta, Georgia, USA; and Nevins, R. and P. Gagge (1972) The new ASHRAE comfort chart. *ASHRAE Journal*, 14, 41–3.

7 Nicol, J.F. and Humphreys, M.A. (1973) Thermal comfort as part of a self-regulating system. *Building Research and Practice* (J CIB), 6 (3), 191–7.

8   Humphreys, M.A. (1976) Field studies of thermal comfort compared and applied. *Journal of the Institute of Heating and Ventilating Engineers*, 44, 5–27.

9   Nicol, J.F., Raja, I., Allaudin, A. and Jamy, G.N. (1999) Climatic variations in comfort temperatures: the Pakistan projects. *Energy and Buildings*, 30, 261–79.

10 Humphreys, M.A. and Nicol, J.F. (1998) Understanding the adaptive approach to thermal comfort. *ASHRAE Technical Data Bulletin: Field Studies of Thermal Comfort and Adaptation*, 14, 1–14.

11 See both: Humphreys, M.A. (1976) Field studies of thermal comfort compared and applied. *Journal of Heating and Ventilating Engineers*, 44, 5–27, and: Humphreys, M.A. (1978) Outdoor temperatures and comfort indoors. *Building Research and Practice* (J CIB), 6 (2), 92–105.

12 Auliciems, A. and deDear, R. (1986) Air conditioning in Australia I: human thermal factors. *Architectural Science Review*, 29, 67–75.

13 Humphreys, M.A. and Nicol, J.F. (2000) Outdoor temperature and indoor thermal comfort: raising the precision of the relationship for the 1998 ASHRAE database of field studies. *ASHRAE Transactions*, 206 (2), 485–92.

14 Leaman, A.J. and Bordass, W.T. (1997) Productivity in buildings: the 'killer' variables. *Workplace Comfort Forum*. London.

15 Baker, N.V. and Standeven, M.A. (1995) A behavioural approach to thermal comfort assessment in naturally ventilated buildings. *Proceedings CIBSE National Conference*. Eastbourne, published by the Chartered Institute of Building Service Engineers, London, pp. 76–84.

16 Nicol, J.F. and McCartney, K.J. (1999) Assessing adaptive opportunities in buildings. *Proceedings of the CIBSE National Conference*, published by the Chartered Institute of Building Service Engineers, London, pp. 219–29.

17 Nicol, J.F. and Kessler, M.R.B. (1998) Perception of comfort in relation to weather and adaptive opportunities. *ASHRAE Transactions*, 104 (1), 1005–17.

18 Nicol, J.F. (2000) Time and thermal comfort, evidence from the field renewables: the energy for the 21st century, *Proceedings of the Fourth World Renewable Energy Congress*, Brighton, edited by A. Sayigh, part 1. Oxford: Pergamon Press, pp. 477–82.

19 McCartney, K.J. and Nicol, J.F. (2002) Developing an adaptive algorithm for Europe: results of the SCAT's project. *Energy and Buildings*, 34 (6), pp. 623–35.

20 Keatinge W.R. and Donaldson, G.C. (2000) Cold weather, cold homes and winter mortality. In J. Rudge and F. Nicol (eds), *Cutting the Cost of Cold. Affordable Warmth for Healthier Homes.* London: E&FN Spon, p. 17; see also Keatinge, W.R., Donaldson, G.C., Cordioli, E., Martinelli, M., Kunst, A.E., Mackenbach, J.P., Nayha, S. and Vuori, I. (2000) Heat-related mortality in warm and cold regions of Europe: an observational study. *British Medical Journal*, 321, 670–3.

21 Bull, G.M. and Morton, J. (1978) Environment, temperature and death rates. *Age and Ageing*, 7, 210–21.

22 Curwen, M. (1991) Excess winter mortality: a British phenomenon? *Health Trends*, 22, 169–75.

23 Collins, K.J. (2000) Cold, cold housing and respiratory illnesses. In J. Rudge and F. Nicol (eds), *Cutting the Cost of Cold. Affordable Warmth for Healthier Homes.* London: E&FN Spon, p. 45.

24 Keatinge, W.R. and Donaldson, G.C. (2000) Cold weather, cold homes and winter mortality, p. 18.

25 Khaw, K.T. (1995) Temperature and cardiovascular mortality. *The Lancet*, 345, 337–8.

26 Collins, K.J. (2000) Cold, cold housing and respiratory illnesses, p. 46. See reference 23.

27 Kilbourne, E.M. (1992) Illness due to thermal extremes. In J.M. Last and R.B. Wallace (eds), *Public Health and Preventative Medicine.* Norwalk, CT: Appleton Lang, pp. 491–501; Keatinge, W.R., Coleshaw, S.R., Easton, J.C., Cotter, F., Mattock, M.B. and Chelliah, R. (1986) Increased platelet and red cell counts, blood viscosity, and plasma cholesterol levels during heat stress, and mortality from coronary and cerebral thrombosis: *Am. J. Med.*, 81, 795–800.

28 Epstein, Y., Shani, Y., Moran, D.S. and Shapiro, Y. (2000) Exertional heat stroke – the prevention of a medical emergency. *Journal of Basic Clinical Physiology and Pharmacology*, 11, 395–401.

29 Fonseka, M.M. (1999) Heat stroke in young adults. *Ceylon Medical Journal*, 44, 184.

30 Havenith, G., Inoue, Y., Luttikholt, V. and Kenney, W.L. (1995) Age predicts cardiovascular, but not thermoregulatory, responses to humid heat stress. *European Journal of Applied Physiology*, 70, 88–96.

31 Wilkinson, P., Landon, M. and Stevenson, S. (2000) Housing and winter death: epidemiological evidence. In J. Rudge and F. Nicol (eds), *Cutting the Cost of Cold. Affordable Warmth for Healthier Homes.* London: E&FN Spon, p. 27.

32 Help the Aged (2001) *Addressing Excess Winter Deaths: The Causes and Solutions.* London: Help the Aged.

33 Curwen, M. (1981) *Trends in Respiratory Mortality, 1951–75 England and Wales.* OPCS, DHI, no. 7. London: HMSO.

34 Boardman, B. (1986) Seasonal mortality and cold homes. In *Unhealthy Housing Conference*, Institution of Environmental Health Officers and Legal Research Institute, University of Warwick, 14–16 December.

35 Boardman, B. (1991) *Fuel Poverty: From Cold Homes to Affordable Warmth.* London: Belhaven Press.

36 Rudge, J. (1994) Coal Fires, Fresh Air and the Hardy British. MSc thesis, London: University of East London.

37 Sakamoto-Momiyama, M. (1977) *Seasonality in Human Mortality.* Tokyo: University of Tokyo Press.

38 Henwood, M. (1997) *Fuel Poverty, Energy Efficiency and Health: A Report to Eaga CT.* Keswick: Eaga Charitable Trust, p. 29.

39 Sartor, F., Snacken, R., Demuth, C. and Walckiers, D. (1995) Temperature, ambient ozone levels and mortality during summer, 1994. *Belgium: Environmental Research*, 70, 105–13.

40 Huynen, M., Martens, P., Schram, D., Weijenberg, M. and Kunst, A.E. (2001) The impact of heat waves and cold spells on mortality rates in the Dutch population. *Environmental Health Perspectives*, 109, 463–70.

41 Katsouyanni, K., Trichopoulos, D., Zavitsanos, X. and Touloumi, G. (1988) The 1987 Athens heatwave. Letter in *The Lancet*, ii, 573.

42 Whitman, S., Good, G., Donoghue, E.R., Benbow, N., Shou, W. and Mou, S. (1997) Mortality in Chicago attributed to the July 1995 heat wave. *American Journal of Public Health*, 87, 1515–18.

43 Hajat, S., Kovats, R.S., Atkinson, R.W. and Haines, A. (2002) Impact of hot temperatures on death in London: a time series approach. *Journal of Epidemiology and Community Health*, 56, 367–72.

44 Skinner, C.J. and Kuleshov, Y.A. (2001) Association between thermal stress and elderly mortality in Sydney – a comparison of thermal sensation indices. *Proceedings of the 2001 Windsor Conference on Thermal Comfort,* Cumberland Lodge, published by the Thermal Comfort Unit, Oxford Brookes University, Oxford, pp. 262–72.

45 Lowry, S. (1991) *Housing and Health.* London: BMJ Books.

46 Collins K.J. (1986) Low indoor temperatures and morbidity in the elderly. *British Journal of Hospital Medicine*, 38 (6), 506–14.

47 Enquselassie, F., Dobson, A.J., Alexander, T.M. and Steele P.L. (1993) Seasons, temperature and coronary disease. *International Journal of Epidemiology*, 22 (4), 632–6.

48 Goodwin, J. (2000) Cold stress, circulatory illness and the elderly. In J. Rudge and F. Nicol (eds), *Cutting the Cost of Cold. Affordable Warmth for Healthier Homes*. London: E&FN Spon.

49 Raw, G. and Hamilton, R. (1995) *Building Regulation and Health*. Garston, Watford: Building Research Establishment.

50 Wilkinson, P., Landon, M. and Stevenson, S. (2000) Housing and winter death: epidemiological evidence. In J. Rudge and F. Nicol (eds), *Cutting the Cost of Cold. Affordable Warmth for Healthier Homes*. London: E&FN Spon.

51 Aylin, P., Morris, S., Wakefield, J., Grossinho, A., Jarup, L. and Elliott, P. (2001) Temperature, housing, deprivation and their relationship to excess winter mortality in Great Britain 1986–1996. *International Journal of Epidemiology*, 30, 1100–8.

52 Kilbourne, E.M (1992) Illness due to thermal extremes. In J.M. Last and R.B. Wallace (eds), *Public Health and Preventative Medicine*. Norwalk, CT: Appleton Lang, pp. 491–501.

53 Sierra Pajares Ortiz, M., Diaz Jemenez, J., Montero Robin, J., Alberdi, J. and Miron Perez, I. (1997) Daily mortality in the Madrid community during 1986–91 for the group between 45 and 64 years of age: its relationship to air temperature, in the Spanish Review of Public Health. *Review Espania Salud Publica*, 71, 149–60.

54 Faunt, J.D, Wilkinson, T.J., Aplin, P., Henschke, P., Webb, M. and Penhall, R.K. (1995) The effete in the heat: heat-related hospital presentations during a ten day heat wave. *Australian and New Zealand Journal of Medicine*, 25, 117–20.

55 Lye, M. and Kamal, A. (1977) Effects of a heatwave on mortality-rates in elderly inpatients. *The Lancet*, i, 529–31.

56 Christoffel, K.K. (1985) Effect of season and weather on pediatric emergency department use. *American Journal of Emergency Medicine*, 3, 327–30.

57 Kilbourne, E.M. (1989) Heat waves. In M.B. Gregg (ed.), *The Public Health Consequences of Disasters*. Atlanta, GA: US Department of Health and Human Services, Centers for Disease Control, pp. 51–61.

58 Semenza, J.C., Rubin, C.H., Falter, K.H., Selanikio, J.D., Flanders, W.D., Howe, H.L. and Wilhelm, J. (1996) Heat-related

deaths during the July 1995 heat wave in Chicago. *New England Journal of Medicine*, 335, 84–90.

59 Naughton, M.P., Henderson, A., Mirabelli, M., Kaiser, R., Wilhelm, J., Kieszak, S., Rubin, C. and McGeehin, M. (2002) Heat related mortality during a 1999 heatwave in Chicago. *American Journal of Preventative Medicine*, 22, 221–7.

60 Clarke, J.F. (1972) Some effects of the urban structure on heat mortality. *Environmental Research*, 5, 93–104.

61 Oke, T.R. (1997) Urban climates and global environmental change. In R. Thompson and A. Perry (eds), *Applied Climatology: Principles and Practice*. London: Routledge, pp. 273–87.

62 Henschel, A., Burton, L., Margolies, L. and Smith. J. (1969) An analysis of the heat deaths in St Louis during July 1966. *American Journal of Public Health*, 59, 2232–42.

63 Schuman, S.H. (1972) Patterns of urban heatwave deaths and implications for prevention: data from New York and St Louis during July 1966. *Environmental Research*, 5, 59–75.

64 Rooney, C., McMichael, A.J., Kovats, R.S. and Coleman, M. (1998) Excess mortality in England and Wales, and in Greater London, during the 1995 heatwave. *Journal of Epidemiology and Community Health*, 52, 482–6.

65 Katsouyanni, K., Trichopoulos, D., Zavitsanos, X. and Touloumi, G. (1988) The 1987 Athens heatwave letter. *The Lancet*, ii, 573.

66 Jones, T.S., Liang, A., Kilbourne, E., Griffin, M., Patriarca, P., Wassilak, S., Mullan, R., Herrick, R., Donnell Jr, H., Choi, K. and Thacker, S. (1982) Morbidity and mortality associated with the July 1980 heat wave in St Louis and Kansas City. *Journal of the American Medical Association*, 247, 3327–31.

67 Sheridan, S. (2003) Heat, mortality and level of urbanization. *Climate Research*, 24, pp. 255–65.

68 Hales, S., Kjellstrom, T., Salmond, C., Town, G. and Woodward, A. (2000) Daily mortality in Christchurch New Zealand in relation to weather and air pollution. *Australian and New Zealand Journal of Public Health*, 24, 89–91.

69 Smoyer, K.E. (1998) Putting risk in its place: methodological considerations for investigating extreme event health risks. *Social Science and Medicine*, 47, 1809–24.

70 Kunst, A., Looman, C. and Mackenbach, J. (1993) Outdoor air temperature and mortality in the Netherlands: a time series analysis. *American Journal of Epidemiology*, 137, 331–41.

71 Katsouyanni, K., Pantazopoulu, A., Touloumi, G., Tselepidaki, I., Moustris, K., Asimakopoulos, D., Poulopoulou, G. and Trichopoulos, D. (1993) Evidence of interaction between air pollution and high temperatures in the causation of excess mortality. *Archives of Environmental Health*, 48, 235–42.

72 Shumway, R., Azari, A. and Pawitan, Y. (1988) Modelling mortality fluctuations in Los Angeles as functions of pollution and weather effects. *Environmental Research*, 45, 224–41.

73 DETR (2000) *English House Condition Survey* 1996, *Energy Report*. Published by the Stationery Office, London.

74 Moore, R. (2001) Personal communication.

75 Nevrala, D. (1979) The effect of insulation, mode of operation and air leakage on the energy demand of dwellings in the UK. *Ventilation of Domestic Buildings*. Published by British Gas, London.

76 Eurowinter Group: Keatinge, W., Donaldson, G., Bucher, K., Cordioli, E., Dardanoni, L., Jendritzky, K., Katsouyanni, K., Kunst, A., Mackenbach, J., Martinelli, M., McDonald, C., Nayha, S. and Vuori, I. (1997) Cold exposure and winter mortality from ischaemic heart disease, cerebrovascular disease, respiratory disease, and all causes in warm and cold regions of Europe. *The Lancet*, 349, 1341–6.

77 Rudge, J. (1996) British weather: conversation topic or serious health risk? *Int. Journal of Biometeorology*, 39, 151–5.

78 Collins, K., Exton-Smith, A. and Dore, C. (1981) Urban hypothermia: preferred temperature and thermal perception in old age. *British Medical Journal*, 282, 175–7.

79 Koppe, C., Jendritzky, G., Kovats, R. and Menne, B. (2003) *Heatwaves: Impacts and Responses*. WHO, Copenhagen.

80 Kovats, S., Wolf, T. and Menne, B. (2004) Heatwave of August 2003 in Europe: provisional estimates of the impact on mortality. *Euroserveillance Weekly*, 8 (11), 11 March 2004.

81 House of Commons Hansard, 20 December 1999, Column 436; http://www.parliament.the-stationery-office.co.uk/pa/cm199900/cmhansrd/vo991220/text/91220w33.htm#91220w33.html_spnew4.

82 Auger, N., Kosatsky, T. (2002) Chaleur accablante: Mise à jour de la littérature concernant les Impacts de santé publique et proposition de mesures d'adaptation. Montréal, Régie régionale de la santé et des services sociaux de Québec, Direction de la santé publique.

6 HOW WET WILL IT GET?

Water is the most fundamental building block of life itself and as we approach the years of the water wars an excess, or lack, of water may present the greatest hazards we face in building durable settlements in the future, even in 'rainy' Britain.

PRECIPITATION TRENDS IN BRITAIN

Britain is fortunate in its verdant landscapes and its future predicted climates. While the changes to predicted precipitation over the next decades appear to be severe for us, they are survivable, with prudent and judicious management.

Winter precipitation in the UK is predicted to increase for all periods and for all climate change scenarios. By the 2080s, this increase ranges from between 10% and 20% for the *Low Emissions* scenario (depending on region) to between 15% and 35% for the *High Emissions* scenario. Conversely the summer pattern is reversed and almost the whole of the UK may become drier, with a decrease in rainfall for the *Low Emissions* scenario of up to 35%, and for the *High Emissions* scenario of a staggering 50% or more. The highest changes in precipitation in both winter and summer are predicted for eastern and southern parts of England, while changes are smallest in the northwest of Scotland.[1] What we are looking at here is the increasing risk of summer droughts and winter flooding.

Annual average precipitation changes across the UK may decrease slightly by between 0% and 15% by the 2080s, although there are likely to be large regional and seasonal differences in the changes.

It should be noted that these are averages. If one were to take extreme events into account, according to an analysis published in *Nature*[2] in 2002, there is a consensus in the results from all the 19 major climate change models around the world that the chances of a very wet winter in Britain could increase fivefold by the end of the century. This means that flood events are likely to show a dramatic increase in frequency, and this has been reflected in the work being undertaken under the Foresight scenarios initiative in Britain (see the section on scenarios on the website: http://books. elsevier.com/companions/0750659114).

Rainfall is likely to also become more intense. Figure 6.1 shows that in both winter and summer the patterns of rainfall will change enormously, except perhaps for northwest Scotland. The figure shows there is over a 50% probability that more or less intense rainfall will be experienced in a given year and season for the different regions of the country. So for the southeast in particular, in winter, there will be much more rain, falling more intensely, leading inevitably to much higher flood risks for the region.

Snowfall amounts will decrease significantly through the UK, perhaps by between 30% and 90% by the 2080s. There will be less snow over the whole UK and for all scenarios, with the largest percentage reductions, up to 90% or more by the 2080s for the *High Emissions* scenario, around the coast and in the English lowlands. In relative terms the Scottish Highlands will experience the smallest reductions, but even here total snowfall by the 2080s might decrease by 60% or more relative to present-day totals. Some areas of the UK are increasingly likely to experience quite long runs of snowless winters.

Humidity

As the climate warms, the specific humidity, the absolute amount of moisture in the atmosphere, will increase through the year, although the relative humidity may decrease, especially in the summer. Cloud cover in summer and autumn may decrease, especially in the south. Summer sunshine and solar radiation may correspondingly increase.

SEASONAL CHANGES

By the 2050s, typical spring temperatures may occur between one and three weeks earlier than at present (this statement relates to the means for the 1990s rather than 2003 which was already exceptional) and the onset of present winter temperatures may be delayed between one and three weeks. This is likely to lead to a lengthening of the growing season for plants.

The heating and cooling requirements of buildings will also change, with less energy being needed to heat buildings in the

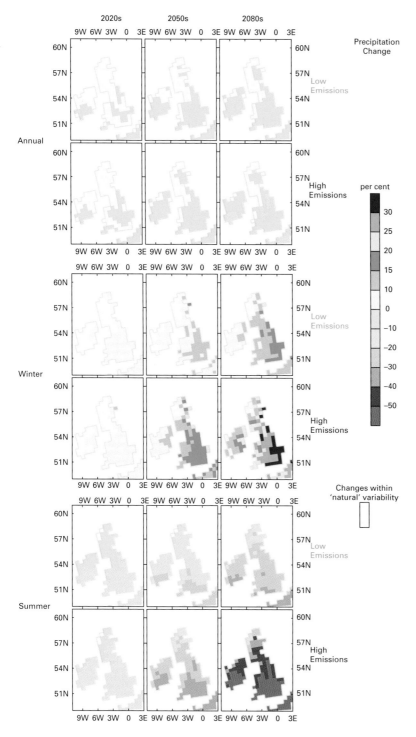

6.1.
Per cent change in average annual winter and summer precipitation for the 2020s, 2050s and 2080s for *Low Emissions* and *High Emissions* scenarios showing that the southeast of England will be very wet in winter and very dry in summer. (*Source:* UKCIP02 Climate Change Scenarios, funded by DEFRA, produced by Tyndall and Hadley Centres for UKCIP)

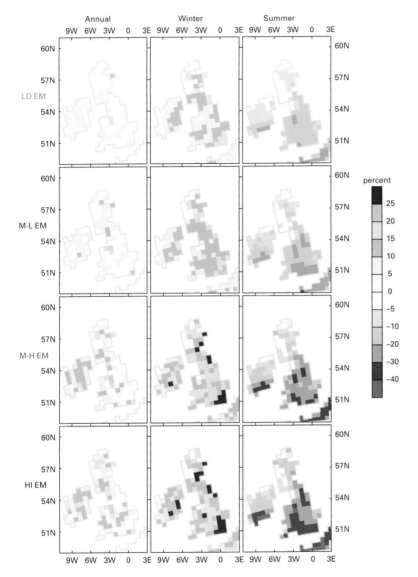

6.2.
Percentage change in the 2080s in the maximum daily precipitation amount which has a 50% chance of occurring in a given year, showing that dry summer weather in the south of England and Ireland will be a problem by the 2080s. (*Source:* UKCIP02 Climate Change Scenarios, funded by DEFRA, produced by Tyndall and Hadley Centres for UKCIP)

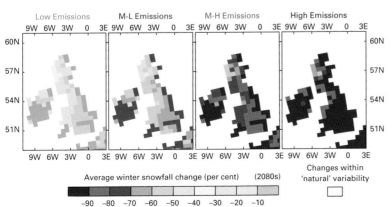

6.3.
Percentage change in average winter snowfall amount in the 2080s showing that White Christmases will be a thing of the past in most places by the 2080s. (*Source:* UKCIP02 Climate Change Scenarios, funded by DEFRA, produced by Tyndall and Hadley Centres for UKCIP)

UK through the winter and more energy needed to cool buildings, particularly ones that are poorly designed for the climate.

CHANGES IN WEATHER EXTREMES

High summer temperatures will become more frequent and very cold winters will become increasingly rare. A very hot August, such as experienced in 1995, and the record breaking summer of 2003, with average temperatures many degrees above 'normal', may occur as often as once in five years by the 2050s and three years out of five by the 2080s for the *Medium High Emissions* scenario. Even for the *Low Emissions* scenario about two summers in three may be as hot as, or hotter than 1995 by the 2080s, or even perhaps than 2003. The Southeast of England is predicted to become 50–60% drier in hot summers.

One consequence of the drier summer climate will be that summer soil moisture by the 2050s may be reduced by about 30% over parts of England for the *High Emissions* scenario and by 40% or more by the 2080s. This has obvious implications for soil shrinkage and related building damage. This will be further exacerbated by significant regional differences in rainfall and the southeast of England, where the clay soils are particularly susceptible to shrinkage and will be badly affected.

Drought could even increase the flooding risk: in Amsterdam in summer 2003 the drought conditions weakened a raised river embankment so much that it gave way, causing localized flooding. In Shetland in summer 2003, prolonged drought conditions weakened the peat covering a hillside, and when there was a heavy shower of rain it resulted in a peat slide which engulfed several houses.

Extreme winter precipitation will become more frequent and by the 2080s daily precipitation intensities that are experienced once every two years on average may become up to 30% heavier, and that means the increasing likelihood of flooding, and increased severity of flooding.

Very dry summers, like 1995, may occur in half the years by 2080, while very wet winters may occur on average almost one a decade for the *Medium High Emissions* scenarios. The combination of hot and dry conditions in summer will also become more common and by the 2080s virtually every summer over England and Wales, whether for the *Low Emissions* or *High Emissions* scenario, may be warmer and drier than the summer of 2001.

A number of basic precautions need to be taken for individual buildings to protect them from very wet or dry spells. For periods of heavy rainfall wide storm gutters should be provided, walls, and especially their feet, should be protected from driving rain and

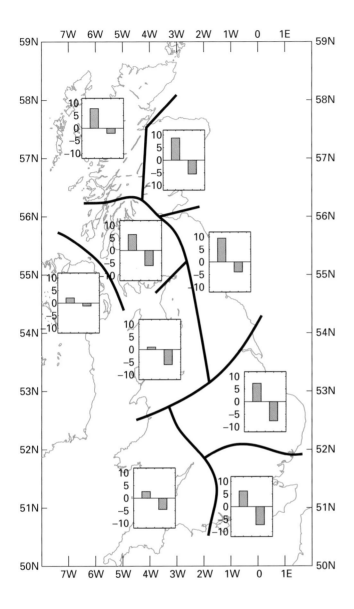

6.4.
The trend will be for winters to become much wetter, and summers drier, but this will vary significantly in the different regions of the United Kingdom. This figure presents the trend (1961–2000) in the fraction of the total seasonal precipitation contributed by the 'most intense' precipitation events in winter (*left hand bars*) and in summer (*right hand bars*) for a number of regions. Positive (*blue*) numbers indicate an increasing trend in the proportion of the total precipitation that comes from the 'most intense' events, i.e. the most intense events are increasing either in intensity or frequency. (For more detail see note 3.) (*Source:* Figure produced by Tim Osborne. UKCIP02 Climate Change Scenarios, funded by DEFRA, produced by Tyndall and Hadley Centres for UKCIP)

splash back, rain water retention features should be designed in like green roofs and absorbent ground surfaces and water storage facilities for individual buildings or localities.

It is difficult to imagine Britain as suffering from a 'drought' problem but images of nearly empty reservoirs filled our papers in the UK in the winter of 2003 and are becoming commonplace. One manifestation of the increasing scarcity of water in the UK system is the rising prices, with charges for water and sewage set to rise by an average of over 40% by the end of the decade. Another is subsidence.

SUBSIDENCE

While the actions of planners in allowing development in flood plains are a concern, perhaps an even bigger concern is the outlook for future subsidence exposures. Subsidence claims currently cost insurers an average of £1 million per day, and this is likely to increase. At least planners frequently consult with the Environment Agency about flood risks, but there is no obligation on them to consult with the British Geological Survey (BGS) about subsidence risks. Not only is there the issue of increasing droughts due to climate change causing subsidence on shrinkable clay soils, there are also issues of building on unsuitable ground. There are planning policy guidelines for unstable land (PPG14) and contaminated land (PPG23A), but often the ground conditions stem from very old workings where only BGS, with their huge archive of 640 000 borehole samples, are aware of problems. The 1991 Building Regulations under the 1984 Building Act focus on the structure, not the site, and the only regulations relating to the site are those dealing with Radon gas (BR211).

The government has said that to save using too much agricultural land, 60% of the 3.8 million projected new houses will have to be built on 'brownfield sites'. Many of these sites will contain made up ground, landfill, old mine workings and contamination. While the government has indicated that assistance may be available to remediate some sites for housing, many authorities are too small to have the expertise or the finance to obtain the information needed about the site. If the planners do not know of the problems and do not ask about them, then adequate remediation will not take place, and the planning policy guidelines will not be applied. The issue of increasing subsidence risk caused by climate change-induced droughts has already been outlined in this study; this risk would be greatly compounded if there are many more houses built on unsuitable ground. This could create major problems for insurers, and there is a very real danger that irresponsible local authorities may earn such a bad reputation for this that all new housing in their area might become an unacceptably high risk for subsidence cover.

The potential scale of this problem was outlined in October 2003, when the city of Shanghai announced that the land of the city was subsiding at a rate of 2.5 cm a year because so many new tower blocks were being built and so much water was being pumped from the underground reserves to provide drinking water for the exploding population of over 20 million people. These problems may be significantly increased with changing rainfall patterns.[4]

In the UK an indication of the growing problem was given in the long hot summer of 2003, when the Direct Line Insurance company stated that, owing to the six dry months experienced in the south and east of the country, they saw increases in subsidence claims of 38% in June and 15% in July compared to the same periods in 2002.[5]

These are some of the problems faced by the UK. How much worse for those countries of the world where there is already a chronic water shortage, causing civil unrest and threatening war!

CIVIL UNREST

Civil unrest because of water is a growing problem in many countries, as the following examples confirm.

In Spain there have been a number of bitter demonstrations over the diversion of a staggering 30% of the waters of the river Ebro in the northeast of the country through a new canal to the parched southeastern provinces of Murcia, Valencia and Andalucia where the great tourism centres of the Costa del Sol are based. Six dams have flooded the unique wildlife habitats in the north and the flatland habitats of the Ebro delta are disappearing at an alarming rate. Over 80% of the total Spanish budget for environmental projects has recently been channelled into the canal scheme, which is designed to take water from what is seen as the poorer provinces to fill the swimming pools of the rich in the south.[6] One of the main problems with the project, objectors claim, is that the calculations of river flows were done based on historic climates from the middle of the last century, while conditions in the 21st century will be very different, leading to potentially catastrophic consequences for the future of the whole of eastern Spain.

The fact that water shortages can lead to local environmental crime waves was highlighted by the strange case of stealing water in Australia during a drought of 2003. Robbers used a range of equipment, including earth movers, to steal water in over 146 reported cases, often from neighbouring dams and billabongs. One of the advantages of stealing water from neighbours is that it gets around the draconian Australian water laws that put very strict conditions on the drilling of bore holes or taking water from rivers, so the law may, as here, encourage environmental crime. Statistics in Australia suggest that some 40 000 jobs have already been lost because of the 2003 drought and it is expected to cost the country over £1.3 billion in that year alone.

WATER WARS

When incidents occur within national boundaries the unrest is dealt with by law. When the incidents involve two countries then that may trigger a war. The global Water Wars have long been predicted and there are a number of flash points for such conflicts around the world from the Mekong to the Rhône.

One high profile region where chronic water shortages combine with political instability is around the River Jordan. Despite a far-sighted programme to bring Jordanian, Palestinian and Israeli hydrologists together to improve water quality in the river, and manage water demand and supply in the region, water availability will inevitably remain a flash point, particularly as populations in the regions continue to grow rapidly and rainfall can be virtually non-existent during periods of drought and, under conditions of drier summers with climate change. One hope lies in the development of desalinating technology, such as already supplies much of the water for the city of Eilat, with its population of 56 000 people, and the 80% of the water requirements of the Kibbutzim of the Negev desert[7] adjacent to the Dead Sea that has already dropped a massive 17 metres since 1975 according to the *Times Atlas of the World*.

On an even larger scale, the Aral Sea has been described as the worst environmental disaster in the world and it is predicted that within ten years it will be the cause of armed conflict. The saline inland sea, divided between the former Soviet Republics of Kazakhstan and Uzbekistan, has been drying up for the past 25 years since the former USSR began a vast irrigation scheme drawing water from its two tributary rivers to grow cotton and rice in the desert. The irrigated area expanded from 6 million hectares in the 1960s to 8 million hectares and the sea began to shrink. It is now reduced to three separate parts and is still evaporating. The shore-line has

6.5.
Droughts are increasingly threatening not only agriculture but also the availability of water from ground and surface sources. It is settlements on the land between the desert and the sown that will dry first, and those where ground water pumping has caused a sudden dropping of the water table, as in the villages around the central Persian desert. (*Source:* Sue Roaf)

receded on average by 250 kilometres and the salinity has increased dramatically, making the water a viscous salt paste in many parts, containing pesticides and minerals. High levels of liver and kidney cancer around the sea have become commonplace. Although an action plan has been introduced there seems to be little agreement between the five countries that border the lake on how to move forward and a proposed dam to the north of the sea, to be built by Kazakhstan, may prove the final straw that leads to an inevitable water war in the region.[8]

Again and again such examples can be shown, as in the constant struggle between Turkey, Syria and Iraq over the waters of the Tigris and Euphrates rivers. India plans to divert large quantities of water from major rivers, including the Ganges and Brahmaputra, threatening the livelihoods of more than 100 million people downstream in Bangladesh. The ambitious plans to link major rivers flowing from the Himalayas and divert them south through drought-prone areas are still on the drawing board but so concerned is Bangladesh that they are considering appealing to the United Nations to redraft international law on water sharing. The project is vast and projected to cost between £44 and £125 billion and will take at least 14 years to complete. If the project goes ahead Bangladesh may have to build a huge network of canals to irrigate the farmlands now watered by the Brahmaputra but they claim the whole scheme would have catastrophic effects on their country. Another water war brewing perhaps?[9]

BORE HOLE WATER

One of the problems with bore hole drilling is that it leads to a reduction in the resource. Groundwater is the main supply for more than 2 billion people in the world and is diminishing almost everywhere. Beneath Mexico City the water table has fallen on average 2 m and in the American Mid-West water tables have fallen 3 m in a decade and 30 m in some places. So much has been pumped from beneath Florida that in some places the aquifers are at risk from being flooded by sea water. Twelve cities of more than 10 million people rely on underground water reserves, including Shanghai, Bangkok, London and Calcutta. Water is used for the rapidly growing global population, in industry and agriculture. It takes 1000 tonnes of water to grow a tonne of wheat, 2000 tonnes to grow a tonne of rice, and small farmers in many regions will be the first to suffer as aquifers dry up. The estimated percentages of populations dependent on groundwater for different regions includes 75% in Europe, 32% in Asia Pacific, 29% for Central and South America and 32% for the world on average.[10]

WHO OWNS THE WATER?

Here we have the problem of who owns the water in the ground, a question rather like who owns the air? One thing is for sure – that it is not Coca-Cola. In Kochi, India, in December the local 'Davids', in the form of a group of villagers, took the 'Goliath' of the major soft drinks corporation Hindustan Coca-Cola Beverages, to the Kerala High Court to direct it to stop drawing groundwater for use in its bottling plant at Plachimedu in the Palakaad district. David won, and the court directed the local council and the state government to ensure that the plant does not extract groundwater after a specified time. The court decreed that the groundwater beneath land is not owned by the landowner. Normally, every landowner can draw a 'reasonable' amount of groundwater which is necessary for their domestic and agricultural requirements. But here, 510 kilolitres of water was extracted per day, converted to products and transported out of the state, thus breaking the 'natural water cycle', and causing the drying up of village fields for miles around the plant. Extraction of the groundwater, even up to the admitted limit by the company, was illegal, the court held. The company had no legal right to extract this much natural wealth and the Panchayat and the government were bound to prevent it. The court held that the groundwater belongs to the general public and the company had no right to claim a huge share of it. The government also has no power to allow a private party to extract such a huge quantity of groundwater, the result of which could be drying up of water tables. So let the buyer beware for high water use industries in the future.[11]

The Coca-Cola case is an issue of the over-exploitation of the capacity of the environment to provide enough water to sustain both soft drink production at the required level, while supporting the expectations of the traditional local community. This basic calculation of capacity should have been done and reviewed at the planning stage of the factory development.

WHO OWNS THE WATER PROBLEM?

There are two issues here:

* The first is unsustainable development – the project exceeding the environmental capacity of the area to support it. This should, from what we have seen in the Coca-Cola case above, be done using calculations of current water resources, under future climate scenarios, to evaluate the reducing capacity of the environment to support too great a demand on it. The capacity calculations should be produced at the planning stage as part of the sustainability statement of a project and the decisions

to reject plants like that at Kochi taken before too great a loss is incurred.

- The second issue is that clear laws should exist on the apportioning of the available water to ensure that the basic human right to clean water is maintained for as long as is humanly possible.[12]

But these issues are pertinent even here in Britain, where the government should be asked questions like:

- Was the chronic water shortage in the Southeast, now and in the future, taken into account when permission was given to build the Thames Gateway development, east of London, with 200 000 new homes?
- What are the extra infrastructural costs of placing those new homes in the Southeast, where new dams and water plants have to be built to cope with the increase, as opposed to the Northwest where there will be more water in summer, and the long term costs will be lower for the ordinary householder and who pays for them?
- Does the ordinary householder agree to pay the increase water bill costs so that those extra 200 000 can live in the Thames Gateway?
- How has the serious problem of more homes exacerbating summer droughts in the Southeast been dealt with in the planning process?
- Will farmers who have less and less water available to them, and who are already suffering from drought stress in arable crops, with irrigation water having to be saved for higher value vegetable and salad crops,[13] be able to claim compensation from the politicians who unwisely approved developments that exceeded that capacity of the regional environment to support them?

FLOODING IN BRITAIN

Flooding is an increasingly chronic problem globally. In the UK it is predicted to significantly increase due to:

- Increased winter rainfall.
- Higher sea levels, in conjunction with higher wave heights and bigger storm surges.
- More intense and frequent winter storms. It is difficult to predict storm incidence and while the Hadley Centre model predicts an increase, a number of other models do not. It is safe to say that storms will be wetter, however.

In the UK an estimated 1.7 million homes are situated in the flood plains, with up to 200 000 of them thought to face a 1 in 75 chance of flooding (a once in a lifetime risk). The insurance industry has agreed to continue to cover homes with better than a 1 in 75 risk and homes with flood defences due to be put in place by 2007. Home owners in the Severn and Thames valleys and other parts of the Southeast of England could see their premiums rise, with excesses going up to £1000–5000, and they may even be denied cover. It will become more difficult to sell such homes, particularly if lenders require insurance cover. In 2000, 10 000 homes were flooded and rainfall, under climate change scenarios, is set to rise considerably.[14]

The fabric of buildings prone to flooding is also a cause for concern as developers move to wider use of timber frame buildings. Where major new developments, such as that proposed for the Thames Gateway development, carry a risk of future flooding, the use of unsuitable materials that absorb water, and may succumb to infestations of mould and wet rot when 'drying out' should be regulated.[15]

In an attempt to reduce the impacts of flooding on citizens, property developers faced a multi-million pound 'flood tax' to counter

6.6.
The River Dee at Maryculter, November 2002 – one of a series of photographs taken by Aberdeenshire council officers from a helicopter at the height of the flooding. The council boundary runs down the middle of the river with Aberdeenshire on the right and Aberdeen City on the left. Note the flooded caravan site in the centre of the picture. The normal path of the river can be seen near the top of the picture, where the farmer had constructed riverside flood banks. The Aberdeenshire strategy is generally to encourage farmers to remove flood embankments beside rivers. It is more sustainable to allow fields to flood, thus storing flood waters and attenuating the downstream flow to reduce flooding elsewhere. (*Source:* Reproduced with the kind permission of Aberdeenshire Council)

the spiralling costs of climate change. A DEFRA (Department of Environment, Food and Rural Affairs) report in January 2003 recommended that developers who build on the flood plain should be made to pay a one-off fee to help raise over £20 million to construct coastal and river defence systems. Spending on flood protection will rise from £411 million in 2002 to £564 million by 2005 although this falls far short of the investment required to protect people in areas vulnerable to flooding from the increased risks they face due to climate change. Environmental groups at that time objected to the conclusions of the report, which they said was actually encouraging development on flood plains while the Housebuilder's Federation warned that the proposed charges would exacerbate housing shortages by pushing up the market prices of homes.[16] The tax, of course, was not introduced.

Another major problem that may also result from flooding is the contamination of land. A key feature of many pollutants is that they are more likely to move in wet, than in dry soil. Many sites on flood plains with a history of soil toxicity may become more toxic if the soil is flooded. In this case, even if a portion of the topsoil has been removed and replaced, if regularly flooded, pollutants may leach through the new topsoil towards the surface. So the worst conditions are provided by a combination of contaminated land and regularly inundated sites, highlighting the problems of containing contamination from industrial sites on flood plains.

A major concern in Britain, prone as it is to flooding, continues to be that of new developments in flood plains being permitted regardless of the impacts they will have in increasing flood risks in adjacent areas. A number of problems heighten risks of flooding

6.7.
Not only are settlements vulnerable to river and coastal flooding but also transport routes, agriculture and health from the spread of pollution and sewage. The scale of the problem is hinted at by this view of the River Severn in flood. (*Source:* R.L. Wilby, Environment Agency)

resulting from these new developments: one is that many planning officers and members of committees on local councils simply do not understand the issues involved because they are not presented with adequately explained information; a second is that the methodologies for evaluating the knock-on risks for local communities of such decisions are not available to them; and thirdly human nature is such that it is often more convenient for people to bury their head in the sand and ignore such real problems, perhaps due to a lack of imagination in many.

Even the 'experts' do not agree on how to correctly calculate flood-related impacts, as is evidenced by a bitter battle being fought over a series of new developments by Kohn Pederson Fox, RMJM and Nicholas Grimshaw & Partners on the banks of the River Clyde in Scotland. The project requires the filling in of some dock basins, which it is claimed will increase the risks of major flooding in Glasgow, according to a report by Clyde Heritage Trust. The report concludes that Glasgow may be at risk of floods similar to those that caused extensive damage in Prague and Dresden in 2002. All of the riverside developments cumulatively add to the narrowing of the river, which reduces its flood water storage capacity pushing water elsewhere in the city. The Clyde Heritage trust also demanded a comprehensive and robust flood plan to be integrated into the overall redevelopment of the city, similar to the construction of the Thames Barrier in 1984.[17]

The developers and experts disagree with the findings of this Report and the battle rages. But there is an ethical issue here: on what side does one come down, on the precautionary side that would tend to hold off from committing to a project that may have catastrophic impacts for the surrounding communities, or on the side of increasing the value of the whole area through fashionable development? Two groups of people will have to suffer any disastrous consequences from such developments: the local council-tax payers and those whose buildings would lose their value if flooded. It would appear that there is a moral onus on ensuring that both groups properly understand the calculations on each side of the argument so they can best decide on their own future. Developers have no vested interest in the long-term well-being of the community in the area but the insurers of those properties will, however, be involved in the future of such developments, and that is why their take on such developments is crucial.

Urban flooding is on the increase around the world, as cities expand and water-absorbent fields and forests give way to impervious roads, buildings and car parks. Torrential rains can lead to flash flooding with devastating consequences and the phenomenon of urban flooding is becoming a problem in cities that for centuries have been untouched by it previously.[18] This is largely due not only to more hard surfaces, but also to the continuing practice of building on the flood plain and the increasing intensity of rainfall with climate change. Failing storm water and sewage infrastructure is also a problem in the UK and many councils now employ SUDS, 'Sustainable Urban Drainage Systems', to reduce the risk of urban flooding, although it should be noted that these do not work on flood plains where there is nowhere for the water to go, as any water 'sinks' are often already below the water table during flood events. A key problem with urban flooding is also the speed of run-off and the 'flash flood' effect that catches people unaware and is responsible for many of the drowning deaths associated with floods as people try to escape in their cars down flooding roads. For an excellent bibliography on the subject see the Reading list on the subject of flooding provided by David Crichton on the companion website http://books.elsevier.com/companions/0750659114.

Rising sea levels

The problem of flooding in the southeast of England is made worse by the fact that the land mass is sinking in the region and by the fact that relatively large areas in the Southeast are already prone to coastal and riverine flooding. Many regions of the world share this problem.

Worldwide, approximately 400 million people live within 20 m of sea level and within 20 km of a coast, worldwide, around 23%. However, this figure is difficult to calculate properly from existing data. Eleven of the world's largest cities are on the coast and in the United State a staggering 53% of the population live near the coast and may therefore be vulnerable to surges in sea levels.[19]

Venice is one of the many cities that face the same problem as London, that as sea levels rise the city itself is sinking on its alluvial soils. In 1900 the central area of Venice around St Mark's Square flooded around ten times a year. Today it is closer to 100 times a year and over the century Venice has actually sunk by around 20 cm. If scientists are right and sea levels will rise between 40–60 cm over the next century and the city continues to sink at the same rate then the eventual inundation of the city is inevitable and will, it is predicted, be uninhabitable by 2100.[20] Many are sceptical that the proposed barrier around the lagoons of the city will ever materialize, not least because of its cost, which is put in the billions rather than millions.

6.8.
Many of the great British reservoirs were built during the drought years of the late 19th century, like the dam at Craig Goch Reservoir, one of a series in the Elan Valley, Mid-Wales built to provide Birmingham with a safe water supply, 72 miles away. The scheme was the brainchild of the late Victorian Mayor of Birmingham and has a reservoir capacity of 2000 million gallons of water. The Elan valley dams are now owned by Welsh Water. (*Source:* Charles Knevitt)

WATER QUALITY

Water quality will be very much affected by climate change:

- Decreased summer rainfall will affect water availability and quality, increasing also the concentrations of CO_2 and pollutants in river, dams and lakes.
- Higher sea levels will interfere with natural drainage patterns, coast lines and water and sewage supply networks.
- More intense and frequent storms may pollute water supplies.
- Changing groundwater levels affect water supply.
- Increased water temperatures will accelerate the growth of water-borne bacteria, plants and fungi.
- Decreased oxygen levels in water with higher temperatures and less water in rivers may kill river species, including fish, which are also physiologically temperature-sensitive in their habitats.

High levels of rainwater run-off from increased levels of rainfall and storm incidence will exacerbate pollution incidences in built-up areas.

An example where a combination of factors is killing large stretches of water is occurring in Lake Tanganyika in Central Africa where the nutrient balance of the lake's water has been so altered that due to a lack of vital nutrients fish stocks have fallen drastically, with a dramatic impact on the local fishing economy. In an area where between 25% and 40% of the protein needs of local people in the four bordering countries traditionally come from the lake, the slumping of the fish numbers, in a large part due to higher water temperatures and changing wind patterns, will have a catastrophic effect on local populations.[21]

DAMS AND RESERVOIRS

Levels of precipitation, and periods of droughts and rain have direct impacts on the infrastructure of our water catchment, storage and supply systems. Climate change may well prove a real threat to the integrity of such systems.

There is, for instance, a very real and hidden problem in many countries of the over-topping of dams, reservoirs and canals. On 2 November 1925 there was a blow-out of the lower section of a portion of the Eigiau dam in the Conwy valley in North Wales. The water scoured a channel 70 feet wide and 10 feet deep, as 50 million cubic feet of water surged down to the Coedty reservoir below. The reservoir was nearly full at the time and the spillway had to cope with a surplus discharge well in excess of its designed capacity. The dam was overtopped, washing away the embankment, and the core collapsed. There was an almost instant release of 70 million gallons of water. A wall of water, mud, rock and concrete hit the village of Dolgarrog at 9.15pm that Monday evening.

Fortunately many of the villagers were attending a film show at the village Assembly Hall, out of the path of the flood, and 200 workers were working late in the nearby aluminium factory, otherwise more lives would have been lost. As it was, ten adults and six children were killed and many houses were destroyed.[22]

Huge boulders, the size of houses, can still be seen in the village. It later transpired that the general manager and board of directors of the company which owned the dams knew that there were defects in them from the beginning, but chose to keep the facts secret. No one was ever held to account, and two of the streets in the rebuilt village were named after directors of the company.[23]

It should be emphasized that no lives have been lost in the UK from dam failure since the Dolgarrog disaster in 1925, however failures do occur around the world. In 1959 the Malpasset dam in France failed resulting in the deaths of 421 people, and in 1963 the overtopping of the Vaiont dam in Italy caused by a landslide caused 1189 deaths, even though the dam itself remained intact. In 1972 a dam in West Virginia, USA, failed causing 125 deaths. Modern dams and reservoirs are designed and built to very high standards in Britain, but in the future, the safety margins will increasingly be eroded by climate change. So far as current safety standards are concerned the main concern is the secrecy surrounding the condition of dams and raised embankments. There are also concerns about the secrecy surrounding dam break inundation maps, and the lack of preparedness of the emergency services in dealing with a catastrophic failure.

The information in the public domain is enough to illustrate the scale of the issue.[24] The Reservoirs Act, 1975, applies to all reservoirs holding or capable of holding more than 25 000 cubic metres of water. There are over 2500 such reservoirs in the UK, of which 530 are large enough to be included in the World Register of Large Dams. Owners of dams covered by the Act are obliged by law to have them inspected every ten years by a civil engineer from a special panel, but the law does not specify the details of the inspection nor that the results should be published. In practice, the thoroughness of the inspection depends almost entirely on how much the dam owner is prepared to pay, and the author is not aware of any case where the results have been published, or even given to local authority emergency planning officers or the emergency services. Dam owners also refuse to issue dam break flood inundation maps. This could mean, and indeed this has happened, that planning officers for the local authority might grant planning permission for new housing developments within the area which would be flooded if the dam failed, simply because they did not know that the area was within the danger zone.

By contrast, in France, everyone living in areas at risk from dam break is fully aware of the fact, and these areas are subject to frequent evacuation exercises. Informal comments from engineers would seem to indicate that they believe the British are more likely than the French to panic if they were given such information.

Climate change could well lead to an increased risk of failure of British dams, some of which are more than 200 years old. Failure can be caused by many factors – for example, climate change could lead to subsidence of the dam foundations, landslip into the reservoir, or overtopping due to heavy rainfall.

Around half of the 2500 large UK dams have earth embankments, most of them constructed before heavy soil compaction equipment was available. Little is known about the content of such embankments, especially the core, or the extent of internal settlement or disturbance, for example from rabbit burrows.

Droughts could lead to cracking of the embankment wall, and climate change will lead to more droughts in the summer, followed by more rain in the autumn. This could impose additional loads, which were not considered when the reservoir was planned. There could also be additional loadings from increased snowfall in upland areas, followed by rapid snowmelt due to rainfall. Higher windspeeds over the reservoir surface could cause more frequent overtopping, leading to erosion of earth embankments unless suitably protected.

Other possible causes of failure include vandalism of valves, pipe work or controls, terrorism, or aircraft crash. Many dams are in or near urban areas, for example there is a large reservoir in Brent in London which is very close to housing and aircraft flight paths. Most UK dams are over 100 years old. A detailed record is kept of defects in dams but this is not published. The reasons for the secrecy surrounding the condition of the nation's dams is not clear, but prudent insurance underwriters are always inclined to assume the worst when information is withheld. The record of dam safety in the UK has been excellent since 1925, but climate change fears might cause some underwriters to reassess the situation. It would seem quite likely that there are people living and working within the danger zone of large dams in the UK. In the United States, where information is more readily available, it is known that there are more than 2000 communities that have been identified as being at risk from dams that are believed to be unsafe.

Growing population and wealth, especially in the Southeast of England, will lead to greater demand for water, while supply will be reduced by summer droughts. Demand management controls such as water meters can only have a limited effect and ground-water abstraction is near its limit. It is therefore likely that more dams will need to be built, and in Southeast England these are likely to be near urban areas. Meanwhile, in 2000, government intro-duced a research programme for dams, with some of the survey work subcontracted to the Transport Research Laboratory because of their expertise in checking earth embankments.

More dams are likely to be built because of climate change, either retention dams as part of flood alleviation measures, or reservoirs for hydro power (in response to the moves away from fossil fuel power generation) or water supply (in response to increasing sum-mer droughts).

Meantime, so long as dam condition reports and inundation maps remain secret, insurance companies may be increasingly likely to assume that properties near to reservoirs may be at risk of flood-ing from a breach, particularly in the case of older earth embank-ments, or concrete dams constructed more than fifty years ago.

CANALS AND WATERWAYS

British Waterways owns and manages over 540 km of navigable rivers and 2600 km of canals which in turn interact with the major river basins and land drainage systems of the UK.[25] Most of the canals were constructed more than 200 years ago, and are very vul-nerable to flood events. Often the waterways cross different catch-ments and can thus transfer flows from one catchment to another.

British Waterways also own and manage 89 reservoirs in the UK, some of which are managed entirely for flood storage. Canals are usually 'still' waters, and do not clean themselves as with flowing rivers, so pollution is a particular problem, for example from sewage back-up from drains, and one that is exacerbated in hot summers.

Canals generally operate with only 300 mm of freeboard, and there are over 650 km of embankments to be maintained. Overtopping of embankments, especially those over 200 years old, can lead to failure, which could have a catastrophic impact, especially in urban areas.

British Waterways is very aware of the risk and has a system of sluices, weirs, pumps and floodgates to control the flow into canals. They have a thorough system of emergency procedures that have worked well so far, but climate change, with the predicted increasingly intense periods of rainfall, is going to impose a major challenge to our 200-year old network of canals, and this challenge does not yet seem to be fully recognized by government.

The levels of rain and snowfall in many regions have a wide-ranging effect on our built environment and have the potential to create significant hazards for homes and settlements in every region. The drive to reduce exposure to those hazards may increasingly influence the location of populations in the future, just as major steps need to be taken to reduce the vulnerability of individual buildings to those hazards, around the world.

What is impossible to do, however, is to move away from the track of a storm.

NOTES AND REFERENCES

1   Hulme, M., Turnpenny, J. and Jenkins, G. (2002) *Climate Change Scenarios for the United Kingdom: The UKCIP02 Briefing Report*. Tyndall Centre for Climate Change Research, School of Environmental Sciences, University of East Anglia, Norwich, UK. Available in pdf format on: http://www.ukcip.org.uk/publications/pub.html.

2   Palmer, T.N. and Rälsänen, J. (2002) Quantifying the risk of extreme seasonal precipitation events in a changing climate. *Nature*, 415, 512–14.

3   The lower boundary to the class of 'most intense' events is defined (separately for each season and region) by an amount (mm) calculated from the 1961–90 period, namely the daily precipitation exceeded on a minimally sufficient number of days necessary to account for precisely 10% of the seasonal precipitation.

4 *Guardian*, 6 December 2003, p. 21.

5 *Observer*, Cash, 31 August 2003, p. 5.

6 *Guardian*, Society, 27 November 2002, pp. 8 and 9.

7 *Guardian*, 14 November 2002, p. 25.

8 *Guardian,* 29 October 2003, p. 13.

9 *Guardian*, 24 July 2003, p. 15.

10 http://www.unep.org/Documents/Default.asp?DocumentID= 321&ArticleID=4026.

11 http://timesofindia.indiatimes.com/articleshow/362916.cms.

12 'The human right to water entitles everyone to sufficient, affordable, physically accessible, safe and acceptable water for personal and domestic uses', states the Committee document. 'While uses vary between cultures, an adequate amount of safe water is necessary to prevent death from dehydration, to reduce the risk of water-related disease and to provide for consumption, cooking, personal and domestic hygienic requirements', http://www.globalpolicy.org/socecon/ ffd/gpg/2002/1127water.htm, see also the Indigenous Peoples Kyoto Water Declaration, from the Third World Water Forum, Kyoto, Japan, March 2003, http://www.treatycouncil.org/new_ page_52112111.htm.

13 *Guardian*, 27 August 2003, p. 10.

14 *Observer*, Cash, 12 October 2003, p. 11.

15 The Environment Agency's 'What's in your backyard' feature on the Your Environment page of its website shows the flood risk in Britain at any particular post code at http://216.31.193.171/ asp/1_introduction.asp. The Environment Agency service only applies to England and Wales, but there is a commercial website that provides a free postcode search facility for the whole of Britain. It can be found at: www.home-envirosearch.com.

16 *Observer*, 5 January 2003, p. 2.

17 *Building Design*, 13 September 2002, p. 2.

18 Roaf, S. (2004) *Closing the Loop: Benchmarks for Sustainable Buildings.* London: RIBA Publications, ch. 19, 'Flooding'. On SUDS in particular see: North East Scotland Flood Appraisal Group (2002) *Drainage Impact Assessment: Guidance for Developers and Regulators.* Stonehaven: Aberdeenshire Council. Available from Aberdeenshire Council, telephone 01569 768300, ask for Ms Hilary McBean or email: hilary.macbean@ aberdeenshire.gov.uk (due to go on their website shortly). Keep an eye out for *Floods and SUDS: A Guidance Note for Local*

Authorities on SUDS Issues by David Crichton, not yet published, but available free by email from david@crichton.sol.co.uk. See also two important new websites: Foresight Flood and Coastal Defence Report, launched on 22 April 2004, looks 30–100 years ahead and uses the UKCIP02 Climate Change Scenarios and Foresight Future socio-economic scenarios. It outlines the possible risks for the UK from flooding and coastal erosion, and highlights the decisions that need to be made to protect people, homes, businesses and the environment in the future. In each scenario, if flood management policies remain unchanged, the risk of flooding increases significantly, and the damage could be very costly. Under the most extreme scenario, annual cost of damages could increase 20-fold from the current level. Copies of the report can be downloaded from http://www.foresight.gov.uk/fcd.html. Also Flooding and Insurance – Information and Advice from ABI. The Association of British Insurers has developed a dedicated Web page as a gateway to information on flooding and insurance issues, including details of ABI's views and reports, and a flood resilience fact sheet with information for householders on how they can reduce flood damage. Visit www.abi.org.uk/flooding.

19 http://www.giss.nasa.gov/research/intro/gornitz_04/.

20 *Guardian*, G2, 18 September 2003, p. 3.

21 *Independent*, 14 August 2003, p. 11.

22 Thomas, D. (1997) *Hydro Electricity in North West Wales*. Llanrwst: National Power plc.

23 Draper, C. (2002) *Walks in the Conwy Valley*. Llanrwst: Gwasg Carreg Gwalch.

24 See: The Babtie Group and the Centre for Ecology and Hydrology (2002) *Climate Change Impacts on the Safety of British Reservoirs*, Report commissioned by the Department of the Environment, Transport and the Regions (DETR) now DEFRA, through their reservoir safety research programme (unpublished) and Hughes, A., Hewlett, H., Samuels, P., Morris, M., Sayers, P., Moffat, I., Harding, A. and Tedd, P. (2000) *Risk Management for UK Reservoirs*. Construction Industry Research and Information Association (CIRIA) Research project report C542. London.

25 Much of this section is based on the following paper: Sim, S., Morgan, L. and Leftley, D. (British Waterways) (2002) British Waterways' role in flood mitigation and emergency response. *Municipal Engineer*, 151, 305–11.

7 WINDSTORMS

THE DESTRUCTIVE POWER OF WIND

Of all the hazards that the climate can throw at us, none equals the power of an angry storm. Despite the fact that there is much greater uncertainty about future changes in wind speed and direction, recent studies have demonstrated that the UK is becoming windier and storm incidents are increasing. This reflects a pattern throughout the world, in which hurricanes and storms are not only increasing in number and intensity but storm seasons are extending into months where storms were previously unrecorded.

According to the reinsurance company Munich Re, between 1980 and 2002, world wide more than a third of all natural disasters were caused by windstorms. It also accounted for a third of all fatalities and economic losses from natural disasters. 'The evidence points

7.1.
Wind damage is responsible for the largest payouts from the insurance industry in Britain and globally. A cause for further concern is that for the first time in recorded history a tropical hurricane arose in December in the Caribbean in 2003, indicating an unprecedented lengthening of the storm season for the Americas. (*Source:* Sue Roaf)

to critical extreme wind speeds and precipitation being exceeded with increasing frequency, so that for this reason alone there will inevitably be a stark increase in the loss burdens as well.'[1]

Munich Re also calculates that out of the 37 natural disasters costing insurers more than one billion US dollars in the 1980s and 1990s, only two were earthquakes and the rest were due to atmospheric extremes, mainly windstorm. Indeed, 27 of the 37 such natural disasters occurred in the 1990s, showing a dramatic increase in costs.

A windstorm provided the most obvious example of the importance of using resilient construction techniques. The great British storm of October 1987 caused £1400 million of damage claims for insurers. The storms in January and February 1990 cost insurers £2500 million. Yet these storms were not particularly severe, compared with the Braer storm in 1993.

The Braer storm was probably the most severe storm to hit Britain in the past 300 years.[2] It lasted continuously for 22 days (17 of which were at severe storm force 12 or higher) with an atmospheric pressure at a record-breaking low of 915 mb, the equivalent of a category 5 hurricane (Hurricane Andrew in the United States in 1992 was only a category 4, with an atmospheric pressure of 924 mb, but caused US$30 billion damage). By comparison, the October 1987 UK storm was trivial: it lasted only 24 hours, with atmospheric pressure only down to 960 mb. Yet the damage from the Braer storm, apart from the damage to the ship after which the storm was named, was negligible to the insurance industry.

One of the reasons for this is resilient construction. It has been calculated that the damage caused by Hurricane Andrew would have been reduced by 40% if buildings had been constructed to current building codes.[3] The Braer storm mainly affected the Shetland Islands, where traditional Scottish or Scandinavian designs are used, and all the building companies are local. As a result, almost all the buildings are constructed of thick stone walls and Welsh slated roofs, with sarking boards.

The use of sarking boards has two major advantages. First, if the roofing tiles or slates are blown away, there is a secondary covering underneath to prevent the wind from entering the loft. Secondly, the smooth surface of sarking boards means that each tile or slate has to be individually nailed in place or it will fall off during construction. Without sarking boards, tiles can simply be hooked onto battens and will stay in place without nailing, so the absence of fixings is not noticed until the wind blows. Unfortunately, sarking boards are rarely used now, at least in England and Wales, yet the cost of using them during construction is relatively low.

During 1997 and 1998, the Department of Environment, Transport and the Regions, and The Scottish Office, funded a project with the Building Research Establishment in Scotland to review the impacts of climate change on the construction industry and on building standards.[4] The report highlighted the need for the design and planning of new buildings to change to 'future proof' new construction, and that failure to adapt existing buildings to cope with future climate would result in increased maintenance and repair costs, and inevitable increases in insurance premiums. Further research and impact assessments were required. Unfortunately little has been done since then.

Perhaps this is because of the widely held perception that older buildings are more vulnerable to storm damage than new ones, especially if they have not been well maintained. The Building Research Establishment was stating this as recently as 2003, but how much of this is fact and how much is assumption? David Crichton was only able to find one UK research project based on the large insurance industry database of storm damage cases, and this shows that the perceptions may be wrong. Research for the Loss Prevention Council (now part of the Building Research Establishment) in 1998 shows that:

- Poor maintenance is not a major factor.
- It is not old buildings that are vulnerable, but new ones, especially those built after 1971.

There is a desperate need to carry out further research into this, using insurance claims data. Before the days of building standards, local builders tended to 'over engineer' buildings, in the light of local knowledge. They also used local stone and timber, plus heavy Welsh slate. Now with building codes, the construction industry builds to the code, which only has a 10% cushion for extreme events. This could explain why older buildings that have already survived many storms are likely to be more resilient than brand new buildings built to the standards set out by codes but no higher.

Work at the University of Aberdeen, part supervised by David Crichton and funded by the Loss Prevention Council, involved a detailed impact assessment of the vulnerability of different types of buildings to windstorm. Using insurance claims data, the research[5] indicates that modern housing may even be more vulnerable, particularly housing built after 1971. One reason for this could be the introduction of prefabricated rafters around this time. Originally rafters were installed without cross bracing, and if subjected to sideways pressure, could collapse like a set of dominoes, bringing down the gable wall. It is interesting to note that after the October 1987 storm, a study[6] found that between 60% and 80% (depending on area) of houses damaged had roofing damage, and 'an unusually high proportion of gables had both leaves of masonry sucked out'. In recent years the insurance industry around the world has suffered from mounting losses from wind damage. In the United States, it has been found that the majority of damage has occurred in conditions where the mean recurrence interval was less than 50 years.[7] There has subsequently been a whole programme of measures from the US insurance industry to reduce vulnerability of buildings to windstorm.

In a supplement to the Aberdeen study mentioned above, in the UK, damage was found from wind speeds that had a recurrence interval as low as three or four years in the case of modern buildings. So far the insurance industry has left it to local government to ensure proper construction through the adoption and enforcement of appropriate building codes. If the findings of the Aberdeen study are representative – and more work is clearly needed to establish if this is the case – this would indicate that building codes and enforcement may already be inadequate in the UK. Unless major changes are made to the Building Regulations to make buildings more resilient to windstorm (and this is very unlikely in the short term), then insurers will have to be more selective in their pricing. They can do this using their detailed data on designs and types of building stock, combined with very sophisticated windstorm models.

Windstorm modelling by insurers has improved significantly in the past decade. The latest techniques now model the geostrophic wind first, that is the wind at an altitude where it is not affected by surface roughness factors, and then vary the model for local conditions where gusts are affected by the topography and the nature of the buildings. This work is being undertaken by a number of reinsurers, insurers and reinsurance brokers independently. However, the job is so large that there really is a need for some central expert body, with access to large scale computing power, to provide definitive answers on behalf of the whole insurance and construction industry.

INSURANCE AS A TOOL TO IMPROVE RESILIENCE

The built environment will have to become more resilient to natural hazards. As shown above, research has indicated that UK building stock in some areas is particularly vulnerable to windstorm, for example. Insurers could potentially have an important role, using premium incentives and other means, to help to raise standards of construction and inspection of new buildings, and retrofitting older ones. To target these efforts, more data is needed about what happens in a flood or windstorm.

At present, when an insurance customer reports storm damage, insurers capture just enough information to enable them to deal with the claim. It would be much more far-sighted to start to capture additional information about the local wind conditions and the reason for the failure of the structure. A database of even just a few thousands of such claims could be of value to the engineers reviewing building standards. In the UK in 1987, the industry had 1 million storm claims, in 1990 it had 3 million. If details of each of these claims had been captured along with local wind speeds, insurers would be in a much better position now to understand what needs to be done to improve building resilience to storm damage. When the next major storm happens insurers would be no better placed to capture such information than they were in 1990.

WHEN THE EXTREME STORM HITS

Getting out

Many have lost their lives because, when a storm hits, they simply could not get out of buildings in time. One of the most vulnerable of all building types to storm dangers is, surprisingly, the most 'modern' type: the thin, tight-skinned, air-conditioned building with no opening windows and no escape route onto the roof. If such buildings are located on a flood plain where there is any risk of water rising to block the only doors on the ground floor, then people have no way out. If the air conditioning then fails, if there is, for instance, a blackout or the plant room is in a flooded basement, and there is little breathable air in the building (this happened in New York during the August 2003 blackout), then things become critical. If you add to this situation exposure to pollutants, perhaps a broken sewage mains or gas pipes damaged in the basement as furniture is banged against it by flood water, or similarly broken toxin containers, then that building may be a death trap, in which, unless occupants are willing and able to smash a glass cladding panel (virtually impossible with some modern 'bomb proof' glasses) they could well die. Risk assessments encompassing such likelihoods should be done for all buildings of this type.

Another problem, that has caused deaths during the flooding associated with wind storms is the location of the means of escape underground, in a car park or an exit route or a subway, as these flood first and trap occupants within a building – or kill them on their way out. During floods in Huston, Texas in 2001 a secretary was travelling down in a lift when a power blackout occurred, and as is standard in many lift programmes, the lift lowered her gently to the basement, which was full of water and she drowned.[8] The advice is, during floods and storms, as in fire, do not use the lifts.

Also, buildings on flood plains must be increasingly closely regulated. Experience has shown that it should be compulsory for bungalows to have escape routes, with accessible windows fitted in their roofs to enable occupants to clamber onto the roof in the case of a rapid inundation of their homes.

People in ordinary buildings can also be very vulnerable to storms. This was shown in December 2003 when five people died in a torrential rain storm with 90 mph winds in the south of France in a region that had suffered catastrophic floods the winter before. One elderly man was found drowned in his basement flat while others were killed as their cars were washed off roads. Some 8000 people were evacuated from their homes, roads and railway lines were closed. Flood waters caused two buildings to collapse in Marseille, where 47 people were evacuated to a local sports centre. In Lyon 200 people spent the night in a gymnasium after their train was cancelled. ASN, the National Nuclear Authority, closed four Rhône valley nuclear reactors because of the storm, as a precaution, showing again, as during the drought of August 2003, the vulnerability of this technology to extreme weather events. Floods also disabled a water purification plant in the Haute-Loire region leaving 4000 without drinking water.[9] These events give a taste of the range of impacts that can accrue from a bad storm. A detailed report on the causes of the event, requested by President Chirac, cited global warming as a cause. Chirac ordered that solutions to the problem of flooding be found that would reduce the scale of the impacts in future years.

Floods, logging and landslides

Every year 90 000 square kilometres of forest are being lost due to logging, the equivalent area of the British Isles according to the *Times Atlas of the World*, for use in industry, commerce and for cooking and heating. During wind and rain storms, the slopes exposed by logging are washed away, and then major landslips occur that, in recent years, have been claiming increasing numbers of lives around the world.

For instance, when Hurricane Mitch hit land in 1998, the highest numbers of casualties were caused by landslides, a direct result of logging. Officials estimated about 7000 had died in the region. The greatest losses were reported in Honduras, where an estimated 5000 people died and 600 000 – 10% of the population – were forced to flee their homes after the storm as floods and landslides erased from the map many villages and households as well as whole neighbourhoods of cities. In neighbouring Nicaragua, the death toll was also high. Official preliminary figures showed 1330 dead and 1903 missing nationwide. As many as 1500 people may have died in mudslides when the crater lake of the Casitas Volcano collapsed, sending a wall of mud and debris onto villages below.[10]

In November 2003 a staggering 72 people were killed by a flash flood that washed through a tourist resort on the island of Sumatra, Indonesia, sparked off by several days of heavy rain in the Leuser National Park. The river Bohorok overflowed its banks washing away many of the flimsy buildings of the area and leaving only around 10% standing. Officials claimed that the flood was caused by 'massive logging' in the Leuser National Park, a widespread problem in many regions of the world,[11] including, in recent years, Spain, Italy, France and Switzerland. Hence maintenance and replanting of forests may be one way of saving lives during storms.

EVACUATION

In his excellent book *Florida's Hurricane History*, Jay Barnes, former Director of the American National Hurricane Center in Florida, described his concerns about the increasing population of the State and the decreasing ability of people to be evacuated from it in the case of a major hurricane.[12]

Even though Florida has been battered by hurricanes many times over the years, most Florida residents today have not experienced a major hurricane. Barnes sums up his concern:[13]

Certainly Andrew in 1992 was a tremendous wake-up call for South Florida. The Panhandle had Eloise in 1975 and most recently Opal in 1995, but the peninsula itself has been spared during the last twenty-five years. As we look back at Florida's hurricane history, we find a flurry of activity in the late 1920s, 1930s, and 1940s. There was the powerful 1926 hurricane in Miami, the 1928 storm that killed many people at Lake Okeechobee, and the fierce Labor Day storm of 1935 that swept across the Florida Keys. Then a series of major hurricanes rolled through the Florida Peninsula in the 1940s. From 1941 to 1950, eleven hurricanes struck, seven of which were category 3 or greater. Of course, most of them didn't have names. Few people talk about them anymore, largely because most Florida residents weren't around back then. Some have been forgotten and are no longer part of Florida's 'hurricane culture.'

Florida has always been vulnerable to hurricanes, but the explosive growth that has occurred in the past few decades has made the coastal areas even more precarious. The population has more than doubled in the past 40 years, and in many communities, it has been that long since the last significant hurricane. Many coastal areas are especially vulnerable because of their unique evacuation problems. In the Keys, for example, only one highway offers escape for many thousands of residents. The 1935 hurricane, which moved through the central Keys on Labor Day, illustrates the evacuation dilemma. As it approached Andros Island in the

7.2.
The Royal Palm Park in downtown Miami was littered with boats and debris after the September hurricane of 1926.
(*Source:* Photo courtesy of Special Collections Department, University of South Florida Library, Tampa Campus)

Bahamas it was a category 1 storm. It took just over 40 hours to become a category 5 storm and was the strongest ever to hit the United States. Today, the time required for evacuation of the Keys is more than 24 hours, and evacuation times for the southeastern and southwestern counties may exceed 40 hours. For many of these areas, the lead time required is too great and the population too large for the highway system to handle all of the traffic.

What I fear most is a scenario similar to what happened in 1935 – a storm that approaches Florida as a minimal hurricane, then explodes in intensity as it accelerates toward the coast. Andrew and Opal were somewhat like that, although fortunately Opal weakened before it came ashore. If a rapidly intensifying hurricane strikes an area that has a long evacuation time, thousands of residents could be caught in the storm's path, where they might be trapped in their cars or forced to remain in inadequate shelters. This is the nightmare that hurricane forecasters live with.

Unfortunately hurricanes are increasing in intensity and severity right along the Eastern seaboard of North America and this fear has yet to be tested.[14]

Is there time to make it?

When Jay Barnes joined the National Hurricane Center staff, the average forecast error in a 24-hour period was 120 nautical miles,

and when he left 25 years later it was only down to about 110 miles. During this time, the population of Florida's coastal areas was exploding. The increase in population has far exceeded any small improvement we have made in our ability to forecast hurricanes. Jay considers it unlikely that there will be any major breakthrough in the forecasting of hurricanes in the future. The atmosphere is too complex to allow the kind of precision forecasts that people who live on the coast today need.

A similar lack of precision in forecasting was a hallmark of the Great 1987 storm when forecaster Michael Fish famously said that there was no hurricane coming on the 6pm news before the rapidly developing storm struck early next morning. Here the unpredictability, as in Florida, becomes a factor in how many do, or could, die.

The basic reason for this is that it is still too difficult to forecast the weather accurately:[15]

We must remember, too, that the mathematical models used in numerical weather forecasting, though remarkably successful, can never fully represent the complexity of the real atmosphere. And complete observational coverage of the atmosphere over the oceans west and south of the British Isles will probably never be achieved.

The question here is will people be given enough warning time to evacuate an area. In some cases, the answer is no.

Evacuation plans

Whom to contact in emergencies

Many buildings and communities at times of flood do get cut off
from their escape routes by the rapidly rising water and need to
know an emergency number to call, such as the British service
'Floodline' – the Environment Agency Emergency hotline.[16] An
added risk factor, however, is that if an electricity blackout occurs
mobile phone systems can also go down and this should be
factored in to escape plans.

Where to go

Another factor to consider is that people have to know where they
can go to be safe. They should be told in advance that at times
of flood, fire, heat and storms that a safe centre has been established at a particular location that has links with the emergency
and health services, perhaps heating or cooling, dry clothes, bed-
ding and food. Every community should have an emergency centre identified, where access is possible without electric swipe cards
or locking systems, and everyone should know who is in charge.

Evacuation strategies for urban neighbourhoods

The problem in cities is that there are so many people to evacuate,
at times of crisis, that sheer numbers becomes the problem, particularly when urban neighbourhoods are already overcrowded. In
London it may be possible to cope with 300 extra commuters every
morning at rush hour on the existing tube system, but if the local
population increases by perhaps 2000, or even 10 000 people from
a couple of new tower blocks on a street (100–200 people a floor
on 50 floors), then transport services may not cope with them even
without an emergency. This problem was seen in the World Trade
Center, where the capacity population of the Twin Towers was around
20 000 people, and although less than half full, there was a significant problem with getting the people away from the towers, one
of which collapsed within three-quarters of an hour.

There is currently planned in Shanghai a super scraper called the
Bionic Tower that is designed to house 100 000 people. This is a
city prone to floods and typhoons, sitting as it does at the tip of
the Yangtze river, and as its mayor has admitted, it is badly prepared for any such emergencies[17] and could be struck by widespread flooding at any time, although it is hoped that the Three
Gorges Dam upstream will significantly reduce the risk to this
burgeoning city from fluvial flooding in the future.

Overpopulation problems result in 'funnelling' effects, for instance
of multiple commuters from district lines converging on single

stretches of line at particular hours of the day/week causing grid-lock. It is the 'surge' of moving people that debilitates systems of movement around a city, and before any new buildings are constructed in a city a very detailed study of the 'carrying capacity' of a city, and calculations of the optimal evacuation strategies for every locality, should be undertaken.

The problem is that not only are there too many people in one place but that the routes into and out of the city are dysfunctional. The mathematician Nickos Salingaros outlined how such movement systems work in his paper on 'urban webs'.[18] Salingaros outlined structural principles for urban form. The processes that generate the 'urban web' involve nodes, connections and the principles of hierarchy. Among the theoretical results derived from his work was a pattern of 'multiple connectivity', in which a city needs to have a variety of 'connections' so that people have a range of alternative routes through the city to avoid the problem of bottlenecks.

He investigated the city in terms of the types of uses the buildings are put to in the different areas of the city and a key risk factor he identified is that areas of the city become dominated by 'monofunctionality', a prime example being that of the single use 'megatower', or skyscraper. Not only do these create a 'mathematical singularity' where one or more quantities become extremely large or infinite, so detracting from the quality of the streetscape and city, but because such towers do, en masse, one thing only, as a result their occupants will behave en masse, needing to be evacuated all at the same time, if at all.

We have also learnt much from 9/11. The idea that any building could be evacuated three floors at a time (the principal on which building evacuation strategies for large buildings are now designed), after 9/11 is ludicrous. As soon as an emergency happens (like the blackouts of August 2003) everybody thinks it may be another 9/11 and gets out of the building straight away, regardless of what is said on the loud speaker system because, after 9/11, no one has faith in what they say on loud speakers. Also many building evacuation strategies are based on having 'pressurized' staircases, that in reality do not work once three or four doors onto that staircase are opened, and would not work once the energy in the buildings fails. This is an apparently clever idea that has to be rethought.

On a street, large monofunctional buildings drown out any of the human outflows from adjacent buildings in a district, when evacuation of an area is necessary, because of the sheer force of their outflow, rather as a gas or liquid would behave under the laws of fluid dynamics. Other people emerging from smaller adjacent buildings would need to find a quiet space in the slipstream of the dominant flow to hang onto, in order to have the chance of being carried away from the event. Put several such towers together and basically no one will get out safely because of the confusion, or turbulence, created at the meeting of major flows. Certainly the occupants of any smaller building between them would have to fight hard (so retarding the outflow of the major building) to have a chance of escape at all. So it is the nature of the interactions of people outflows from adjacent buildings (determined by mathematics), during periods of evacuation, as well as the simple numbers versus route ways calculations (determined by mathematics) that will determine who escapes from an area, as well as the fighting abilities of the evacuees. More men than women would probably escape, because they are stronger and the urge to survive is deep, so to some extent this could be modelled; but then British men may, perhaps, be more chivalrous, so this also would have to be factored into the equation.

In answer to a question from a major employer in a city on whether people will get out of the organization's building safely, many issues will have to be factored into the response including:

- What is the carrying capacity of the existing routes and transport systems in the city?
- What are they escaping from, e.g. floods, fire, bombs, excessively hot indoor temperatures etc.?
- Are their escape routes likely to be blocked?
- How long is the warning time they will get?
- What are the adjacent buildings like?
- Who are the people who want to escape?
- What is the use pattern of the building?
- Where will they go?
- Do they know where to go and how to get there?

Such planning is essential, not only for employees who want to survive, but for councils and businesses who need to demonstrate they have behaved responsibly in the face of risk, for insurance companies who need to know they are containing the risk they cover and for the government which needs to contain the growing risks of climate change, and terrorism.

The stakes are high. For instance, in the case of London, recent estimates suggest that if a tidal surge comes over the top of the Thames Barrier, the cost would be in the region of £30 billion, or 2% of UK GDP.[19] What would be the cost of paying for loss of life resulting from what could have been predicted by proper planning? Where does the legal buck stop in such an event?

Due to the increasing unpredictability of global storm tracks, no new, or existing, development or neighbourhood should now be without a strategy for dealing with the eventuality of encountering an extreme windstorm, no matter where in the world they are built.

NOTES AND REFERENCES

1 See http://www.munichre.com/pdf/TOPICSgeo_2003_e.pdf.

2 Stirling, R. (1997) *The Weather of Britain*. London: Giles de la Mare.

3 http://www.ibhs.org/publications/view.asp?id=455.

4 Garvin, S.L., Phillipson, M.C., Sanders, C.H., Hayles, C.S. and Dow, G.T. (1998) *Impact of Climate Change on Building*. East Kilbride: Building Research Establishment.

5 Mootoosamy, V.K.S. and Baker, M.J. (1998) *Wind Damage to Buildings in the United Kingdom*. University of Aberdeen, Department of Engineering. Published by the Loss Prevention Council, Paper LPR 8: 1998, Watford.

6 Buller, P.S.J. (1988) *The October Gale of 1987: Damage to Buildings and Structures in the South-East of England*. Watford: Building Research Establishment.

7 Sparks, Peter (1990) *Defending Against the Wind*. Paper presented at the National Committee on Property Insurance Annual Forum, Boston, MA, December 1990.

8 *Guardian*, 4 November 2003, p. 16.

9 *Guardian*, 24 September 2001.

10 http://www.turkishdailynews.com/old_editions/11_04_98/for2.htm.

11 *Guardian*, 4 December 2003, p. 19.

12 Barnes, J. (2003) *Florida's Hurricane History*. Chapel Hill, NC: University of North Carolina Press (first edition 1998).

13 http://www.ibiblio.org/uncpress/hurricanes/fl_foreword.html.

14 Goldenberg, S.B., Landsea, C.W., Mestas-Nunez, A.M. and Gray, W.M. (2001) The recent increase in Atlantic hurricane activity: causes and implications. *Science*, 293, 20 July.

15 http://www.met-office.gov.uk/education/historic/1987.html.

16 See www.environment-agency.gov.uk/floodwarning; the British Floodline is on 0845 988 1188.

17 http://www.china.org.cn/english/12537.htm.

18 Salingaros, N. (1998) Theory of the urban web. *Journal of Urban Design*, 3, 53–71. For the full paper see http://www.math.utsa.edu/sphere/salingar/urbanweb.html. © Taylor & Francis Limited. See also Kunstler, J.H. and Salingaros, N. (2001) The end of tall buildings, on http://www.peoplesgeography.org/ tall.html.

19 *Guardian*, 9 January 2004, p. 11.

8 SEA LEVEL RISES

Since the end of the last Ice Age, some 18 000 years ago, sea level has risen by over 120 m. On average, sea levels may have risen at a rate of 0.1–0.2 mm per year over the past 3000 years globally, but in the 20th century this increased to 1–2 mm per year.

In 1995, 2.2 billion people lived within 100 km of a coastline, nearly 39% of the world's populations, and many of these people will be directly affected by rising sea levels in three ways:

- As seas rise many areas of the coast will be inundated.
- With increasingly severe and frequent storms and wave damage, shoreline retreat will be accelerated.
- Catastrophic flooding events may be caused by a combination of climate events such as heavy flooding, high tides, windstorms in combination with higher seas.

This issue of how much of a low-lying shoreline retreats with increases in sea levels is a complex one and depends very much on the behaviour of incoming currents, wave patterns, the structure, materials and form of the shoreline, and wave heights in that area and the care with which the coastline is managed.[1]

While sea level is predicted to rise almost everywhere, there is considerable spatial variation; in some regions the rise is close to zero, while others experience as much as twice the global average value. The predicted patterns show large increases in sea level in parts of the north Pacific and to the west of Greenland. Confidence in the regional sea level rise predictions, that indicate global rises of between 30 and 80 cm by 2100, is not as great as for temperature predictions.[2]

As the world warms, it is predicted that global average sea levels may rise by between 7 and 36 cm by the 2050s, by between 9 and 69 cm by the 2080s and 30–80 cm by 2100. The majority of this change will occur due to the expansion of the warmer ocean water. The UKCIP team does not consider it likely that the melting

(a)

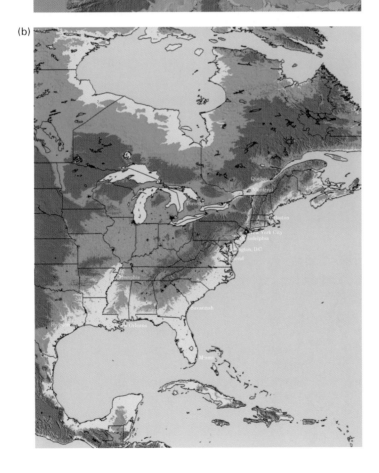

(b)

8.1.
Computer models of what
(a) Europe and (b) North America
may look like if the global ice
reserves melted raising the sea
levels by 100 m. (*Source:*
Laurence O. Williams (2002)
An End to Global Warming.
Pergamon, reproduced with
permission)

of the West Antarctic ice sheet will contribute much to sea level rises in the 21st century, although its impact, if it does melt, would be catastrophic in the 22nd century, making sea levels rise as much as 70 m. Indeed, the Antarctic, by acting as a storage area for snowfall, will continue to help to mitigate rising sea levels for many decades to come.[3]

The temperatures of UK coastal waters are increasing, although not as rapidly as temperatures over the land, with again the greatest warming in the south. Offshore waters in the English Channel may warm in summer by between 2 °C and 4 °C by the 2080s.[4]

The relative sea level will continue to rise around most of the UK shoreline, with the rate depending on the scenario and the

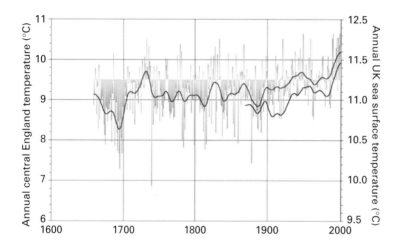

8.2.
As the global climate warms so the seas of the world warm too. This is reflected in this graph showing the warming of the climate in central England (red) and the surrounding UK coastal waters (blue). The deviations here are relative to the 1961–90 average, and not the different scale for each. (*Source:* UKCIP02 Climate Change Scenarios, funded by DEFRA, produced by Tyndall and Hadley Centres for UKCIP)

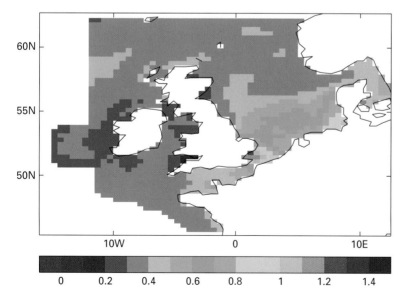

8.3.
One of the most dangerous areas of sea around the British Isles is that between Southeast England and France, where the extreme water height is higher than in any other stretch of British waters. The figure shows the change, by the 2080s, in the height (metres) of the extreme sea level that has a 2% chance of occurring in any given year for the *Medium High Emissions* scenario, with the mid-range estimate of 30 cm global sea level rise. (*Source:* UKCIP02 Climate Change Scenarios, funded by DEFRA, produced by Tyndall and Hadley Centres for UKCIP)

region. This is because some parts of the UK land mass are actually rising, in the northwest of Scotland for instance, while other areas like Southeast England are sinking relative to sea levels. This is due to isostatic rebound in Scotland as the land recovers from the weight of the glaciers of the last Ice Age, leading to a lowering of land in the south due to 'tilting' of the tectonic plate. By the 2080s, and depending on the scenario, sea levels may be between 2 and 58 cm above the current level in western Scotland and between 26 and 86 cm above the current level in Southeast England.

Extreme sea levels, occurring though combinations of high tides, sea level rise and changes in winds, will be experienced more frequently in many coastal locations. For some English east coast locations, for example, a water level that at present has a 2% probability of occurring in any given year, may have an annual occurrence probability of 33% by the 2080s for the *Medium High Emissions* scenario. Sea level rises may also lead to deeper water

Table 8.1. The historic rates of vertical land movement and the estimated net change in sea level by the 2080s using the low end of the *Low Emissions* scenario (9 cm global sea level rise) and the high end of the *High Emissions* scenario (69 cm rise)

	Vertical land change (mm/yr)	Sea level change 2080s (cm) relative to 1961–90	
		Low emissions	High emissions
NE Scotland	+0.7	1	61
SE Scotland	+0.8	0	60
NE England	+0.3	6	66
Yorkshire	−0.5	15	75
East Midlands	−1.0	20	80
Eastern England	−1.2	22	82
London	−1.5	26	86
SE England	−0.9	19	79
SW England	−0.6	16	76
Wales	−0.2	11	71
Northern Ireland	n/a	9*	69*
NW England	+0.2	7	67
SW Scotland	+1.0	−2	58
NW Scotland	+0.9	−1	59
Orkney & Shetland	n/a	9*	69*
Global-average	n/a	9*	69*

*These estimates in the sea-level change exclude the vertical land changes.
Source: UKCIP02 Climate Change Scenarios, funded by DEFRA, produced by Tyndall and Hadley Centres for UKCIP.

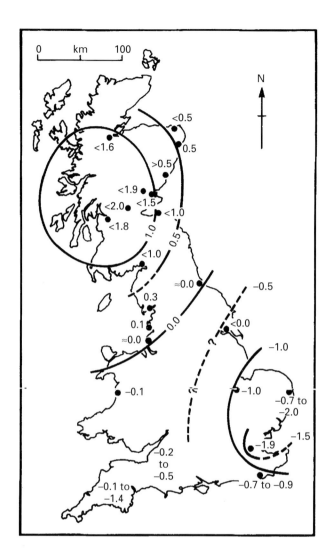

8.4.
Estimate of the present (late Holocene) rates of relative land changes (mm/yr). Positive values indicate relative land uplift, negative values are relative land subsidence. Contours have been drawn by eye. The effects of sediment consolidation are not included. (*Source:* UKCIP02 Climate Change Scenarios, funded by DEFRA, produced by Tyndall and Hadley Centres for UKCIP, and Ian Shennan, 1989)

in the near-shore zone allowing waves greater energy to reach the shore line, so significantly increasing storm damage to shore lines.

Even if greenhouse gases in the atmosphere are stabilized, further substantial increases in sea level over many centuries remain inescapable due to the extremely slow response of the oceans to air temperature.

The question has been raised in the media of the effect of climate change on the 'Gulf Stream', one of the three main ocean conveyors, the great currents that drive the seas – the Atlantic, the Pacific and the Indian Ocean, known also as the 'thermohaline' loops.

The ability of the oceans to convey heat is dependent on the salinity of the water. If the oceans become more saline, they become more efficient in transporting warm water from the equatorial regions to the temperate zones. The North Atlantic Conveyor, also called the North Atlantic Drift but commonly referred to as the 'Gulf Stream', brings warm weather to the UK from the tropics and via the north American and Canadian coasts. It also melts Arctic ice, reducing the amount of sunshine reflected back into space (the albedo) and this has a global warming effect. As the Conveyor becomes more active, more heat is taken from the Southern and Indian oceans. (The South Pole is insulated from the Conveyor by the Antarctic Circumpolar Current and is not affected by this.)

There comes a point where the amount of freshwater from Greenland and Arctic ice melt plus the increase in freshwater flows from rivers in Siberia reduces the salinity to the stage where the flow of heat is reduced or interrupted for a spell. This happened around 1900 in the North Atlantic, for example, and again around 1960 ('The Great Salt Anomaly'). Each time this was followed by several years of unusually cold weather in the UK (1900–05, and 1963–71), a phenomenon also described as 'oceanic flip flop'. There is not yet a scientific consensus on the question of whether climate change will interrupt the flow of the Gulf Stream,[5] but if it did the consequences would be very serious, especially for the British Isles.

The UKCIP studies point to the fact that the Gulf Stream will continue to exert a very important influence on the UK climate. Although its strength may weaken in the future, perhaps by as much as 25% by 2100, it is unlikely that this would lead to a shut down of the Gulf Stream and a resulting permanent cooling of the UK climate within the next 100 years since the warming from the greenhouse gases will more than offset any cooling from a weakening of the Gulf Stream. All of the changes included in the UKCIP02 report reflect this predicted weakening of the Gulf Stream. However,

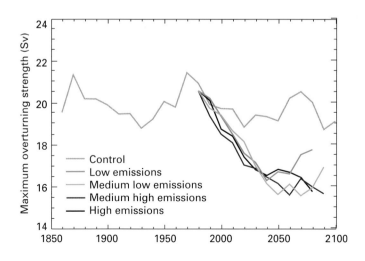

8.5.
Simulations by the Hadley Centre show a weakening of the Gulf Stream during the 21st century although 'flip flop', the shutting down of the flow, is not considered likely this century. (*Source:* UKCIP02 Climate Change Scenarios, funded by DEFRA, produced by Tyndall and Hadley Centres for UKCIP; *Briefing Report*,[15] p. 14)

not enough is known about the factors that control ocean circulations to be completely confident about this prediction, especially in the longer term.

WHAT MAKES SEA LEVELS RISE?

Sea level changes are caused by:

- The thermal expansion of the oceans.
- The melting of glaciers.
- Changes to the major Greenland and Antarctic ice sheets.

The thermal expansion of the oceans

As the temperature of the waters in the oceans rises and the seas become less dense, they expand and will spread, occupying more surface area on the planet causing inundation of low lying areas. Increased temperature will accelerate the rate of sea level rise. Since the end of the last Ice Age, 18 000 years ago, sea level has risen by over 120 m.

The melting of the glaciers

This is occurring at an alarming rate with glaciers, on five major continents disappearing rapidly. The ice cap on Mount Kilimanjaro may be gone in 20 years and the summer of 2003 saw melting of the perma-frost levels in many parts of the Alps destabilizing mountain slopes and closing off the Matterhorn to visitors for the first time in its history. Temperature changes are already causing 90% of the world's glaciers to retreat and some to disappear completely, with potentially catastrophic consequences for communities that rely on melt water for irrigation, hydroelectric power and drinking water, and also communities affected by sea level rises.

In the Alps, where summer temperatures have risen by 2.1 °C since the 1970s, summer flows in glacier-fed rivers have doubled, enabling hydroelectric dams to remain full and power stations to generate at maximum capacity, helping to take up the load slack from the nuclear power stations that, due to low river flow elsewhere, could not generate at full capacity during the heat wave of 2003 in Europe. So there are many other knock-on effects from such melts.

In the longer term many glaciers will only survive at the highest altitudes. Only Scandinavian and Alaskan glaciers are not receding, and in some cases are increasing due to increased snowfall locally, another side effect of climate change.

Another problem is that due to the higher atmospheric pressure experienced in the Alps there is now less snowfall there resulting

(a)

(b)

8.6.
(a) When Mark Lynas's father photographed this fan-shaped glacier in the Jacabamba valley in the eastern Cordillera Blanca in Peru in 1980 he little thought that his son would revisit it 20 years later to find that it had completely disappeared (b). Note the severe thinning of the ice field on the skyline above the lake. (*Source:* (a) Bryan Lynas; (b) Tim Helweg-Larsen in Mark Lynas (2004) *High Tide: News from a Warming World*, Flamingo)

in glaciers not being replenished as before. Scandinavia, by contrast, is in the path of the changed track of the Atlantic depressions, as is Britain, resulting in extra rainfall in these countries. In other regions of the world the picture is much worse; the glaciers of Central Asia are disappearing at a rapid rate threatening severe future drinking water deficits in countries such as Kazakhstan as the river run-off is reduced. A further problem is the mounds of rubble left behind them, in which meltwater accumulates in dams that could burst and cause catastrophic flooding to settlements downstream.

Changes to the major Greenland, Arctic and Antarctic ice

At very high northern latitudes, in and around the Arctic sea, ice loss will be dramatic although in the southern oceans around Antarctica that rate of ice loss will be slower. The maximum melt of the Greenland ice sheet has increased on average by 16% from 1979 to 2002. The melting in the winter of 2002 to 2003 was unprecedented, in a year when the sea ice in the Arctic was at its lowest level ever recorded. The warming of Greenland and the Arctic is already increasing the rate of sea level rises, mainly due to the dynamic response of the large ice sheet rather than just the melting of the ice. For every degree increase in mean annual temperature near Greenland, the rate of sea level rises increases by about 10%.[6]

Monitoring has shown that currently the oceans are rising around 5 cm every ten years. Both sea and glacier ice cool the earth, reflecting back into space about 80% of the spring time and 40–50% of summer time sunshine The winter sea ice cover is extremely important to the global climate as it slows heat loss from the relatively warm ocean to the cold atmosphere and without the large sea ice masses at the poles to moderate the energy balance, global warming will escalate.

At the current rate of thawing the Arctic sea ice could, according to Professor Johannessen of Nansen Environmental and Remote Sensing Centre in Bergen, Norway, disappear completely by the end of the century, having a serious effect on the wildlife of the region, such as the 22 000 polar bears that depend on the pack ice during their seal hunting seasons. The estimated fall in sea ice of up to 60% on Canada's east coast is also having a devastating effect on the seal populations who rely on the ice during the pup rearing season.[7]

The Antarctic Peninsular is one of the three places on the globe that is warming more quickly than initially predicted at the moment. It is the speed of such local warming that could trigger unexpected events. Not only are the breeding grounds for species, such as the penguin colonies, shifting with the warming climate, but the pattern of snowfall is changing and threatening the nesting habits of the birds. Many Antarctic species are susceptible to very small changes in climate.[8]

The Antarctic is the world's largest remaining wilderness region; it is larger than the United States, and drier than the Sahara. Parts of it are covered by 3000 m of compacted ice and snow and the continent is the repository of nine-tenths of the world's fresh water.[9]

IMPACTS OF SEA LEVEL RISES

Inundation of coastal communities

Sea levels will rise almost everywhere but at very different rates, with some areas having very little rise and others over the twice

(a)

8.7.
Arctic perennial sea ice has been decreasing at a rate of 9% per decade. The first image (a) shows the minimum sea ice concentration for the year 1979, and the second image (b) shows the minimum sea ice concentration in 2003. The data used to create these images were collected by the Defense Meteorological Satellite Program (DMSP) Special Sensor Microwave Imager (SSMI). (*Source:* NASA and http://www.gsfc.nasa.gov/gsfc/ earth/pictures/2003/1023esuice/ STILLsea79.jpg)

(b)

the global average rises. The predicted patterns show large increases in sea level in parts of the north Pacific.[2]

Many islands around the world will disappear as sea levels rise. Tuvalu may have the first large inhabited island to be lost forever. It comprises nine coral atolls located between Australia and Hawaii. Their highest point is 5 meters (15 feet) above seal level. As sea level has risen, Tuvalu has experienced lowland flooding. Salt water intrusion is adversely affecting drinking water and food production.

8.8.
Woman carrying a bowl of food through the flood waters in the centre of Funafuti atoll of the South Pacific to a gathering in the nearby community centre. The tidal floods, brought on by rising sea levels, were up to a foot deep in places. (*Source:* Mark Lynas (2004) *High Tide: News from a Warming World*, Flamingo)

Tuvalu's leaders predict that the nation will be submerged in 50 years, but this may be very optimistic as much of the island is already covered by water at regular intervals during the year. In March 2002 the country's prime minister appealed to Australia and New Zealand to provide homes for his people if his country is washed away, but the plight of this nation is being ignored.[10]

Other threatened island nations include the Cook Islands and the Marshall Islands. During the past decade, the island of Majuro (Marshall Islands) has lost up to 20 per cent of its beachfront.

In addition to island nations, low-lying coastal countries are threatened by rising sea level. A 1 m rise in sea level, inevitable under current CO_2 emissions scenarios, would inundate half of Bangladesh's rice land and flood large areas of rice-growing nations such as Vietnam, China, India and Thailand. There are areas of large-scale population particularly vulnerable to sea level rise in the Philippines, Indonesia and Egypt.

The eastern coastline of the United States is also extremely vulnerable to coastal erosion, with shorelines retreating rapidly in some regions, resulting in the narrowing of beaches and washing out of vacation houses, exacerbated by the more frequent and intense hurricanes along the eastern seaboard.

Coastal flooding in the UK

In Britain the impacts of the combination of sea level rises and stormier weather are set to take a high toll. Much of the British coastline will experience rising seas and stormier weather, and amongst others, the National Trust, which owns 600 miles of coast-line, is engaged in a 'managed retreat' from threatened coastlines. A number of its key sites will be threatened; seaside properties in the picturesque villages like Porthleven, Mullion, Birling Gap and Brownsea, as well as major sites like Lindisfarne Castle and St Michael's Mount, are at risk.[11]

Settlements have evolved with defences designed to cope with historic sea levels and extreme heights of flood or storm surges. It is the surge height of a river or ocean wave that causes the most damage and over-tops defences, and this height will be raised above previous historic levels, exacerbated by sea level rises and more intense storms. The risk of London flooding is increasing year on year. The Thames Barrier, built at a cost of £50 million in 1984 to protect the capital from tidal surges until 2030, is clearly not going to be able to protect London from a flood like that of 1953 by then.[12]

This area of Southeast England has suffered throughout recorded history from catastrophic inundations, and London is particularly

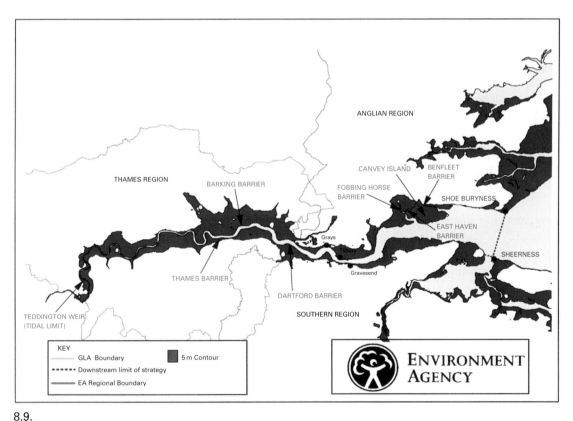

8.9.
The historic flood plain of the lower Thames Estuary showing the areas that have historically flooded during periods of tidal surges. (*Source:* Environment Agency)

vulnerable, being sited on the conjunction of the mouth of the flood-prone Thames river valley and the end of a storm surge-prone estuary (see Box 8.1).

Box 8.1 Some examples of fatal floods in London's history[i]

1236 – Floods caused by a high storm surge tide in November drowned many people and a great number of cattle in the Woolwich area.

1242 – Heavy rain and thunderstorms on 19 November and on many days thereafter; the Thames flooded at Westminster and Lambeth.

1663 – A flood, driven by gales and produced by a high tide that was said not to have been exceeded for more than 200 years submerged Whitehall.

1703 – November: The Great Storm. The tidal flood affecting the Thames on 30 November was associated with this storm, though the tidal storm surge for this event was more significant on the Severn and along the Dutch coast. Twelve warships with 1300 men on board were lost in sight of land, Eddystone lighthouse was destroyed and practically all shipping in the Thames was destroyed or damaged. In London alone 22 people were drowned, 21 people were killed and 200 injured by falling and flying debris. It was estimated that 8000 people lost their lives in the floods caused by the storm in the rivers Thames and Severn and in Holland. The damage due to the storm and flood in London alone was estimated then to be £2 million.

1809 – January: A flood occurred, which may have been tidal in the lower reaches of the Thames, and carried away bridges at Eton, Deptford and Lewisham. Flooding was noted at Windsor.

1953 – 31 January to 1 February: The North Sea Storm Surge. A northerly severe gale/violent storm (mean speeds up to 70 knots/80 mph, with gusts in exposed areas in excess of 100 knots/115 mph) developed as a depression deepened as it moved east-northeast just to the north of Scotland. Then on the 31 January, still deepening, it turned and accelerated southeastwards across the North Sea, making landfall in the Elbe–Weser estuary in northwest Germany late in the evening. As a result of the storm, the ferry *Princess Victoria* foundered during a crossing of the Irish Sea, with the loss of 132 lives. Much damage (loss of timber) was done to afforested areas in Scotland too. The major well-known effect of this storm was due to a combination of events, which brought tragedy to many living in low-lying areas on either side of the southern North Sea. The rapidly reducing pressure allowed a rise in water level; a sharp recovery (or rise) in pressure to the west of Ireland tightened the gradient on the western flank of the low pressure area; the state of the tide (spring/full-moon) and of course the driving of huge quantities of water towards the narrower southern portion of the

North Sea gave rise to severe inundation of coastal areas in England (from the Humber estuary in the north to the Thames Estuary and east Kent coast in the south), Belgium and the Netherlands, with much loss of life. The situation was not helped due to the fact that the rivers were full, attempting to discharge greater-than-average quantities of winter rain-water *against* the wind-driven surge. The UK Storm Tide Warning Service was inaugurated after these floods,[ii] though the Dutch had had a similar service since the early part of the 20th century.

[i] From the excellent site: http://www.booty.demon.co.uk/climate/wxevents.htm).

[ii] The UK Storm Tide Warning Service can be contacted via the Environment Agency General Enquiry line: 0845 9333111; Floodline on 0845 9881188 gives information on all types of coastal and riverine flooding. For specific enquiries email the EA on enquiries@environment-agency.gov.uk).

In light of such an historic record of flooding and given that this area of Britain will see the great rises in sea levels it is easy to understand why so many people are concerned over the plans for the Thames Gateway project for 200 000 homes to the east of London. The development, it is hoped, will provide 300 000 jobs in an area that already has no job shortages and one that is prone to serious flooding and contains some of Britain's most valuable wildlife sites, 42 of them Sites of Special Scientific Interest. It reaches some 40 miles on each side of the Thames east of London and as planned will be one of the biggest construction projects Britain has seen since the post-war boom, with a proposed new airport at Cliffe, a deep-water port at Shellhaven and a second bridge across the lower Thames landing on the south side of the river at Higham Marshes in the EU Special Protection Area.[13]

The Association of British Insurers (ABI), who had not been consulted during the planning stages, were so concerned about the proposed location and the use of lightweight innovative construction methods such as timber and steel frame housing, which has proved to be high risk for insurers in the past, that they had not guaranteed to provide mortgages or house insurance for a single dwelling before plans were passed for the development. In a spectacular example of the lack of joined-up thinking the ABI were requiring that a substantial flood defence be placed around the whole development, possibly a double bund structure. This would inevitably push up flood water levels in the Thames Estuary so flooding other settlements on its coast and possibly, in conjunction with a storm surge and raised sea levels, push water over the Thames Barrier so flooding London. The Thames is the best defended river in the UK, with protection to a design standard of the 1000 year return period event. In The Netherlands they design for a 10000–20000 year event. Perhaps London should do the same. Planners are also concerned that there is only one road in and out of the heart of the Thames Gateway development and not only will this lead to congestion but it also means that in the event of an emergency, evacuation of the region would be slow at best, and at worst be halted by a single road accident.

While confidence in the regional sea level rise predictions is not as great as for temperature,[14] there is sufficient evidence for people to make informed and sensible decisions about where, and where not, to develop 'sustainable' communities. Perhaps the French word here is better. They use 'durable', meaning that they will last.

For instance, in choosing lightweight steel or timber innovative building types the ABI are worried that houses in the Thames Gateway development are too *vulnerable* to damage in the event of a flood, and that they are, being located in this flood zone, too *exposed* to the *hazard* of flooding. Increasingly planning for 'sustainability' will require that the exposure of new developments to such hazards be minimized and this may well mean far tighter planning controls on who lives or works on flood plains, or ultimately moving people to those areas of the country that will not flood and are capable of being evacuated rapidly and safely if they do. We may then see, over the next decades, the migration of populations to less climatically exposed regions of the British Isles.

NOTES AND REFERENCES

1 For a map of where these people live see: http://earthtrends. wri.org/text/POP/maps/196.htm and for a detailed discussion of the impacts of shoreline management see: http://www.survas. mdx.ac.uk/pdfs/3mizutan.pdf.

2 See: http://www.metoffice.gov.uk/research/hadleycentre/pubs/ brochures/B2000/predictions.html.

3 *Guardian*, 4 September 2003, p. 15.

4 Hulme, M., Jenkins, G., Lu, X., Turnpenny, J., Mitchell, T., Jones, R., Lowe, J., Murphy, J., Hassell, D., Boorman, P., McDonald, R. and Hill, S. (2002) *Climate Change Scenarios for the United Kingdom: The UKCIP02 Scientific Report, Appendix 2* published in conjunction with UKCIP, the Hadley Centre and the Climate Research Unit in the School of Environmental Science at the University of East Anglia, by the Tyndall Centre, Norwich. http://www.ukcip.org.uk/publications/pub.html.

5 For a fuller discussion of this phenomenon and related arguments see Crichton, D. (2001) *The Implications of Climate
   Change for the Insurance Industry: An Update and the Outlook
   to 2020.* Garston, Watford: Building Research Establishment.
   See http://www.brebookshop.com. See also for a concise
   website on the subject: http://www.doc.mmu.ac.uk/aric/eae/
   Climate/Older/Gulf_Stream.html.

6 *Guardian*, 11 January 2003, p. 9, quoting the work of Professor
   Konrad Steffan, a geographer at Colorado State University.

7 *Independent*, 10 March 2003, p. 5.

8 *Guardian*, 9 September 2003, p. 9.

9 http://www.antarctica.ac.uk/About_Antarctica/Ice/index.html.

10 For an excellent description of the current state of flooding in
   Tuvalu and a fascinating first-hand description of a wide range
   of climate change impacts around the world see Lynas, Mark
   (2004) *High Tide: News from a Warming World.* Flamingo.

11 http://www.nationaltrust.org.uk/coastline/save/coastal_erosion.
   html.

12 *Observer,* 22 December 2003, p. 5.

13 *Guardian,* Society, 12 March 2003, p. 8.

14 see http://www.metoffice.gov.uk/research/hadleycentre/pubs/
   brochures/B2000/predictions.html.

15 Hulme, M.J., Turnpenny, J. and Jenkins, G. (2002) *Climate
   Change Scenarios for the United Kingdom: The UKCIP02
   Briefing Report.* Published in conjunction with UKCIP, the
   Hadley Centre and the Climate Research Unit in the School
   of Environmental Science at the University of East Anglia, by
   the Tyndall Centre, Norwich.

9 VULNERABILITY, EXPOSURE AND MIGRATION

MIGRATION

Definition (http://www.hyperdictionary.com/dictionary/migration):

1 the movement of persons from one country or locality to another
   the periodic passage of groups of animals (especially birds or
   fishes) from one region to another for feeding or breeding
2 (chemistry) the nonrandom movement of an atom or radical
   from one place to another within a molecule
3 a group of people migrating together (especially in some given
   time period)

Over 175 million people now live outside the country of their birth –
double the figure in 1975. Many are economic migrants, who may
be fleeing poverty and severe deprivation. They are an important
development resource for their home countries, remitting about
US$80 billion per year to developing nations, compared to the $50
billion such countries receive in world aid.[1]

Environmental refugees currently outnumber those fleeing from
war, political or religious persecution and could soon reach 20 million people a year. By 2050 the new Economics Foundation claims
that around 150 million people will be displaced by the impacts of
climate change and such refugees will be a major cause of global
instability and a fertile breeding ground for bitterness and resentments, and terrorism.[2]

The Third Report from the International Development Committee
of the House of Commons, on 'Global climate change and sustainable
development' (2002), stated:[3]

Where vulnerability is extreme, often populations are left with no alternative but to migrate. It is often used as a means of last resort.

Migration is an important traditional coping mechanism to deal with climatic
situations that are not survivable, and as such is an adaptation strategy. But

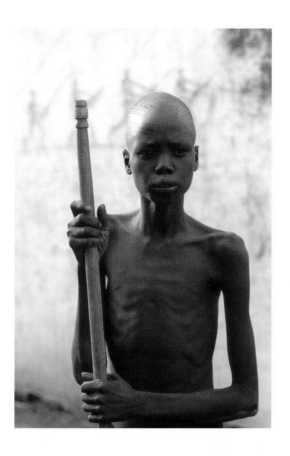

9.1.
Children across the world are becoming climate refugees, such as this young man in Sudan. Would you close the door on his future which is now threatened by a combination of climate change and war. (*Source:* Adrian Arbib)

the right to migrate is increasingly being contested and is a source of conflict in many societies. Many of those displaced in Bangladesh by rising sea levels will migrate to India, exacerbating already high levels of illegal migration. The immigration populations of the Sahel into the Ivory Coast was on such a scale that the Ivory Coast had introduced legislation preventing foreign nationals from owning land. There is no international recognition of environmental refugees; they are not entitled to the same rights as refugees from conflict and persecution. The UK Government has no specific policy to deal with them. The British Bangladeshi Professional Association called for a new convention to protect the rights of environmental refugees in the same way that refugees fleeing conflict or persecution are protected under international law. The need for national and international policies to deal with 'environmental' refugees will become greater as more people are temporarily or permanently displaced from their homes by more frequent and more intense climate disasters or by progressive climate change, such as rising sea levels or desertification. DFID [Department of Food and International Development of the UK Government] was recommended by the Commons committee to push for a policy on 'environmental' refugees. Any policy response must recognize that this issue cuts across several [government] departments.

Migration has traditionally been seen as a 'reaction' to environmental disasters, but in an age where we have the tools and methodologies to predict, and imagine, future impacts the movement of peoples must be developed as a 'proactive' tool. For instance, the inhabitants of Tuvalu, mentioned in Chapter 8, know very well their plight, but even today as their islands flood they have nowhere to go.

Every region and country should have well-developed models of what climate change will do to their industries, populations and ecosystems now, in order that humane political decisions on the movement of peoples in the future can be carefully planned to avoid the later devastation in extreme climate events.

Perhaps one of the most effective adaptation skills our society could develop would be to train enough climate modellers to be able to inform a generation of decision-makers, and the communities they serve, on how to minimize the impacts of climate change on populations. But it would depend on who was being affected, because we all know that humane political decisions often do not win votes, regardless of who is doing the polluting. Such information may also be against the entrenched interests of some politicians and industries.

We know enough already, in many instances, for it to be arguably irresponsible not to act to engineer our future history to minimize the impacts of our actions today on the well-being of the children of tomorrow. The careful, pre-emptive planning, and movement, of future populations is one of the most effective methods we have of minimizing such impacts, across the world or just across a town.

The polluters should pay

The costs of supporting climate refugees is now a matter for open negotiations. Many are now questioning why, when it is the rich countries that are creating the pollution that is driving climate change, it falls on the shoulders of many of the world's poorest countries, and continents, to foot the bill for those peoples displaced by that climate change.

The New Economics Foundation warned in September 2003 that the rich countries of the world must be prepared to take their fair share of the refugees created by climate change, in an extension of the 'Polluters Pay' principal. This states that:[2]

People whose environments are damaged and destroyed and who are losing their livelihoods, should be recompensed and protected by those responsible.

The Foundation suggested that the Geneva Convention should be expanded to include those displaced by environmental degradation.

They argue that, despite widespread denials of liability, where countries continue to pollute when they are fully aware of the damaging consequences, they should be made to reflect their liability by taking in climate refugees. To disregard knowledge should be classed as intentional behaviour, and could be considered as environmental persecution. Environmental refugees currently outnumber those fleeing from war, political or religious persecution and could reach 20 million people a year. The number of refugees taken in, they suggest, should be proportional to the amount of pollution a country generates.

The UK, for instance, produces around 3% of greenhouse gas emissions and of the 20 million refugees created a year they should be liable to take in 300,000. The figure for the United States, which generates 25% of all greenhouse gases, would be 5 million refugees a year. They cite the fact that rich countries spend around £50 billion a year subsidizing fossil fuel industries but around £300 000 helping poor countries manage their emissions and adapt to climate change.

The idea that the impacts and severity of climate change could, over the coming decades, become the subject of international litigation is interesting; that the polluters will have to pay could add billions to the budgets of countries as they face the challenges of footing the bill for climate change in the future. But it is also within countries that the issue of responsibility for paying for climate change impacts becomes critical.

In a desperate attempt to get the Bush administration to accept its responsibilities in relation to climate change, a dozen US states have filed a suit against the US government to force them to act on global climate change.[4] In the current suit the states claim that the agency is ignoring federal studies that demonstrate that climate change is causing 'disease, extreme weather, destruction of shoreline and loss of critical wetlands and estuaries'. What is not cited are the economic and human impacts of the desertification of tracts of the Mid-West and the huge costs of the inevitable, and happening, mass migration of people from stricken areas as agriculture is devastated by the climate.

In the UK could similar charges be levelled? The already stretched water reserves of the southeastern area of England are to be required to supply a massive increase in homes and population in the region, imposed upon them by the current government, so threatening future availability of summer water supplies in the region.[5] Will such decisions be the source of law suits, either from water utility companies that will find it increasingly expensive to make less water go further, or from populations whose water bills rise to insupportable levels because of injudicious decisions by transient governments? Similarly as whole neighbourhoods of a city have their transport, sewerage, water and electricity services compromised to support a monster building, for instance, whose developers have sold, profited and moved on without paying for any of the environmental impacts of that building, will the polluters, in these cases, be made to pay?

One of the core issues here is the extent of the vulnerability of communities to impacts.

VULNERABILITY

Many sources expand on the perception that the impacts of climate change will not be evenly spread across the globe and are likely to fall disproportionately on the poor.[3] Such studies typically outline the potential impacts on the developing world. The Tyndall Centre, of the University of East Anglia, did an excellent study in Vietnam,[6] demonstrating that those already marginalized in the economy were likely to suffer the greatest impacts as they had the fewest resources for coping with adverse change, a finding reflected in a number of other studies.[7]

In the Commons Select Committee report on global climate change referred to earlier, it was repeatedly stressed that climate change has the potential to increase further the inequality between developed and developing countries. As with corruption and HIV/AIDS, they claim, climate change could undermine development investment.[3] However, unlike corruption or HIV/AIDS, climate change is not widely recognized as an immediate problem because many of its impacts have been, to date, gradual and long-term.

9.2.
Regional depopulation may be accelerated by a compounding of issues such as low rain fall, pollution of water, waste, over population and high temperatures. (*Source:* Adrian Arbib)

The relative economic severity of climate events in different regions may be influenced by a wide range of factors from the large difference in the value put on a life in different parts of the world, to multiple impacts resulting from the interaction of different factors and events in a particular region. The relative *vulnerability* of a settlement, as may be demonstrated by cost of property repair or death tolls during droughts or heavy rains, may accrue largely from the compounding of contributory factors to those deaths or damage by, for instance, the incidence of local land and water pollution, as much as to the relative *exposure* of a settlement to a flood/drought *hazard* in the region.[8]

Insurance statistics do not illustrate well the compounding of such physical factors or the interrelationship of more complex human, historic or economic trends that might influence the level of impacts resulting from the slow desertification and abandonment of regions, the sinking of water tables, or many other aspects of climate change that will fuel human migrations. They do not also address the external costs that those regions will have to pay when accepting incoming refugees.

There is also little evidence of work having been done on quantifying the vulnerability of populations to long-term internal costs. If, for instance, the Thames flooded, inundating riverside homes in the capital or fashionable riverside sites, many very rich people, including MPs, could lose their life's savings that are wrapped up in, say, a Westminster flat. How does one calculate the knock-on impacts on an economy of the loss of the lifetime investment of thousands of people?

In the UK, at the time of writing, the Association of British Insurers has said that the current guaranteed availability of flood insurance for areas where the flood risk is less than one in 75 years will be reviewed annually and may cease after 2007. Whether the ABI then decides to insure the homes in an area will depend on whether the government has, or has not, constructed adequate flood defence works in that area by that time and tightened planning controls locally. In many areas such assurances will not be forthcoming and insurance withheld. Where are the economic impacts of that withholding then recorded?

People who have, perhaps £200 000 mortgages on such properties may spend the rest of their working lives paying off such a mortgage on a property that is virtually un-sellable. Such people may no longer be able to afford to live in expensive cities and may have to move to where they can afford housing in the future.

Similarly, insurance companies and banks that have invested in inner city properties that are shown to be increasingly expensive to heat, cool and maintain as the climate warms and the costs of energy rise may find it impossible to sell such 'White Elephant' or 'Dog' buildings, and sections of the markets, where large amounts of equity are placed in real estate, could collapse, taking swathes of white collar workers and their families into poverty. Similar results could accrue from the direct impacts of catastrophic storms that destroy vulnerable buildings, or fires or urban flooding. Buildings, or whole areas of a city, may become subject to negative equity within minutes.

What we learnt in the summer of 2003, as the lights went out in cities around the world (for millions of people in Italy because a single tree blew across a power line in a storm), was that in fact the people in the buildings of New York were the most vulnerable of all during power failures. High rise buildings had to empty within minutes because the air was no longer breathable according to some evacuees. Those in simple traditional buildings in cities in the developing world where the power failed often hardly noticed it, getting on with life as usual until the power went back on. What would have happened if the electricity had failed in New York in a blizzard? Perhaps it is time for the developed nations to look at the issue of vulnerability very closely in relation to their own cities and lifestyles.

As the pressures of climate change bites, the vulnerability of populations to it will spread, from the dried-out Mid-West of America, hurricane-struck Florida, the flooded coastal flats of the Thames Estuary, or to the deserts of Africa and the Middle East. Populations will not stay where they no longer have homes they can afford to live in, food or water enough to survive, and they will bring their anger to town, as has happened throughout history. When the Nile or the Rhine flooded, people came to the nearest towns and cities in hope of surviving there, and were willing to take what they need to survive.

In an interesting study, written in the late 1930s, S.F. Markham, an extremely influential climatic determinist, mapped those areas of the world that could comfortably house European populations without too much heating and cooling.[9] He argued that all those areas without shading in Figure 9.3, above and below the tropics, would require large amounts of energy to keep 'civilised whitemen' comfortable, but, he opined, the domination of the white European in the world would be established with the uptake of air conditioning in those areas where it was too hot to survive in a 'civilised' fashion without it. He also went on to point out that air conditioning, even in the hottest climate, gave people the 'zest' to dance, eat, work, earn and spend money. It is an interesting line of thought to associate global politics, religion and capitalism with the joys of air conditioning. Recent studies, however, have begun to indicate that in some climates people will spend more time out of doors,

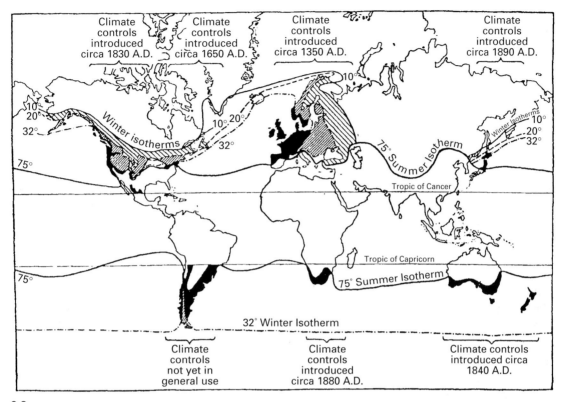

9.3.
Areas of the world where the warmest months do not exceed a mean of 75 °F and the mean for the coldest month does not fall below 32°, 20° or 10 °F. (Tropical areas within these limits have been excluded because of the greater intensity of solar radiation.) These were areas Markham considered of optimal climate, requiring minimal heating and cooling to maintain indoor comfort. (*Source:* Markham,[9] p. 98)

shopping, eating and spending more money, in warmer weather. This is a field where much more work is needed on understanding exactly how such complex inter-relationships between climate, economy and human behaviour can be manipulated to result in decisions with low environmental impacts that can also benefit local and regional economies.

Much is written about 'vulnerability' to climate change. The Commons Report describes it as being: 'determined by social, institutional and economic factors and the sensitivity of populations to climate impacts, as well as by institutional capacity, the ability to adapt, and location. The Commons Report also states that:[3]

As the conditions within a country change, so does its vulnerability. National vulnerability will increase if the main centres providing economic growth are located in vulnerable areas.

Do they mean exposed areas perhaps, or both? For example, those countries whose populations and economically productive enterprises are in coastal zones will face a higher risk.

IPCC Working Group II[10] noted that the communities that are the most vulnerable to climate change were also subject to pressures from population growth, resource depletion and poverty.

Rapid urbanization, land degradation, water pollution, water scarcity, and the destruction of ecosystems are also added pressures. All these factors affect vulnerability to variations in the current climate, as well as to future climate change.

These conditions would appear to be applicable to many coastal cities such as London, New York and Tokyo. What is not mentioned is that the short-sighted actions of politicians can add substantially to this catalogue of risk factors, and the vulnerability of populations, by not taking seriously the challenges of future-proofing buildings, cities and regions against such pressures. MPs who represent local populations should be given key positions on committees making decisions on such developments in their constituencies.

The Commons Report[3] goes on to claim that 'Developing countries have limited financial, human, technological, institutional and natural resources, making them less able to respond to the effects of climate change.' That may be true, but how prepared is the Southeast for the knock-on impacts of three million new homes – the need to find more local waste dumping sites, to make scarce summer water supplies serve hundreds of thousands more people in the region, to increase sewerage capacity and build new power plants in an already well-populated region?

QUIS CUSTODIET IPOS CUSTODIES?

Who guards the guardians? A major problem with the development of solutions to the problem of international climate refugees is that no single international agency, not even the UNHCR (United Nations), exists to promote the rights and interests of environmental refugees.[3]

In the UK no single agency has the remit to promote environmental sustainability at the broad scale. One Department deals with flooding, another with energy, waste and water supply. The Institution of Civil Engineers (ICE) called in 2003 for an Independent Chief Engineer (it could be a person in any profession with the right knowledge) 'to ensure that a co-ordinated, long term, sustainable approach is followed and that actions are not wholly driven by political agendas'.[5]

What has not yet been ostensibly recognized by the British government, despite increasingly sophisticated scenario-based studies of future impacts,[11] is that the vulnerability of many people in the UK to adverse impacts of the changing climate is increasing more rapidly than anyone thought. What will happen to the ski resort communities of Scotland as the snow disappears? How will the agricultural and fishing industries be affected? Will enough water be available to the populations of the Southeast, at an affordable cost, as the summers get warmer and drier? Can the Thames Barrier hold back the tidal surges until the new barrier is built? Will the Thames Gateway development increase vulnerability to flooding of the coastline communities of the whole of Southeast England? Will climate refugees from the lower latitudes bring north with them smouldering resentments, fuelled by hardship and global inequality and will migrations carry with them the potential for spreading political conflict?

To quote from Mark Mawhinney, in the conclusions of his book on sustainable development:[12]

the major issue remains the lack of clear evidence for decisions on development . . . and the risk that arises as a result of this. The lack of clear evidence often leaves humanity with a choice – act before the event using preventative principles or leave it until the evidence is available.

Migration is often seen as a safety net to be used to ease population pressures after a catastrophic event; in fact, it may also be one of the most powerful tools we have for the pre-emptive planning for the mitigation of climate change impacts.

NOTES AND REFERENCES

1 *Guardian*, 30 September 2003.

2 http://www.neweconomics.org/gen/uploads/nld2s2juqs2t34 mdhr31235506122003192037.pdf, see also: http://www.wmo.ch/ web/Press/Press.html.

3 Published on 24 July 2002: http://www.parliament.the-stationery-office.co.uk/pa/cm200102/cmselect/cmintdev/519/51902.htm.

4 *The Ecologist*, December 2003, p. 6.

5 ICE (2003) The state of the nation: an assessment of the state of the UK's infrastructure by the Institution of Civil Engineers. See text on: www.ice.org.uk.

6 Adger, W.N., Kelly, P.M. and Ninh, N.H. (eds) (2001) *Living with Environmental Change: Social Resilience, Adaptation and Vulnerability in Vietnam*. London: Routledge, pp. 314.

7 IPCC (2001) Third Assessment Report: Impacts, Adaptation and Vulnerability.

8 A range of publications are available on planning for disaster mitigation and response. See Freeman, P.K., Martin, L.A., Mechler, R., Warner, K. and Hausman, P. (2001) *Catastrophes*

and Development: Integrating Natural Catastrophes into Development Planning. Washington: World Bank. See also www.worldbank.org/dmf/files/catastrophes_complete.pdf, and the International Federation of Red Cross and Red Crescent Societies (2002) World Disasters Report: Focus on reducing risk (www.ifrc.org/publicat/wdr2002/chapter8.asp).

9   Markham, S.F. (1944) *Climate and the Energy of Nations.* Oxford: Oxford University Press.

10   Report of IPCC Working Group II: Summary for Policy Makers, 2001 (available from www.ipcc.ch/pub/spm22-01.pdf).

11   A number of different agencies are undertaking excellent studies and scenarios of a range of impacts in a more or less coordinated fashion, but how the results of this work is fed to the general public or feeds into the political decision-making process is less clear. See for instance http://www.foresight.gov.uk/; http://www.ukcip.org.uk/publications/pub.html; http://www.rcep.org.uk/energy.html.

12   Mawhinney, M. (2002) *Sustainable Development: Understanding the Green Debates.* Oxford: Blackwell Science, p. 171.

10 AIR CONDITIONING – THE ULTIMATE SOLUTION?

But surely, before we start moving people around, the solution to keeping comfortable in a hotter future already exists – air conditioning! S.F. Markham in 1939 realized the power of air conditioning, as he pointed out, to a world unfamiliar with it, the miracle of this new technology.[1] And it was a miracle, because it enabled people, adapted to the colder climates of Europe, to colonize the world. Indigenous people had always populated most parts of the globe, as we saw in Chapter 2, from the Arctic to the Equator, from the high valleys of the Himalayas to the great below sea level basins of the Dead Sea and the Turfan Oasis in China. Intrepid European entrepreneurs and imperial armies had penetrated most of the far-flung corners of the globe by the end of the 19th century, but Markham saw that if Westerners could actually live all year in cool buildings, regardless of the climate outside, they could truly export their 'civilization', and their god, on a massive scale to 'heathen' lands, exploit economically untapped regions and capitalize on the wealth of even the most uncomfortable nations on the planet. And this is exactly what has happened, for better or worse.

And if air conditioning could be used to enable people to be comfortable in hotter regions than they are adapted to, surely it can be used to keep people comfortable in a hotter future?

AIR CONDITIONING HAS BEEN WITH US FOR OVER 150 YEARS

Air conditioning was first used on a large scale at the turn of the 20th century to cool food but as early as 1748 William Cullen at Glasgow University experimented with evaporating ether under a

SUSTAINABLE SETTLEMENTS

HIGH ENERGY BUILDINGS

PASSIVE BUILDINGS

2000

1980

1950

1900

REGIONALLY APPROPRIATE BUILDINGS

AIR CONDITIONING

10.1.
The evolution of buildings changed dramatically with the advent of air conditioning, which significantly increased the electricity demands of buildings. (*Source:* Sue Roaf, digitally produced by Claire Palmer)

partial vacuum. It was not until 1805 that Oliver Evans, an American, caused water to freeze using a similar process, and the possibility of cheap coolth appeared. At that time many were also experimenting with freezing mixtures and the great natural ice trade was at its peak. In 1834 a closed cycle system was patented by Jacob Perkins and in the mid-1840s the use of room coolers was pioneered independently by physician John Gorrie, who used ice to cool air in hospital wards in Florida and Charles Piazzi Smyth, a Scot. Gorrie was not able to capitalize on his idea, being thought a crank by many, and he died a pauper, never dreaming that his invention would one day dictate the forms of buildings around the world.[2]

In 1862, at an International Exhibition in London, crowds were amazed to see hot-looking steam apparatus churning out miniature icebergs and one of these machines, made by Seibe (Ferdinand Carre produced the other) was bought by the Indian government and sent to relieve the suffering of the troops in India. In the 1870s a few ice production factories were set up in cities and provincial towns but they were expensive and took time to become established. In 1877 a breakthrough was made when meat from England was first exported to America in refrigerated ships, and in the 1960s many cities around the world still got their main ice supply from cold storage plants from which one bought blocks of ice. Fridges were not routinely designed into UK council houses until as late as the 1960s.

Early examples of air-conditioned office buildings were being experimented with in the UK and the United States in the 1890s and by the 1930s large buildings in the States were being more routinely air-conditioned. Hotels had their main public rooms air-conditioned by the early 1930s and by the 1940s every room in the best hotels had 'conditioned air'.[3] What air conditioning did was to liberate architects and engineers to create 'modern buildings' in which the internal climate is completely disconnected from that outside. In them, people are isolated in increasingly thin-skinned, fixed envelope buildings that can only be occupied if the air conditioning system is operating, and are un-occupiable if the machines stop!

'MODERN' BUILDINGS

The growth of the 'modern building' paradigm was made possible only because of the advent of air conditioning, fuelled by cheap fossil fuel energy, and based, until perhaps now, on the belief in the availability of limitless energy to power the machines that provided buildings, wherever in the world, with, to use Corbusier's words, 'une respiration exacte', that is to say a controlled indoor climate – air conditioning with precise controls.

Corbusier, arguably the greatest of the Modern Movement architects, published his influential book *Vers une architecture* in 1928.[4] In this he expounds his theories of a new sprit, for 'architecture, stifled by custom'. In his writings in search of 'l'esthétique de la vie moderne' he developed, already by 1926, his ideas based on what would become known as 'The Five Points Towards a New Architecture':

1 The pilotty is elevating the mass off the ground.
2 The free plan, achieved through the separation of the load-bearing columns from the walls subdividing the space.

3   The free facade, the corollary of the free plan in the vertical plane.
4   The long horizontal sliding window.
5   The roof garden, restoring the area of ground covered by the house.

Of those five points only the roof garden can improve the thermal performance of a building in many climates. To raise a building off the ground is to decouple it from the stable temperatures of the ground and expose the sixth face to the unstable climate of the air. The deep plan building makes mechanical air conditioning a necessity as only relatively shallow plan buildings can be naturally ventilated. The free facade has turned traditionally robust walls with sensibly sized windows into sheets of glass that increase the vulnerability of the building occupants to any external climate by an order of magnitude, and impose huge energy penalties onto building owners to try to stabilize internal climates into a controlled 'comfort' zone. The long horizontal sliding window, as we saw in Villa Mala Parte, almost eliminates any easily usable connection between the inside and outside climates and has led to the virtual elimination of usable windows from modern buildings, be it houses or offices. The green roof is the only feature that provides a modicum of thermal protection for a building as it is now being developed to provide good thermal resistance and rain water run-off control in roofs. These tenets by Corbusier continue to inspire generations of young architects who appear never to have questioned their applicability to the very different societal or environmental conditions of the late 20th, let alone the 21st, century.

In *Vers une architecture*, Le Corbusier wanted to make it clear why

'the engineer's aesthetic' is far more successful than architecture. Engineering takes advantage of the latest and most innovative building types, technologies and construction systems, based on mass-production, standardization and industrialization.

Architecture, if it wanted to embrace the 'new spirit', needed to embrace these modern methods of technology and progress away from the static 'safe' traditional architecture. Le Corbusier encouraged economy and mechanical precision in architecture, as this was the driving force in engineering's success.[5]

Here Corbusier acknowledges the increased 'risk' of modern buildings, referring to traditional buildings as 'safer'. The extent to which he recognized that they increased the vulnerability of occupants to the external climate is not clear, however he did not use his European design models when he built in Chandigar in India.

His famous statement that 'a house is a machine for living in' he justifies by stating that a house requires efficiency, economy, simplicity, elegance, and most of all, a form that is clear with regard to the function. He does not mention the need for comfort in all seasons, a sense of safety, quietness, low energy and mainte-nance bills. If his idea of economy and simplicity related to his demonstrated search for a 'minimalistic appearance' inside and out, rather than to efficient heating and cooling systems and structures, why were his buildings riddled with cold bridges and over-glazed facades? If his grasp on the physics of building had been greater then perhaps 20th century architecture would have been different, but he was an upper middle class professional for whom elegance held a high priority, and infinite energy was apparently assured.

The Second World War was followed by a rebuilding programme, the scale of which exceeded anything built before, as whole cities were 're-planned'. Increasing numbers of buildings were built in the 'modern' style using modern construction methods, which were innovative, untried and apparently unquestioned. Because modern construction methods enable very rapid and large-scale projects, the impact on our cities was immediate and often devastating as the old hearts of cities were torn out and replaced by concrete and steel and prefabricated structures as never before.

It was a changed Britain to which I returned: in just four years many towns and cities had been transformed [wrote Rod Hackney of his home-coming to Manchester in 1968]. The guts had been torn out of them, and new buildings had been carried out at an alarming rate ... Whole areas were unrecognisable – acres of terraces had been razed and replaced by

10.2.
Flats in Singapore on a new residential estate without air conditioning in 1963. Today almost every dwelling on the island is air-conditioned. (*Source:* Sue Roaf)

new tower block estates. In the city centres, where I remembered rows of individual, small old shops, there was now a concrete slab precinct. All sense of scale and perspective had been lost.

It was not only the look of these places that had changed. People's attitudes had too. They had begun to protest against their new homes and environments. In Denmark I had grown used to informed dialogue between the public, the architects and the state. In Britain there were two simultaneous monologues – the public in opposition to official policy. Faith in the state machine had been badly shaken.[6]

What has not failed is our belief in the air conditioning machine.

THE SIZE OF THE AIR CONDITIONING INDUSTRY

The air conditioning industry is one of the most powerful industries in the world, dwarfed only by the financial, insurance and motor industries. The US market for industrial air conditioning, refrigeration and heating (HVAC) machinery grew 3.5% from 2001, to a value of US$28.1 billion in 2002. The market for industrial air conditioning, refrigeration and heating machinery in the United States is relatively fragmented, with the top four players accounting for only 30.9% of sales in 2002. In 2002 the top four players

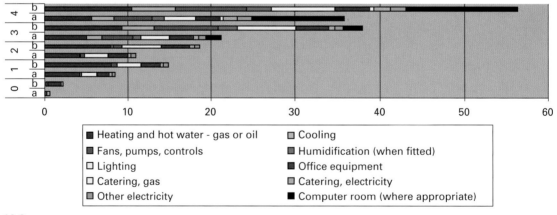

10.3.
Air-conditioned offices use significantly more energy to operate than naturally ventilated ones. This figure shows office building types and their annual carbon emissions (kg carbon/m² Treated Floor Area) with (a) best practice and (b) typical. Type 1 is the traditional office building, shallow plan, naturally ventilated and typical of the traditional 19th and early 20th century buildings. Type 2 is open plan and naturally ventilated buildings, such as became increasingly used after the 1950s when the demand for urban office space grew rapidly. Type 3 is typically a deep or shallow plan, standard air-conditioned building and Type 4 represents the typical 'prestige' or 'fashionable' air-conditioned, probably deep-plan office building of the type increasingly popular with 'modern' architects and developers. Type 0 has been added by us (with apologies to Bill Bordass) to represent what we hope 21st century, shallow plan, naturally ventilated or mixed mode (using air conditioning only at the hottest times of the year) buildings will look like with type 0a operating on renewable energy where possible. (*Source:* Bill Bordass, 1990[11])

in the market spent nearly US$1.5 billion on research and development. As the US market grows increasingly competitive and a lack of pricing power limits overall market value growth, many manufacturers have focused on overseas expansion to drive future sales, no doubt many looking to Iraq as a potentially fertile market for expansion for instance. The US market is expected to grow by just over 26% during the 2003 to 2007 forecast period, reaching a value of US$37 billion by 2007.[7]

The UK is not yet so addicted to air conditioning that it plays such a central part in the economy, but things are changing fast. Today around one-third of all UK office blocks have air conditioning of one form or another, despite the fact that we know that air-conditioned prestige offices consume four times the energy of traditional shallow plan naturally ventilated buildings, as were ubiquitous in the UK before the 1970s, and despite the fact that we do not actually need to cool well-designed buildings in these islands.[8]

The problem is that air conditioning is a fundamental cause of climate change, the symptoms of which it was design to address, creating a 'vicious circle' that we have to break if we are to survive. Buildings consume over 50% of all energy generated around

(a)
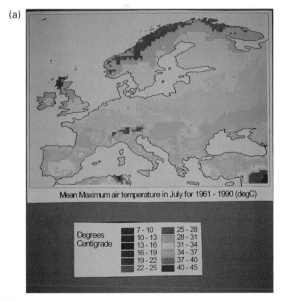

(b)
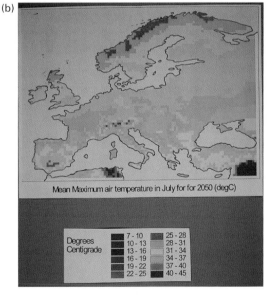

10.4.
The mean maximum temperatures for July in Europe recorded for (a) 1960–90 and (b) predicted for 2050. This figure shows that Britain is predicted to remain with fairly moderate maximum temperatures well into this century and temperatures that mean, in a well-designed passive building, air conditioning will not be needed for the foreseeable future. (*Source:* Climate models by G. Kenny[8])

the world and produce over half of all climate change emissions globally. In the United States alone air conditioning uses around 30–40% of all building-related energy, so say a fifth, or 20%, of all energy in the United States is used for air conditioning. The United States uses around 25% of all the world energy: that means that potentially around 5% of all the greenhouse gases in the world come from US air conditioning systems alone.

In the past two decades there has been an exponential growth in European sales of air conditioning that has been in the double-digit percentage growth during most of this period. The market for packaged air conditioning in Europe grew by 20% in 1998 and 11% in 1999. The most rapidly growing EU markets are in Greece, Spain and Italy.[9]

Two significant trends in the sale and design of air conditioning markets are:

• It is common for engineers to oversize air conditioning plant 30–50% to future-proof buildings against climate change.[10]
• Building usage patterns are changing in ever-shorter cycles, for example from office to apartment, shop to restaurant and power station to museum, requiring the market to develop more flexible, adaptable, systems with shorter payback periods to reflect shorter life cycles.[11]
• This trend for smaller systems, more often changed, also has a significant impact on the embodied energy of the systems, typically made with high embodied energy materials such as aluminium, tin and steel.

What is hard to understand is why modern buildings have evolved in a form that requires expensive and unnecessary energy wastage in air conditioning when we knew as early as the 1950s that the 'modern building' had serious design problems, including creating uncomfortable indoor conditions that would require air conditioning to alleviate, and as early (and later studies) have shown people often do not actually like working in air-conditioned offices.

LIGHTWEIGHT, OVER-GLAZED AND VULNERABLE BUILDINGS

It is important to deal with one of the key climatic design problems of 'modern' buildings, and that is the excessive use of glass in their external envelopes. We have for nearly fifty years known that there is a problem with over-glazed facades, and these problems will be significantly increased in a changing climate.

Early uses of 'Building Performance Appraisal'[12] techniques in offices in the UK were originally developed as diagnostic tools to understand the emerging problems of buildings that were changing from the traditional 'British' building to the larger, more complex 'modern' building type in the 'international style' that began to dominate the urban environment from the 1950s onwards.

In 1966, few air-conditioned buildings existed in London, and Flora Black and Elizabeth Milroy, working at the Building Research Station in Garston, completed a review and survey of the 'experience of air-conditioned buildings' in London.[13] Air conditioning was not then considered climatically necessary in the UK, and remains so in some buildings. Recent studies have shown that traditional passive buildings may be robust enough to provide comfort conditions for several decades to come, even with the changing climate, without year-round air conditioning.[8]

Black and Milroy's study was designed to use feedback from office workers to optimize working conditions in future offices by understanding emerging performance problems as the paradigm changed. The results echo many, not dissimilar, studies done more recently,[14] namely that air-conditioned offices are perceived to be cleaner and quieter (the buildings studied were new with fixed windows), and in very hot weather were preferred to naturally ventilated buildings, but in 'less extreme weather, the thermal environment in the A/C buildings was in many ways less favoured than that in offices with opening windows'.

One reason suggested for this was the type of building, 'the heavier more conventional construction being more comfortable than the lightweight building with large areas of glazing'. This study was done to gauge the human impacts, and in turn the design imperatives, of the changing market in 'building types' with a view to informing regulations on the issue. Such early studies were, in effect, a 'kind of quality control writ large'.[15]

A second study published two years later indicates how rapidly the office market was developing[16] in the UK in the 1960s. The paper by A.G. Loudon at the BRE resulted from the increasing problem of overheating in buildings due to excessive glazing. In the 1960s the style of building was changing rapidly as more glass and lighter-weight buildings replaced the traditional heavier type, and a survey by Gray and Corlett[17] showed that in pre-war offices the window areas averaged around 20% of the floor area and 85% of occupants wanted more sunshine in their offices, while only 9% were concerned that it should not be too hot. By 1961 a survey by Loudon and Keighley[18] in post-war offices showed that as many as 40% of the occupants were sometimes too hot in summer and was widely published in professional as well as research circles.[19]

The probable reasons for this increase were given as greater use of glass, with windows over 50% larger in the 1961 survey

(a)

(b)

10.5.
(a) There are still cities in the hottest parts of the world where few buildings are air conditioned. View over down town Yangon, in Myanmar. (*Source:* Sue Roaf) (b) Man leans over a balcony in Yangon: windows are an important link between life inside buildings and that in the community outside. To close the window is to cut that link. (*Source:* Sue Roaf)

than in the 1948 survey. Moreover, 80% of the internal partitions on post-war buildings were lightweight, warming up quickly, and in the pre-war buildings they were heavy. The fact that there was more traffic noise in the later survey, making people keep their windows shut, was also thought significant, and more complaints about over-heating were recorded near busy traffic routes.

This study concluded that buildings of heavy construction could have up to 50% of the external wall glazed, but that unless sun controls were provided, glass areas in buildings with lightweight internal walls and ceiling should be restricted to 20% of the wall area, if they face south and are not shaded. If temperatures of 27 °C were considered acceptable then this area could be extended to 30% of the wall area in noisy areas and 50% in quiet ones for lightweight buildings. If more glass was required for reasons of introducing sunlight or the view then excess heat could be removed by air conditioning, however this was expensive and should be considered as a last choice after proper building design and the use of external shading. This study was one of the building blocks from which the 'admittance method' was developed.[20]

The performance of passive and low energy cooling systems is, by their very nature, much more sensitive to climate than is the performance of refrigeration-based systems and the low energy cooling systems require higher levels of internal thermal mass in buildings and will never be successfully applied in lightweight, over-glazed buildings that get too hot to handle without throwing vast amounts of energy at them to cool them on hot days.[8] What the admittance method shows is that mass is essential to sensible, passive building design.

A clear symptom of over-glazing in modern office buildings is that the blinds are so often closed, resulting in higher lighting energy use and not reducing the over-heating problem. Once solar radiation has passed through glass, it is absorbed and re-emitted at a different wavelength at which it can no longer travel back out through the glass. This phenomenon is the basis for the greenhouse effect, and means that even with the blinds down, the building overheats.

That glass buildings with little or no shading cause severe overheating is an international problem. From the Gulf, where the inside temperatures recorded on glass walls often reach over 60–80 °C, to many fashionable modern buildings where internal temperatures soar on hot days, even with the air conditioning on. It appears as if, for some architects, the penny has not dropped that it is extremely difficult to live comfortably in a 'greenhouse'. That is without the added problems of the hotter climate and the rising energy costs of trying to keep such buildings cool.

10.6.
Downtown Buenos Aires, Argentina: like many cities in the world, the evolution of the low energy buildings of the early 19th century, with their sensibly sized windows, shade, blinds and shutters and awnings, gave way over the decades to the thin, tight-skinned, highly glazed buildings most commonly built today. There is little density change in the number of people occupying adjacent buildings but the modern buildings may well use four or five times more energy to keep occupants no more comfortable for many months of the year. (*Source:* Sue Roaf)

Many attempts have been made to reduce internal temperatures with ingenuity, famously in the National Library in Paris, designed in the late 1980s by architect Dominique Perrault. This grand monument eventually cost the French people US$1.3 billion, and an undue amount of trouble. The towers contain more than one design flaw. For example, it was realized too late that a library built from transparent glass would provide little protection for the books from sunlight; and that in fact, excessive sunlight would actually overheat the towers (and pose a risk of turning them into blazing infernos!). To remedy this the architect specified timber shutters to line the whole of the four towers to be made from top grade mahogany from the Brazilian rainforests. In addition, the glass design failed to account for condensation, another threat to delicate books. These issues were remedied by the architect only after the construction had been started, and at considerable additional expense to the French public.[21] It is difficult to think of a modern 'monument' that does not suffer from similar problems, although the British Library, fortunately, was designed sensibly to avoid such a foolish mistake.

But there are a range of other well-known problems with 'shiny' and over-glazed buildings, and some of these are illustrated in Boxes 10.1 and 10.2. A number of the examples have been contributed by, amongst others, members of the American Society of Building Science Educators (SBSE), teachers of environmental science in US Schools of Architecture.[22] Collectively that show that tight, thin, lightweight and over-glazed buildings are a chronic problem today – and air conditioning can never be a solution to all their problems.

INDOOR AIR QUALITY

Buildings are becoming increasingly 'sick'. In the United States the office worker on average takes a day a month off work suffering from 'Sick Building Syndrome', a figure unimaginable in Europe where we are less dependent on air conditioning.

Indoor air quality can be worse in an air-conditioned building than in a comparable naturally ventilated one. Worryingly, researchers are finding that the filters, ducts and plant of air conditioning systems are often filthy, introducing air that is dirtier than if one simply opened the window, even in the city.[23] Ducts can harbour potentially killer chemicals and bugs, such as *Legionella*, moulds and particulates that are released back into the ducts from the filter. This happens particularly when the weather changes, for instance, on getting warmer and wetter in a warm front.[24] Such changes happen every time a warm front moves across a region, only not in such a marked fashion.

Many internal ducts are not only seldom cleaned but also impossible to get at to clean, and to make matters worse actually give out toxic fumes from the plant, seals and duct work itself. Often uncleaned filters and long dirty duct runs collect passing toxins and store them until ambient conditions become warmer and/or more humid. In addition, already dirty duct air is then mixed with the cocktail of volatile organic compounds, formaldehydes, moulds, fungi, dust mites and potentially toxic cleaning materials already inside rooms. This may be one good reason why in air-conditioned buildings many more people succumb to sick building syndrome.[25] Furnishings and finishes that are made of natural materials reduce the problem of excessive toxin levels in the room air.

Air conditioning units also cannot filter out some of the most harmful of pollutants in the air, such as diesel and other particulates, PCBs and any substances below approximately 9 ångström in diameter. The poor location of air inlets often means that, in inner city locations in particular, the air circulated in air-conditioned buildings is of a lower air quality than if the occupants had simply opened a better-placed window. The claim is often made that particular buildings such as laboratories, museums and hospitals should have air conditioning as a matter of course, but on the contrary, while there is a need for particular very clean spaces in such buildings studies have shown that office workers, artefacts and patients are happier, last longer and get better sooner in naturally ventilated spaces.

WILL SYSTEM EFFICIENCY HELP?

There are a number of ways to ameliorate the negative impacts of air conditioning, including:

- Don't use it.
- Use it only at the hottest times of year.
- Make the hardware more efficient.
- Make it run on renewable clean energies that do not lead to global warming.
- Design better buildings that keep solar gain out, generate minimal heat and are slow to heat.
- Make the controls more intelligent, so they are not just set on one indoor temperature for the whole year (as happens in many systems) but can track outdoor temperatures, so saving up to 50% of their running costs.

The importance of moving away from a dependence on fully, inefficiently, poorly controlled, air-conditioned buildings has been widely recognized. There have been experiments in different countries with methods of changing the traditional approach to air conditioning a building – with varying success:

- **Market forces.** The theory that environmentally friendly technologies will be increasingly used over more damaging ones does not seem to apply with air conditioning. Here, market forces appear to work in favour of 'prestige solutions'.[26]
- **Guidance.** Guidance measures, however strong, appear to be useless. For example, in the UK for the engineering and architectural professions strong guidance not to use air conditioning systems has had minimal effect on the standards of environmental design of typical office buildings or their energy consumption. British Standard BS 8207:1985 the British Standard Code of Practice for Energy Efficiency in Buildings, Appendix B, has in Table 2 on the check-list for Design Teams Point 7: 'Only specify air conditioning where it is essential to do so.' The RIBA in 1989 in its policy Guidelines advised its members against the unnecessary use of air conditioning and the Chartered Institute of Building Service Engineers has as Item 1 on it Code of Professional Conduct devised to promote ethical practice: 'Avoid the use of refrigeration where natural and mechanical ventilation is a feasible alternative.' Negligible attention has been paid to such guidance in the UK.
- **Legislation.** This works well. In the Canton of Zurich, Switzerland, a law was introduced practically overnight in the late 1980s, banning the use of air conditioning in buildings unless it could be proven to be absolutely necessary. Surprisingly, building designers adapted to the new challenge very rapidly.[27] The drawback has been that the building industry has learnt since then how to argue credibly that air conditioning is essential in new buildings. The real problem here is that it is very easy to design an air-conditioned building that more or less works, but it takes great skill and expertise to design a good passive building, skill that, frankly, many modern architects simply do not have. The experience of Zurich has proved that they can learn fast, although even there architects and engineers are now finding ways around the pioneering regulations, showing that enforcement is as important as the legislation itself.
- **Political management of the problem.** A major drawback is that in most countries there is no single authority with jurisdiction over the control of energy use in, or CO_2 emissions from, buildings – neither the planning nor the building regulations departments – and hence there is no related authority to

10.7.
The non-air-conditioned buildings around the 'Padang' in central Kuala Lumpur light up for 'Merdeka', the independence day celebrations in 1958. (*Source:* Sue Roaf)

control the use and performance of air conditioning systems. With the increase in significance of CO_2 emissions from buildings, and their commoditization as an internationally tradable unit and legally controllable substance under international law, legislation for the control of energy use in buildings, and by countries, will inevitably be considered and eventually implemented in most countries.

AIR CONDITIONING IS HERE TO STAY

We live in the air conditioning age and a number of books have been written about the importance of air conditioning to the American way of life and economy in particular. Gail Cooper points out:[28]

[the three different kinds of air conditioning in America] – the custom designed systems, the plug in-appliance, and the standardized installation for the tract home – illustrate the difficulties involved in integrating technical expertise into commercial products.

None of these systems fit *[sic]* perfectly the interests of the engineer, the company, and the aggregated groups known as the consumer ... The customer-designed system produced the most technically rational design but surprisingly afforded the user little flexibility. The plug-in appliance privileged the consumer, but its complete divorce from the building compromised its performance. The standardized installation of the tract development provided affordability and performance, but in a buildings that was dependent upon its mechanical services and alarmingly inefficient in energy consumption.

The extent of the dependence of building users on inefficient air conditioning systems in poor buildings in American was also a conclusion drawn in another classic work on air conditioning America, by Marsha Ackermann, who concludes by mentioning that Lewis Mumford, at the age of 75, wrote that air conditioning was deeply complicit in our society's authoritarian tendencies towards control. Ackermann adds:[29]

The counterpart of technologically enabled control is dependency, and the history of air conditioning provides it in full measure. Air conditioning has made it possible to erect structures that must be evacuated when the power fails, to make buildings in which people get sick. It gulps electricity; roars, wheezes, and whines; makes urban heat islands even hotter with the exhaust of a million air-conditioned cars and thousands of sealed buildings.

It has led to a human society that is increasingly unable to adapt to change, because of this dependency, but she adds:

For better and for worse, our world tomorrow will be air conditioned.

In Chapter 12 we look at the growing problems of oil and gas depletion that may, in the not so distant future, challenge this premise. Inevitably, we will all, sooner rather than later, have to 're-structure our expectations and our habits' to refocus our efforts and investments on the provision of our basic needs: shelter, health, real comfort, security and survival. We need to extricate ourselves from the market place that sells comfort and air quality as a product rather than an 'attribute' or property of the building itself. Comfortable and healthy indoor conditions are created by good building design, and by truly good architects and engineers. Rather than wasting time discussing and rewarding small incremental

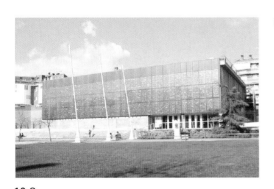
(b)

10.8.
The Mataro Library, powered by Desiccant Solar Air Conditioning designed by ICAEN, the Catalonian Energy Institute. (*Source:* Rodrigo Leal, ICAEN, Barcelona)

improvements in the efficiency of a dated and profligate technology we urgently need to reorganize the 'normality' of what constitutes a good building, if we are to survive.

Air conditioning may be with us for quite a while longer but changes in the industry will have to be as radical as those in the motor industry 15 years ago to meet the rapidly improving performance targets we need to achieve if we are to stabilize climate change. The US air conditioning industry, in particular, is monolithic, outdated and already losing out, as it has in the car markets, to foreign manufacturers who realized a decade ago that deep efficiency and quality of product would be what mattered in the 21st century, and they were right. Developing countries will have to be very wary in the future of having outmoded technologies dumped on them as the First World decides it can no longer use such wasteful products at home.

Rather than tinkering with small incremental improvements in the efficiency of air conditioning systems, we need a step change to new paradigms for cooling buildings. Just as with the cars, we need super-low-consumption, dual fuel, eco-buildings that are naturally ventilated in spring, winter and autumn, and in summer are run on solar air conditioning when the sun is out topped up by small amounts of grid electricity when it is not. This is the way forward.

We have to move away from the chronically inefficient 'modern', thin, tight-skinned, over-glazed and over-serviced buildings to robust, heavier, shallow plan buildings with opening windows. To do this we need to wean ourselves from the 'path-dependency' we have for the provision of inadequate products in the place of what we really need – the genuine attributes of 'comfort' and a 'healthy working environment'.[30] Perhaps the age of the HVAC engineer and the 'modern' architect is over if we want such new building paradigms, just as people will very soon require estate agents who actually know what the annual energy running costs, comfort levels and sick building syndrome history of a buildings is. Such knowledge will contribute to identifying the high-impact and high-risk buildings, amongst which will be many of the worst environmental offenders, such as those dinosaurs of the Modern Movement, tall buildings, which form the subject of the next chapter.

Box 10.1 People who live in glass houses . . .

Despite the known problems with over-glazed buildings, glass continues to be used more and more widely today. Apart from the issues of thermal comfort which are the main concern of Chapter 5, other problems with over-glazed buildings include:

- Loss of privacy: fellow workers can see untidiness, wall charts or flip boards that are being discussed, heated meetings!
- Difficulty of arranging furniture against glazed walls – for instance, desks placed against glass are impossible to use by women who wear skirts. This caused a famous engineering firm to replace the lower half of the glass windows on their new HQ building with frosted glass – no one had thought about this at the design stage!
- The excessive daylight and glare make it difficult to read computer monitors. Engineers cite the fact that some monitors are now so bright they can be seen in full daylight, but at what cost in energy and eye strain? Glare is also the reason why so many highly glazed buildings have their blinds full down and all the lights on, making the indoor conditions poor and energy use in them expensive.

These types of ostensibly trivial gripes are the sorts of factors that can make the difference between being 'happy' at work or not.

Box 10.2 Reflectance, glare and 'singing buildings'

Reflectance of light and heat from metal and glass finished buildings can often cause chronic problems, to motorists, pedestrians and to adjacent buildings. The Hooker Building, built by Occidental Chemicals in 1980 in Niagara Falls, NY, was one of the first double-skin buildings in North America. It was designed with highly reflecting airfoil type movable shading devices on all sides that were supposed to reflect sunlight/daylight deeply into the interior. The reflection of the sun off these foils was so bright as to blind the motorists crossing the Rainbow Bridge from Canada to the US. Within 4 months of the building being occupied they were refinished white to eliminate this problem.

The Ontario Hydro building in Toronto, on the corner of College and University Avenue, actually focuses the sun's rays onto the sidewalk in front. It has a concave curved front with reflective glass. The focusing effect of the sun at a particular time of year not only causes glare problems but intense solar heating. Luckily the front faces northeast so this occurs only for a short period during the summer in early morning, but it is obviously a generic problem that should be avoided. Curved buildings also have acoustic issues, as they can magnify sound as they reflect the sound waves within the curve.

This raises the issue also of 'singing buildings'. The glass and steel TD Bank tower designed by Mies Van der Rohe, with a black envelope, like the Seagram tower in New York, was 55 storeys high and the first true skyscraper in Toronto. It was designed for thermal expansion on the south, east and west sides of the building to make allowance for the effects of the sun on those facades, particularly as black metal is highly affected by heat. When a new glass tower was built immediately to the north of the building it reflected so much heat back at the TD Bank tower that its occupants were greatly alarmed by the loud creaking and groaning that the building started to exhibit due to the unexpected solar thermal expansion on its northern facade. Steps were taken to control this unexpected movement in the building and the groans stopped, but at an enormous cost to the Bank.

The Hancock Tower in Boston was built in the early 1970s and won the 'most beautiful piece of architecture in Boston' award. It is also a textbook example of problems with glass in buildings. The 60-storey building framed in steel was totally clad, floor to ceiling, in two layers of reflective glass separated by a lead spacer soldered to the glass sheets. The inner surface of the outer glass light, or sheet, facing the cavity has a layer of silver reflective coating on it.[i]

Problems started from early on in the project and the first of four disasters struck. The foundations caused serious settlement of buildings in the surrounding streets. The second problem occurred when a windstorm hit Boston on 20 January 1973 and a number of glass panels being erected in the tower blew out. The falling panels caught in the air turbulence around the building hit and cracked a number of other panels, which had to be replaced. Experts who were called in identified the fact that the tower itself was not safe in windstorms and to remedy this the steel frame stiffness in the long direction was reinforced with 1650 tonnes of extra diagonal steel bracing. The final problem in construction, that of a number of glass panels cracking, was explained by the fact that the lead spacer had developed fatigue because the bond obtained between the melted lead spacer between the reflective coating and the outside light and that between the reflective coating and the lead sealer did not yield, and thus transmitted the motions from thermal expansion to the outer light, cracking it first. The seal was too strong. All the 10 344 identical panels of the Hancock Tower were replaced with single-thickness tempered glass. The cost of the building rose from US$75 million to US$175 and its opening was delayed from 1971 to 1976.[ii]

But the Tower's problems were not over. The building reflected so much heat into the adjacent Copley Square Hotel that the hotel sued the John Hancock building owners to pay for increased air conditioning equipment and operation costs. The owners of the Tower ended up purchasing the Copley Square Hotel to settle the issue, which was sold on recently for a sum of over $900 000.

External building elements can also cause temperature problems. The REJ building in Austin, Texas was designed with attractive curvilinear, specular light shelves that would project light deep into the interior of the building. Unfortunately, this meant projecting light into hallways that were then impossible to walk down when the sun was shining just so. To fix this the building operator hung blinds permanently in front of the offending light shelves, making them into expensive plant shelves. Office furniture was also not installed as specified by the architects, further blocking the light shelves.[iii]

Many leading architects have predicted the need for more careful design of areas of glazing in buildings and the 'BetterBricks Daylighting Lab' in Washington has done a series of studies on the 'environmental' impacts of the new OMA-Koolhaus Central Seattle Library glass reflections. An extensive series of model studies were done on the nearly all-glass building. OMA spent a great deal of time and money working with Schott Glass in Germany in developing a multi-layered glass system to reduce solar gain, glare and, hopefully, reflected sun problems while admitting as much light as possible from the overcast sky. It will be for the building users and visitors to determine if this has proved successful.[iv]

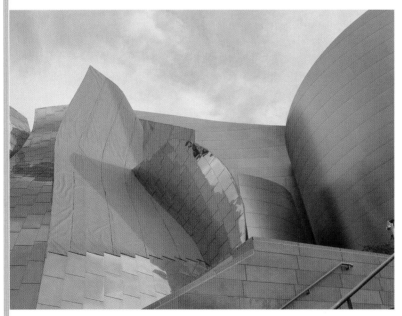

10.9.
Gehry's Walt Disney Concert Hall has had to be covered up due to the excessive levels of glare experienced from its highly reflective metal surface (*Source:* Bill Bordass)

Another building to have major reflectance problems is the new Walt Disney Concert Hall, designed by Frank Gehry and owned by the County of Los Angeles, which has had to call in experts in an attempt to reduce the glare and thermal issues surrounding (literally) the building. There are convex and concave stainless steel surfaces, in some cases brushed, and in some cases polished. In late June

2003, when the builders peeled off the film used to cover the steel during construction, the owners of condo apartments opposite began to complain. In mid-afternoon the glare from the steel became so intense they had to leave their balconies, close the curtains and put on the air conditioning for three hours till the sun went off that face of the building. The temperatures in their apartments went up by up to 15°C because of the added glare off the building. Gehry blamed the builders. The county put a $6000 mesh over the steel as a stop-gap remedy, demonstrating a proactive approach to solving the problems to neighbours of heat and light pollution caused by a building they commissioned. Modifications of the external reflective surfaces have been completed in order to change the reflectance of some of the surfaces and more work will have to be undertaken, although this not a building that can be easily or lightly modified.[v]

[i] Levy, M. and Salvadori, M. (1992) *Why Buildings Fall Down*. New York: W.W. Norton, pp. 197–205.
[ii] http://www.mit.edu/afs/athena/course/1/1.011/www/1.011-hancock-bostonglobe-290403A.pdf.
[iii] A report on this can be found in Song, S., Haberl, J. and Turner, D. (2002) Sustainability assessment of the Robert E. Johnson State Office Building, submitted to the Texas State Energy Conservation Office, Energy Systems Laboratory Report No.ESL-TR-02/01-02, Texas A&M University, 139 pp (April).
[iv] The report on this project can be found on:
http://www.lightingdesignlab.com/daylighting/daylighting_studio.htm
[v] sbse.org/newsletter/issues.sbsenewssp04linked.pdf.

NOTES AND REFERENCES

1 Markham, S.F. (1944) *Climate and the Energy of Nations*. Oxford: Oxford University Press.

2 Beamon, S.F. and Roaf, S. (1989) *The Ice-Houses of Britain*. London: Routledge, pp. 138–49.

3 http://www.hevac-heritage.org/papers/papers.htm.

4 Le Corbusier (1986) *Towards a New Architecture*. London: Dover Publications (Mineola, New York). This is a translated reprint of Corbusier's original book *Vers une architecture*, first published in 1928 in Paris.

5 http://www.geocities.com/rr17bb/LeCorbusier5.html.

6 Hackney, R. (1990) *The Good, the Bad and the Ugly*. London: Century Hutchinson, p. 37.

7 http://www.euromonitor.com/Industrial_air_conditioning_refrigeration_and_heating_machinery_in_USA_(mmp).

8   Haves, P., Roaf, S. and Orr, J. (1998) Climate change and passive cooling in Europe. In *Proceedings of PLEA Conference*, Lisbon, James & James Science.

9   Roaf, S. (1992) Ozone loopholes – a case study of air conditioning in Britain. *Proceedings WREC Conference*. Reading: Pergamon Press, pp. 1870–6.

10 BSEE (2000) Technology and market demands drive booming European air conditioning market. *Building Services & Environmental Engineer*, vol. 10, December.

11 Bordass, B. (1990) Appropriate methods and technologies for new build and refurbishment: offices. *Global Responsibilities of Architects*. London: RIBA Publications, pp. 15–17.

12 This term was coined in the early 1970s. Baird, G., Donnne, M., Pool, F., Brander, W. and Aun, C. (1984) *Energy Performance of Buildings*. Boca Raton, FL: CRC Press, p. 7.

13 Black, F. and Milroy, E (1966) Experience of air conditioning in offices. *Journal of the Institute of Heating and Ventilating Engineers*, September, pp. 188–96.

14 For a typical study of this type see a number referred to on the following website that covers the methodology used for such studies: http://www.learn.londonmet.ac.uk/packages/mulcom/comfort/thermal/.

15 Leaman, A. (2004) Post-occupancy evaluation. In Roaf, S. with Horsley, A. and Gupta, R. *Closing the Loop: Benchmarks for Sustainable Buildings*. London: RIBA Publications.

16 Loudon, A.G. (1968) Window design criteria to avoid overheating by excessive solar gains. Building Research Station Current Paper 4/68, published by the BRS.

17 Gray, P.G. and Corlett, T. (1952) A survey of lighting in offices. Appendix 1 of Postwar Building Research No. 30. London: HMSO.

18 Loudon, F.J. and Keighley, E.C. (1964) User research in office design. *Architect's Journal*, 139 (6), 333–9.

19 Loudon, F.J. and Danter, E. (1965) Investigations of summer overheating. *Building Science 1*, 1, pp. 89–94.

20 The evolution of the admittance method is illustrated in Danter, E. (1965) Periodic heat flow characteristics of simple walls and roofs. *IHVE Journal*, 28, pp. 136–46. And a worked example is available on: http://www.esru.strath.ac.uk/Courseware/Class-16458/.

21 http://www.pps.org/gps/one?public_place_id=350.

22 www.sbse.org/newsletter/issues/newsw03weblinked.pdf.

23 Clausen, G., Olm, O. and Fanger, P.O. (2002) *The impact of air pollution from used ventilation filters on human comfort and health*. Proceedings of the 9th International Conference on Indoor Air Quality and Climate, Monterey, vol. 1, pp. 338–43. www.indoorair2002.org.

24 Mauderly, J. (2002) *Linkages between outdoor and indoor air quality issues: pollutants and research problems crossing the threshold*. Proceedings of the 9th International Conference on Indoor Air Quality and Climate, Monterey, vol. 1, pp. 12–13.

25 Bjorkroth, M., Asikainen, V., Seppanen, O. and Sateri, J. (2002) *Cleanliness criteria and test procedures for cleanliness labelling of HVAC components*. Proceedings of the 9th International Conference on Indoor Air Quality and Climate, Monterey, vol. 1, pp. 670–4.

26 Tselepidaki, I. and Santamouris, M. (1991) Statistical and persistence style analysis of high ambient summer temperatures in Athens for cooling purposes. *Energy and Buildings*, vol. 17, pp. 243–51.

27 Meierhans, R. and Zimmermann, M. (1991) Slab cooling and earth coupling. *Proceedings of the Future Buildings Forum – innovative cooling workshop*. International Energy Agency, organized by Oscar Faber, May, pp. 1–24.

28 See for example the excellent: Cooper, Gail (1998) *Air-conditioning America: Engineers and the Controlled Environment, 1900–1960*. Johns Hopkins Studies in the History of Technology. Baltimore, MD: Johns Hopkins University Press.

29 Ackermann, Marsha (2002) *Cool Comfort: America's Romance with Air-conditioning*. Washington, DC: Smithsonian Institution Press.

30 An excellent book that looks at the problems with viewing comfort as a product rather than a quality is Shove, E. (2003) *Comfort Cleanliness + Convenience: The Social Organization of Normality*. Berg: Oxford.

11 TALL BUILDINGS

The age of skyscrapers is at an end. It must now be considered an experimental building typology that has failed.[1]

SIZE MATTERS

Size matters, and always has mattered. It represents power, and dominance within a group. There are strong subliminal drivers for the idea that to be 'above' is better. In terms of defence the further you can see the sooner you know that the enemy approaches. In early warfare there were significant physical advantages to being 'above' when lobbing sling bullets, spears or cannon shot at the enemy, although this advantage is hardly relevant when the enemy is a disgruntled colleague, the hubris of the CEO of a large organization, or an anthrax spore.

In animal groups, dominant males strengthen the 'family line' through the idea of selective breeding, where the 'strongest' men, in a particular ecological niche, will win the fair hands of the strongest wives and so have the strongest children, so fortifying the 'line' in perpetuity within that niche, be it because they can run faster, earn more or survive the cold. We also enjoy 'looking down on' people, from lofty 'heights', be they intellectual, financial or simply the seat of a great big SUV. In many settlements the best houses were raised above the unhealthy masses in the cleaner fresher air that wealth affords. We are also impressed by looking up at people, and their edifices, the ultimate symbol of great achievement. This tendency is reflected in a charming poem written in Cairo in the 14th century, about a windcatcher, which demonstrates that human nature changes little over centuries:

> A house resembling as-Samaw'al's castle has come to brag
> About one of its architectural features, saying:
> 'I see my windcatcher rise up high in the air,
> Being mightier and taller than those who go after it'.
>
> (Ibn Abi Hajalah at-Tilimsani, 1325–75)

Since the race to build the tallest building began, first won in the late 1920s by the Empire State Building[2] at 381 m and 102 storeys, over the Chrysler Building, at 319 m and 70 storeys, the title of the 'owner of the tallest building in the world' has also been a goal of very powerful men. The Twin Towers of the World Trade Center held the title for a time.

(a)

(b)

(d)

(c)

11.1.
Huge buildings in America were run with and without air conditioning in the 1930s and 1940s, still using careful climatic design, thermal mass, opening windows and shading. Here we see four: (a) The Hotel Lincoln in New York; (b) the Merchandise Mart in Chicago – an early 'mall' and the largest building in the world at that time; (c) the Stevens Hotel, Chicago, with circulating iced water in every room; and (d) the Chrysler building in New York, with a pioneering air conditioning system. (*Source:* S. Ross, postcard collection)

Currently Taipei is now ahead in the skyscraper stakes, housing 12 000 people in 101 Office block, which at 508 m has overtaken the Malaysian Petronas Towers, and is designed to survive a 9/11-type attack. It has more escape stairs than the Petronas towers, not a small consideration, and can endure extreme winds and an earthquake above 7 on the Richter scale. Severe storms and tremors are common in Taiwan. It also has the world's fastest lifts, that travel at 37 mph and take passengers to the 90th floor in 39 seconds – when the electricity is on, that is.[3]

The 88-storey Jinmao tower, China's tallest building, is located in Shanghai. London's tallest building, Canary Wharf, is someway behind in the stakes, at 235 m high and 50 floors.[4] The 'Shard of Glass', which has recently got planning permission, designed by Renzo Piano at 305 m high, is to be located in Southwark. The UK's highest residential building, a 157 m high, 47-storey glass tower, is to be built in Manchester. The height was dictated by the fact that Manchester airport sets a 160 m height limit on buildings in the city. It will be 30 m taller than the Barbican tower in London. It will cost £150 million to build and buyers have already reserved £60 million worth of space in it.

Some architects actively promote tall buildings

Richard Rogers is one who supports tall buildings, as was demonstrated by his recent attack on the UK Centre for the Built Environment's[5] decision to oppose permission for the high rise glass 'shard' building designed by Renzo Piano for London. Despite much opposition, by those who said that the building did not do enough to improve the public realm in the area, Richard Rogers, stated:

To stop a massive development because some people think the public domain is not as good as it should be is an absolute mistake ... It is completely throwing the baby out with the bathwater ... I don't believe that all tall buildings need public space.[6]

In his evidence to the planning inquiry for the building he claimed that the building was:

a masterwork of architectural design, sited in the right place to maintain London's status as a world city. Its impact on London's protected skyline, as a part of a cluster of towers will be entirely positive, and will not harm statutorily protected views or harm the setting of St Pauls.[7]

A number of architects supported the tower, which was variously described as 'very special', 'audacious' and a 'true masterpiece', and declared that it would be embraced by Londoners for its 'meaning and elegance', though what that meaning was is still unclear. Those voicing strong opinions were notably those who make a living out of big buildings, one notable claiming that this building in particular 'sensitively reflects its local context', in contrast to CABE's concerns over its scale, form, detail, design references and the grain of the development. How do people justify such statements? What would sensitive mean in this context?[8]

In London, the Mayor Ken Livingston promoted the idea of high buildings to trumpet the international status of the city.[9] A number of new tower blocks had been proposed for London, including a 30-storey tower for the Southwark Estate and a number of other multi-storey developments in Greenwich,[10] Mill Harbour,[11] Docklands, and the City.[12] One developer was even told to make his tower a number of floors higher, even though calculations showed that above 18 floors they would begin to lose money.

Many people think tall buildings are not a good idea

A number of groups, such as English Heritage, have raised objections at the planning stage to these developments, while other groups have not only supported the building of these new tower blocks but also vilified the objectors. Livingston famously likened English Heritage to the Taliban of British Architecture for its objection to the London Bridge scheme.[13]

Richard MacCormac and Sir Norman Foster have voiced their reservations about new tower buildings in the City of London, that can 'so easily become ghettos, just a series of fragments floating apart and looking after themselves'.[14] Sir Norman Foster sensibly called for 'less hysterical debate – The issues need to be discussed rationally.'[15] There are a number of people calling for a new look at the potential for 'ground scrapers', and low rise, high- and medium-density developments.

And some cities resist them

Paris has one of the most untouched skylines of any city in the world, and is now considering lifting a 30-year ban on skyscrapers at the edges of the city. In 1974 they outlawed the building of any building above eight storeys over an area of 40 square miles. The move comes at a time when there is growing pressure on space, but plans are only being considered for new higher buildings in the city's outskirts, not in the historic centre, where the only high buildings are the Eiffel Tower built in 1889 to a height of 324 m[16] and the Montparnasse Tower, with 58 floors. It may be that major corporations that are now extremely concerned not to be situated in, or near 'target' buildings, may in future favour more 'secure' cities, free from such buildings.

11.2.
Cities all around the world grew within a couple of decades to their soaring current forms. When the author was a girl in Sydney the highest building was the AMP building, at 28 storeys and the radio weather programme would report occasionally that snow had been spotted on the top of this huge building! It can be seen behind the ferry by the wharf. (*Source:* Sue Roaf)

SPACE PLANNING PROBLEMS

A high rise building usually consists of a shaft and elevators surrounded by living units on each storey. The properties of openings in the south (sun: solar gain) and north (cold wind: infiltration) and the very limited opportunities for the floor plans, with restricted walk distances to fire exits and access shafts, drastically reduces the organizational possibilities of the plan.

Such are the conditions of a high rise form that, because of its very height, can severely disadvantage people who suffer from vertigo, a recognized condition in which individuals are psychologically frightened of being 'too high'. The enclosed access conditions for tall buildings may also trigger agoraphobia, a condition that can be exacerbated by high temperatures. Many people cannot work in such buildings for this reason, which would be a problem if they were a key worker in an organization. It is unclear how employers can insist on employees only occupying 'high' offices, where their business is located, when this work condition would contravene employment law against the discrimination against individuals or 'minorities' with such conditions. How does a person climb the corporate ladder in a tall building when they suffer from vertigo?

The form also has climatic design limitations, magnified because they occur on every floor in a rigid plan form. It has been proven nigh on impossible, for instance, to prevent all south-facing apartments in high rise buildings from overheating in summer and all north-facing ones being cold in winter due to radiant gains and losses. It is very difficult to attach solar shading to the outside of a sheer building face without increasing the risk of failure at the point where the shade connects to the buildings and controlling them in high winds where the wind pressure is significantly amplified with the height of the building. However, currently this problem is being looked at by some firms interested to try to achieve apartments that can have access to both facades.

The geometric properties of towers make it difficult to utilize solar hot water systems for occupants because of the low ratio of the external building surface area: unit/person. A rule of thumb for solar hot water system design is that there needs to be about 1 m^2 per person in the UK. This means that the tall building simply cannot generate sufficient solar hot water and/or solar electricity to heat and power its occupants, particularly in a deep plan building. However the need, and challenge, of incorporating renewable energy into buildings is currently being explored by a number of practices who are experimenting with wind generators, transparent PVs for window areas and geothermal pile foundations. Such work is increasingly important if one looks forward to a time when every building will have to be at least 10% (by 2010) to 100% (by 2050?) powered by new energy, or surprise sources, under conditions described in Chapter 14. Early calculations show that 50–60% of energy for recent designs could be generated onsite for high rise buildings and it is maintained that the rest could come from off-site green sources.

Vertical circulation is also a problem that has traditionally been dealt with by using fast lifts. However, at times of crisis these lifts become a problem, with people becoming trapped in them being a major hazard when the power fails. Lifts are not used during fire events. Travel times in buildings are another issue arising from building height. For instance, the 'street door to destination' travel time for a visitor arriving at the building and then travelling up to say the 5th or the 100th floor will obviously exceed the travel time in a low to medium rise building of the same floor plan. This increases the stress associated with the visit and one consequence of this is the alienation of visitors, particularly in times of emergency evacuation, whether simulated or real. Similarly increased travel times experienced by the staff may increase the wasted time during the day experienced for everyday operation, and hence costs, for the business in question. Such travel times can be critical in buildings such as hotels and hospitals, and offices, as we now know from the Twin Towers, in times of emergency. It took people from the top floors some 3 hours to evacuate the building in 1993 when one of the towers at the World Trade Center was damaged by a bomber.

A related factor is that the high rise by its very nature piles floor upon floor, and people one on top of another. Hence when the building is catastrophically damaged causing collapse everything above the damaged floor falls, as we saw in New York. If the same space is arranged in a low rise form, such as at the Pentagon, only a part of the building collapses. If the Pentagon had been a high rise building most of the people in it would have died, and because of its robust, low rise form, far fewer occupants were affected when the structure was hit by a plane. In addition, the sheer amount of material generated by the collapse of the Twin Towers was exponentially higher than would have accompanied the collapse of say a 10-storey building of the same size due to the force of the collapse.

However, it was not only the main buildings of the Twin Towers that collapsed but six adjacent buildings also had to be demolished as part of the aftermath of the 9/11 attack. The decision to demolish the former Deutsche Bank building that overlooks the World Trade Center site was taken as late as June 2003. The 40-storey skyscraper became known as the 'widow' because of the black netting hung over it to prevent debris from falling onto passers-by. The building, constructed in the 1970s, was severely damaged, with a 24-storey-high gash rent in it by collapsing steel from the South Tower. Worse damage was inflicted by a mould infestation, caused by the sprinkler system going off and standing water going stagnant, making the building uninhabitable. The reason it has stood for so long untouched is that the insurers could not agree that it could not be salvaged. It was calculated to cost US$100 million alone to demolish, a sum that would cover the removal of asbestos and other contaminants from the building.[17]

Workplace Security and Business Continuity Planning experts also warn corporations, not surprisingly, to be wary of taking space next to 'high-risk' buildings in view of the impacts they may have on adjacent buildings if targeted in terrorist events, and the value of buildings adjacent to new high profile 'target' buildings may be adversely affected by such trends in the business community.[18]

PSYCHOLOGICAL PROBLEMS

When high rise buildings were first commonly built in the UK a number of studies were done evaluating and reporting on the often chronic problems amongst tower dwellers, including many psychological and social problems, such as slower motor development among children who are prevented from spending time outside without adult supervision; distress and alienation, especially amongst groups of certain ages or genders who spend many hours indoors – women, the elderly and children; dissolution of social connections; a higher crime rate relative to the same phenomena in lower buildings, particularly around lift shafts and stairways in poorer areas, where the lifts are often broken and irregularly maintained due to the low priority of the task for already overstretched budgets.[19,20]

There are now methodologies for including within the life cycle costings for a building the increased costs to the UK National Health Service of different types and conditions of housing by post code.[21] New studies could be instigated on the health costs of existing high rise housing, so they can be incorporated in the cost planning on new towers for which they seek planning consent.

There is also, currently, real concern raised about the after-effects of the Twin Towers event in terms of psychological damage and the impact on the minds and even productivity of people who now occupy high rise buildings around the world.

Voices raised against the skyscraper include that of the architect and urbanist Constantine Doxiades:[22]

My greatest crime was the construction of high-rise buildings. The most successful cities of the past were those where people and buildings were in a certain balance with nature. But high-rise buildings work against nature, or, in modern terms, against the environment. High-rise buildings work against man himself, because they isolate him from others, and this isolation is an important factor in the rising crime rate. Children suffer even more because they lose their direct contacts with nature, and with other children. High-rise buildings work against society because they prevent the units of social importance – the family ... the neighbourhood, etc. – from functioning as naturally and as normally as before. High-rise buildings work against networks of transportation, communication, and of utilities, since they lead to higher densities, to overloaded roads, to more extensive water supply systems — and, more importantly, because they form vertical networks which create many additional problems – crime ...

BUILDING, OPERATIONAL AND MAINTENANCE COSTS

The higher the building, the more it costs to build, operate and maintain. The primary increase in build costs, per metre square, results from the increased structure and construction required to support the building, earthquake-, fire- and weather-proof it and the increased systems needed to operate it, including lifts, escalators, water pumping and electrical systems. These high costs can only pay back if higher than average prices are paid for the floor area, housing or offices than would be the case in a lower rise building. So to put social housing up in the air is to ask the poor to pay over the odds for the simple provision of housing.

In addition, the higher the building, the more it costs to run because of the increased need to raise people (lifts), goods, and services and also, importantly, because the more exposed the building is to the elements the more it costs to heat and cool. The higher the building, the higher the wind speeds around the building, the more difficult to keep it out, and the more the wind pressure on the envelope sucks heat from the structure, particularly as with many 20th century tower blocks the envelope leaks. The higher the building, if standing alone, the more exposed to the sun it is and the more it can overheat. And hence the higher the building the more it costs to keep the internal environment comfortable.[23]

So in effect, by making the simple decision that those with less money will live in the air in social housing 'towers', their quality of life will be compromised: they will struggle to pay their utility bills and for the service charges for their lifts and for caretakers necessary to keep such buildings safe and clean. Local councils in the UK now have to charge home owners what it costs them to run a building people live in. Previously such service charges were absorbed in the general council charges, so making all tenants and council tax payers pay to run the lifts in high rise buildings that others occupied; now individual house holders will have to foot the bills for the costs of their own homes. So individual council tax payers and tenants foot the bill for a politician's choice to go 'high'.

Lifts are very energy-expensive and costly to run, maintain and replace. Lifts alone can account for at least 5–15% of the building running costs and the higher the building, the more it costs.[24]

The higher the building, the greater the annual maintenance costs to keep it clean, repaired and safe. The failure of a single building element can be catastrophic. For example, the silicon mastic used to weatherproof glazing panels was given in its early forms only a 15 year performance guarantee. If mastic fails, it can result in the need to remove and/or repair every single glazing panel in the surface of a building, which in a high rise building would prove to be a crippling expense. Day-to-day maintenance of buildings can be similarly expensive and where building envelopes are problematic to access, they can have enormous annual cleaning costs. One famous tower block in the City of London has allegedly proved impossible to sell because of its astronomical maintenance and running costs, and even relatively lower rise buildings such as the Greater London Authority headquarters can run up annual window cleaning bills in the tens of thousands of pounds.

Many tower blocks have fallen into a very poor state of repair because their owners cannot afford their upkeep. The historical reality has proved that it is often cheaper to blow up tower blocks than repair them. 'Tower blocks are only for the rich', said Mike Holmes of Arup Associates, so why is anyone considering them for social housing at all, particularly when, with climate change, wind speeds, storms, flooding and solar intensity will increase significantly over the next decades, so speeding up their deterioration. Particularly vulnerable to a more extreme climate will be leaky envelopes, typical of concrete panel tower blocks, and glass and steel structures that suffer from very high levels of solar gain, are very difficult to shade high up and have traditionally had extreme cold bridging problems through the structure. Tower blocks also typically have to have air conditioning, as they are of sealed envelope construction, a decision that can quadruple energy costs at a stroke, and in turn gives them a disproportionately high carbon emitter status, at a time when carbon taxes for home owners are being spoken of. So on top of high running costs homeowners would have also to consider that they may have to pay far higher carbon taxes associated with high rise buildings in the future.

OVERPOPULATION OF DISTRICTS

The concentration and compaction of high rise buildings permits intensive land use but causes population over-crowding in localities, at certain times of the day/week. This can result in drastic affects on open areas, streets and parks, and places excessive strain on the existing infrastructure, such as parking, roads, transport, sewerage, water and energy.[25] If one breeds bacteria in a test tube they can double and double in number many times with no noticeable impact on their population until the test tube is half full and when they double again the test tube becomes full. A single doubling incident becomes the point at which the habitat ceases to become viable as its capacity is exceeded.

Leon Krier has referred to this as 'urban hypertrophy', making the additional point that overloading any given urban centre tends to prevent the organic development of new healthy, mixed urban fabric anywhere beyond the centre.[26] Bear in mind, too, that some of the sturdiest and even aesthetically pleasing tall buildings of the early 20th century are only now approaching the end of their so-called 'design life'. What is their destiny? The worst offender in this urban destruction is the monofunctional megatower, which paradoxically has become an icon of modernity and progress. This issue has also been dealt with in Chapter 7, in consideration of effects on infrastructure and evacuation.

SOLAR, WIND AND LIGHT ACCESS RIGHTS

There are real issues of solar rights with high rise buildings that have to be addressed and agreed. The higher a building is the greater the shadow it casts on the buildings around it.[27] The shadow cast by a two-storey building is larger than the shadow of a one-storey building of identical floor plan by 2%. A building of 16-storeys casts a shadow 43% larger than a one-storey building, at noon on the winter solstice.[28] A high rise building will cast a shadow over a huge area of a city. Naturally, if the building is close to the high rise it will be shadowed most of the year and if it is distant it will be shadowed perhaps for only a period in the day, however this could be when the solar energy is most needed. Solar rights legislation is being passed in cities around the world and an excellent example is that of the Solar Law of Boulder, Colorado[27] where legislation has been enforced to ensure that buildings do not steal the sunlight from adjacent properties. There is also a case to be made for wind rights to ensure that new buildings do not cut off the air flow around buildings that may be needed to power ventilation systems or generate electricity.

In a world where power failures will become more common, the use of non-grid-connected solar or wind generation systems for, for instance, failsafe security and fire alarms and lighting, electric garage doors, UPS systems for computer networks and emergency lighting will increase, enhancing the need to protect the solar and wind rights of buildings. In the less energy-secure future we will have to rely increasingly on emerging energy generation technologies, such as wind, solar and hydrogen systems, to run our buildings for hot water, space heating and electricity.

The higher up one gets, the higher the wind speed, and so on the facades of high rise buildings there will be huge potential for wind generators. There is much interesting work currently being done by Dr Derek Taylor at the Open University on how to power individual buildings using the wind. Again there will be optimal levels of building surface available in relation to building volume and occupancy to be explored here and optimal wind-driven building forms will emerge and be exploited. But again we come to the problem of stealing other buildings' energy, and if a series of wind generators are built on city buildings, and an adjacent tower block is erected in the direction of the prevailing wind, the wind energy of the first building is substantially reduced. There are also problems of generator vibration, passing through to the structure of a building, that will have to be solved in high buildings and the necessary structural reinforcements would have to be factored into the system and running costs.

There are increasingly high profile legal issues in allowing one building to steal the sun, light, wind and sound from one or many other buildings. Shanghai's Urban Planning Administrative Bureau has proposed curbing the height of tall buildings in the city.[29] Over the past decade the Chinese city has witnessed an extraordinary

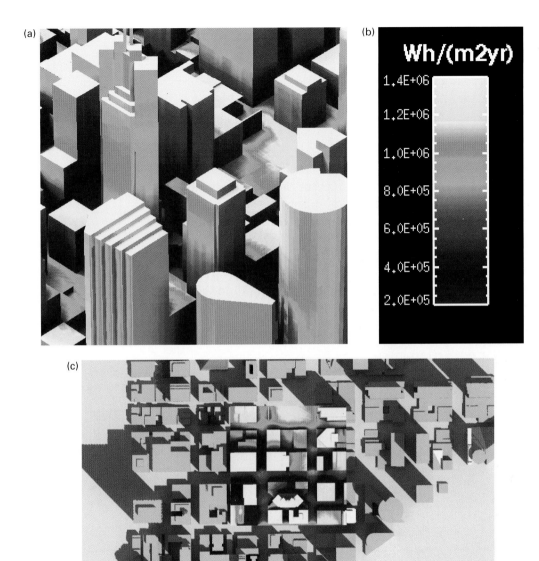

11.3.
Simulation of an aerial view of San Francisco showing the surfaces that get most solar gain over a year and the shadows that buildings of different shapes and heights cast across an area of the city. (a) Predicted total annual irradiation incident on building facades in San Francisco; (b) Irradiation scale; (c) View from above of the 3D model of San Francisco with an overlay map of total annual irradiation for the study area. (*Source*: John Mardaljevic, Institute for Energy and Sustainable Development, De Montfort University; see www.iesd.dmu.ac.uk/)

construction boom – the Chinese government's plan for Shanghai to replace Hong Kong as the financial hub of East Asia is thought to be on schedule. But a consequence of the city's growing prominence has been a steep rise in land values, which in turn has contributed to the construction of a large number of tall buildings in the city. Now, with a growing number of civil court cases alleging that tall buildings can block light and raise the city's temperatures, it has been proposed that buildings should not exceed 30 storeys. The proposal is unlikely to please developers. Land prices have risen as high as US$1500 (RMB 12 000) per square metre.[30] There are also concerns that the quality of some tall buildings is not high enough.

Two conditions conspire to make daylighting difficult in high density buildings. One is how wide they are, from one external wall to another. Once the width of a building increases beyond about 12 m it is difficult to daylight it. Not withstanding the depth of a building, the amount of daylight reaching an interior is dependent on how much clear sky is visible from any particular window. The more sky which can be seen from a window, the greater the amount of daylight that can enter a room. In a dense urban setting, it becomes clear that windows close to the ground will not provide significant daylight to interiors in high rise districts.

WIND-PROOFING BUILDINGS

Peter Blake, in *Form Follows Fiasco*, condemned megatowers on several points. One was the disastrous wind shear that their surfaces created; another was fires that had burned out of control in two skyscrapers in Latin America. He warned the world that:

The first alternative to Modern Dogma should obviously be a moratorium on high-rise construction. It is outrageous that towers more than a hundred storeys high are being built at a time when no honest engineer and no honest architect, anywhere on earth, can say for certain what these structures will do to the environment – in terms of monumental congestion of services (including roads and mass-transit lines), in terms of wind currents at sidewalk level, in terms of surrounding water tables, in terms of fire hazards, in terms of various sorts of interior traumata, in terms of despoiling the neighborhoods . . .[31]

Perhaps the worst climatic impacts that are associated with high rise buildings result from the wind. The increasing height of a building results in two major factors:

1 The speed of the wind increases the higher it is off the ground resulting in higher air pressure experienced on the surface of the building.
2 The higher the pressure at the top of the building the greater the difference in pressure between the top and the bottom of the building increasing the speed of the wind between the apex and the base of the building.

The increasing high level air pressure causes accelerated air speeds on the surface of the building significantly increasing air penetration into the building, and out on the leeward side of the building through openings and cracks.[32] This can substantially increase the heating or the cooling load of an exposed high building over the loads of a low to medium rise building, often requiring expensive systems of climate control to even maintain a comfortable indoor climate the higher up the building one goes, but perhaps the potentially most severe impacts of wind discomfort occur in the outdoor spaces around high rise buildings.[33] Many of us will experience such discomfort daily. In the city of London, for example, it is difficult not to notice the significantly increased wind speeds on an ordinary summer's day in say, Threadneedle Street, adjacent to a high rise tower.

Wind becomes an annoyance at about 5 m/s, by causing clothes to flap and disturbance to the hair. At 10 m/s it becomes definitely disagreeable and dust and litter are picked up and by 20 m/s it is likely to be dangerous. In studies the Building Research Establishment found that wind speeds of 5 m/s were exceeded less than 5% of the time in areas of low rise developments but were exceeded over 20% of the time in areas with high rise buildings.[34] With the increasingly deep low pressure systems currently being associated with climate change and their associated increases in wind speeds, the ground level turbulence and wind speeds in city streets may become increasingly less tolerable for the ordinary citizen in areas adjacent to tower blocks.

Higher wind speeds at street level are also associated with higher wind chill factors, making the outdoors even more uncomfortable. Where today problems of outdoor air comfort may result from wind flow down and up from high rise buildings, they may in future climates become the cause of increasingly dangerous street conditions as wind speeds increase.

There are a number of laboratories in the UK where the wind impacts of new city developments can be tested on models in wind tunnels or through simulation, as for instance at the Universities of Cardiff, Sheffield, Cambridge, UMIST and at the Building Research Establishment and the National Physical Laboratory. Such wind testing is required by local authorities, by independent bodies, but for current climates only, and not future wind environments.

The highest percentage of the 85 UK construction-related deaths between 2001 and 2002 were caused by falls from height and a report on Health and Safety on sites concluded that 'designers are often abdicating their responsibility to reduce risk in relation to work at height by leaving it to the principal contractor without first considering how they could change the design in a way that would make it safer to build, clean or maintain'.[35] Increased wind speeds at height, with a windier climate, will significantly increase the risk of construction worker deaths to the point where building firms may become reluctant to put their workforces under such risks during certain seasons of the year.

SECURITY

There are four ways in which high rise buildings will impact on the security of individuals, a business or a district. The first is obvious, being the security threat posed by occupying a 'target' building, occupied particularly by other target companies. In the current anti-globalization atmosphere in current politics the larger the building the bigger the trophy. In New York it was the highest symbol of American Imperialism that was targeted by Islamic fundamentalist bombers. In London the Irish bombers chose again the district that represented the 'heart of the beast' to plant their largest bomb in the capital – Canary Wharf.

The second security issue is less obvious but may have more bearing on the everyday lives of people. It is the increasing wind speed at street level detailed above that has, and will increasingly have, the general effect that people avoid the streets. This impacts on street businesses as people begin to move out of doors less and less, leading to a general reduction in the quality of street life. American studies also show that lower numbers of people on the streets increases the levels of crime and violence, so reducing the security of whole districts.

In addition, studies of high rise housing estates have shown that they are subject to higher levels of crime generally and can have disastrous impacts on society and culture. The problems of access

11.4.
Just as financiers and pension holders alike have 'taken a bath' on the 'Dog Funds' that lost their value overnight, so many buildings may also say *Cave Canem* – 'Beware of the Dogs'. To avoid them look for signs of vulnerability to a range of hazards in a particular building.
(*Source*: www.moloss.com)

and psychological alienation of high rise housing have been well studied. Such was the scale of the problem in Hulme in South Manchester that the Chief Housing Office of the city actually quit his job in the 1970s to write a PhD on access in housing estates.

The third security issue is that of biological warfare. In buildings with fixed windows and extensive air circulation systems there is an increased hazard from biological agents. Ventilation ducts have proved to be a route of infection; at the Pentagon 31 anthrax spores were found in the air conditioning ducts of the building.[36] The problem here is the bigger the building, the bigger the risk. Many tall buildings have centralized circulation, servicing and air handling units that make them very vulnerable to attack from many different sources.

A fourth issue we could add is nature's 'biological warfare' on us. For example, after more than a year, Hilton Hawaiian Village reopened in September 2003 after paying $55 million dollars in repairs that saw the building closed for 14 months, because a single tower block became infected with mould throughout its air-handling system, exacerbated by very high humidity within the building. The mould *Eurotium aspergillus* was said to be to blame, the same kind of mould seen on bread or cheese. It has no effect on most people, but some people get minor irritation of the nose around it, the symptoms abating as soon as one moves away, while a very few people have severe symptoms that in rare cases can be life-threatening. This is not confined to the tropics, and indeed a problem similar to what Hilton experienced was found in hospitals across Canada in recent years.

Hilton has sued virtually every contractor that had anything to do with the construction of the Kalia Tower, including the architect, all the consulting engineers and other specialists on the project, and even the company that provided the lanai glass doors. It has argued that both the design and the construction of the building made it a 'greenhouse' for growing mould. The entire HVAC system was rebuilt, mostly to ensure a more frequent turnover of drier air. The insurance industry has subsequently withdrawn 'mould coverage' from many policies and it is claimed mould will be the 'new asbestos' in terms of payouts. The severity of the problem is reflected in the size of the payout to one family in a mould case, when a Texas jury awarded a family $32 million in a single toxic mould lawsuit against Farmers Insurance Group in June 2001.[37] Such outbreaks may become more prevalent with a warmer, wetter climate, which will make buildings more susceptible to systemic infestations of naturally occurring toxins within large-scale air-handling systems.

ENERGY SECURITY

The height of a building affects its internal climate. A building develops its own internal micro-climate, and heat from the lower floors will rise by natural buoyancy, making the higher floors hotter. The higher the building the greater this problem of thermal stratification and the more energy that has to be thrown at cooling the upper floors.

In a high rise building, where so many people are dependent on machinery for their very survival, there are severe repercussions from system failure. If a chiller breaks down and a part has to be obtained from Japan the systems of the whole building may be put at risk. In February 1998 in Auckland, New Zealand, all four main cables into the central city failed, cutting electricity to offices and more than 5000 apartments. Backup cables also failed, due in part to the extreme summer temperatures[38] and for up to 8 weeks there was chaos in the city buildings, where temperatures soared to over 50 °C and allegedly in the top floors of tall buildings to over 80 °C, making their habitation impossible. So taller means hotter at the top and more energy to heat and cool the building – a factor when floors are metered and lessees have to pay for the energy they use on their own floors. Businesses with all their eggs in one building basket will be very vulnerable to the impacts of energy outages, particularly in thin, tight-skinned buildings with no opening windows that have to be immediately evacuated because the air indoors becomes unfit to breathe once a blackout begins.

A 100-storey office block in the centre of London with a 50 m by 50 m floor plan would, if it was inefficient, use in the region of 1000 kWh/m^2/annum of primary energy to run if it was of a business-as-usual design. This would translate to around 115 W/m^2 ($1000/(24 \times 365)$ W/m^2). Tall buildings, by their very nature of being tall, can use twice as much energy as equivalent low buildings – to raise people, goods, water etc. throughout the building. Therefore peak demand from the building could be say 250 W/m^2 or 62.5 MW. A typical UK power station today has a rated output capacity of about 1 giga watt. So one more 1 MW power station would have to be built to cope with 16 new high rise buildings in the City of London for instance, and this would be paid for from the bills of the ordinary electricity consumers of a region. Is this fair people may begin to ask, and especially when energy security is increasingly a core requirement of UK government policy.

Such buildings are a large part of the energy security problem in that they draw down so much of the energy in an area they can jeopardize supplies to buildings around, particularly where the power supply infrastructure is weak. The need to turn off or turn down buildings was seen in the case of the factories and shopping malls of Shanghai that had to be 'turned off' during brownouts (severe drops in voltage that cause the lights to dim).

Many towers are advertised as 'energy efficient' or 'green', and such claims could be taken with a pinch of salt. However, mitigating against reductions in air conditioning use with efficient technologies is the fact that standards of environmental design of building envelopes are decreasing continually, as evidenced by the fairly universal trend in office buildings in the 1990s, and increasingly in residential properties in the United States, towards thin, tight-skinned buildings, often with non-opening windows.[39] The lack of insulation in the external envelopes of such buildings, often coupled with poor thermal fabric storage internally, increases the heating and cooling loads of the buildings. With increasingly poor standards of environmental design, including widespread excessive use of glass in envelopes, and rapidly increasing levels of equipment use, and in particular of computers, air conditioning becomes more and more essential.[40]

FIRE

A designer of the Twin Towers stated on TV the day after the event that if they had designed in sufficient escape stairs for the building then there would not have been enough office space left to make the building economically viable. It is increasingly recognized that in such cases, in tall buildings, everyone above the fire is likely to die. As a result of this open acknowledgement of the risks of occupying high rise buildings, the Building Research Establishment has been pressing UK ministers to tighten building regulations related to fire and have written to the Department of Transport, Local Government and the Regions raising the issues.[41] The current regulations do not take into account the provision for illegal acts, catastrophic fires or terrorism, nor was there sufficient provision in the guidelines for very tall buildings. The increasingly stringent costs of building in new standards for fire precautions may affect the financial viability of high rise projects.

Statements were also made after the 9/11 event that no building could have withstood the forces of the two aircraft and the associated catastrophic fires after their crashes. What we know from the Pentagon impact, however, is that in a robust, securely designed, low-rise building fatalities can be reduced. After 9/11 the whole way in which fire engineers calculate survival risks in cases of fire has changed. Traditionally they estimated on the notion of phased evacuation where the floor of fire and the one above and one below evacuates first. Today we know that in any fire event in a high rise building people will think '9/11' and all scrabble to evacuate simultaneously. There would never be enough fire exits in any high rise to enable that to happen within the minutes that may be available. We also know now that the fire engineers' theories about 'pressurized' escape stairs are flawed and that it is impossible to maintain a pressurized escape when more than a few doors are opened into it at the same time.

The New York fire department say that a fully clothed fire fighter can reach and operate effectively to around the tenth floor, but not higher up, so people who need attention on floors higher than this may never be reached.

We also know that in catastrophic fires, explosions and blackouts, sprinkler systems and fire lifts can fail. We now know that the increasingly hot summers will increase general fire risks out of and inside cities and that they are often associated with wide-scale power failures. And we know that fires can be caused for many reasons, and 'insecurity' will increase the risk of them being triggered. On 1 February 1974, in São Paulo, Brazil, a fire caused by electrical faults broke out in the upper storeys of a bank building and killed 189 people, many of whom leapt to their deaths. On 31 December 1986, in San Juan, Puerto Rico, fire in the Dupont Plaza Hotel set by three employees killed 96 people, largely due to occupants breaking windows at the point of 'flashover', when a fire ball explodes, instantly killing many of the victims. On 23 February 1991 a fire broke out on the 22nd floor of the 38-storey building known as One Meridien Plaza in Philadelphia. The fire began in a pile of oil-soaked rags left by a contractor. It burned for 19 hours, eight floors were gutted and three firefighters lost their lives.[42] In the August 2003 blackout in New York the city fire brigade were called to numerous fires caused by candles used for light.

WHAT IS THE FUTURE FOR TALL BUILDINGS?

In an increasingly insecure word, do we really need to live in more insecure buildings? What would common sense tell us about how high a building should go?

- High enough not to be a 'target' building – to nestle beneath the canopy of the city skyline to escape storm winds and not shade the buildings next door from the sun – this depends on the area of a particular city.

DEAD END

HIGH ENERGY BUILDINGS

11.5.
Buildings with extremely high energy costs and exposure to extreme winds and solar gain may be one of the evolutionary types of buildings that die out first as the climate changes and the costs of energy rise over the next decades. (*Source:* Sue Roaf, digitally produced by Claire Palmer)

- High enough that a fire fighter could run up fully clothed to people in a fire – so no more than ten floors.
- High enough to be comfortably naturally ventilated – say fifteen floors.
- High enough for occupants to be able to carry bags, and water, up and down the stairs safely if a blackout occurs – say three floors.

So, a compromise would be around six to eight storeys, but its anybody's choice and anybody's guess. A sensible choice may be found in the city of Paris, which has a canopy built to these heights. So interestingly, the French, with their 'Beaux Arts' tradition and few notable low energy buildings at all, may have a model for a low risk city. What will the market benefits of that be over the coming decades?

Perhaps the days of size mattering are over and our building choice in the future will be dominated by the desire to ensure that what we build from now on has the smallest impacts and lasts the longest time rather than making the biggest impression today. Whatever form of building we chose to live and work in, in the future, one thing must be sure: that the occupants can survive in it when the lights go out, because, in the last decades of the fossil fuels age, energy insecurity will drive many of our lifestyle choices. It is to this we turn next.

Box 11.1 The impact of '9/11'

The thrill of tall buildings has, to a large extent, been dampened for New Yorkers, and many others around the world, by the events of and after 11 September 2001. Some 70 million square feet of office space was destroyed on 9/11. Two months afterwards the demand for office space in Lower Manhattan was almost negligible because commerce and industry had moved out of the area to what they consider to be safer premises, lower and less prestigious perhaps, outside the city centre.

The Empire State Building, one of the city's prime pieces of real estate, has become less prestigious and desirable.[i] Once again New York City's tallest structure, it has lost a number of its 880 tenants since September 2001, and others have said they are thinking about new locations. Many business owners who are staying in the Lower Manhattan area have numbers of employees, and their back-up information centres, located elsewhere due to their fears of further terrorist attacks. Others found they were losing money because of their location.

In New York it is not only the big players in the property markets who suffer, but also the florists, the grocers and the restaurants, many of whom are also moving out having lost everything, to try to start again elsewhere. They have lost tens of thousands of well-heeled customers in the space of a couple of blocks due to the event and out-migration of workers and there is not enough business left in the area to keep many afloat. Economic migration is already happening in downtown New York.

'The attacks on the World Trade Center and the Pentagon changed everything – and have created immediate and intense visibility for Corporate Real Estate.' This quote from Cathy Guilbeault, Workplace Resource Director, Sun Microsystems Inc.[ii] shows how importantly businesses are taking 'Workplace Security and Business Continuity Planning' in light of 9/11 and 'planning for the survival of the Enterprise' now includes obvious risk mitigation, such as:

- Shifts in preference from signature buildings in traditional business development plans to low visibility facilities in dispersed or less popular locations.
- Shift from high-rise to low-rise buildings with a preference for lower-level offices.
- Less visible external signage.
- Greater emphasis on building safety, with more pressure on corporate real estate to ensure that they have done everything possible to provide for the safety and security of employees.
- Shift to medium-sized cities (in the UK this would favour places such as Manchester, Birmingham, Bristol, Newcastle and Leeds).

In London, businesses are apparently also wary of occupying high profile, high rise buildings, because, in part, of the perceived terrorists risks. At Canary Wharf, rents fell steadily over 2003, with around 15% of the office space empty in the summer, and some of the tenants having deals letting them give back rented space without paying financial penalties despite the fact that Middle East investors were shifting their attention from US markets to Britain and Europe.[iii] The half-empty Swiss Re tower building proved a problem for its owners when it became very difficult to let the other half of the 600 000 square feet of building at St Mary Axe in the heart of the City of London (Swiss Re had taken the bottom floors of the building). Many reasons were given for this, including that the shape of the space was difficult to use, no doubt fear of occupying a 'target' high profile building did not help, nor what were then the highest rents in the city. At stake was half of the £2.5 million a year rental costs if no occupant for the top half of the building could be found. At that time around 20 million square feet of business space was available in central London, presumably a further disincentive to the building of major new high rise developments.[iv]

Just like the 'Dog' Bonds that financiers can't sell because they lost nearly all of their value over night we now look as if we may have a generation of 'Dog' Buildings. Here we see the issues, writ large, that it is not the micro level considerations of how the BMS system works or what the 'u' value of the walls is, but the fundamental market image of the building that drives sales. There is money to be made from this realization.

[i] http://www.newsday.com/business/local/newyork/ ny-bzcov182469047nov18.story.

[ii] www.corenetglobal.org/pdf/learning/9_11_impact.pdf, loaded on 2 October 2002. This site shows how importantly businesses are taking 'Workplace Security and Business Continuity Planning' in light of 9/11 and 'planning for the survival of the Enterprise'. There are many websites, mainly US, that can offer valuable insight, including guidelines

from the Federal Protective Service on How to Make Buildings Safe etc. for instance on: www.gsa.gov.

iii *Observer*, Business, 24 August 2003, p. 4.

iv *Evening Standard*, 19 March 2003, p. 20.

Box 11.2 Ghettos in the sky

There is no industry-wide policy of not offering mortgages on high rise flats and different lenders have their own policies as to what they will lend on. There are a number of issues that lenders will take into account when considering whether to lend on a flat. These will include whether the area, and the block, is predominantly owner-occupied, whether there is likely to be ongoing demand for the property and what the short- and long-term maintenance costs are likely to be.

Large maintenance bills can be a particular issue in tower block flats. Some borrowers have been faced with bills of £30 000 if major refurbishment is carried out on a block. If there were any possibility that a borrower will be faced with a bill of this order it would severely restrict their ability to pay their mortgage and affect the security of the loan, so older, poorly maintained, blocks are not favoured by lenders.

The fact that a lender is not prepared to accept the property for mortgage purposes may have as much to do with the fact that there is little or no demand for such properties in a particular area as with an individual property's specific physical condition.

The type of construction is also an issue. Individual lenders will have their own policies on the types of construction they are prepared to lend on. Concrete panel construction has caused problems in the past, including cold bridging and air leakage problems through the envelope, and a number of lenders are reluctant to lend on this type of property. However, if the construction type is an unfamiliar one or there are doubts about its durability, the lender will often ask for a recent structural report. If the potential borrower is unwilling to pay for this then the mortgage will be refused even though the property may be acceptable. This associated risk is also amplified by the experience of large payouts from the insurance industry related to a single event, such as the gas explosion in a single flat at Ronan Point, London, resulting in the collapse, and subsequent demolition of, an entire tower block.

For poor people in Glasgow there is little chance of ever getting a mortgage in a tower block on a council estate. This is one reason why famous tower blocks that have dominated the Glasgow skyline for over 40 years are being demolished. They had become synonymous with crime, poverty and urban decay in Britain's unhealthiest city and billions of pounds will be spent over 10 years to transform the bleak landscape of Scotland's biggest city, which has the highest concentration of public owned housing in Europe. Most of the 250 blocks of flats will be knocked down to make way for thousands of new, purpose-built homes after the city's 94 000 flats are transferred from council control to community housing trusts. The plans are backed by the Scottish Executive and Chancellor Gordon Brown, who has promised to write off the city's £1 billion housing debt if the transfer is successful. Under the plans, the Glasgow Housing Association will be given a £6 billion budget to deal with dilapidated housing stock, including the tower blocks.

Housing consultants estimate the cost of refurbishing flats at Red Road, Glasgow, to a standard that would last for the next 30 years would amount to more than £70 000 per home. They say it will be cheaper to get rid of them and start again.[i]

For the same reason many other cities across Britain are blowing up their tower blocks, including Birmingham where all the 315 tower blocks are planned to be demolished. Officials confirmed that finance for the transfer is based on a programme to demolish 100 tower blocks in the next five years, and almost all of the remaining 215 blocks before 2018.[ii]

Although some lenders have a greater appetite (and capacity) to take on loans which are considered a greater risk than others, and will insure some tower flats, only a few will expose themselves in this market and this is why it is very important that tenants who are considering whether to exercise their right to buy should be advised of the additional risks involved in purchasing a tower block flat and the possible problems they may have if or when they come to resell it.

Some local authorities may be willing to buy back the property under the 'Buy Back Scheme' introduced on 1 April 1999, where local authorities are able to buy back homes from leaseholders or others who are in difficulty or are having problems selling their property. It allows local authorities to regain a property which can then be re-let, but it is doubtful if many authorities would do this for such high-risk properties, which is one reason why Glasgow has chosen to demolish its tower stock. Alternatively, individuals could seek a cash buyer or someone who would see it as an investment property, as an investor may take a different view of the risks posed.

However, there are too few houses in Southeast England, and thus forced high house prices, meaning ordinary working families are unable to afford to live near their work and have to commute, sometimes for hours, to get to work. Local councils are increasingly asking for a higher percentage of 'social' or 'affordable' housing in all developments, up to 40–50% from some councils.

Developers reap less profit from social housing and are very reluctant to build more than the minimum they can get away with.

In April 2003, London Mayor Ken Livingston threatened to block Broadway Malyan's 50-storey apartment block in Vauxhall as its 25% affordable homes was insufficient.[iii] He has developed a formula, dubbed the 'Kenculator', that responds to a range of factors to arrive at a reasonable figure for what numbers of low cost houses, up to 50%, should be included in every new development. Developers are reluctant to lose such a substantial percentage of their profits by providing low cost housing that gives them lower profit levels, and worryingly the architects are lending weight to the developers' arguments by openly doubting if the formula would work. Further, if a higher percentage of units were social housing then mortgage lenders may be less willing to provide loans to buy such houses due to their rules of thumb of the proportion of owner-occupiers they require in a block to agree to lend on it.

However, some of the 1960s and 1970s tower blocks are being refurbished. Two 15-storey tower blocks on Conway Street, Liverpool, were in such poor condition that they seemed fit only for demolition, but having successfully renovated two similar blocks on Manchester's Wythenshawe Estate one developer saw an opportunity to provide affordable homes. He bought the two towers for £1 million each and is spending eight times that amount to transform the 1960s towers into flats with purchase prices starting at £49 500. The difference in the refurbishment costs estimated by Glasgow's consultants of £70 000 and the money spent on these blocks begs the question on how long the refurbishments here will hold and, once they fail, will these blocks just turn into ghettos again?

[i] http://society.guardian.co.uk/housing/story/0,7890,565387,00.html.
[ii] http://society.guardian.co.uk/housingtransfers/story/0,8150,632697,00.html.
[iii] *Building Design*, 17 April 2003, p. 6.

Box 11.3 Stealing sound and vision

In 1997 the House of Lords refused a claim by 700 residents of east London who claimed that their television reception had been severely affected by the building of Canary Wharf. While the court accepted that this did amount to quite severe interference to their enjoyment of their properties and could reduce their market value, there was still no legal basis to award compensation.[i] There is, however, hope for such residents who have suffered as the result of radio and TV wave shadows in that the approach taken by the courts is regarded as unlikely to survive the introduction of the Human Rights Act.[ii] If the loss of TV and sound quality from the erection of a tall building constitutes 'severe interference' to the enjoyment of properties then it does indeed constitute a 'material consideration' and councils are obliged by law to consult with those so affected in the planning process. So perhaps the residents affected could sue the councils for failing to meet their statutory obligation to consult with all those who will in future be affected by a development.

i All England Law Reports: 1992, p. 426; *Hunter* v. *Wharf*, available from: http://www.lib.nus.edu.sg/linus/96oct/llbcdnew.html.
ii *Guardian*, Money, 16 February 2002.

NOTES AND REFERENCES

1 Kunstler, J.H. and Salingaros, N. (2001) The end of tall buildings. At: http://www.peoplesgeography.org/tall.html. See also Salingaros, N. (1998) Theory of the Urban Web. *Journal of Urban Design*, 3, pp. 53–71. See http://www.math.utsa.edu/sphere/salingar/urbanweb.html.

2 The Empire State Building was the brain-child of John J. Raskob, the vice-president of General Motors, who wanted this new building to exceed the height of the Chrysler Building, still under construction, when the plans were released on 29 August 1929. The site had previously housed the 'twin hotel' of Waldorf–Astoria (Waldorf Hotel 1893, Astoria Hotel 1897, both by arch. Henry J. Hardenbergh), both built by the Astor family and eventually connected by a wide hall. After a fire the buildings were demolished, a new Waldorf–Astoria built farther uptown and the construction of the Empire State Building was started on the site. The excavations for the foundations were begun on January 1930, work on the steel framework in March of the same year, and the building was completed on 11 April 1931.

3 *Guardian*, 18 October 2003, p. 20.

4 *Independent*, 28 October 2003, p. 9.

5 CABE is the Commission for Architecture and the Built Environment – whose stated aim is 'inspiring people to demand more from their buildings and spaces'. CABE's home page states:

We believe that well designed homes, streets, parks, work-places, schools and hospitals are the fundamental right of everyone. We use our skills and resources to work for a higher quality of life for people and communities across England, with particular concern for those living in deprived areas. We do this by making the case for change, gathering hard evidence, providing education opportunities and through direct help on individual programmes and projects.

We motivate those responsible for providing our buildings and spaces to design and develop well. We demonstrate to those clients that investment in excellence will pay back many times over through a more productive workforce, more contented customers and a healthier bottom line.

6   *Building Design*, 9 May 2003, p. 1.

7   *Building Design*, 25 April 2003, p. 4.

8   *Building Design,* 25 April 2003, p. 4.

9   http://www.london.gov.uk/view_press_release.jsp?releaseid= 210.

10 *Building Design*, 6 July 2001.

11 *Building Design,* 5 October 2001.

12 *Building Design,* 22 July 2001.

13 *Building Design,* 6 July 2001.

14 *Building Design,* 6 July 2001.

15 *Building Design,* 6 July 2001.

16 *Guardian*, 3 November 2003, p. 16.

17 *Guardian*, 21 June 2003, p. 28.

18 www.corenetglobal.org/pdf/learning/9_11_impact.pdf.

19 Newman, O. (1973) *Defensible Space.* London: The Architectural Press.

20 Alexander, C. *et al.* (1977) *A Pattern Language – Towns, Buildings, Construction.* New York: Oxford University Press, pp. 114–19, 468–76.

21 Rudge, J. and Nicol, F. (2000) *Cutting the Cost of Cold: Affordable Warmth for Healthier Homes.* London: E&FN Spon.

22 Blake, P. (1974) *Form Follows Fiasco: Why Modern Architecture Hasn't Worked.* Boston: Little, Brown. See also an interesting discussion around the subject on: http://www.geocities.com/ Athens/2360/jm-eng.fff-hai.html.

23 Meir, I., Etzion, Y. and Faiman, D. (1998) *Energy Aspects of Design in Arid Zones.* J. Blaustein Institute for Desert Research, Ben-Gurion University of the Negev, p. 115.

24 Al-Sharif, L. (1996) Lift and escalator energy consumption. *Proceedings of the CIBSE/ASHRAE Joint National Conference*, Harrogate, pp. 231–9.

25 Meir *et al. Energy Aspects of Design in Arid Zones*, p. 115.

26 Krier, L. (1984) *Houses, Palaces, Cities.* New York, St Martin's Press.

27 Littlefair, P. (1998) Solar access, passive cooling and micro-climate in the city: the polis project. *Proceedings of EPIC 98, the 2nd European Conference on Energy Performance and Indoor Climate in Buildings.* Lyons, p. 984. See also the solar ordinances of Boulder Colorado, 1991, on: http://www.sustainable.doe.gov/municipal/codtoc.shtml. The City of Boulder's solar access ordinance guarantees access to sunlight for homeowners and renters in the city. This is done by setting limits on the amount of permitted shading by new construction. A solar access permit is available to those who have installed or who plan to install a solar energy system and need more protection than is provided by the ordinance. For new developments, all units that are not planned to incorporate solar features must be sited to provide good solar access. They must also have roofs capable of supporting at least 75 square feet of solar collectors per dwelling unit. Non-residential buildings have similar requirements for siting. When applying for a building permit, a simple shadow analysis must be submitted to the City's Building Department.

28 Meir *et al. Energy Aspects of Design in Arid* Zones, p. 116.

29 Viljoen, A. and Bohn, K. (2000) Urban intensification and the integration of productive landscape. *Part One, Proceedings World Renewable Energy Congress VI.* Oxford: Elsevier Science, pp. 483–8.

30 *RIBAWorld*, Issue 231–232, Friday 23 August 2002, 16:17:10 +0100 RIBAWorld@inst.riba.org.

31 Blake, *Form follows Fiasco*, p. 150. See also http://www.peoplesgeography.org/tall.html.

32 Meir *et al.*, *Energy Aspects of Design in Arid Zones*, p. 115.

33 Lawson, T. (2001) *Building Aerodynamics*. London: Imperial College Press.

34 See Geiger, R. (1965) *The Climate Near the Ground*. Cambridge, MA: Harvard University Press; Oke, T.R. (1978) *Boundary Layer Climates*. London: Methuen & Co.; Penwarden, A. and Wise, D. (1975) *Air Flow around Buildings*. Garston, Watford: Building Research Establishment Digest.

35 *Building Design*, 9 May 2003, p. 3.

36 *Guardian*, 18 October 2001.

37 More results from www.bizjournals.com.

38 http://www.helio-international.org/Helio/anglais/reports/newzealand.html.

39 Robertson, G. (1992) A case study of Atria. In Roaf, S. and Hancock, M. (eds) (1992) *Energy Efficient Building: A Design Guide*. Oxford: Blackwell Scientific.

40 Bordass, B. (1990) Appropriate methods and technologies for new build and refurbishment: offices. *Global Responsibilities of Architects*. London: RIBA Publications.

41 *Building Design*, 5 October 2001.

42 For a detailed analysis of this event and its implications for the fire hazards posed by tall buildings see http://www.iklimnet.com/hotelfires/meridienplaza/html.

12 THE FOSSIL FUEL CRISIS

The future of such energy-profligate buildings as skyscrapers is limited because we simply no longer have enough energy to run them. We now have to start designing and planning for the buildings to house us in the Post Fossil Fuel Age.[1]

The huge structural cracks already opening up in the fossil fuel economy are reflected in the 2003 White Paper on Energy Policy put out by the UK Department of Trade and Industry, the key aims of which were to:[2]

- Put the UK on a path to cut the its carbon dioxide emissions – the main contributor to global warming – by some 60% by about 2050 with real progress by 2020.
- Maintain the reliability of energy supplies.
- Promote competitive markets in the UK and beyond, helping to raise the rate of sustainable economic growth and to improve our productivity.
- Ensure that every home is adequately and affordably heated.

The fact is that oil and gas resources are finite, outputs of both are plateauing and will subsequently fall, and global demand is increasing. It is the gap between the fossil fuels we use, and the exponential rise in this demand for energy, that is already resulting in the energy insecurity that will be a hallmark of life, in all countries, over the next decades.

The other problems are that the emissions of greenhouse gases arising from our burning of fossil fuels are driving climate change and must be reduced dramatically if we are to have any chance of stabilizing the changing climate, and avoiding the $150 barrel!

OIL

Current estimates of how much oil we have left range from 30 to 40 years, but the nature of oil reserves, exploitation and reporting is very complex.[3] Colin Campbell gives some insight into the complexity

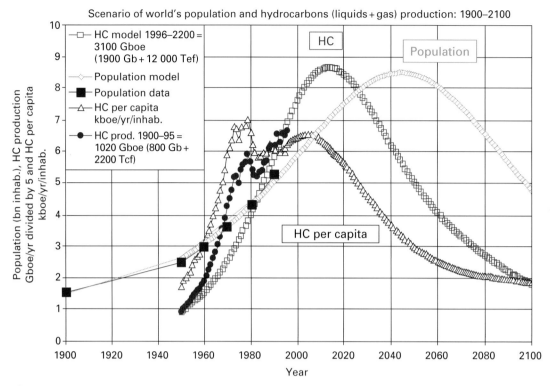

12.1.
Increases in the world population, coupled with the decrease from now on of fossil fuel availability will cause energy prices to skyrocket. (Abbreviations: Gb = billion barrels; Gboe = billion barrels oil equivalent; Tcf = trillion cubic feet (5.5 Tcf = 1 Gboe); HC = hydrocarbons). (*Source:* www.energy crisis.com)

of the forces at play in the industry in his very interesting piece called 'The Heart of the Matter',[4] and his many published works offer a fuller outline of the mechanics of the oil supply industry.[5]

Since the futurologists of the 1970s oil crisis began to warn us of 'the end of oil' based on estimates from fairly crude field surveys, the industry has become very proficient in identifying potential oil fields, locating, quantifying and exploiting them with extremely sophisticated equipment and technologies. The industry can now identify the 'needle in a haystack'[6] and high levels of confidence are placed in the validated figures they come up with.

HOW MUCH OIL LEFT IS THERE?

There are two kinds of commonly defined sources of oil and gas:

* **Conventional** – which is considered, roughly, to be all the sources that are not:
* **Non-conventional:**
  - Oil from coal and 'shale' (immature source rock)
  - Bitumen and extra-heavy oil (<100 API)

12.2.
Image from the cover of Colin Campbell's book *The Essence of Oil and Gas Depletion*.[5] Campbell was the first to highlight the global problem of 'Peak Oil' and alert the world to the coming energy crisis that he now believes may occur as soon as 2008. (*Source:* Bill Hughes, Multi-Science Publishing Co., Brentwood, Essex)

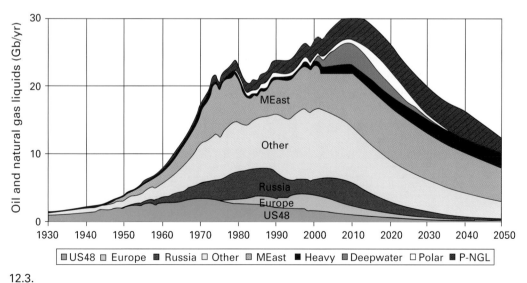

12.3.
Showing the available global fossil fuel reserves (2003) and indicating how badly off the United States and Europe are in relation to their dwindling stocks (Gb = billion barrels). (*Source:* www.peakoil.net)

- Heavy oil (10–17.5 API)
- Polar oil and gas
- Deep water oil and gas (500 m depth)[7]

There are some 20 000 conventional oil fields around the globe. Technical estimates of the size of a field are relatively constant although they evolve as knowledge grows. These confidential estimates are tested by drilling, and a plan for the exploitation of a field then developed. Oil companies report estimated reserve sizes, but are prudent in typically underestimating them to ensure investors are impressed by the rising outputs from a field. The process of reserve reporting is a finely balanced one, and one that is easy to get wrong, as both BP and Shell know to their detriment. In 2001 BP Chief Executive Lord Brown announced that output would be only 3% up on the previous year rather than the 5.5% growth promised. This was the third time he had slashed his estimates in a single year and he personally lost considerable market credibility in having to do so[8] and in January 2004 came the astounding news that Shell was downgrading its known reserves by 20%, a shocking admission that led to a rapid fall in its price on the markets.

In reality, the reserves in any field are finite and output from oil fields roughly follows a bell-shaped curve with a plateau that represents the peak output of that field. One of the great challenges over the past decades has been to develop technologies that were able to get as much of the available oil out of the ground as possible and

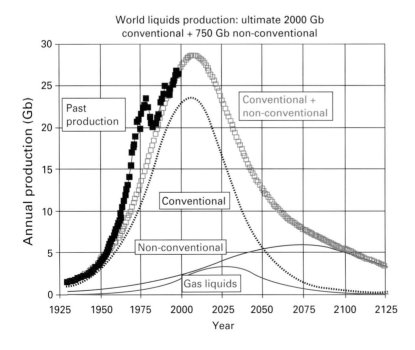

12.4.
Annual recorded and predicted global oil production of conventional and non-conventional liquid gas and oil liquids production from 1925 to 2125 (Gb = billion barrels). Note when production 'peaks'. (*Source:* www.energycrisis.com/)

enormous advances in extraction methods have taken place. However, it is unrealistic to expect that new technologies will release vast amounts of new conventional oil.[9,10,11]

A further major problem arises because the majority of the remaining reserves of oil are located in areas of the world where demand is not greatest, as in the Middle East, Eurasia, Africa and Latin America. Half of what remains lies in five Middle Eastern countries: Abu Dhabi, Iran, Iraq, Kuwait and Saudi Arabia. At some point when the gap between supply and demand has ceased to be cushioned by these swing states contributions, and the gap between what we can produce and what we need yawns, the market will react, probably in proportion to its preparedness for that transition. The result may well come in the form of oil shocks, not in a gradual decline in supply as Bartsch and Muller predicted in 2000:[12]

It is not that we will not have enough oil to take us to 2020 but that the road is likely to be bumpy and subject to a number of economic and political shocks.

Another real problem for Western users is the location of the oil reserves geo-politically. The United States in particular is having problems exerting sufficient influence to stabilize and secure the oil production and transport facilities it would ideally want. The civil and political forces in Latin America, Asia, the Middle East and Africa have proved difficult to overcome, even for a super-power.

GAS: 'THE NEW OIL?'

Reserves of natural gas are far more abundant than those of oil but it is a far more mobile material, which means it leaks from its traps. More of it is recoverable from reserves than oil, around 75%, and its depletion profile gives a constant supply over a long period before coming to an abrupt end, when production plummets and prices soar.

It is also much more difficult to model gas depletion, because its profile is dictated more by market forces than by the immutable physics of the reservoir. The middle point in production is estimated by Campbell to come at around 2020. The United States, and in the not too distant future, Canada, are facing chronic gas shortfalls. Europe faces the same general future but has the advantage of being ably to tap, by pipeline, into the reserves of the Middle East, the former Soviet Union and North Africa, politics permitting.

Britain is predicted to have around 3 years' supply left, but insufficient to meet its own total demands. In November 2003 the first flow of gas *into* the UK via the gas interconnector pipe from Belgium occurred, accompanied by a sharp hike in the cost of UK gas (by up to 10% higher than the weeks before), making prices for natural gas in the UK some of the highest in the developed world. Before that the interconnector had been supplying gas *to* the Continent, at a time when UK prices were, even then, more than a third higher than the equivalent elsewhere in Europe.[13]

Gas is a 'cleaner' fuel, emitting less carbon dioxide per unit of 'delivered' energy produced, and hence politically a more popular fuel for the generation of electricity than coal or oil. It is also mainly located in politically interesting territories.

In November 2003 Shell signed a historic deal to explore a region of Saudi Arabia for gas. Shell's stated belief is that gas will overtake oil as the primary source of energy in the world, and already gas is playing an increasing role in meeting the world demand for energy. It will overtake oil some time after 2020 as the 'preferred' fuel,[14] although no doubt through necessity rather than actual preference.

However, gas supplies are decreasingly secure as UK imports of gas grow to meet growing demands and dwindling supplies from UK sources. A £5.8 billion plan to develop Norway's Ormen Lange gas field, to be operated by Shell, will, the UK government claims, 'secure' UK's long term supplies via a 1200 km pipeline to

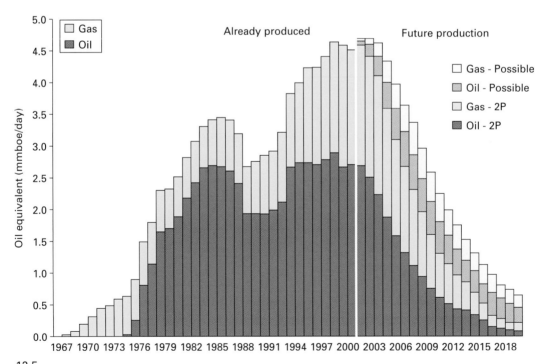

12.5.
Produced and predicted oil and gas reserves for the UK (mmboe = million barrels oil equivalent). (*Source:* UK Department of Trade and Industry, via www.peakoil.net)

Easington in Yorkshire.[15] This field is structurally difficult and expensive to tap and extract,[16] with questions over the reservoir quality of the gas according to Norsk Hydro, who are developing the field.[17] Putting lots of British eggs in this particular gas basket is not a risk-free stratagem for the UK government.

There are a number of new developments in the area of reducing pollution from related generation. Although CO_2 sequestration technologies are coming on line that will reduce the greenhouse gas emissions from gas plants, particularly carbon dioxide, they will actually require 10–20% more energy to produce the same amount of electricity as a result, so here we have the question of whether it is more acceptable to reduce climate change emissions and use our dwindling reserves of fossil fuels more rapidly, or the reverse.[18]

ENERGY WILL COST MORE

An inevitable result of such factors will be increasing prices for consumers of oil and gas. In December 2003 came the news that British Gas were going to start to raise gas and electricity prices for its 15 million consumers by 5.9% from 10 January 2004, blaming the sharp rises in wholesale prices and the growing costs of meeting green targets. Powergen's prices were set to rise by 6.9% for gas and 4.9% for electricity.[19] Similar rises were also being introduced by Scottish Power and Scottish and Southern Electric. Wholesale gas prices rose by 15% in 2003 and a further 21% rise was predicted for 2004. The cost of electricity rose by 15% in 2003 with a predicted rise in 2004 forecast at 17%. Opponents of the rises criticized the hikes saying that the significant reductions in wholesale prices over the past few years had not been passed on to the consumers.[20]

Price hikes most affect the numbers of people in fuel poverty, those who spend more than 10% of their net income on energy. Almost 70 000 homes in the UK were disconnected in 2001, 2002 and 2003. The numbers in fuel poverty halved between 1996 and 2001 from 5 million to 2.5 million, a million of which could be attributed to falling prices. But it does not take a great increase in prices to switch someone back into fuel poverty. The UK government has a policy to end fuel poverty by 2010 for the vulnerable and by 2016 for all. This seems an ambitious target in the face of already rapidly escalating prices.

Price increases are also being driven by the need to maintain and modernize power distribution networks to enable more renewables to be included in supplies and to prevent the power outages that have become increasingly common over the past years. In fact the

infrastructure of the privatized and publicly owned energy industries around the world is weakening as plant comes to the end of
its life and maintenance practices slip.

The impact of such neglect was demonstrated in 1998 when an
explosion ripped through Esso's natural gas plant in the southern
Australian state of Victoria, killing two workers, injuring eight others
and shutting off energy supplies throughout the state for at least
a week. One union official confirmed that the number of maintenance workers at the 30-year-old plant had been halved over the
past six years, and cited this as a possible contributory factor to
the explosion.[21] Such accidents could cripple whole regions for
long periods.

Such neglect is evidenced not only by the widespread power
outages in August 2003 but also by the unprecedented loss of supplies of gas which occurred in the UK on 17 and 18 June that were
blamed on maintenance problems at the Bacton import terminal in
Norfolk.[22]

COAL

There are sufficient reserves of coal left to last for over 200 years.
Coal currently provides only 26% of the world's primary energy
consumption, very much less than in 1950 when this figure was
59%. There are abundant reserves of coal in the ground, estimated
to be capable of lasting over 200 years. Over 50% of the reserves
are in the United States, China and Russia. The coal industry does
have the additional problems of poor working conditions in some
mines and the high costs of transport for the fuel. In France it is
expected that all mines will be closed by 2005.

The main problem with coal now is that it is a dirty fuel and contributes 38% of CO_2 emissions from commercial fuels. It is also a
major source of sulphur dioxide and nitrous oxide emissions as well
as particulates and other emissions. The UK government struggled
to find ways of accommodating the EU's Directive on sulphur emissions, which threatened the future of Britain's coal industry. Other
European sources of coal have a lower sulphur content (Britain's
coal is dirtier) and therefore could comply with the directive.

Under the Directive the UK would have to reduce sulphur dioxide emissions 575 000 tonnes per annum, the bulk of which would
come from the electricity industry. The impact of these savings was
seen to be to close much of the UK coal industry, posing a further
real threat to the security of energy supply. The solution discussed
was to further tighten up on emissions control from power station
chimneys, but the government's only public comment on the issue
was to state that they would go for the lowest cost option for

industry to solve the problem, implying that national security of supply to them was not high on the list of priorities when making such decisions.[23]

NUCLEAR POWER

Nuclear energy at present provides around 25% of the electricity supplied in the UK and is claimed not to contribute to atmospheric CO_2, although such claims do not take into account the energy costs of the buildings and transport associated with the industry.

The ageing and fragile nuclear power industry is on its way out in Britain and has, worryingly, been sold off in part to American buyers.[24] The UK plants are leaking, poorly maintained and the problem of what to do with the radioactive waste from the plants has not been solved.

Another major problem with nuclear power is that it is too expensive to produce. The UK government, or more accurately the people of Britain, have been bankrolling the industry for decades, to the tune of billions of pounds over that time. In September 2003, British Energy, the nuclear power generator, close to bankruptcy having been bailed out to the tune of £650 million by the government, suffered further heavy financial losses due to shutdowns at two power stations. The company produces 20% of UK electricity. A problem at Sizewell B in Suffolk in 2003 resulted from leakages from two welds in the generator. The other shutdown was at Heysham 1 plant in Lancashire, caused by a failure in a sea-water cooling pipe in the plant's turbine hall,[25] and lasted well over a month. Friends of the Earth said at the time, 'This is a classic example of why a future based on nuclear power is a bad idea'. The huge power supply outage would have to be replaced by dirty coal as gas prices are already too high to compete with the coal powered stations.[26]

Nuclear energy suffered another major setback when British Nuclear Fuels announced that it was to close its Sellafield's Thermal Oxide Reprocessing Plant (THORP) on the 25 August 2003. It was estimated that there would be around £3 billion worth of cleaning up to be completed to make the site safe. It was opened in 1994 and was expected to close in 2010, two years before the proposed closure of a much older reprocessing works, built in the 1950s by the Ministry of Defence to separate plutonium for nuclear weapons. This latter plant will stay open until 2012, when all the old Magnox nuclear power stations, which currently produce 8% of the UK's electricity, are closed. All these stations are currently running at a loss but are needed to keep the lights on.[27] The Sellafield site was condemned as 'unsafe' to occupy in August of 2003, due to the poor condition of buildings and the leaking of highly polluted water and radioactivity from the structures.[28]

Although it was claimed that the widespread blackouts around the world in the summer of 2003 meant that the UK government was forced to reconsider the role of nuclear energy in terms of provision of high levels of energy supply, limited greenhouse gas emissions and the need to keep lights on,[29] climate change has already proved to be threatening the proper operation of the French nuclear power stations because of lack of cooling water for the plants.

In France in August 2003 the scorching temperatures caused the nuclear plants to overheat and then have to be shut down. In a plant in Fessenheim, near Strasbourg, staff were forced to hose down the building to cool it as temperatures rose to 48.5 °C, only 2 °C below the point at which an emergency shutdown would be triggered.[30]

As temperatures across France continued at 40 °C for the second week running French nuclear plants were granted permission late in August to pump their cooling water into the nearby rivers at higher temperatures than usual to allow them to continue generating electricity. Demand for electricity soared as people turned up the air conditioning and fridges and rushed out to buy fans. In some regions river water levels dropped so low that the vital cooling processes in the stations had become impossible, while water temperatures downstream of the cooling process exceeded environmental safety levels.

That the UK cannot rely on French supplies to tide it over in difficult periods was then demonstrated during the heat of August when, in an attempt to conserve energy for the nation, France, Europe's largest energy exporter, cut its power exports by more than half on 12 August 2003, causing a shortfall in supplies to the UK.[31] This is another indication that cross-border dependency on fuel leads to insecurity of power supplies.

It is difficult to see nuclear power playing the role of the fairy godmother for our extravagant lifestyles either, although it may well plug the energy gaps as we get used to doing more with less and as new solutions come online. Already, the UK Government has delayed the decommissioning of some older stations by five years, to give them more time to achieve their targets on greenhouse gas emissions, but no new UK stations are planned. This is part of a global trend, with Germany having committed to phasing out their nuclear industry within 20–30 years. However with the approaching oil crisis the UK government may well have to review this policy. It is difficult to see how we will cope without nuclear power, but selling off the nuclear industry to the highest bidder can cause problems in the future when the high costs of the plant have to be recouped. Cutting corners can have catastrophic impacts in this industry. On 15 April 2003, Tokyo's main power company, Tokyo Electric Power Co (Tepco) shut down the last of its 17 nuclear reactors for safety checks after a series of accidents and scandals concerning lax safety procedures. Tepco was ordered to suspend operations for a safety review after it was found to be hiding structural problems in the plants and obstructing government inspections.[32] The shutdown caused serious problems because Tepco produces around 40% of the power used in the Tokyo area, and about 30% of Japanese energy overall is nuclear.

Countries that have abandoned nuclear power include Italy, Denmark, Ireland, Greece, Luxembourg and Portugal. Construction of nuclear plants has stopped in Spain. However, most of the world's big industrial powers still rely, to a greater or lesser extent, on electricity generated by nuclear reactors, including the United States, Russia, Britain, Japan and France. Whether this is a judicious move or not is open to question and Sweden, which made great play of the fact that it was going to close down its nuclear plants, soon found out that it would have to import electricity from dirty coal plants in Denmark and has subsequently reversed its policy.

RENEWABLE ENERGY

The advantage of renewable energy is that it is infinite. Add to that the clean energy it produces, and the fact that people now want it. The UK Energy policy has established outline targets for the production of 20% of energy from renewables by 2020, and to achieve these targets we will have to integrate solar and wind generators into buildings, as well as locating them in the countryside. This means a revolution in the way we supply energy in the UK, because if we are to do this then it will be necessary to re-engineer the UK energy supply network to accept contributions from millions of small power stations instead of a hundred large ones. The only solution is to rewire Britain.

Hydro power

Hydro power is currently the world's largest renewable source of electricity, accounting for 6% of worldwide energy supply or about 15% of the world's electricity. In Canada, hydroelectric power is abundant and supplies 60% of the electrical needs. Traditionally thought of as a cheap and clean source of electricity, most large hydro-electric schemes being planned today are coming up against a great deal of opposition from environmental groups and native

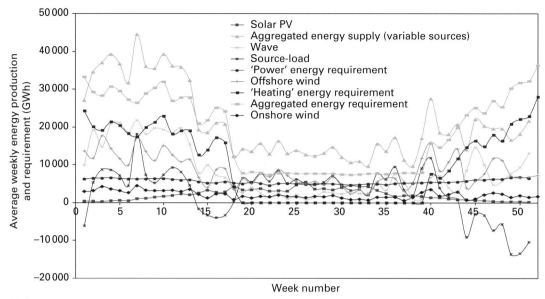

12.6.
A study done by researchers in the CREST centre for renewable energy shows that regionally we may well be able to meet most of our annual demand from a cocktail of renewable energy sources over time. (*Source:* Catherine Streater, by courtesy of David Infield, CREST, Loughborough University)

people.[33] Over the long term, silting of large dams has also been a significant problem for larger schemes.

Hydro power is particularly susceptible to climate change, both to unprecedented spells of drought and flooding. In March 2001 Brazil faced wide scale blackouts after two years of drought because the reservoirs that fed the hydro plants were less than a third full. Brazil generates about 70 000 megawatts (MW) of electricity annually, and consumes all but an estimated 5% of total output. Ninety per cent of Brazil's electricity comes from hydro power and although there was some ability to import extra energy from Argentina the country had no option but to ration energy and accept a rolling programme of blackouts.[34] Similar situations have arisen in the hydro-dependent economies of Tasmania and New Zealand.

Solar energy

Solar energy has many advantages as an energy source of choice for buildings, being the easiest to integrate onto buildings and cities. PV (photovoltaic) systems provide clean electricity while producing no CO_2. It is estimated that for every kilowatt hour (kWh) of PV electricity that is produced 0.6 kg of CO_2 is saved, with this figure rising to 1 kg/kWh when the PV replaces off-grid diesel. In ordinary UK houses, for instance, it has been shown to be possible to reduce

CO_2 emissions by up to 60% with energy efficiency measures, but using photovoltaics (PVs), solar hot water and passive solar systems, 90% reductions in emissions can be achieved, enough, in the view of the Royal Commission on Environmental Pollution, to stabilize climate change,[35] if such reduction were achieved across the buildings board.

The energy supply is located at the point of demand so there are little or no losses incurred in transporting the electricity, and therefore enhancing security in the supply. PVs can supply electricity to locations remote from a traditional grid. PV electricity supply can be isolated from the grid supply and so provide a reliable back-up at periods of grid failure. This factor is already important because over 3 billion people today are connected to conventional electricity supply systems and PVs offer the opportunity for them to have such back-ups when the power fails, although the connection mechanisms are not well developed to achieve this yet. Thus solar energy will become increasingly important as conventional grid supplies become less reliable.

In many parts of the world brown-outs (reductions in voltage that dim the lights) and blackouts already occur at the times of day when power is most needed. An example of this is in hot countries when the surge of demand on hot summer afternoons means that blackouts shut down air conditioning systems. In sensible low energy buildings cooling may be easily achieved with PV-powered ceiling fans or passive cooling, so making buildings, in many climates, comfortable again. PV systems cannot run large air conditioning systems, although great advances have been made in the field of solar cooling. Solar systems are quiet, robust and require little maintenance or repair. They often actually form part of the building skin itself, so reducing the cost of installation. When properly integrated into a building, solar systems can also perform other functions, such as rain screen cladding, roofing, sun shades, covered walkways, brise-soleil, roof tiling systems or solar slates, and PV generation systems on motorway barriers. PVs often have few or no moving parts, and so are potentially very durable systems. There are many knock-on effects that may be important in a changing climate, such as the fact that a solar roof is 'slippier' than one of conventional construction so may not have to be so steeply pitched in areas vulnerable to heavy snowfall, making large construction savings. Also, because each slate is attached to the roof with firm fixings, it is less vulnerable to storm damage than some common roofing systems.

PV systems actually become less efficient as temperatures rise above their test condition temperature of 25 °C and so although they will respond well to more solar radiation they do not perform well during heat waves.

Recent work has shown that in fact Britain is very well suited for solar technologies and will increasingly be so because of the predicted rise in solar availability and intensity with climate change. Domestic solar PV systems could save half the annual energy needs for an individual home, for an average saving of £100 a year, says the UK Energy Saving Trust. PV systems can generate up to 25% of a home's total energy requirements over winter months.[36]

Wind power

Wind energy has become a major player in the energy generation field and will become even more so with a planned increase in wind markets over the coming years. On 18 December 2003, the Department of Trade and Industry and the Crown Estate announced that 12 successful developers have been offered 15 site leases, with a potential combined capacity of 5.4 to 7.2 GW of offshore wind energy.[37] New wind farms should provide enough power for about one in six British households by 2010, and will help to meet the renewable target of 10% of UK energy from renewables by that date. The government hopes Britain will get 20% of its electricity from renewables by 2020 and not only are the power companies enthusiastic about the boost for wind power but also the government predicts that local communities will also benefit as it is estimated that the manufacturing of the wind turbines, the construction and maintenance of the off-shore wind farms would employ about 20 000 people.[38]

Large firms with little experience in energy generation are also getting in on the market. BT, the Telecoms group, is considering plans to build wind turbines on its own land and invest in other renewable energy schemes in an attempt to meet its own targets for reducing greenhouse gases. The company believes that unless something drastic is done the (self-imposed) target of 10% from renewables by 2010 will not be met; action is needed promptly to counter the shortage of capacity in production of renewable energy.[39] The government needs a huge shake-up in the way it approaches the renewable energy sector, including more public finance, according to a Report in October 2003, commissioned by British Telecom (BT) from Forum for the Future, a sustainable development charity. The Forum recommended that BT commission a detailed audit of its buildings and land to see where it would be feasible to install its own on-site renewable energy generating facilities, and urged BT to investigate the potential for investment in the renewable technology sector, one that has grown at a rate of 20–30% per annum over the past decade. This is an example of a major company actually delivering on its own Corporate Social

Responsibility Commitments and using renewable energy as a high profile, and cost-effective, means of doing so.[40]

Domestic wind generation is also coming a step closer, with the design of Britain's first small-scale domestic wind generation unit, which the company who is selling them, Windsave, claims can produce up to 15% of the domestic needs of an ordinary Scottish home. The machine is a 3 ft by 2 ft sealed box with three blades that face into the prevailing wind and can be attached to the walls or roof of an ordinary house. It tops up the existing mains supply and, unlike bigger systems, it cannot sell power back to the grid. The cost of the system is £750 and there are government subsidies available for installation of the machine.[41]

Wind power is popular to UK investors because it has a relatively quick return on the investment. However, it cannot, in itself, replace fossil fuels because it is very weather-dependent. There is also the real problem that wind farms are perceived to spoil areas of natural beauty, and this is already resulting in a significant backlash from the public. The people of Shetland were delighted when their single wind turbine was eventually scrapped and such public concern has also led to the increasing emphasis put in the UK on the development of the offshore wind potential in these 'windy Isles'.[42]

Wave power

The UK has an incredibly long coastline. Just one Scottish county, Argyll and Bute, has a longer coastline than the whole of France. While wave power is weather-dependent (though less subject to the short-term vagaries of weather as are wind and solar), it could provide an important source of energy in the future, although the technology still has some way to go. Under existing policy and economic constraints, there is little to be expected from wave power over the next decade or two. Perhaps it is the development of offshore barrages, still fraught with technical and funding difficulties, that holds out the best promise of large-scale wave power contribution.

Tidal power

Following the oil price crisis in 1976, the government set up the Severn Barrage Committee to assess the feasibility of a tidal barrage across the Severn. According to evidence from this Committee to the Parliamentary Select Committee on Climate Change in March 1999, just this one barrage could make a significant contribution. It would cost around £10 000 million to build, but it would produce 6% of the annual electricity demand of England and Wales, and reduce annual greenhouse gas emissions by 16 million tonnes. A more ambitious scheme could generate even more power.

A tidal barrage would create more benign conditions in the Severn estuary and one recent proposal for the Severn estimated that a barrage could lead to 40 000 new jobs in the area. Such a barrage could be operational within 15 years of getting the funding to proceed. A tidal barrage across the Severn could reduce the tidal flood risk upstream, although measures might be needed to prevent excessive siltation, provide for disposal of effluent from Bristol and Cardiff, and safeguard wetland wildlife.

The biggest stumbling block to such a project is the length of time it would take to pay back the large capital costs, but as pressure grows for more 'clean energy' sources, the project becomes increasingly attractive.

Combined heat and power (CHP)

Large-scale CHP plants are usually sized according to the base load heat demand of the buildings or area they are supplying. Their overall efficiency and commercial success depend on the combination of heat transfer efficiency and electrical generation efficiency, and the demand cycles for electricity and heat. Thus, CHP is not necessarily more efficient than the alternative of stand-alone heat and grid-supplied electricity. CHP is most attractive when the price of grid electricity is high and fuel for the plant, e.g. gas, is low.

In a fairly revolutionary development the world's first commercially available domestic CHP plant, the 'WhisperGen', has been developed jointly with Whisper Tech in New Zealand, and Powergen in the UK. It fits under the worktop in a kitchen, like a dishwasher, and provides hot water like a normal boiler. However, it contains a generator powered by a Stirling engine, which produces electricity from the same gas supply and any surplus electricity will be fed back into the National Grid and bought back from consumers by Powergen.[43] Some estimate micro CHP systems will power up to 20% of all homes by 2020.

Bio energy

With current technology, for the UK, biomass energy crops arguably have the greatest potential of all non-nuclear renewable energy. As less and less farmland is needed for growing food crops, or rearing livestock, more is available for growing biomass. In addition, British Biomass have calculated that there is more than enough land currently not suitable for conventional agriculture but which could be used to grow biomass crops.

Biomass includes wood, especially willow, or other plants, which can be harvested for energy. Forestry and agricultural residues can also be used. This is an area where UK expertise is world class. Although biomass burning releases carbon dioxide, a greenhouse gas, no more is released than is absorbed during growth, or would be released if the material was allowed to rot naturally, so the energy is virtually carbon dioxide neutral. Experiments by the Forestry Commission on 'short rotation coppicing' have shown that biomass can provide a continuous supply of fuel for small-scale local power stations. Biomass is much less weather-dependent than, say, wind or solar power and, in the short term, biomass planting could give governments a further breathing space by acting as a carbon dioxide sink for the purposes of the Kyoto Protocol.

Ethanol

The importance of ethanol (alcohol) is that it can be used to power petrol and diesel engine vehicles with minimal modification – just a computer chip in the fuel system and a fuel line made out of slightly different materials. It is a relatively clean fuel with a higher octane rating than petrol, but is less of a fire risk, and it can be produced anywhere plants can be grown. The burning of ethanol results in release of the carbon trapped by the plant, but this is far better than releasing the carbon formerly trapped in fossil fuels for millions of years because it is a truly renewable form of energy, that can be re-grown rapidly year on year, rather than being a finite resource like oil and gas.

ENERGY FUTURES: THE NEW AGE OF DARK CITIES

In the transition from the fossil fuel age to whatever comes after it, energy prices will rise and the hardest hit buildings will be those built in the last half of the twentieth century when energy was abundant and size of building and energy profligacy were signs of success. The era of Big is Beautiful has already passed, and as we saw in Chapter 11, the smart money is already moving out of big buildings and out of the hearts of big cities.

You cannot occupy a tall building when the power fails. You cannot power a tall building on solar energy, but you can power a robust, well-designed, low rise building using renewable energy in Britain. Similarly, you cannot run a HVAC system in a thin, tight-skinned building in a hot country from photovoltaics, but you can run ceiling fans from them in well-designed passive buildings in the same climate.

We will rapidly have to implement the step changes needed to create a 21st century generation of deeply passive buildings, that can be run largely on renewable energy supplies, because in settlements around the world the lights are already going out. Some say we are, even now, at the threshold of a new Age of Dark Cities.

NOTES AND REFERENCES

1   Pout, C.H., McKenzie, F. and Bettle, R. (2002) *Carbon Dioxide Emissions from Non-domestic Buildings: 2000 and Beyond.* Garston, Watford: Building Research Establishment and Department for Environment, Food and Rural Affairs, p. 10. This publication shows that buildings in the UK use around 46% of all energy produced simply to heat, light, cook and run equipment, without the energy costs of materials and transport being taken into account.

2   http://www.dti.gov.uk/energy/whitepaper/index.shtml; and see also http://eeru.open.ac.uk/natta/renewonline/rol46/9.htm for information on UK energy consumption and policies

3   For more on the science of remaining reserves, see the companion website http://books.elsevier.com/companions/0750659114 and also the excellent Peak Oil and Energy Crisis websites: http://www.peakoil.net/ and http://www.energycrisis.com/.

4   http://www.energycrisis.com/campbell/TheHeartOfTheMatter.pdf.

5   See the following classic works on the subject: Campbell, C.J. (2003) The Peak of Oil: an economic and political turning point for the world. In Low, N. and Gleeson, B. (eds), *Making Urban Transport Sustainable.* Basingstoke: Palgrave Macmillan, pp. 42–67. Campbell, C.J. (2002) *The Essence of Oil and Gas Depletion.* Brentwood: Multi-Science Publishing. Campbell, C.J. (1997) *The Coming Oil Crisis.* Brentwood: Multi-Science Publishing. See: also: Youngquist, Walter (1997) *Geodestinies: the Inevitable Control of Earth Resources Over Nations and Individuals.* Portland, OG: National Publishers. Deffeyes, Kenneth (2001) *Hubbert's Peak: The Impending World Oil Shortage.* Princeton, NJ: Princeton University Press. Hoffman, Peter (2001) *Tomorrow's Energy: Hydrogen, Fuel Cells and the Prospect for a Cleaner Planet.* Cambridge, MA: MIT Press.

6   Campbell, *The Peak of Oil*, p. 44.

7   Campbell, *The Peak of Oil*, p. 45. API stands for American Petroleum Institute; degrees API is an oil-industry term used as a measure of density.

8   *Observer*, Business, 3 November 2002, p. 3.

9   http://www.hubbertpeak.com/deffeyes/. See Deffeyes, *Hubbert's Peak*.

10   Campbell, *The Peak of Oil*.

11   See also www.opec.org.

12   Bartsch, U. and Muller, B. (2000) *Fossil Fuels in a Changing Climate*. Oxford: Oxford University Press.

13   *Financial Times*, 11 November 2003, p. 6.

14   *Guardian*, 17 November 2003, p. 25.

15   *Guardian*, 5 December 2003, p. 23.

16   http://www.hydro.com/en/press_room/news/archive/2002_09/ormen_iland_en.html.

17   http://aapg.confex.com/aapg/barcelona/techprogram/paper_83493.htm.

18   Singh, R. (2003) Costing carbon. *European Power News*, July, London, pp. 23–4.

19   *Guardian*, 5 December 2003, p. 23.

20   *Guardian*, 9 December 2003, p. 17 and *Guardian*, 5 December 2003, p. 23.

21   http://www.wsws.org/news/1998/sep1998/gas-s29.shtml.

22   *Daily Express*, 15 August 2003, p. 2.

23   *Guardian*, 17 November 2003, p. 25.

24   http://www.guardian.co.uk/nuclear/0,2759,181325,00.html.

25   *Guardian*, 27 November 2003, p. 22.

26   *Guardian*, 31 October 2003, p. 32.

27   *Guardian*, 26 August 2003, p. 1.

28   *Guardian*, 26 August 2003, p. 4.

29   *Guardian*, 22 October 2003, p. 22.

30   *Guardian* 5 August 2003, p. 3.

31   *Guardian*, 13 August 2003, p. 13.

32   *Guardian*, 16 April 2003, p. 13.

33   http://www.iclei.org/EFACTS/HYDROELE.HTM.

34   http://eces.org/archive/ec/np_articles/static/98575920040789.shtml.

35   http://www.re-focus.net/news_archive/index.html.

36   http://www.re-focus.net/.

37   http://www.rcep.org.uk/newenergy.html and http://www.dti.gov.uk/energy/renewables/technologies/offshore_wind.shtml.

38 http://www.enn.com/news/2003-07-15/s_6554.asp.

39 *Guardian*, 17 October 2003, p. 24.

40 Roaf, S. (2004) Corporate Social Responsibility. Chapter 4 in *Closing the Loop: Benchmarks for Sustainable Buildings.* London: RIBA Publications.

41 *Guardian*, 24 November 2003, p. 5. See: http://www.windsave.com/main.htm.

42 See: http://www.offshorewindfarms.co.uk/ for a full outline of sites and programmes of development for offshore wind farms.

43 http://www.whispergen.com/.

13 FUEL SECURITY: WHEN WILL THE LIGHTS GO OUT?

In many developing countries it is accepted that 'brown-outs' and blackouts will and do occur. This typically happens during periods of peak electricity demand, which in hot countries are usually in mid-afternoon to coincide with peak air conditioning demand at the hottest times of day and year, and in cold climates in the evening and mornings, before and after work.

However, in a turnaround, in November 2003 the UK National Rail Enquiries blamed power blackouts in Britain for their decision to move 600 call centre jobs to Bangalore, India from Cardiff, Derby, Newcastle and Plymouth. Rail Enquiries claimed that they had had ten blackouts in this year alone in the UK and that the Indian electricity supply network would be more reliable than in Britain. Obviously the fact that Indian workers are paid considerably less also played a part in the decision to move the jobs abroad, but that the issue of energy insecurity in Britain has become an economic negotiating card in this fashion is interesting.[1]

WEATHER-CAUSED OUTAGES

Over the hot summer of 2003, the UK had 'insufficient systems margins' seven times, that is inadequate reserve capacity to provide a cushion for expectant demand surges, and each time generators stepped in to provide extra power.[2] Suppliers paid as much as £1000 a megawatt-hour one day, on peak tariffs, in the 2003 winter as opposed to normal wholesale prices of £17 because the UK energy supply system simply does not have the capacity to cope with severe weather.

A report commissioned by Brian Wilson, the then Minister at the Department of Trade and Industry, from the independent consultants British Power International in May 2002, warned that several UK companies might not be able to cope with a widespread

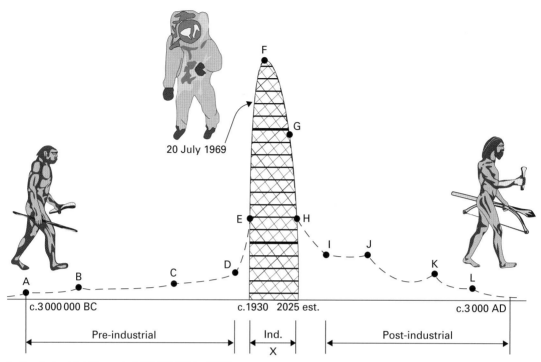

1. Pre-Industrial Phase (c.3 000 000 BC to 1765)
   - A Tool making (c.3 000 000 BC)
   - B Fire used (c.1 000 000 BC)
   - C Neolithic agricultural revolution (c.8 000 BC)
   - D Watts steam engine of 1765
2. Industrial Phase (1930 to 2025, estimated)
   - E Per capita energy use 37% of peak value
   - F Peak energy use
   - G Present energy use
   - H Per capita energy use 37% of peak value
3. Post-Industrial Phase (c.2100 and beyond)
   - J, K, and L = Recurring future attempts at industrialization fail

Other scenarios are possible

13.1.
Time for lights out. An image that represents the concerns of many of the public politicians around the world: the impact of per capita consumption patterns over the coming decades. (*Source:* www.dieoff.org)

storm, because a number relied on the same pool of contractors to provide mobile generators, engineers for overhead lines and the technology to handle surges in calls. The contractors would only be able to respond to one call at a time and would thus have to leave some areas uncovered if the devastation caused by some storms was widespread.[3] This report came in the wake of the storms which left more than 20 000 customers of 24Seven, the utility that covers parts of London and East Anglia, without power for more than a week, as a result of staff cuts and bad management, although they claimed that the continuing failures were due to stronger winds in their region. 24Seven ended up paying over £2 million in compensation to its customers but some of the blame for cuts was also passed on to the Regulator, who in 1998 placed a price cap on firms making it necessary to introduce cuts for staff and tree maintenance programmes.

Weather-related blackouts are a major cause of outages. Hurricane Isobel in late September 2003 plunged 4.5 million people in the Washington area into darkness as trees fell onto cables around the city.[4]

Italy experienced power cuts in mid-August 2003[5] caused by massive surges in demand due to very hot weather and the unprecedented use of air conditioning systems.[6] The weather was also responsible for the Italian blackouts of 2003, when 57 million people were plunged into darkness on 28 September. The problem started when a tree, uprooted in a storm, tumbled onto a power line in Switzerland, cutting out 3–4000 MW of supply and setting off a cascade effect of failures throughout the Italian grid. The impacts were catastrophic:[7]

- Planes were grounded.
- Some 110 trains were halted, some for over 12 hours, with 30 000 travellers on board.
- Lifts stuck.
- Stores and underground car parks were unable to open their security gates.
- Electric turnstiles failing trapped people in buildings.
- Traffic lights failed causing numerous accidents.
- Mobile phones failed.
- Hundreds of elderly people were hospitalized after falling over in the dark.
- Sales of coffees, food and ice creams worth 50 million euro were lost.
- Frozen food worth 70 million euro spoiled in freezers.
- Hospitals ran out of fuel for their emergency generators.
- Water pumping systems stopped, causing water supply problems in cities.
- Sewage plants stopped operating causing effluent build ups.

On a smaller scale, the impacts of a local blackout can be just as disruptive, as this anecdotal story shows. When the power failed one morning in a school in Scotland, no one in the building knew what to do because the emergency plan and all the emergency contact numbers, parents' phone numbers etc. were on the computer, so the children could not be sent home. The school could not supply lunch but the children had used their lunch money to top up their magnetic swipe cards, which they would normally use to buy lunch, so they could not even go to the shops for a sandwich. They all had to leave the school buildings because the fire alarm had no battery back up, and so they stayed in the playground for hours until the electricity was fixed. Here the weather was good but imagine what would have happened in a storm! Our dependence on electricity is so pervasive that nothing seems to function if the power fails nowadays.

SYSTEM FAILURE

The UK's biggest power cut in 25 years hit large parts of London in the early evening of 28 August 2003. The 37 minute blackout was caused by the failure of a single piece of sophisticated equipment that shut down when power surged through it. There was also a problem with a transformer in Kent and further blame for the severity of the blackout – which involved the loss of 20% of the capital's power – was levelled at the slow response time of France's EDF electricity grid company, in responding to the surge in demand.[8] This in its turn was caused by the high demand experienced in France due to very hot weather and the poor performance of the nuclear reactors in the extreme heat.

The effects on London during the evening rush hour were dire. The Underground and rail networks were paralysed. The problem for people trying to find other ways home was exacerbated by the fact that automated cash machines were down, preventing them from getting access to the additional cash they needed to, for instance, pay for taxis. Pubs benefited in the city though, as many commuters avoided the grid-locked streets and over-crowded buses with the pleasure of a slow pint on their long way home.[9]

On Thursday 14 August, in the United States, where US Energy Secretary Abraham said:

Reliable electric power is the lifeblood of the economy for both the United States and Canada. ... It's more than just a personal convenience – it's essential to the health and safety of the two countries' citizens.[10]

50 million people were hit by America's and Canada's worst power failure. The effects of the blackouts were particularly felt in cities like New York, Cleveland (Ohio), Detroit (Michigan) and Erie (Pennsylvania) as well as in many Canadian cities such as Toronto, Ottawa and Niagara Falls.

New York City suffered badly when office buildings were evacuated shortly after 4pm. The events of 11 September 2001 were on people's minds. Many were convinced, wrongly, that terrorists had struck again. On the Thursday night, thousands of stranded commuters slept on the streets and in bus and train stations rather than venture on long walks home. In hotels guests had to sleep outside on the pavement because there was no electricity to operate its electronic room keys and knock-on

13.2.
The lights go out in New York in August 2003 and in cities around the world, at a time of unprecedented global heat waves. (*Source:* Associated Press)

effects also included:[11]

- During the night from Thursday to Friday New York suffered 60 serious fires, mostly caused by people lighting candles in the dark.
- Nine nuclear reactors in four US states were taken offline, contributing here to the problem of fuel insecurity rather than solving it.
- The US federal Administration halted flights into six airports – three in the New York area, one in Cleveland, and two in Canada.
- Sporadic looting was reported in at least four areas of the Canadian capital, Ottawa, and 26 people were arrested for looting in Brooklyn, New York.
- The blackout closed the Detroit–Windsor Tunnel, which links the United States and Canada and is used by 27 000 vehicles daily.
- In the Canadian mining town of Sudbury some 100 miners were trapped underground until power could be restored.
- Detroit's 15 major car plants closed down until Monday 18 August 2003.

A US–Canadian government investigation of the massive power outage in the Northeast singles out a series of operators' mistakes, computer failures, violations of grid rules and inadequate maintenance by FirstEnergy Corp., the Akron-based utility serving northern Ohio, as the primary causes of the largest blackout in North American history.[12]

POOR MANAGEMENT OF SUPPLIES

California is perhaps the prime example of a region where mismanagement of energy supplies has caused widespread hardship, and death. In California, the supplies across the whole state have been affected by rolling blackouts over the past three years, due in part to poorly managed privatization of the electricity industry and an inflexible legislative system. Very high energy demand from buildings, for instance in the heat wave of 2000, caused a surge in demand and private companies, once a price cap was lifted in June, raised their prices by up to three times in a matter of months. Poor management, in part by the Enron Corporation, and the State, resulted in outages in many cities and settlements. Reasons given for these failures included:

- Excessive energy demand at peak period consumption, related in a large part to high air conditioning use in very hot weather.
- Lack of energy conservation measures in buildings and equipment.
- Poorly managed energy tariff systems.
- Lack of coordination of plant outages on an emergency basis.
- Lack of back-up generating capacity.
- Poor State management of the sector.
- Corrupt private utilities.

By contrast, in New England in the US the electricity supply problems are different. The plans to increase the percentage of electricity generated by gas-powered stations from 16% in 1999 to 45% by 2005 proved unrealistic, not only because of the soaring cost of gas in the United States but also because:

- During peak demand some advanced gas turbine plants would not be able to switch quickly enough to their back-up oil supplies to avoid temporary outages.
- The existing gas pipeline capacity in the region would potentially be insufficient to supply the demand of the 45% increase in gas-generating plants at peak periods, a fact that caused gas supply problems in 2003.
- The pipeline construction, and power generation companies are not one and the same.

There is concern that the New England power supply system, like that of California but for different reasons, will not be able to meet demand within a matter of years. The Boston area is particularly vulnerable as the ageing grid in the area is considered, as in many other areas of the United States, to be on the brink of failure. The competitive market is failing also as suppliers are pulling out of the market rather than jumping in. The problem was highlighted in spring 2000 when an unexpected heat wave forced the power companies to call Boston customers to cut down on electricity use in order to prevent blackouts. Other cities have similar problems, such as New York where 2000 residents lost power in 1999 prompting the city to plan to install 10 mini-power plants as back-up to its main lines – a seemingly pointless gesture in the face of the scale of the 2003 blackouts.

It would appear that to improve their fuel security, what America needs, as well as better energy infrastructure, is to use less energy.[13]

We are moving into an era in which we can no longer, in any country in the world, presume 100% security of delivered energy supplies. In the UK the old research facilities of the Electricity Industry at Capenhurst, where work on the optimization of power supply and demand was undertaken, have been closed and such research is no longer being undertaken in a coordinated fashion by the UK government.

This results in a lack of long-term, in-depth, knowledge, skills and planning on such subjects, that will manifest itself as our supply and demand systems are increasingly placed under pressure from new developments, climate change and energy scarcity.

The UK government's move to privatize 100% of the UK energy supply market has exacerbated our energy insecurity. For instance, part-privatization of the London Underground was blamed for exacerbating the August 2003 failure that brought the transport system to a standstill and affected tens of thousands of tube passengers who were stuck in tunnels as trains stopped. In 2002 London Underground's 97-year-old independent power station, Lot's Road, was shut, and responsibility for powering the tubes was handed over to a new consortium, Seeboard Powerlink, in a private finance deal under which the tube now gets all its power from the National Grid. Seeboard provided a back-up power station at Greenwich, south London, for use in emergency, but the arrangements failed, leaving dozens of trains stranded, raising again with the unions, and many others, the question of the advisability of handing over to private finance contractors the responsibility of key public services. Senior Seeboard executives had decided not to start up the Greenwich generator when the 28 August blackout began at around 6.30pm at the height of the rush hour, hoping to switch supply from other parts of the grid that were still working. Questions were later asked as to why it had been felt necessary to change a system that had kept the Underground working all through the Blitz.

The move away from state-owned generating companies has sent prices tumbling around the world over the past decade but privately owner power stations have not been investing in new plant or infrastructure because they see their profit margins being squeezed, and they have been shutting down what they see as excess capacity to maintain their profits. Global warming is resulting in more unpredictable weather and tending to result in massive surges in demand for power.

The summer 2003 crisis in Italy highlighted its chronic dependency on foreign sources of energy. GRTN, Italy's grid manager, draws in power not just from France and Switzerland, but also from Austria, Slovenia and even Greece via an underwater cable. Sixteen per cent of Italy's requirements are met from outside the country. At that time a bill to increase Italy's generating power by a quarter had been stalled in Parliament for months and calls were being made to restart the nuclear programme that had been abandoned after a referendum in 1987. Its four remaining nuclear plants are currently being dismantled. More than 75% of electricity generated in Italy comes from oil, gas and coal and producing it accounts for 25% of Italy's greenhouse gas emissions. The need for energy efficiency measure to damp the summer air conditioning peak was clear in this instance.[14]

Massive power cuts in Denmark in late September 2003 were said to be caused by damage to the power transmission lines linking Sweden and Denmark, from where Denmark obtains much of its power. Some even claimed that the lines had been sabotaged by terrorists.[15] This transboundary dependency for energy is increasing the risk of political as well as physical and economic insecurity.

Public concern also acts as a restraint on the operations of the privatized utilities in their efforts to ensure supplies. President Bush's plans to exploit the Alaskan oil fields were thwarted by a 52 to 48 vote in the US Senate on 20 March 2003, when Democrats and eight Republicans voted to block, for at least a year, drilling for oil over a 600 000 hectare area of the wilderness refuge of Alaska. The US uses around 7 billion barrels of oil a year and the government estimated that as many as 16 billion barrels could be found in Alaska.[16] In the face of mounting oil shortages in the United States it is only a matter of time before the interests of environmentalists will, inevitably, have to give way to the need of Americans to feed their growing dependence on oil, and in turn, electricity, an issue that has already led to civil unrest on the streets.

Shanghai, a city with a booming population soaring above 20 million people and the leading city in the Chinese economic revolution, is now facing an energy crisis. As the population flocks from the country to the city to cash in on the £2900 average annual income available to workers, more and more tall buildings have emerged to house the population and provide them with workplaces. However the energy infrastructure is unable to meet the rapidly growing demands for power and in December 2003 the municipal authorities ordered many factories to move to night shifts because energy supplies were unable to meet the soaring daytime demand for electricity.[17]

Tens of thousands of factory workers were affected and ordered to work nights because of power shortages caused by the rapid growth of China's economy. Shanghai also urged shop owners to turn down thermostats and conserve electricity. Such moves not only embarrassed government officials but also presaged a battle for energy supplies in Asia. Car ownership in the city is rising at 25% a year. It has the world's first commercial magnetic levitation train. But on 4 December the city announced that unless it took drastic action to overcome the energy problems the trains might not run and the street lamps and skyscrapers may be blacked out.

As mid-winter approached the city authorities calculated that the city was 2 million kilowatts short of the 11.6 million it needed to meet peak demand. Although the city buys electricity from the new Three Gorges Dam, and plans to buy an extra 1 million kilowatts from there, it was still facing major problems. The city planned to shut its most energy-intensive small factories and change work shifts to midnight to 8.00am in energy-intensive industries. Many of the population can now afford electric heaters in winter, and one of the main problems has been identified as the gleaming new shopping malls, where 0.4 million watts could be saved by lowering the temperature in them alone. Power pricing is changing to encourage people to use less during the day (highlighting the need to use thermal storage in buildings).

China's general power consumption rose by 15% to 1.88 trillion kilowatts in 2003. More than half China's provinces have been hit by shortages and the government has warned that the energy shortfall could hinder growth, despite more plant being brought online, and shortages would remain chronic until at least 2006. China was an energy exporter for three decades but is now one of the world's biggest oil importers.[18]

Such necessities of reducing consumption, rapidly and on a large scale, also exist in the UK. In the face of the blackouts in August 2003, the National Grid company Transco denied that there was any risk that inadequate generating capacity in the power stations would lead to power shortages in the winter, although it did admit that it had written to some of its largest industrial customers to offer inducements for lower usage contracts in August 2003. The suggestions, sent to major manufacturing plants, as owned by Rio Tinto and the aluminium manufacturer Alcon, and other heavy power users, include inducements for accepting 'interruptible' contracts where the grid can reduce supply at 24 hours' notice to enable the Grid to free up capacity to meet regional peaks in demand. The contracts can be worth as much as £56 000 an hour, a bonus at a time when electricity prices are expected to rise by as much as 30% over the next year for the renewal of such contracts.[19]

OTHER CAUSES OF POWER OUTAGES

There are two further major threats to the security of supplies. The first is terrorism. The blowing up of power lines and plants is such an obviously effective means of bringing a region to its knees and inflicting major economic damage that it significantly influences the thinking of politicians on the subject of future fuel mixes. The second, and it has happened already, is when a country simply can no longer afford to pay for the oil and gas to run its plants.

EMBEDDED GENERATION

The electricity blackouts around the world in 2003 demonstrated clearly that many countries have become absolutely dependent, for the ordinary functioning of society, on a constant, and high quality, supply of electricity. Quality of supply can be considered to have three elements:[20]

- Reliability – long- and short-term interruptions of power supply.
- Power quality – frequency and voltage stability, waveform abnormalities.
- Service – response time and restoration time.

Not only do we need a constant supply of electricity for basic functions like street and domestic lighting, that can operate under quite varied voltage conditions, but the advanced electronic equipment found in modern working environments often requires a high level of reliability from the incoming electricity supply.

For example, today's complex manufacturing processes rely heavily on microcomputers, variable-speed drives and robotics devices to achieve high levels of product throughput and product quality. This leads to higher expectations of electricity end consumers, who place increasing demands on electricity suppliers to meet the demand for quality of supply. Evidence for this is given by the large market for power quality measurement and analysis systems.

National regulations dictate the minimum quality of electricity and, if these are complied with, the needs of most consumers will be met. In the case of consumers with special requirements, or in areas where quality measurements give rise to concerns, there are methods of ameliorating shortcomings in the electricity supply. However, some of these methods can themselves have an effect on the supply network.

The winds of change?

There are new factors that raise several issues with regard to the current distribution regulatory arrangements, which were not considered 20 years ago. The industry is changing, with greater emphasis on:

- Quality of supply.
- Security of supplies.
- Environment.

In recent decades, Great Britain has relied almost exclusively upon electricity generated by large, traditional power stations that are connected to the higher voltage national transmission system. In line with this, distribution networks, the lower voltage part of the system, have largely been concerned with delivering electricity in one direction, from the transmission network to customers' homes. However, structural changes are ahead, including the anticipated growth of 'distributed' generation – that is, small, local power generators, particularly of renewable energy – to underpin the 'rewiring of Britain'.

What is embedded generation?

Embedded generation (also known as distributed, embedded or dispersed generation) is electricity generation connected to a distribution network rather than the high voltage transmission network. Distributed generators are mostly – though not exclusively – those generating power from environmentally friendly renewable energy sources (including small hydro, wind and solar power) or from combined heat and power (CHP) plants.

Historically, distribution networks have been designed to take electricity from the high voltage transmission system and to deliver it to customers. The management of this one-way flow of energy has been termed 'passive'. In order for the networks to accommodate increased levels of distributed generation energy flow in both directions will have to be managed – both to the customer and from the distributed generator. This is termed 'active' management. This move from 'passive' to 'active' management is a major challenge.

The nature of distribution networks today means that many smaller generators find it difficult and expensive to connect to networks that were not designed to accommodate them. The output from photovoltaics (PVs) from a single house into the grid is little more than noise on the line, but when the whole street has solar hot water systems and PV arrays then the solar contribution to powering houses down the street becomes significant, especially if the householders are out all day at work during the week but at home during the week-end. Matching the load profiles to the electricity supply becomes a real challenge.

Naturally, the large distribution companies involved find it is much easier to deal with the outputs from a handful of major generators, but in the changing climate, with resource pressures developing year on year, a strong theme of the UK government's White Paper on Energy is the need for energy security, and it is widely felt that the sole reliance on the mega-grid for the supply of future energy would be a very high-risk strategy to follow.[21]

Future grid scenarios need to be built to also cover the potential for 'renewable energy cities, suburbs and streets' within which a relatively high proportion of, for instance, the domestic load is locally generated, during spring, summer and autumn, from building-integrated solar hot water, micro-wind, CHP systems and PV systems that supply unpredictable energy, depending on the weather of the day and the month. For such small-scale embedded generators, work is focusing on 'micro-grid' systems where power demand and supply are controlled within a local grid, separated from the main grid by a power gate that can be shut off in times of power supply emergencies to ensure security of supplies within the main grid system.

Within such micro-grids, it is envisaged that a cocktail of different generating sources could be located, from a range of solar, wind, hydrogen fuel-cells, CHP plants, hydro plants and other sources. Such systems can work well at the level of the 'campus', where a single owner is responsible for the plant inside the power gate and the management and control of energy supply and quality within the mini-grid. One example of such a campus site that has a two-way power gate into the national grid is that at the Centre for Alternative Technology at Machynlleth, Wales, that has a range of embedded generators including wind and solar, within its micro-grid. As part of its active energy management system the site has a bank of batteries to provide energy storage, and a buffer against fluctuating supply and load situations.

If distribution networks are to accommodate increased quantities of embedded generation, from a PV roof or a solar street, to an aluminum smelting plant's power station, then they will need to be managed as 'active' rather than 'passive' systems. This not only means installing complex control systems, but also equipping transformers with tap changers that can control voltage locally. If the cost burden that different sources of generation imposes on networks is not recognized early on by the charging arrangements, then the most efficient network/generator configurations are unlikely to be implemented and charges to customers will be higher than need be in the long term as oil and gas prices rise. Insufficient investment at the right time may cause future supply systems to be even less secure.

Energy storage

The generating capacity available must be able to meet the peak demand and, as demand is below peak for most of the time, a significant amount of generating capacity is under-utilized. It has been estimated that the average utilization of generating capacity is around 50%. One way of improving generator utilization is to use 'off-peak' electricity in energy storage schemes.[22]

There are some very large schemes, for example, the Dinorwic pumped hydro scheme, in Wales, where electricity generated at off-peak times can be pumped back up to the reservoir and used to generate again at peak periods. Despite there being suitable technology available, for example regenerative fuel cells, as yet there is little storage in the current supply chain.

It is often considered that renewable generation is of two types, despatchable and stochastic. **Despatchable generation**, such as conventional hydro or that powered by biofuels, can be made to provide electricity in a manner which is related to demand. **Stochastic generation**, such as that powered by wind or wave, fluctuates in a manner that is unrelated to demand. However, stochastic generators can provide electricity that contributes coherently to the demand cycle if they are associated with appropriate energy storage systems.

The trading system for Great Britain was designed to enable competitive markets to develop, but critics claim that it is extremely complex to implement, creating problems for users.[23]

The main technical problem to be overcome in moving to embedded generation from the traditional grid system is that of providing constant, high quality, electricity from unpredictable sources. The lack of back-up energy storage facilities in the UK systems will be exacerbated by the increased use of generators powered by fluctuating (stochastic) renewable energy sources, such as wind and tide. Many of the proposed technical solutions will also mean significantly increased costs of energy to the consumer.[24] As fossil fuel prices rise, the marginal costs of this storage capacity will decrease relative to the cost of the 'delivered' energy, that enters a building through the meter.

For many power generators, downtime, when power outages occur in plant, including its hidden costs, can represent 5–10% of annual revenue and potentially 30–40% of annual profits, and outage optimization regimes are increasingly central to the management of the energy supply system to make sure that neither mechanical nor human error causes unnecessary blackouts.[25]

CONCLUSIONS

We face a future in which we will no longer be able to rely on a constant, reliable, high-quality supply of energy. 2003 gave us a taste of what is to come. Key issues are:

- **Quality of supply.** How important is quality if there is no supply? How will the inevitable 'rewiring of Britain' to accept renewables affect the quality of supply? Will we have to adapt to using lower quality energy, as well as to using less of it?

- **Security of supply.** This will be increasingly challenged by the end of the fossil fuel age; the rise of embedded generation; micro-grids, privatization, de-regulation; lack of investment in the industry; geo-political insecurity; extreme weather, and a plethora of other forces are gathering to test our ingenuity in keeping the lights on for as long as possible.

- **Environment.** This must be the driver: energy use is dependent on weather and our warmer and more extreme weather has proved to be the wild card that carries the poker game. The blackouts in August were caused in large part by high demand in a hot summer, the sort of hot summer we will increasing expect ever year or two in the future.The other critical factor is that of the global environmental impacts of energy generation, the burning of fossil fuels that is driving the climate to change. Those who maintain that the problems of a changing climate can be solved simply by throwing more energy at them – that energy-profligate buildings will provide bastions of comfort for those who can afford it – are mistaken.

The Institution of Civil Engineers, in their State of the Nation Report 2003,[26] pointed out the chronic structural problems the UK faces:

- Over 95% of the country's present generation mix is made up of coal, nuclear and gas supplies.
- Emissions constraints means that the remaining UK coal plants will close within 15 years.
- Only one nuclear power station will remain open after 2020.

They asked for:

- Increasing investment in infrastructure (including – I would add – the knowledge infrastructure).
- Investment in developing the full range of fuels.

Add to this the need for more long-term storage of fuels in reserves. France, Germany and Italy have storage of more than 20% of annual consumption – more than 70 days' worth. The UK has less than 2 weeks' worth.

Add to this the need for stringent demand side management policies to make consumers use less.

Add to this the need to store more energy in the thermal mass of buildings, where the thermal capacity of a building offers the potential for providing a significant reservoir for heat or coolth.

Add to this the urgent need to re-wire Britain to accept emerging energy technologies.

And finally add to this the imperative to design buildings in which we can survive when the lights do go out.

NOTES AND REFERENCES

1   *Guardian*, 13 November 2003, p. 9.

2   *Guardian*, 13 August 2003, p. 16.

3   *Guardian*, 15 November 2002, p. 9.

4   *Guardian*, 20 September 2003, p. 16.

5   *Guardian*, 13 August 2003, p. 16.

6   *Guardian*, 29 September 2003, p. 3.

7   *Guardian*, 29 September 2003, p. 3.

8   *Guardian*, 11 September 2003, p. 2 and *Guardian*, 29 September 2003, p. 3.

9   *Guardian*, 29 August 2003, p. 7.

10   http://www.citymayors.com/news/power_blackout.html.

11   http://news.bbc.co.uk/1/hi/world/americas/3152985.stm.

12   http://www.washingtonpost.com/wp-dyn/articles/A62280-2003Nov19.html.

13   IPG (2001) *International Power Generation*. DMG World Media, UK, March.

14   *Guardian*, 30 September 2003, p. 15 and *Daily Telegraph*, 29 September 2003, pp. 1, 3 and 21.

15   *Guardian*, 29 September 2003, p. 3.

16   *Guardian*, 21 March 2003, p. 18.

17   *Guardian*, 6 December 2003, p. 21.

18   *Guardian*, 5 December 2003, p. 18.

19   *Independent*, 25 August 2003, p. 16.

20   The following sections come largely from the IEE Policy Statement on the issue. For a full text on the subject see: http://www.iee.org/Policy/Areas/EnvEnergy/embedgen.pdf.

21   http://www.dti.gov.uk/energy/whitepaper/index.shtml.

22   http://www.ofgem.gov.uk/elarch/retadocs/golive_explained.pdf.

23   http://www.ofgem.gov.uk/ofgem/shared/template2.jsp?id=4221.

24   http://www.ofgem.gov.uk/ofgem/index.jsp.

25   International Power Generation, November/December 2002, p. 17.

26   ICE (2003) The State of the Nation: An assessment of the state of the UK's infrastructure by the Institution of Civil Engineers. See text on: www.ice.org.uk.

14 THE PLAYERS

Buildings are in the front line of the battle against climate change. Either they change fast and radically or we lose the war. We must, with all speed:

- Reduce the production of greenhouse gases that are driving climate change.
- Adapt our buildings and cities so that as many people as possible can survive as comfortably as possible in them, for as long as possible.
- Build buildings today that will last for as long as possible, with minimum of maintenance and refurbishment because the energy embodied in the construction, operation and demolition of buildings, and the manufacture and transport of materials is perhaps globally the major source of greenhouse gases, pollution and waste.

In every country on earth,[1] regardless of class, creed or wealth, buildings are threatening the quality of our lives, either because of the emissions they generate, or the impacts they have on our lives through extreme weather trends and events. You cannot buy your way out of a cyclone.

Books on the subject tend to try to fudge the problems. They dwell on particular uni-dimensional aspects of the problem, such as how a micro-grid works, or changing the building controls system, adding shading or changing the glass type.[2] They do not challenge the heart of the beast, the fundamental paradigms of the buildings which cities and the market place accept as inevitable today; it is these paradigms that are destroying our planet.

The market mantra of 'you get what you want' is but a hair's breadth away from the chilling 'you get what you deserve', and 'buyer beware' – take the consequences of your own poor decisions. The time has come for buyers to educate, and future-proof themselves, against climate change implications. Do you really want to buy a house that will flood? Or work in a building you cannot get out of when it does? Or is under the path of a runway where the air will become extremely polluted in a heat wave? Or live where the drain in your drive will spill out raw sewage every time there is heavy rain?

To change the current paradigms will require a revolution, because of the deeply entrenched positions of the key players in the built environment. The need exists to restructure the political, professional, business, industrial, academic and media roles in our built environment, as touched on below. But this may well happen faster than any of us anticipate because the 21st century markets are very different from those even a couple of years ago.

The smart high-end movers and shakers have already moved on, left town, become more efficient, reduced their impacts, re-invested in quality leaving many of the good old boys to hawk their new 'modern' ideas, and dated products, to their cronies, to the ill-informed, or to the developing world. The problem with the construction industry, as in the American computer industry, is perhaps it was all too easy and they just got sloppy.

HIGH TECH MISSIONARIES OF SLOPPINESS

In her very influential online paper entitled 'High Tech Missionaries of Sloppiness', Cheryl Aim, writing for *Salon Magazine*,[3] pointed out the reasons why 'India is going to eat the American computer industry for lunch', including:

- The US computer product is not reliable. (Modern buildings are often not reliable, and in the UK insurance premiums are higher for post-1971 houses because they fail more than the ones that are centuries old, with the ABI considering some of the highest-risk homes being the 'innovative' prefabricated types being promoted by the current government.)
- The industry had come to see their product reliability problems as an inevitable side effect of what they excelled at – innovation at top speed. ('Innovate' – why?)
- The 'Don't Worry, Be Crappy', philosophy, which holds that the way to sell is to 'ship, then test' and 'Act fast and fix the problems later'. (We are pulling down a 'ship fast' generation of buildings from the 1960s, 1970s and even the 1980s all over the country.)
- Being first to market with new products is exalted as the highest goal. (Make sure you have good lawyers.)
- 'Glitchy software' bugs are talked of as mere annoyances when they are in effect defects and should be labelled so. (Can you get the Advanced Building Control System to work properly?

Some of the leading engineers cannot even control the climate in their own buildings.)

- As in the automobile industry, where Japanese car makers grabbed nearly a third of the US market and much of the international market, why would a foreign company want to buy outdated inefficient American air conditioning if it could get reliable super-efficient, low impact, Japanese (or Scandinavian) air conditioners for the same price?

- The era of 'playful creativity' governing the design and manufacture of PCs is over, and has got to give way to one in which computers are seen by their creators as being more like bridges and tunnels than, say, the houses of Frank Lloyd Wright or Le Corbusier. (Could we bear to live in a world without Architect as Maestro? Do we actually know how to build buildings worthy of Brunel?)

- A High Dependability Computing Consortium (HDCC) was planned with an 'In thee we trust' mission.

- Carelessness freely wastes these firms' own resources.

- High-tech products . . . [often] have more style than substance — what computer scientists are calling 'feature-itis', 'glitzware' or, in a pointed reference to the products of late-1950s Detroit, 'tail fins' and 'flashy chrome bumpers'.

- 'Not until the consumers demand [quality] and get it from overseas (or less tech, low impact, lower cost, providers of reliable product?) will the reigning companies believe – American computer and software companies are making too much money in the current environment to care.'

This article should strike a real chord in the building design world, as in many other industries, where many have had their eye off the ball for a while, and increasingly look to a bemused public as if they have lost the plot. Where is the 'firmness, commodity and delight' our forebears were so proud of, in the modern 'minimalistic' paradigm? It certainly appears as if people have been cut out of the design equation in many cases. Perhaps building users would be more forgiving if the buildings worked well, but the sloppiness has begun to bite, poor performance and high costs and impacts have added extra coffin nails that are gradually being eased into place. Industries come and go, the wool industry, the shipping industry,[4] and the aircraft industry will too, when the oil runs out. No Chief Executive Officer should be too confident that their business cannot fail. But why is more not being done to ensure that the designing professions and the construction industries survive, thrive and contribute to the Climate Change War?

GOVERNMENTS

The Kyoto process has theoretically been extremely influential in creating targets for emission reductions, and Europe is leading the world in the imposition of biting targets for greenhouse gas emissions. On 12 August 2003, the European Commission unveiled tough proposals to cut emissions of particular potent greenhouse gases by a quarter before 2010, a really ambitious target.

This may well have been spurred on by the realization of the growing financial costs to governments of not taking such steps. The costs of the floods in Europe in 2002 were astronomical, as were those of the heat wave of 2003 where governments were forced to provide significant handouts of subsidies for stricken sectors. The German government, for example, arranged emergency aid to farmers in conditions that were described as 'desert like' by one agricultural leader.[5] Climate change is really beginning to hurt major economies.

The problem for governments is how to turn the requirement to reduce impacts into a requirement to deliver target reductions. The faster, cheaper, mentality, characteristic of the height of the fossil fuel era, favoured privatization, and the more efficient delivery of goods and services that would make them cheaper for the voters. But that idea is evaporating as water and fuel become scarcer and corporate profit requirements are paid for by the person in the street.

The 'rate' of change may also work against success. In 1950s and 1960s Britain the momentum for urban reform resulted in the destruction of the hearts of many well-loved towns and cities beneath a carpet of brutal concrete and bitumen. Labour's current declared policy of building new towns in the green belt was challenged by, among others, Richard Rogers, who said that Deputy Prime Minister John Prescott's agenda to 'go fast' in building new towns was wrong, and that we have made the same mistake before and had to pull the lot down. New development, he argued, should be concentrated in places like Birmingham and Milton Keynes, echoing the trend amongst leading global businesses to move to provincial centres and away from 'target' buildings.[6] As John Prescott said, 'The Green Belt is one of the great success stories of the Labour Party and we intend building on it.'

What is needed by the government quite simply is a mechanism by which the contribution of every building to meeting those targets can be recorded and improved where necessary, and here the 2001 European Building Directive will provide the means by which such accounting can be made through annual building performance audits and audits of performance at point of sale of both houses and offices.[7]

The European Commission Directive 2002/91/EC, adopted in December 2002, designed to result in savings of 45 million tonnes of CO_2 by 2010, requires that member states:

- Apply a general framework for calculating the energy performance of buildings.
- Apply minimum standards of performance for all new buildings.
- Apply minimum standards of performance for existing buildings over 1000 m^2 that are subject to major renovation.
- Ensure that boilers, heating systems and air conditioning are inspected regularly.
- Ensure that when a building changes occupants an energy performance certificate is made available and displayed in all public buildings plus those visited by the public.

The intention is to place a clear responsibility on those selling a property to provide information about that property at the point it is put on the open market. The domestic information will form a Home Information Pack (HIP), and will include a Home Condition Report (HCR) undertaken by a Home Inspector as well as evidence of title and local searches. For offices and buildings over 1000 m^2 where the general public can enter, a Performance Certificate, required to be updated annually, must be publicly displayed after 2006.

Other provisions under the Directive cover the accreditation of those carrying out inspections, publication of the scheme and governance. It is also a requirement that the methodology for calculating energy performance is reviewed regularly, at least every 2 years. Member states have a maximum of 3 years in which to implement the provisions, by 4 January 2006. A further period of 3 years is allowed for the introduction of full certification and inspection of existing buildings if there is a lack of accredited experts to carry out the work.[8] However one big issue has been ignored in the Bill, which is whether these inspectors will be legally liable for the consequences of incorrect advice, and whether they will be able to afford professional indemnity insurance.

PRIVATIZATION

Chapter 13 touched on the impact privatization has had in destabilizing the security of the energy markets. In the United States, in particular, privatization has undermined the reliable provision of, for instance, energy in California, spurred on by corporate greed and corruption, famously flag-shipped by the Enron scandal. The trend to privatize pervades many different aspects of the way we design and manage our built environment.

One example is the loss of long-term theoretical research from the public to the private sector. Formerly publicly funded research establishments, such as the UK's Building Research Establishment, and the research centres of British Rail and the Electricity and Gas industries, have been sold to the highest bidder or the attached industries, so losing for the nation an invaluable powerhouse of expertise that would be essential in future-proofing Britain against the exigencies of the coming decades. In their place we have a 'product oriented' research community dependent on short-term research contracts handed out by a government increasingly interested in getting 'added-value' for their research investments by favouring research that is co-funded by industry. That means that instead of investigating theoretical or generic issues, priority is given to testing products, in a manner that promotes the agendas of the funders, that is, industry. Gone are the researchers with decades of experience on 'the big issues', replaced by a hustling research market place, dealing in diminishing research funds, with large tranches of tax payers' money being paid directly to the privatized service industries to do with as they like to promote, and hopefully effect, environmental impact reductions. The conflicts of interest between the industry, the regulators and the research community must be dealt with and delineated, and contraventions of the bond of trust placed in these bodies staunchly defended through the courts.

MARKET FORCES

We have seen elsewhere that for the air conditioning industry market forces are driving the exponential increase in the very air conditioning systems that are one of the major sources of carbon dioxide emissions to the atmosphere. The use of 'Guidance' programmes and publications without legislative teeth have traditionally proved ineffectual in the face of the urge to stay cool in a poorly designed building.

When the Royal Institute of British Architects urged their members against the unnecessary use of air conditioning and the Chartered Institute of Building Service Engineers includes in its Code of Professional Conduct the admonition to 'Avoid the use of refrigeration where natural and mechanical ventilation is a feasible alternative', both professions continue to move indiscriminately to almost universal use of air conditioning in their larger buildings.

However, it is hoped new initiatives will prove more successful. Many local councils recognize that they have to play a larger part in tackling climate change. The Local Government Association has teamed up with the Energy Saving Trust to fund a senior project officer to work at the Greater London Authority on sustainable energy and climate change and to update the Association's policy on such matters, in light of climate change developments and the government's White Paper on energy that requires a 60% CO_2 emissions reduction by 2050.[9] It may well be that people will come to recognize the urgency of acting promptly, and the growing uptake of the tenets of Corporate Social Responsibility will encourage people to 'do well by doing good'.[10]

REGULATION AND LEGISLATION

Without strict regulation and laws to ensure the:

- maintenance of air, land and water quality, and
- reduction of waste production, water consumption and energy emissions

they simply will not happen. Recent revisions to the Building Regulations have been significantly watered down in response to effective lobbying by related professions and industries, at the expense of the quality and sustainability of the built environment and society in general.[11]

Imaginative new methods are being explored to give extra teeth to the regulatory process. In the Introduction to the new Housing Bill introduced on 8 December 2003, John Prescott said one of its objectives was to:

replace the housing fitness regime with an evidence-based risk assessment process, carried out using the Housing Health and Safety Rating System (HHSRS), enabling local authorities to address more effectively the hazards to health and safety in dwellings

although in considering health and safety, there is very little regard paid to the risk of your roof being blown away, or flood water coming in through your walls.[12]

The ability of governments to modernize regulation effectively and rapidly, to deal with emerging challenges, will be an important adaptive mechanism in the 21st century.

PLANNERS

The planning system is in the front line of the forces making sustainability happen. Unfortunately planners, although many are very pro-active on such issues, are simply not equipped with the knowledge, or the statutory teeth, to deal with 'unsustainable' developments.

In the current planning process, there is generally no statement on the thermal or environmental performance of a proposed building given to councillors for consideration before it is granted planning permission. So the planning member who decides if the building will get permission may have no idea of the potential environmental impacts of the building on, for instance, greenhouse gas emissions, traffic generated pollution, or health of the occupants and the quality of life for those in the building. Planning members, the elected councillors, generally judge a building by what it looks like, and what they are, or would like to be, familiar with. Committees can give approval for fashionable, un-shaded, all glass and steel buildings with huge air conditioning systems, and remain blissfully ignorant of the task they have passed on, down the road in the process, to the Building Control officer to try to, at least make it appear to, conform to UK Building Regulations.

Even the pioneering steps taken by the London Borough Council of Merton, who require that a 'Sustainability Appraisal' be submitted with the proposals for building over 1000 m^2 describing how the building has been designed to reduce its environmental impacts over its lifetime, are meeting with resistance from the government, who are, incredibly, challenging the need for the use of such sustainability statements on a case by case basis, rather than promoting their generic use in the system.

If the government intends to meet the reductions targets of the EU Directive it is difficult to see how this will be achieved without organizations, albeit the planners, or the Environment Agency, having statutory teeth. Buildings will have to meet the required standard *before* they are given planning permission, not afterwards.

As the climate changes buildings will have to incrementally upgrade their defences against the sun and wind, with awnings, shades, solar systems, shuttering features and even wind turbines and it will be necessary for the planning organizations to decide the rules for their generic application, and to re-train planning officers in relation to their applications.

Many of these adaptations require fast tracking through the planning system, and in particular in relation to the need to put shade awnings on the south- and west-facing windows of the rooms of all elderly and disabled people who may be bed-ridden or find it difficult to move. These are the groups who are, along with young children, the most vulnerable to heat stroke, as the French found out in August 2003.

For larger buildings, requirements on the ordinary untrained citizen who is elected to sit on planning committees to pass or reject a building are onerous. It would be rare to find a councillor who is qualified to make such a decision on performance grounds. Even when they do make intuitional decisions that their voters would not like a particular building in their backyard, they can be overruled at appeal by those higher up in government whose interests may lie elsewhere than with those of the local community.

The complexity of the impact and performance issues involved are difficult to deal with for overworked planning officers who are not routinely trained to understand issues of building physics and impacts, but from now on perhaps they should be. Without such knowledge how are they, within their planning targets, to consider, for instance:

- The solar access implications of the building?
- The wind impacts of the building?
- The impact of the building on the local and regional public transports system, parking and road usage?
- Energy implications for the local and regional energy supply systems, and emissions from the City in relation to the agreed Kyoto targets for the City of London and the renewable energy potential of the development?
- The impacts of the development on local council facilities and finances, such as heath care, education, sewerage, water, gas and electricity supply, implications of bio-regional material sourcing policies, policing, building cleaning, maintenance and demolition costs?

There is a strong case for every planning department to have a trained sustainability officer to deal with such issues for most applications.

The disaster mitigation services in England and Wales also need urgent revision to deal with emerging climate-related events (the system in Scotland has already been revised). Neither the Emergency Powers Act 1920 nor the Civil Defence Act of 1948, both effected through the planning system, have been updated in England and Wales since the end of the Cold War.

Under the Civil Contingencies Bill, local councils in England and Wales, including planning departments, will form core 'Local Resilience Forums', tasked with emergency planning, providing information to the public, risk management advice and ensuring that businesses continue to operate. For the first time councils in England and Wales will have a statutory duty with respect to emergency planning as 'First Tier responders',[13] although many see this Bill as potentially impinging on the civil liberties of people.[14]

County, metropolitan, unitary and London borough councils, unlike districts, receive direct funding in the form of a civil defence grant but its value, even in the face of climate change, has been falling year on year, until 2000 when it rose from £5 million a year to £19 million, and has stayed at this level since then. Studies have showed that in fact the actual expenditure on emergencies in England and Wales is over twice this, and flood-prone regions are disproportionately penalized, particularly by floods over the past few years. These sums cover facilities such as the serious casualty access teams, chemical spills and mobile decontamination centres, the latter developed for the nuclear industry leakages.

Some counties, at the hub of transport networks also bear an undue burden of emergency planning costs. Surrey has developed a strategy for a super-jam on three busy motorways that pass through the county. Helicopters would be used to rescue the injured and vulnerable motorists and provide information to stranded motorists. Such response capabilities require significant investment, taking money from other core services.

THE COMMUNITY AT LARGE

Many different local pressure groups and national organizations are working on every aspect of how to make their locality more sustainable. These range from groups working on water, waste, pollution, transport and energy, to fuel poverty and helping the aged who are, without doubt, the most vulnerable in our society.

Some groups are even working on projects to reduce carbon dioxide emissions from buildings. CRED (which stands for carbon reductions) is the name given to an initiative, launched in August 2003, by a group of scientists at the University of East Anglia. They are concerned that although the UK government has signed up, in its February 2003 White Paper on Energy, to reducing carbon dioxide emissions by 60% by the year 2050, it has provided no clues as to how it intends to get there, let alone develop plans for effective strategies to do so. The government has begun a programme of activities to reduce emissions locally, including the installation of wind generators, night classes to teach people how to make solar panels, doing environmental audits for local companies, holding community meetings to advise people on how to conserve energy in their homes, providing low emissions travel advice etc.[15]

For large-scale emitters of greenhouse gases there is also the EU Emissions Trading Scheme (EU ETS), a mandatory greenhouse gas emission trading scheme, arising from European legislation that came into force in October 2003. It is due to begin in 2005, the first phase running from 1 January 2005 to December 2007 and subsequent phases lasting 5 years.

The main targets of the greenhouse gas trading scheme are the largest individual emitters of carbon dioxide, including electricity generators, oil refineries, the iron and steel industry, the mineral industry and paper, pulp and board manufacturing. However, other non-industrial sites could fall within the scope of the scheme as a result of the size of their combustion facilities (any installation that operates combustion facilities, for example boilers, above the threshold of 20 MW will be included in the scheme).

All installations covered by the scheme must hold a greenhouse gas emissions permit, or will be liable to financial penalties. Permits were to have been obtained by 31 January 2004. Although the scheme may be expanded in the future to cover other greenhouse gases, for the initial phase it only covers carbon dioxide.

The scheme will work on a 'Cap and Trade' basis. EU member state governments are required to set emissions limits or 'caps' for all sites (known as installations) in their country that are covered by the scheme. Each installation will then be allocated allowances equal to that cap for the particular phase in question. For the first phase (2005–07) all allowances will be allocated free of charge. The allowance allocations for each installation for any given period (the number of tradable allowances each installation will receive), will be set down in a document called the National Allocation Plan (NAP). This plan will cover the whole of the UK. The overall allowances for the period for each installation will then be broken down into annual amounts.

Installations that reduce their annual emissions to below their allocation of allowances can trade their surplus allowances on the market or bank them (storing them for use in future years). Installations that need additional allowances to cover their annual emissions will be able to buy them from the market. A reconciliation of allowances and emissions will need to take place on an annual basis, completed by 30 April each year, for the preceding calendar year.

Many city and town councils also have excellent programmes aimed at carbon emissions reductions, including Enfield, Merton, Leicester, Nottingham, Oxford, Brent and Bristol. A quick trawl through their websites will give a good flavour of what they are trying to achieve in their different ways to reduce emissions.

INDIVIDUALS

People can save lives in the changing climate, and behaviour patterns will have to adjust with the changing conditions. People should be able to wear more or less than usual, or go home early, or take a few days off. In the heat wave of 2003 security guards at the Louvre in Paris no longer tried to prevent tourists from soaking their feet in the fountains because as one said, 'at this temperature we understand that people have to get cool', and across the Channel Londoners were jumping into the fountains in Trafalgar Square.

A range of techniques for coping with, and surviving climatic extremes are available and should be taken on board by a generation who will have to get used to it, whether they be a train driver in Paris in the August 2003 where heat wave speed limits were imposed in an effort to reduce the levels of ozone, or a facilities manager who takes the decision to shut down the Treasury building in London and send everyone home because it is too hot to work.

THE INTERNET AND THE MEDIA

The Internet is the most amazing source of future-proofing ideas, opportunities, strategies and experiences in the world. It is so fast-moving and all-pervasive that new ideas become universally available instantaneously. It can also peddle agendas and well-disguised lies, in the form of apparently 'high-end' information and guidance that effectively promotes the interests of the funding organization of a site. It also works for the truth, in that a search engine like Google sorts information according to patterns of its use, a system that can be manipulated by clever Webmasters. With determined interrogation, however, that is, looking through all the pages on a subject, many sides of a discussion will be aired and a broad perspective on a subject can be enjoyed in the comfort of one's own home.

The press is also very important in educating the public with key messages, such as the fact that when watering gardens, one sprinkler uses in an hour what a family of four consumes over a week. Such information could change habits.[16]

Many of the references in this book come from papers, journals and the Internet. That is because of the rapid developments in the field, which means that books resulting from events of recent months are not yet published and the Internet, newspapers and monthly magazines are thus very important where speed and flexibility of response are an adaptive opportunity. However, the downside is that the 'opinion forming' journalists need to be very well versed in the issues, and to provide first class copy on those issues if they are to help turn the 'zeitgeist' of the general public, and the ship of government, in more sustainable and effective directions.

The architectural press has unfortunately suffered from too many journalists who are trained in related disciplines such as philosophy, art history and history, or are architects who perhaps never completed their studies or practised and have little grasp of how buildings 'work'. It is not uncommon to read articles in which buildings are described solely by how they 'look', on the 'philosophy' or 'symbolism' of a building, as seen by the journalist. This 'opinion-based' reportage reflects the way assessment of work goes on in Schools of Architecture, as staff and students proffer opinions on design. An example, in the reporting of Will Alsop on going round Tate Modern (a great example of a recycled building) gives real cause for concern. He was reported as saying that it was like 'going round a shopping centre', and his analysis of the single greatest threat to modern architecture being the local planning authorities was that it put power in the hands of a group who 'by and large don't have a lot of vision'. And, demonstrating the breadth of his own vision perhaps, he also called the Georgian architecture of Bath 'boring . . . too many hanging baskets' and he said that it is a better time to be an architect in the UK than it has been for years because 'there is no predominant style any more'. 'Suddenly ... there would appear to be no rules.'[17]

What many architectural correspondents, and architects for that matter, find difficult to do, perhaps because they are not trained to do so, is to report on how buildings 'perform'. The comparison of the energy consumption per square metre of the buildings of Bath against those of a modern development would be interesting and useful, providing some 'evidence' for use in improving future designs.

One valid defence for such low levels of reporting is that architects and engineering firms often will not brook open criticism of their buildings in the press. At least one, well-known, British architectural journalist was effectively banned from candid commenting on buildings by her editor, because a 'great man' of architecture slapped a writ on his desk the morning after she had dared to voice a criticism of his latest masterpiece. The press has quite effectively been gagged by the powers that be in the profession, and therefore many ordinary readers will continue to be surprised that there appears to be little intelligent discussion in the newspapers about buildings.

QUANGOS

The government has tried, in part, to remedy this by funding CABE,[18] the architectural industry watchdog designed to help raise standards of building and architectural design in the industry. In February 2003 its influence on the building markets was strengthened when its £4.4 million budget was increased to £10 million. It was also given a series of new responsibilities to ensure that the 200 000 new homes in the Communities plan would meet a high design standard. This include the massive £466 million investment planned in the Thames Gateway area and the £164 million for Milton Keynes, Ashford and the M11 corridor. Tony Blair has promised to personally oversee the Thames Gateway development.[19]

CABE now has its fingers in many architectural pies, and in November 2003 also proposed that the Building Listing Process, by which buildings are protected under the law from demolition because of their architectural merit, be passed over, as its retention would block a significant regeneration project. This proposal was soundly rebutted by the traditional defenders of the British landscape, both English Heritage and the RIBA.

RIBA President George Ferguson rejected the idea saying:

The RIBA believes that the sole criteria for listing should be those of architectural, cultural and historic importance and that matters of viability and economy should be dealt with solely by listed building consent.

He maintained that CABE's proposal would 'corrupt' the listings system and distract English Heritage from its main role in assessing the historic significance of any building.[20] But CABE has useful roles and has acted as a funnel for funds into improving quality in the built environment and education on it. Unfortunately its tenets of what constitutes 'good design' are based on the opinions of members of its panels, such as the fashionable architects who are biased in favour of the fashionable paradigms of design, which they promote in their own work. CABE is ultimately no more nor less than a 'high profile' government quango, led by individuals who control money and therefore have power.

What comes out of such a cocktail of interests will hopefully be independent of who signs the cheques. The money may have been better spent in completing Post Occupancy Evaluations of all the major buildings in London to see how well, or how badly they actually perform, an exercise that would educate us far more than hearing what a particular CABE member thinks of a particular building. In March 2004 one senior member of CABE was investigated for a conflict of interest, after people raised concerns that developments proffered by his own company for review by CABE design quality panels always came out with high marks for excellence, unlike a number of other developments.

ARCHITECTS

What ethical and moral responsibilities does the profession have? In his book *Streets for People*, in 1969, Bernard Rudofsky wrote, and no doubt in part as a response to the brutal redevelopment of many city centres at that time:[21]

Unlike physicians, today's architects are not concerned with the general welfare; they are untroubled by scruples about strangling the cities and the misery that this entails. Architects never felt the urge to establish ethical precepts for the performance of their profession, as did the medical fraternity. No equivalent of the Hippocratic oath exists for them. Hippocrates' promise that 'the regiment I adopt shall be for the benefit of my patients according to my ability and judgement, and not for their hurt or for any wrong' has no counterpart in their book. Criticism within the profession – the only conceivable way to spread a sense of responsibility among its members – is tabooed by their own codified standards of practice. To bolster their egos, architects hold their own beauty contests, award each other prizes, decorate each other with gold medals, and make light of the damning fact that they do not amount to any moral force ...

In fact, since this was written the Architect's Registration Board, the body with the Statutory responsibility of registering UK architects, as opposed to the Royal Institute of British Architects which is really a professional club, included in its Code of Conduct an implied professional Duty of Care relating to their wider social responsibilities,[22] stating that:

Standard

In carrying out or agreeing to carry out professional work, Architects should pay due regard to the interests of anyone who may reasonably be expected to use or enjoy the products of their own work.

5.1 Whilst Architects' primary responsibility is to their clients, they should nevertheless have due regard to their wider responsibility to conserve and enhance the quality of the environment and its natural resources.

What teeth such matters have in law is unclear, although architects do have a tried and tested legal Duty of Care, under the Laws of Tort, to avoid injuring someone, damaging their property, or causing financial loss due to inadequate expert advice.

Design at what cost – a moral issue?

We have seen in the previous chapters that modern prestige buildings often carry a very high environmental cost, in terms of the energy they use and, in many, the risks they pose to their occupants and owners, including the financial penalties of being landed with very high cleaning and maintenance costs. This disregard for the 'cost' of a building to its owners is reflected in the growing tendency for buildings to come in well over time and over cost on building budgets. This disregard for the client's welfare first shocked the British public when they were forced to pay for what turned out to be the billion pound 'Millennium Dome' fiasco. Hackles have been kept raised by the sheer audacity of the insouciance of architects to the implications what such costs may mean.[23]

The proposed £750 million design of the new Wembley stadium will ultimately be reflected in the ticket price fans have to pay for a seat in the stadium.[24] The University of Birmingham had to cancel its landmark library following a dramatic rise in the estimated budget from the original £100 million to £170 million in September 2003. Is it ultimately the students through their fees who will in future have to cover the cost of doing expensive designs that are then scrapped? Is it the people of Wales who will have to pay for the rapidly escalating costs of the Welsh National Assembly in Cardiff, where uncontrolled spending led to a ban on regular monthly payments to designers, which was replaced by the Assembly's agreement to pay only when individual work packages are complete. The move followed the Audit Commission's investigation into why the original cost of £12 million had risen to over £30 million in an attempt to stop the practice of what some saw as the signing of blank cheques for those firms involved in the construction of the project.[25]

The most publicized over-spend to date is where the people of Scotland will pay for decades for the new Scottish Parliament building at Holyrood, designed by the Catalan architect, the late Enric Miralles. The cost of this building has risen from £37 million to £375 million, that is, around £150 for every one of the 2 345 000 homes in Scotland.[26] The fact that the designer knew nothing about the British climate, people and building industry of Scotland must surely have added to these ridiculous costs and also to the risk of future building failure. Miralles designed many complex windows that stand proud from the face of the building, and which will at every joint potentially fail. This may have been a mistake, exacerbated by the fact that it was such a 'tricky' solution that many of the windows as built did 'not quite fit'. In addition, future maintenance and cleaning bills on the structure will be very high, each of those outstanding windows forms a cold bridge out into the chill winds of the windy city, and will deteriorate fairly rapidly, particularly in the increasingly wet and windy, and scorching, future climates we expect. Perhaps here a wrong decision on the wrong building will be made worse by a changing climate.

Competitions

Many have questioned the role of the 'Design Competition' in some of the above over-spends. For example, in May 2003 the European Commission received a 20 page complaint about the Scottish Parliament building claiming that the competition that was won by Miralles disadvantaged some entrants unlawfully; so suggesting that there were breaches in EU regulations on the letting of contracts and secrecy and political bias over the selection of the site.[27] Some believe that it was solely on the preference of the then Scottish leader, the late Donald Dewar, that the project was given to the late Enric Miralles.

What we do have is a system in which the judges of fashionable competitions often include many fashionable architects whose life work has been devoted to the promulgation of a later 20th century paradigm of prestige architecture. Reflections of their own style convictions will become apparent in their choices of competition winners, so setting the benchmark standards of what constitutes 'great architectural masterpieces'. Unfortunately, the greater the 'masterpiece', typically the greater its environmental impacts. Issues of environmental performance figure nowhere in the requirements of such competitions and the resulting buildings, often 'evaluated' for their performance after construction, prove to be 'nightmare' buildings.

In October 2003 the Laban Dance Centre in Deptford, southeast London, won the £20 000 Stirling Prize for Architecture. The judges were Julian Barnes, novelist, Justine Frischmass, singer from the band Elastica, and others. Technical competence to evaluate the performance of the buildings was obviously not a core requirement of the judging panel. Designed by the Swiss team of Hertzog and de Meuron, it was a popular win. The sealed-envelope, fully air-conditioned building on a waterside site could easily, and very pleasantly, have been naturally ventilated, in parts at least. There was no consideration of its environmental performance taken into account in the judging and the current and long-term running costs of the building were never discussed by the press or the judges of the competition.[28]

Exhibitions

Well-known architects get high profile exhibitions at the best venues. It is a fact of life, because certain designers dominate the architectural press, the competitions and the zeitgeist of the late 20th century public who consider them to be the 'maestros' of architecture. The fact the famous often sit on the panels that choose the designs of famous offices, often their own, for display is merely an indication of their global excellence – perhaps?

The education of architects

Engineers are crucial to the solution of these [climate change] problems, but it might be that they could be avoided in the first place if the education and training of engineers was to include a bit more about the globe's essential life-support systems. It is after all these systems which ensure the habitability of our planet as it spins in the vast spaces of the universe.

HRH Prince Philip, writing in the January 2000 edition of the magazine
Ingenia, the Journal of the Royal Academy of Engineering

What about the basic concerns of the designing professions, in terms perhaps of their 'wider responsibility to conserve and enhance the quality of the environment and its natural resources' or even the interests of their clients.

On one aspect of their professional liability they have been shown to be wanting. Architects are, apparently, currently poorly educated in their duties under the law with regards to Health and Safety. A study by the Health and Safety Executive (HSE), published in May 2003,[29] looked at designer's compliance with the Construction Design and Management (CDM) Regulations of 1994 and found architect's awareness of their duties woefully inadequate. The highest percentage of the 85 construction-related deaths between

2001 and 2002 were caused by falls from height and the report concluded that 'designers are often abdicating their responsibility to reduce risk in relation to work at height by leaving it to the principal contractor without first considering how they could change the design in a way that would make it safer to build, clean or maintain a building'.[30]

Many students in schools of architecture around the world are poorly taught on issues of building performance. In her doctoral thesis, Marianne Ryghaug did a detailed study in Norway of how architects view environmental issues such as energy efficiency and found that it has a very low status in the teaching of the subject. Architects were perceived as more 'artistic' than engineers and more preoccupied with design and form. She put the blame for this partly on architectural education, where in many schools energy and environmental courses were optional. She also identified the need for stricter regulations and funding for demonstration buildings, although perhaps more funding for Post Occupancy Evaluations of the actual, not the predicted, performance of buildings would be money better spent, as the 1990s was a decade of extensive demonstration building funded by the EU. The study was done of the Norwegian markets, but could apply anywhere.[31]

A report funded by CEBE, the Centre for Education in the Built Environment, found that sustainability is rarely considered in the design curriculum and, when it is, the subject is treated as a one-off project or tagged to an existing brief. The majority of schools have one or two lone individuals who teach students to use sustainable design features such as energy efficiency, and healthy materials, but the RIBA and ARB, the validating bodies for the schools, it argued, should insist that the subject is demonstrated on all design projects. One Head of School said that he thought it was a matter of opinion whether sustainability should be the driving force for architectural education, and his view reflects those of many heads of architecture schools in Britain.[32] The environment is not an issue to most design teachers in schools of architecture, who may, or may not, feel threatened by what they know nothing about themselves.

Teaching staff over the years have often been downgraded in schools of architecture so where a school had individuals teaching lighting, services, construction and structures they may now have one or two generalists, who will often teach by case studies rather than getting students to grips with the basic principles of building physics and performance. This may be because they really do not have a firm grip on the basics themselves, and/or because the 'lighter touch' of this approach complements the studio teaching style prevalent in many schools.

So what do they teach in schools of architecture?

Some of the best teaching on environmental issues takes place in the American Schools of Architecture,[33] often not greatly encouraged by some heads of school. This was the impression given by an extraordinary website that has recently been pulled that showed how distressed students at the Department of Architecture at the University of California at Los Angeles were losing their rights to pragmatic teaching in favour of a 'highly' theoretical approach to design – the kind that has resulted in many visually arresting buildings around the world, the kind of buildings known as the 'pointy', the 'falling over' and the 'blob'.

Many of the counter-intuitive forms of such buildings have been largely influenced by 'deconstructionism'. The following section on deconstructionism was inspired by an important recent paper on the subject by Nikos Salingaros.[34]

Deconstruction is a method of analysing texts based on the idea that language is inherently unstable and shifting and that the reader rather than the author is central in determining meaning. It was introduced by the French philosopher Jacques Derrida in the late 1960s.[35]

Deconstructionism disaggregates a specific text or building and then reassembles the components in a manner that makes the viewer look at the building not in terms of its formal function but asks the question why the architect designed it in that particular way. It is about the 'signature' of the designer.

Deconstructionism's most visible manifestation is in architecture, in a building style characterized by broken, jagged and lopsided forms, evoking physical destruction. Salingaros states that architectural theory has embraced deconstructionism in order to reverse architecture's main *raison d'être*: to provide shelter. Architecture's goals happen to be precisely what ostensibly Derrida rejects: aesthetics, beauty, usefulness, functionality, living and dwelling. The randomness of the buildings this approach produces[36] is the antithesis of nature's organized complexity. Housing buildings such as scientific departments, university buildings and museums, whose function is to enhance and complement the order of the universe, in chaotic jumbles of form, is an often unnoticed irony.

Otherwise knowledgeable clients, including academics, have been seduced to commission tortuous buildings in the deconstructionist style, applauded by fellow architects and considered ugly, odd and useless by ordinary people. Salingaros builds up a careful picture of how forces combine to make such buildings apparently 'acceptable' to those commissioning buildings, including its incomprehensibility, the silliness of people who do not want to appear not to understand it, the desire of architects to ride a

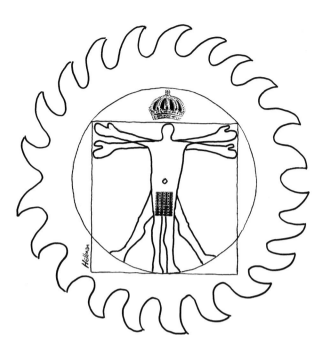

14.1.
'The Emperor has no clothes!'
(Copyright Louis Hellman 2004)

wave of stylistic fashion for fame and profit, the desire to reject the 'context' of a building, and the desire of some architects to be seen as 'leading edge' and 'innovative', hiding behind phrases such as fractals, complexity, emergence, chaos as well as their more conventional and perhaps more potentially questionable late modernistic terms, such as transparency.

Roger Scruton[37] pointed out that:

deconstruction . . . should be understood on the model of magic incantation. Incantations are not arguments, and avoid completed thoughts and finished sentences. They depend on crucial terms, which derive their effect from repetition, and from their appearance in a long list of cryptic syllables. Such incantations are a part of a ritual of indoctrination used to recruit followers, attracted by the extreme scepticism and disbelief that lies at the heart of the theory; this cult demands total emersion,[38] and human beings seem to be inclined to fall into a kind of uncritical group-think.

One should not underestimate the destructiveness of deconstructionism that is now becoming institutionalized, particularly in the academic faculties of architecture in universities around the world, where the impact of the theory is compounded when the administration also then commissions a high profile decontructionist building which effectively turns the whole school, and the university, into a training ground for decontructionists. Few people, designers, clients or architects, are keen to look foolish by admitting they were wrong, and now when the style is already nearing its sell-by date, those buildings that were commissioned two or three years ago are coming to site and the bandwagon rolls on.

After their initial infatuation with deconstruction, some architects have turned to other wider influences for design inspiration, such as 'blobs' or 'folding', a reflection of the fact that deconstruction is not a style that can be adapted or evolve to meet changing needs and as such is already *'passé'* with some architects.

Cities around the world are now seeing the next generation of 'blobs'. In the UK the first famous blobs were the four silver metal blobs of the Sheffield Centre for Popular Music, that was so inappropriate for its surrounding brick terraced streets.[39] Nearly a decade on the buildings remain getting dirtier and dirtier as local groups cannot afford the high cleaning costs. The Centre folded, although people have tried to use these funny building forms for different activities subsequently, none very satisfactorily. Like the Dome, the shapes are not quite right for anything.

The largest UK blob is four storeys high and wrapped in a skin decorated with 15 000 spun aluminium discs painted blue. It is the new Sainsbury's supermarket in the Bull Ring redevelopment in Birmingham, designed by Future Systems and opened in the summer of 2003. It was described as 'Top of the Blobs' by Jonathan Glancy of the *Guardian,* and it makes no gesture at all to 'fit in' to its context of surrounding buildings. It was hailed by Glancy as 'architectural entertainment'.[40]

14.2.
The Museum of Popular Music in Sheffield. (*Source:* Steve Sharples)

Any end of year show at an architecture school will be dominated by blobs and shards, not least because many of the teaching staff are skilled at teaching blob design, which relates largely to digital simulation skills. The computer images of blobs look stunning and many schemes are marked in schools by the quality of the digital presentation, rather than whether they illustrate a building that would work, could be used, or would be liked by its clients or its surrounding community, let alone what its impacts would be on the local, regional and global environment. More than a few teachers in schools of architecture would not consider it necessary, desirable or conscionable to mention the actual construction or performance of a building, its buildability or functionality, during the studio tutorials, and in some cases students can pass though five years of architectural education being virtually illiterate on performance-based subjects. They then emerge into the offices of unsuspecting practitioners who are expected to educate them in the boring realities of how buildings work and are built, while paying them for the privilege.

Peter Cook, head of the Bartlett School of Architecture, and a blob designer himself, was very worried about the increasing obscurity of his students' work:

Some of Britain's brightest students are producing work that not even their experienced tutors can understand, never mind clients, planners and the public . . . During last year's summer exhibition I was often puzzled and bemused by the obscurity of intention, of brief or nature of the pursuit . . . lovely stuff that you had to play guessing games with . . . we are in danger of collective headiness sustained within a 'bubble' of arcaneness.

Cook said that he would in future personally check that work is better declared and described.[41]

In the UK, however, this is changing fast as the RIBA and the ARB have got together to ensure that teaching standards across the board are of an adequate standard, and if not they withdraw their recognition from that school in an effective system of policing standards in education.

One of the most effective 'exclusionary' techniques used by 'theoretical' teachers and deconstuctionists alike is to brand traditional architecture as bad, retrograde, non-innovative and an impediment to progress, eliminating solid traditional buildings from consideration in the teaching studio, or the market place.

Leon Krier expressed the view that architects like Rogers and Foster, arch proponents of the great British 'glass box' tradition, in particular 'have too much power', and in agreeing with him Robert Adam said it was 'offensive that they are so dogmatic . . . They believe the future is theirs and there is no other way. You are a traitor to the future if you disagree with them. It is intolerant.'[42] Unfortunately, adaptability and flexibility are two of our survival mechanisms, and it may be that just as we end up with white elephant buildings our changing environment will result in white elephant architects as well.

Salingaros states that 'It is unlikely that those converted to deconstruction can be persuaded to abandon their irrational path. Sanity and rationality, however, are likely to be restored among a future generation of architects.' We return here to the notion of conventional wisdom, represented by the established theoretical 'design'-driven teachers in schools of architecture:[43]

Keynes, in his most famous observation, noted that we are ruled by ideas and by very little else . . . But the rule of ideas is only powerful in a world that does not change. Ideas are inherently conservative. They yield not to attack of other ideas but to the massive onslaught of circumstances with which they cannot contend.

The economic and environmental context, around the glass houses, the shards and the blobs, is changing rapidly, and it is this need to respond to these changes that will drive society back to demanding robust buildings rather than 'architectural entertainment', because the former are capable of adapting to those changes while the latter are not.

The most celebrated proponents of deconstruction are American-trained architects, trained to design sealed, highly serviced buildings. The buildings are little more than timber or steel frame structures with cut or bent plywood-like materials, metal or plastics bent and moulded as thin, tight skins over the framing structure. Windows are often difficult to insert in this type of building and they are few and far between. These air-conditioned and artificially light structures are built more like a boat hold than a building. Cold bridging and insulation in such buildings are real problems and, due to their lack of opening windows, they are impossible to occupy during the power cuts. They thus use extremely high levels of energy and are responsible for high levels of emissions. They are in the very high-risk category of building in the 21st century, up there with the steel and glass boxes.

In light of the importance of 'future-proofing' our buildings and cities against climate change the time may well have come to split architectural education into two distinct arms, one for those primarily interested in learning graphic and digital skills and another for those interested in becoming more pragmatic building designers who are specialist in, for example, designing low energy and low impact buildings. Then it would be clear to students, who will increasingly have to pay for five years of their university education themselves, exactly what they are getting for their money.

POWER IN THE BUILDING INDUSTRY

There has been, in the term of this current UK government, a lot of support for high-end 'design' and the works of fashionable architects who were seen to represent 'Cool Britannia'. Tony Blair has put considerable personal effort into lobbying for large design firms. He stepped in to help Foster and Partners and Arups scoop a £1.2 billion commission to extend Beijing airport in Autumn 2003. At a face-to-face meeting with Chinese prime minister Wen Jiabao on his summer trip to Beijing, Mr Blair asked Wen Jiabao and president Hu Jintao to recognize the expertise of the UK in prestigious landmark projects around the world. His decision to do so came when two UK firms, Fosters and Vector Management, were put on the short list of three. Top-level lobbying for the work by the government had gone on for two years.[44]

Powerful firms carefully place key men in key positions of political influence. Marco Goldschmied, a Director of Richard Rogers Partnership, and ex-president of the RIBA, put in a bid to advise Tony Blair directly on sustainable development as one of 15 experts who will provide advice as part of a Sustainable Development Commission,[45] chaired by environmentalist Jonathon Porritt,[46] but he was not chosen. This followed on from the work done by Richard Rogers himself, former Chair of the Government's Urban Task Force, who was also the Mayor's Chief Adviser on Architecture and Urbanism and the Chairman of Richard Rogers Partnership (RRP). He was originally appointed by the Mayor of London to this post as a consultant in April 2001, supported by a small group in the Architecture and Urbanism Unit (A+UU). Unfortunately there arose during his time there a range of 'conflicts of interest', including the weight given to his deliberations on the future of tall buildings in the capital. Other minuted conflicts of interest arose over his bids for work in a range of projects, although particular care was taken to ensure that he 'stepped outside' when such conflicts arose during meetings.[47]

Real concern about too much design work going to a few large firms was also voiced by the Office of Fair Trading, which was asked by the Better Regulation Task Force in May 2003 to launch an inquiry into the government's procurement policy because they claimed that small and medium-sized design and construction firms were being excluded from government construction contracts.[48] Both larger and smaller firms however will have to address the needs for providing more resilient buildings and so climate change issues cut right across the industry.

ENGINEERS

It is not surprising that in an age of 'machines for living in' engineers dominate the building process. Architects, who seem to be happy to pass on as much design liability as possible to anyone who will take it, often transfer their challenging designs to engineers and rely on them to make them work. The engineers who had to try to make the original design of the GLA headquarters building work, had their work cut out for them. They had to design out much of the glass on the roof, and try to control the indoor air temperatures with the sun beating down through the envelope into the building from above – a task that can only be done by using not insignificant amounts of energy to remove the heat once in the building. One could certainly ask whether there is a place for glass roofs in the design of 21st century buildings.

A great consolation for engineers over the past decades since 'modern' offices started to overheat in the 1950s, is that engineers are typically paid according to how much plant and duct work they can get into a building, so the more environmentally 'innovative' the project, the more they get paid to rectify the basic design mistakes of the architect.

If we are ever to get green buildings we must ensure that this contractual arrangement is promptly changed to ensure that engineers are fairly paid to reduce energy consumption, not encouraged through their contracts to increase it. Engineers should work side by side with the architect, from the first days of the brief, to ensure that the form and the fabric of the building itself is used to minimize its costs and impacts, not expensive machines.

Terry Wyatt, an inspirational President of the Chartered Institute of Building Service Engineers in 2003/04,[49] in his inaugural speech entitled 'Adapt or Die', outlined the exciting possibilities for engineers who will have to re-tool for a business climate in which the traditional work of building services engineers is shrinking while they will have to bear the brunt of pressures to reduce waste in the construction industry by 30%. He identifies that work such as calculations, sizing, positioning and coordination, specification, costing, manufacturing and the construction and fitting out of the building with traditional air conditioning systems will diminish. This work he regards as the 'filling in a sandwich' between one 'slice of bread' that involves the briefing, footprint design, concepts and budgets for the building and the other slice that includes operation and maintenance work to keep the building functioning well and to make future change possible.

He identified two key pressures affecting the traditional work of building services engineers as globalization and standardization. However, he represents the industry that makes buildings work, and this design knowledge will be increasingly important in the building design process. Engineering work could thus become more central rather than less so in this process. He demonstrated how farsighted companies are increasingly well positioned in the market place, such as Colt in solar shading, Nuaire in efficient air-systems equipment and Thermomax in solar thermal collectors, as engineers become key players in increasing building efficiency.

The biggest opportunity, he saw, as actually being offered by climate change was government efforts to reduce carbon emissions by 60% by 2050, accompanied by targets for energy efficiency and renewable energy over the next 20 years. He describes the recent Energy White Paper as throwing down the gauntlet. Carbon management offers huge opportunities for services consultants and the wider industry, and the building services industry has a major opportunity to be at the forefront of carbon management within buildings. He even suggested that engineers would be well placed to become key players in the carbon trading markets, as well as growing into the role of building-related renewable energy specialists using, for instance, wind, solar, biomass and water power.

Hear we see a real visionary, assisting his members to come to terms with the challenges of the coming decades and helping them to strategically position themselves in the emerging market places in what is an excellent example of 'profession continuity planning', an exercise essential to the survival of all professions in the coming decades.

CIBSE has intelligently sought to educate its members with high-quality annual conferences and a wide range of specialist groups who meet to inform the membership of developments, and act fast and effectively to pre-empt the changes happening all around. One of these is the need to begin to calculate the climatic performance of buildings for future climates, and their climate change group has been developing a dataset for future climates so that decisions made today about buildings that will hopefully stand for 100 years, can be tested against future climates. We saw how Spain has courted environmental disaster by basing the calculations for the building of the canal from the Ebro river to the south of Spain on climates of 20–50 years ago.[50] They should in fact have been done on the basis of river flows in 2020 or 2050.

BUILDING OWNERS, OCCUPIERS AND EMPLOYERS

It's 'wake up time' for building owners and users, who have a responsibility to future-proof their own interests against the exigencies of climate change, terrorism and fuel insecurity. All businesses should now have a continuity planning strategy to include emergency procedures for all events. The global corporate real estate network has a range of strategies they promote, including, to list but a few:[51]

- Shift from high rise to low rise with a preference for lower level offices.
- Less visible external signage.
- Careful lobby design.
- Parking strategies.
- Designs for evacuation including location and design of stair wells.
- Security in terminology in leases and insurance policies.

Extreme climate events and blackouts over the summer of 2003 reinforced the need for businesses and building owners to make preparations for the repetition of such events.

It is a requirement under UK Health and Safety legislation that employers may face investigation and prosecution by the Health and Safety Executive (HSE) if they fail to devise suitable contingency plans for emergencies. It is envisaged that claims could arise from workplace accidents caused by the sudden loss of lights, power to lifts or failure of air conditioning systems in hot weather. Panic-induced trampling could occur, particularly if personnel are not promptly informed about the cause of the failure. Stress claims could be brought, particularly if staff suspect a terrorist attack. While many employers have strategies for incidents of fire or terrorist attack, it is now considered necessary, by legal experts in the field, that they should also have an appropriate response to deal with total sudden power loss, under the 1999 Health and Safety Regulations,[52] which requires employers to undertake a 'suitable and sufficient assessment' of workplace risks. Extreme weather events were involved in most of the summer 2003 blackouts and so this issue should be factored into business planning for blackouts in the future.

'There are certainly identifiable dangers associated with swift and protracted power failure at work. Further widespread electricity failures are foreseeable. Accordingly, there is a compelling argument that a risk assessment should address the repercussions of such eventuality,' said Peter James, a health and safety lawyer at Parabis Law in December 2003. Secondary lighting sources, generators and evacuation procedures were cited as primary options, but what it is not possible to do is to provide air conditioning over a long period for a high-energy building with back-up generators alone.

Accidents during darkness, complete or partial, could lead to prosecution. Health and Safety prosecutions are worrying because liability is absolute save for the defence of reasonable practicability and employers might argue that they had done everything that was reasonably practicable if they followed the HSE advice. There is a possibility that if an employer follows the HSE guidance to the letter but there is still a bad accident the employer might seek redress from those liabilities from the HSE.

Lawyers have commented on another dimension of the issue. Under the Building Regulations, fire safety regulations apply to those who build a building in the first place, or modify one. For many years this has meant having an 'appropriate means of escape in case of fire', that is, one that is capable of being safely and effectively used at all material times. But emergency lighting is not mentioned, although it would be hard to argue that an escape route that cannot be safely used when the power fails is 'appropriate'.[53]

Employers also have a 'duty of care' under Fire Precautions (Workplace) Regulations 1997 to provide emergency lighting. Regulatory breach is an offence but does not give rise to civil liability. The quality of the emergency lighting may depend on the property's age, and of course the diligence of the employers in ensuring that the regulations and legislation are complied with. Deep plan offices, with less available natural daylight obviously require more emergency lighting than offices with a shallower floor plan. Regular maintenance of battery systems is also important. QC Graham Eklund warns that legislation has enabled electricity supply companies 'to restrict their liability for economic loss caused by negligence disrupting the supply', so it is likely that 'economic losses consequent on a negligently caused blackout or failure of the electricity supply' will not be coverable.[54] In New York in the August 2003 blackouts it should be noted that both simple and sophisticated systems for emergency lighting failed alike in some buildings.

Questions will arise in the law as to where liability lies where buildings also have to be abandoned in extreme weather events, such as the emptying of the Treasury building in the heat wave of August 2003. We have known since the 1960s that certain building types, those with excessive glazing in particular, overheated in hot weather. It could, and no doubt will be, argued that because of the quantity of related information in the public realm on the subject, that designers could be held liable for buildings that provide unnecessarily uncomfortable temperatures during hot spells. This has yet to be tested in the courts but a good case could be made. Similarly where loss of life occurs during flood events due to insufficient attention being given to the problem at the design stage then designers could again be held culpable.

INSURERS

Insurers know what the problems are, they pay out on them. In relation to flooding they are particularly well prepared. A system has been developed for capturing flood and storm damage data. It has been tested on a number of flood events on a pilot basis, and evaluated and refined by loss adjusters, architects and academics. The system was also used to assist in establishing a national flood claims database for the UK.[55]

The system is called FASTER (Flood And STorm Event Reporting). The FASTER system not only streamlines the inspection of damaged property but provides all the data needed to build a vulnerability database, and has been endorsed by all the key insurance industry bodies.

There is significant reluctance within the claims side of the industry, however, to change existing systems, because the main benefits would be to loss adjusters, consumers and to technical underwriters responsible for rate setting, while the benefits to individual insurers' claims departments are less obvious.

The UK government has indicated that its UK Climate Impacts Programme will now have more emphasis on seeking ways to adapt to climate change, including ways to make buildings less vulnerable to storm and flood damage. Government may have a perception that the insurance industry has considerable detailed data on the effects of storms and floods on buildings from its claims records and may increasingly be looking to tap into such data.

The UK insurance industry could perhaps follow the example of the National House Building Council in the UK and the Institute of Business and Home Safety in the USA, by employing their own inspectors, or training government inspectors. In Australia, insurers and mortgage lenders have gone even further. They have drawn up their own set of standards for certain types of buildings. The standards are called the 'Blue Book' and have in effect made the official standards redundant because all builders know that unless they follow the Blue Book, the building will not be insurable and the bank will not lend money on it.

Another approach would be to classify new housing according to the build quality and specification, which would allow insurers to charge different rates according to vulnerability to windstorm, subsidence and flood. This would be similar in some ways to the different groupings used by motor insurers: it would reflect the risk better, and could lead to public pressure for improved standards.

But in effect the insurance industry stands to be a major loser in the face of a changing climate, not only because of the escalating payouts for which they are responsible but also because a significant proportion of their funds are already invested in what could be surmised to be high-risk buildings. Many of the more glamorous buildings in major cities are owned by the insurance industry, who hold significant stocks in 'prestige' developments. These are what is increasingly being recognized as the high-risk end of the property markets. There is a deadly Achilles' heel in the system. Insurance companies charge similar rates for office space by post code, regardless of the risk an individual building, or space within a building poses. So similar insurance premiums are charged for offices at the top of a very tall 'target type' tower as may be charged to a low rise robust office in a middle-sized city. So people in resilient buildings may be subsidising the risk of the target buildings, the buildings that are perhaps most vulnerable to extreme climate events. This unfair situation will only last until the government decides to legislate that buildings should pay according to the risks they present, or until the first clever insurance company divests itself of its 'white elephant' and high-risk buildings so that it is itself sufficiently unencumbered by a portfolio of high-risk buildings to offer fair, lower premiums to low-risk building owners, according to their actual risk *vis-à-vis* claims related to perhaps extreme climate or power outage events.

This issue also pertains to the 'terrorist' insurance, where office space is charged the same premium at the top of a target building as is charged for robust low provincial offices that are unlikely to be threatened by terrorist events. Hence local councils are paying top dollar around the country for now mandatory terrorist cover to, in part at least, protect the vulnerable 'target' assets of the industry that provides that insurance. This again will only last as long as government does not regulate against this monopolistic practice or until a smart insurance company wakes up to the potential to gain market advantage by charging buildings according to their actual risk.

Architects were actually told by the insurance industry in March 2003 to stop offering clients advice on ways of protecting buildings against terrorist attacks and of providing escape routes because the service has recently been excluded from professional indemnity insurance policies and it is felt by the industry that architects would be stepping out of their area of expertise by doing so. Most insurers have now dropped clauses in their building insurance policies that cover terrorism because insurers feel that it is not something that is insurable without specialist coverage.[56]

This may in part explain why in a year of unprecedented payouts on climate events the insurance industry made a healthy profit in 2003. If architects, or engineers, started to try to quantify the risks associated with the buildings they are involved in it may lead to the growing public awareness of the relative risk of buildings, so requiring a shaking down of terrorist premiums to the detriment of the interest of the insurance industry.

REAL ESTATE MANAGERS

The blame for the inexorable rise in the market for prestige buildings, that are increasingly recognized as 'high risk', can be laid partly at the doors of real estate, and property portfolio, managers. But perhaps 'the higher you rise the harder you fall'. For the larger companies that have accumulated a portfolio of high-end prestige buildings, may well be faced with plummeting rents on vulnerable buildings, with clients gradually tending to prefer more robust, low-cost, low-impact, comfortable and less vulnerable buildings. There was a time in the 1980s and 1990s where the push was for higher-end prestige space in the portfolio. The more a client was charged on a lease, the greater the cut for the property managers so the drive was to push clients towards the high end to optimize profits.

There is an obvious need for the property management industry to start to service the requirement for resilient low-risk buildings in low-risk locations, and the ability to track risk and performance will be an increasingly marketable advantage in the industry. Annual Performance Evaluations will be a key tool of property managers in the coming years as companies try to sort the space sheep from the space goats.[57] The smart companies – who will not be the ones who are locked into long-term, once-favourable leases – will already be beginning to move in the direction of consolidating the 'sustainability' of their portfolio. Management and contract flexibility and adaptability here are two key adaptive skills.

INDUSTRY

Industry will do what it does best, respond to the market place. In simple terms the changing climate will lead to more demand in many areas, and less in others. Marks & Spencer sold fewer overcoats in the 2003/4 winter because it was not cold. In Milan consumption of water in the heat wave of 2003 averaged 900 000 m^3 a day, more than 50% more than normal.[58] Tesco predicted a 100% increase in the sales of ice creams in the heat, taking out 500 lorries to keep stocks supplied around the country. The heat wave of 2003 led to a dramatic increase in the sales of bottled water of 11% on the year before, reaching a record retail value for the marker of over £1 billion a year.[59]

But here again the importance of Business Continuity Planning becomes key. Many industries like the water supply industry are already prepared with their 50 year plans. For smaller bottled water provision companies the 5 year plan with seasonal provision, based on good climate-related data, will need careful thought. For major product distribution services, including those in the building industry, the need to plan for extreme climate events may tend manufacturers towards on-site provision of products, like site ice-cream making facilities at large supermarkets, if gridlock on the roads hampers delivery during periods of peak demand.

Industry, including the building industry, will have to plan carefully over the short, medium and long term to be capable of responding to, and profiting from, demand.

THE 'AMERICA' PROBLEM

The current occupants of the White House are putting huge effort into denying that climate change even exists. In March 2003, a memo was exposed that advised the US Republican Party to avoid 'frightening' phrases such as 'global warming' after an internal memo had warned that it is the domestic issue that George W. Bush is most vulnerable on. The memo, by the leading Republican consultant Frank Luntz, conceded that the party has 'lost the environmental communications battle' and urged Republican politicians that:

The scientific debate is closing [against us] but not yet closed. There is still a window of opportunity to challenge the science.

Mr Luntz wrote in a memo obtained by the Environmental Working Group, a Washington-based campaigning organization:

Voters believe that there is no consensus about global warming within the scientific community. Should the public come to believe that the scientific issues are settled, their view about global warming will change accordingly. Therefore you need to continue to make the lack of scientific certainty a primary issue in the debate.[60]

The White House position that mandatory restrictions on emissions, as required by the Kyoto Protocol, should not be countenanced until further research is undertaken is a popular line from the Administration. Meanwhile the clock ticks on and more and more Americans lose their lives and livelihoods to the climate.[61] What is a major concern is that, not only is the American building type, with its use of inefficient air conditioning systems and thin, tight-skinned, un-shaded, over-glazed, no-weight buildings being exported to many countries, and being imposed on some like Iraq, but also that the American people will be left, when the lights do go out in extreme weather events, trying to survive in highly vulnerable buildings, highly exposed in their 'continental' climate.

CONCLUSIONS

The players in the buildings and climate change equation are too numerous to cover comprehensively, but the reader should by now have an idea of the inter-connectivity of the roles of the players, and the huge step changes in all walks of our lives that need to be taken to if we are to stabilize climate change and manage its impacts and survive with a decent quality of life.

Businesses, services, professions, communities and ordinary people will need 'reorder normality', rearrange the paths they take, and the costs they apportion, to make buildings happen, to plan carefully to future-proof their own lives. Change will touch all of us from the fuel-poor to the corporate executive. The writing is now on the wall, and at the heart of our response to these challenges lies the ever-increasing need for resilient buildings.

NOTES AND REFERENCES

1 The notion that there is a developed and an undeveloped world is dated in our 'global' society. In most countries there are groups of people who live the 'fossil fuel life' and live in big comfortable houses, drive big cars, and are globally 'connected' by cheap flights, cyberspace and growing trends in obesity. There are in most countries, including the United States, pockets of extreme deprivation, where the lack of food to eat could be seen as part, also, of a global problem. The global economy has done nothing to break down the internationally ubiquitous wealth-based class systems, and is widely claimed to be exacerbating the gaps between the rich and the poor.

By 2030 30% of the world's population may well live in slums, according to a UN report released in October 2003. It warned that unplanned and unsanitary settlements may become trigger points for social instability in the future (*Guardian*, 4 October 2003, p. 17), and this is not just in the developing world.

Squatter settlements in the United States and the UK may provide models of what will develop within or around our cities in the future. The authors of the report claim that 'cities have become a dumping ground for people working in unskilled, unprotected and low wage industries and trades . . . the slums of the developing (and developed) world swell' (www.unhabitat.org/global_report.asp).

2 Ekins, P. (2003) *Projects and Policies for Step Changes in the Energy System: Developing an agenda for social science research*. Report of the ESRC Energy Research Conference. Text available on: http://www.psi.org.uk/docs/2003/esrc-energy-conference-report.doc.

Jim Skea, in summing up: 'emphasized the context of the Energy White Paper: the importance of the international dimension, and the need to secure international cooperation on the reduction of carbon emissions; and the importance of assessing energy developments in a broader framework of sustainable development, which includes issues of affordability, reliability and competitiveness, as well as carbon reduction.

'Addressing such an agenda requires a wide disciplinary perspective, in which engineering-economy modelling had an important, but not exclusive, role to play. An emphasis on *evidence* was particularly important in this field: much good research in a variety of relevant areas had been carried out in the past, and this needed to be brought together through systematic reviews and through research into the effectiveness of different policy approaches and into the evaluations of policy initiatives that had already been implemented. There were many issues that still needed further work, including assessment of the geopolitical situation, the need to invest in strengthening the electricity distribution network, the whole relationship between supply chains and the different interests of the actors they comprised, and the nature and role of public engagement. It should not be forgotten that a lot was already known about these issues. It might be that in this situation an investment in networking existing knowledge might be more cost effective than new projects which sought to add to it. It would be good if the new Research Council programmes could bear this in mind.'

3   See http://dir.salon.com/tech/feature/2000/12/06/bad_computers/index.html.

4   Thanks to Terry Wyatt, in his 2003 Presidential Speech for CIBSE, the UK Chartered Institute of Building Service Engineers, for this idea that the building industry could follow such industries into obscurity.

5   *Guardian,* 5 September 2003, p. 3. The fact that some regions that are more severely hit by droughts, or floods, will then have their staple crops disadvantaged in the wider markets was emphasized when the Italian farmers' federation said that due to the extreme drought of the summer of 2003 in 11 of the country's 20 regions, olive oil could go up by 30% in costs, that if passed on to the buyers would kill exports, leading to dire economic consequences in the region (*Guardian,* 5 August 2003, p. 3).

6   *Building Design,* 16 May 2003, p. 2.

7   For coverage of Post Occupancy Evaluations and Building Performance Evaluations see two recent books: Roaf, S. with Horsley, A. and Gupta, R. (2004) *Closing the Loop: Benchmarks for Sustainable Buildings.* London: RIBA Publications; and Prieser, W. and Vischer, J. (2004) *Assessing Building Performance.* Oxford: Butterworth-Heinemann.

8   See http://www.eurisol.com/pages/EPDirective.html and http://www.defra.gov.uk/environment/energy/internat/ecbuildings.htm.

9   See www.lga.gov.uk or ring 0207 664 3131 for more details.

10 Hampton, D. (2004) Corporate Social Responsibility. Chapter 3 in Roaf, S. with Horsley, A. and Gupta, R. (2004) *Closing the Loop: Benchmarks for Sustainable Buildings.* London: RIBA Publications.

11 The effectiveness of lobby groups from the voluntary sector is growing and many NGOs and charities, often funding by far-sighted management of major organizations, are now driving the agenda in related fields. For instance, a report commissioned by BT from Forum for the Future, a sustainable development charity, and published in October 2003, recommended that the government should consider introducing binding national carbon reduction targets on a sliding scale, reaching a 60% decrease on 1990 levels by 2050 (*Guardian,* 17 October 2003, p. 24).

12 Some interesting related Q&As can be seen on: http://www.odpm.gov.uk/stellent/groups/odpm_housing/documents/page/odpm_house_02625706.hcsp TopOfPage.

13 http://www.cityoflondon.gov.uk/our_services/law_order/security_planning/civil_contingencies_bill.htm.

14 http://www.statewatch.org/news/2004/jan/05uk-civil-contingencies-Bill.htm.

15 *Guardian,* 27 August 2003, p. 10.

16 *Guardian,* 5 August 2003, p. 3.

17 *Guardian,* 8 December 2003, p. 5.

18 *Building Design,* 7 November 2003, p. 2.

19 www.cabe.org.uk.

20 *Building Design,* 7 February 2003, p. 1.

21 Rudofsky, B. (1969) *Streets for People.* New York: Doubleday & Co.

22 http://www.arb.org.uk/regulation/code-of-conduct/conduct-and-competence.shtml.

23 Over budget projects are listed on: http://news.bbc.co.uk/1/hi/uk/911317.stm. See also other follies on www.follies.btinternet.co.uk/dome.html.

24 The Professional Footballers Association questioned the wisdom of spending £750 million on a new national stadium at Wembley following news that football chiefs and the government are set to declare that contracts for the controversial project have finally been rubber-stamped, two years after a major game was last played at the famous ground. The £750 million cost of the project will include £352 million to build the

stadium, £120 million to buy land, £50 million for improving infrastructure, £23 million for demolition, £40 million for development costs and £80 million in financing costs. At a time when so many Football League clubs are facing financial crises, Gordon Taylor, Director of the Association, expressed his fears that 'the new stadium could become a 'white elephant', and was not convinced it was the best use of government (tax payers) and FA money at such a time. Wembley had been overtaken by events, such as the collapse of football broadcaster ITV Digital and the serious financial problems of one of the FA's flagship leagues. Cardiff, Manchester and literally dozens of other magnificent stadiums have been created for a lot less and are being used by regular occupants. The fact that money is being borrowed from Germany rather than in this country makes one wonder at the future viability of the scheme. http://www.givemefootball.com/pfa.html?newsID =456.

25 *Building Design* 12 September 2003, p. 2.

26 The cost of the new Scottish parliament building at Holyrood has risen from £37 million to £375 million, while running badly over time. The consultants fees alone are thought to exceed £60 million. £18.5 million were spent on windows that 'don't quite fit' and £14.35 million was spent on extra fees to architects, engineers and cost consultants and for site running and construction management. *Building Design*, 13 June 2003, p. 1.

27 *Building Design,* 30 May 2003, p. 2. In May 2003 the European Commission received a 20 page complaint about the Scottish Parliament building claiming that the competition disadvantaged some entrants unlawfully, also suggesting that there were breaches in EU regulations on the letting of contracts and secrecy and political bias over the selection of the site.

28 *Guardian,* 13 October 2003, p. 10.

29 http://www.hse.gov.uk/construction/designers/index.htm.

30 *Building Design,* 9 May 2003, p. 3. Only 8% of designers surveyed had been trained how to comply with the CDM Regulations. See also www.hse.gov.uk/statistics.

31 CADDET InfoPoint, Issue 2/03, p. 7. See http://www.caddetre.org/newsletter/back_issues.php.

32 *Building Design,* 30 May 2003, p. 7.

33 See the excellent website of the American Society of Building Science Educators (SBSE) on www.sbse.org/.

34 I am indebted to Nikos Salingaros, the American architect, philospher and mathematician for much of the following section on deconstructionism. The full text of his important and thoughtful

paper on the subject is published in: Salingaros, Nikos (2003). The Derrida Virus, *TELOS*, No. 126, Winter, pp. 66–82. Also available online on: http://www.math.utsa.edu/sphere/salingar/derrida.html.

35   See *Encarta World English Dictionary* (1999) New York: St Martins Press.

36   Architects designing in a deconstructionist manner include Peter Eisenman, Frank Gehry and Daniel Libeskind.

37   Scruton, R. (2000) *An Intelligent Person's Guide to Modern Culture.* South Bend, IN: St Augustine's Press. pp. 141–2.

38   Lehman, D. (1991) *Signs of the Times: Deconstruction and the Fall of Paul de Man.* New York: Poseidon Press, p. 55.

39   Apart from the alienating design, the architect chose a very rapidly deteriorating surface to clad the blobs. Sheffield is a very 'dirty' city due to the cold air inversion in the valley and the blobs looked awful within months. One very energetic group in Sheffield put forward a clean-up bid, as reported here: 'A bid to clean the grimy shell of the failed National Centre for Popular Music has been given the brush off. Campaigners wanting to see the tarnished stainless steel drums restored to their gleaming former self have failed to persuade regeneration agency Yorkshire Forward to underwrite a clean up. The group called Pride in Sheffield had lined up a £3000 bargain contract with local firm Stealth Access to restore the glitter to the building – wrong material – wrong shape.' See: http://www.freelists.org/archives/ncpm/102002/msg00017.html. If such inappropriate materials are used in a dirty city their deterioration in a changing climate will be hastened. The importance of local knowledge is emphasized here, including the fact that this building was located in what is not a rich neighbourhood and that the £3000 required was a great deal of money for them. It is a pittance when compared to the tens of thousands of pounds that the Greater London Authority pays simply to clean the windows of its new headquarters blob building every year.

40   *Guardian*, G2, 1 September 2003, p. 13.

41   *Building Design,* 1 February 2002, p. 1.

42   *Building Design,* 1 February 2002, p. 1.

43   Galbraith, J.K. (1963) *The Affluent Society.* Canada: Mentor Books.

44   *Building Design,* 7 November 2003, p. 1.

45   *Architects Journal*, 27 July 2003.

46   www.sd-commission.gov.uk/.

47 www.london.gov.uk/assembly/stndsmtgs/2003/stdoct16/stdoct 16item05.pdf.

48 *Building Design*, 16 May 2003, p. 2.

49 http://www.bsee.co.uk/news/fullstory.php/aid/2733/CIBSE% 92s_new_president_highlights_the_pressing_need_for_a_future _of_change.html.

50 *Guardian*, Society, 27 November 2002, p. 8.

51 http://www.corenetglobal.org/pdf/learning/9_11_impact.pdf. See also the business continuity section PAS 56 on www.thebci.org.

52 http://www.hmso.gov.uk/si/si1999/19993242.htm.

53 When the lights go out, *Independent Review,* 16 December 2003, p. 12.

54 For an interesting case see *AE Beckett & Sons (Lyndons) Ltd and Others* v *Midlands Electricity Plc* http://www.lawreports.co. uk/civdec0.4.htm.

55 Black, A. and Evans, S. (1999) *Flood Damage in the UK: New Insights for the Insurance Industry.* University of Dundee, Scotland (ISBN 0 903674 37 8).

56 *Building Design*, 28 March 2003, p. 1.

57 See Roaf, *Closing the Loop.*

58 *Guardian,* 5 August 2003, p. 3.

59 *Observer,* 13 July 2003, p. 5.

60 The text of the Luntz memo is available to download on the Environmental Working Group website, see www.ewg.org/ briefings/luntzmemo/pdf.

61 Oliver Birkham, Washington, *Guardian,* 28 July 2003, p. 14.

15 THE BATTLE CONTINUES

We have seen the devastation wrought upon us by the changing climate worsening year on year. We have counted the fallen in the climate wars, those who have died from heat, hunger and disease, in the floods and droughts and a myriad of emerging horrors in our warming world. We can no longer give credence to the disbelievers. The war against climate change must be waged with the utmost vigour, but what are the tactics and the weapons that we can take up in the ultimate battle for the planet itself?

THE INTELLIGENCE MUST BE RELIABLE

The first priority when going to battle must be to have available high-quality, reliable intelligence. In the built environment, we are often shielded from the truth by ignorance, or by people who, understandably, are keen not to reduce the market value of their 'product'. While heart surgeons and teachers have their successes and failures demonstrated in league tables in the national press, designers consider it acceptable to be 'immune' from the consequences of the performance of their buildings. A number of leading designers are notoriously litigious. Stephen Brand, author of the excellent book *How Buildings Learn*, had to scrap a whole print run of his book for the UK market because of the criticisms he levelled at one famous British architect, alleging that he produced buildings that were often very expensive to maintain. He was threatened with legal action and withdrew the book, which then had to be altered before reprinting.[1] The libel laws in Britain favour a relatively high degree of control of the media. Step one in our search for resilient buildings must be the flowering of a free, open and well-informed debate.

On the other hand we have excellent intelligence from the scientific community who, remarkably, have the extraordinary skills to foretell the future, using simulations and scenarios,[2] with which we can now design for estimated future conditions and climates. Massive investment will be needed to pay, not only for this science, but also to turn the forecasts into fully fledged battle plans and to enlist every person on this planet in the fight for survival.

NEW WEAPONS ARE NEEDED

Our traditional weapons are losing their power as we face the growing Goliath of the climate. The cheap energy we relied on to buy our way out of the problem is fast disappearing and moreover its use is increasingly seen as the cause of the problem. Everyone recognizes now that new energies must be brought online rapidly.

The problem is that we are battling extreme events, with outdated infrastructure and obsolete products, processes and paradigms. We need effective regional commanders who have the power to call war councils with all the players, to thrash out, and agree, new paths for procurement, and new 'closed' and 'adaptive' systems, capable of rapid modification, improvement and response.

15.1.
Resilient offices may well look more like the ING Bank I Amsterdam than a glass box. (*Source:* Sue Roaf)

The requirement for an annual evaluation of the performance and emissions of every public building is an obvious first start that can be tied into global monitoring systems on the health of the planet, such as carbon taxes and trading, contraction and convergence planning, and the strategic implementation of renewable energy quotas for the built environment.

But early on, we have to face up to the need to plan for the obsolescence of the worst aspects of the enemy, to get rid of a generation of lethal technologies like the completely unnecessary sports utility vehicles (SUVs) and the high-impact, high-emission buildings that have proliferated globally within the short time window of the past 30 years. They are capable of being scrapped and recycled within an even shorter time frame with our improved knowledge, communications and information systems, and the global reach of meta-strategists, exemplified by the armies and actions created by the Agenda 21 movement.

RESILIENT BUILDINGS: THE FRONT LINE OF DEFENCE

In the front line in our battle for survival must be a new generation of resilient buildings, which would:

- Suffer less from the impacts of a changing climate than other buildings, being carefully placed within a robust infrastructure of transport, resources, services, jobs, food, water, and as safe as possible from the excessive stresses of climate change.
- Have fewer impacts on the people and environment around them. Such buildings would:
  - Use as little energy as possible through good design.[3]
  - Provide that energy, where possible, from clean, renewable sources that will not pollute nor run out.
  - Reduce waste in construction, operation and demolition.[4]
  - Be built with goods and materials that produce minimal pollution.
  - Not destroy fragile biodiversity and ecosystems.
  - Promote the health of all.
  - Ensure that people are comfortable, and can survive even in extreme weather within them.

We see unresilient buildings all around us – buildings that are vulnerable to climate change. Many are already uninsurable buildings, like the thousands of flood-blighted homes in the UK, or those already falling prey to a receding coastline. In August 2003 many homes and offices were simply too hot to sleep,[5] work or remain in and over 15 000 people, many in lethal buildings, died in France in August 2003. As insurers respond to the increase in climate-related hazards

Architects:
Sue Roaf and David Woods

PV:
Energy Equipment Testing:
Bruce Cross,
Cardiff with Jeremy Dain,
Inscape Architects, Bristol

Solar hot water:
George Goudsmit, AES Findhorn

Owner:
Susan Roaf

Location:
Oxford, UK, 51°N, 1°W, 40 m
above sea level

Climate:
Temperate

Area:
232 m^2, 250 m^2 including porch
and sun space

15.2.
Resilient dwellings may perform like the Oxford Ecohouse that has minimal carbon dioxide emissions. (*Source:* Sue Roaf, Manuel Fuentes and Stephanie Thomas, *Ecohouse 2*. Oxford: Architectural Press, 2003)

with rising premiums, and the shelving of whole sections of their portfolios of exposed and vulnerable buildings, some have predicted that we may even see the catastrophic collapse of the insurance industry as a result of weather-related claims, if it cannot respond rapidly and effectively enough to the escalating impacts of climate change.

REDUCE THE EXPOSURE AND VULNERABILITY OF POPULATIONS

While it is impossible to move buildings and cities, growing populations can be housed in climate-safe regions, and existing populations shifted to regions where their chances of survival will be improved during the coming decades. Where is the sense in planning for major population growth in Florida or Sydney when there is already insufficient water to meet the existing population's needs? While people are being moved from exposed coastal locations in some countries, in many more, millions of people are still at risk from the rising sea. Regional planning is becoming a global issue. Every country should now have a High Commander for Sustainability with real power to act.

Local authorities, who will have a good working knowledge of where local infrastructures are failing in extreme weather events,

15.3.
Resilient buildings like this
residence at Keble College,
Oxford, designed by Rick Mather,
are well loved by their occupants.
(*Source:* Sue Roaf)

should have a mandate to plan to reduce the impacts of short-
and long-term climate changes.[6] Reducing the vulnerability of the
weakest sections of the population should be a priority for individuals, organizations and governments alike, requiring immediate
action, from the putting of shades and awnings on all south- and
west-facing windows of rooms that house the elderly and young,
to universally providing shaded areas in school playgrounds.

EMERGENCY PLANNING

In the short term, planning and educating for emergency warning,
evacuation and support systems for businesses and communities,
is vital. Much of the loss of life and property in a disaster results
from the lack of effective response to the events, as was reflected
in heat waves in Chicago in 1995[7] and France in 2003, where
blame, in both cases, was placed largely on the shoulders of the
politicians for their slow response to the developing crisis, and the
unpreparedness of local governments in dealing with it.

Existing public institutions such as the emergency services, social
workers and armed forces can do a great deal to reduce vulnerability by careful planning and a quick and effective response. Similarly
insurers, by quick action, can reduce the social and economic damage following a disaster. For many years, fire insurers used to give
discounts for properties located near a fire station, and no doubt
in the future other premium incentives will be available for robust
and resilient buildings where future climate change risks have been
evaluated and effective mitigating strategies have been established.

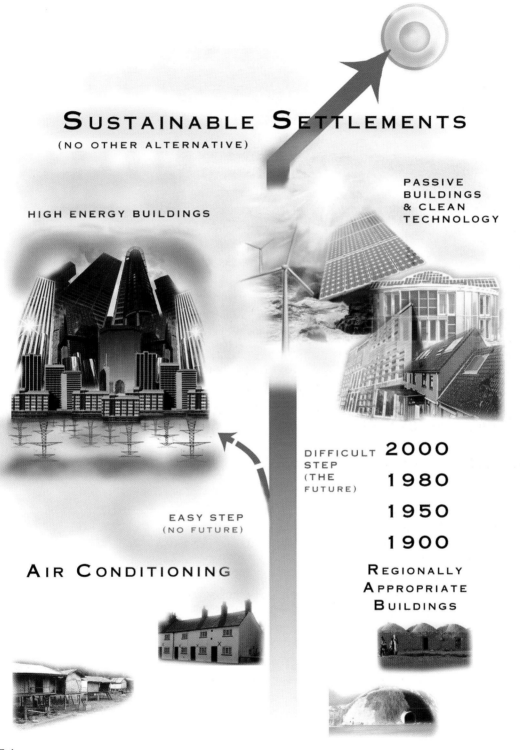

SUSTAINABLE SETTLEMENTS
(NO OTHER ALTERNATIVE)

PASSIVE
BUILDINGS
& CLEAN
TECHNOLOGY

HIGH ENERGY BUILDINGS

DIFFICULT
STEP
(THE
FUTURE)

2000

1980

1950

1900

EASY STEP
(NO FUTURE)

AIR CONDITIONING

**REGIONALLY
APPROPRIATE
BUILDINGS**

15.4.
The future made possible by a new resilient building that can respond to the moving targets of the changing climate.
(*Source:* Sue Roaf, digitally produced by Claire Palmer)

CONTINUITY PLANNING: THE BATTLE PLAN

In the medium to long term, all nations, businesses, councils and government departments, professions and individuals will need to draw up what amounts to a survival strategy and plan of action, and stick to it. The smarter end of the markets have already planned well ahead, in their well-informed Business Continuity Planning Departments,[8] moving to medium-sized cities, away from cities such as London with its problems of flood potential, excessive housing costs, poor infrastructure and large number of 'target' buildings. They have a detailed grasp of 'the big picture', and you will find a lot of 'smart money' already in Reading, Cambridge, Manchester, Wales, and areas where their operations are less vulnerable to climate change, and terrorism, and there is a perceived higher quality of life for many workers and their families.

At a macro-scale it is possible to see how political issues, such as those of land use planning and reform, property, human and employment rights, privatization policies for service industries, will have to be carefully scrutinized and reformed where necessary, as will the balance of power within different political systems, to avoid the problem, currently all too obvious, where small and self-interested minorities can have undue influence in the decision-making processes.

National and regional continuity planning, by governments and councils alike, must take into account that it is not just the hazard that is important, but exposure and vulnerability. If you put a house in the middle of a motorway, you must expect your children to be run over. If you put a house in a floodplain, you must expect it to be flooded. If you put a house on an old rubbish tip, you must expect it to subside. Buildings should not be placed next door to hazardous chemical plants or oil refineries, or downstream of dams or reservoir embankments, or on coastal mud flats known to flood.

Society may not be able to do much to change the hazard, but much can and must be done to reduce our vulnerability, and to some extent exposure, to it. Why are the overdue improvements to our building stock so sadly lacking despite the obvious benefits of early investment in the matter of future-proofing our buildings against climate change, an issue that may amount to no more or less than life and death for many, particularly the most vulnerable in our society?[9]

This defining fight against climate change in the 21st century is not about solving our problems by putting more and more machines into buildings, it is, to a large extent, about reducing the dependence of buildings on machines in buildings, and where there is a need, of finding minimum-impact machines to meet the basic needs of those in the buildings.[10]

For buildings, the 19th century was the age of the great architect, the 20th century that of the great engineer, and the 21st century will be the age of the resilient building designer, one who combines the skills of the building physicist, architect, engineer, urban designer and community planner. Perhaps, it will rather be the age of designs done by cooperatives of high dependability building consortia, in whom we all can trust, and who are capable of new thinking and producing the new solutions we urgently need now to survive.

IS IT TOO LATE?

Rapa Nui, or Easter Island, is a small (166 km^2), inaccessible island in the Pacific Ocean, 2000 miles from the nearest centre of population on Tahiti, where the islanders outgrew their resources and ended up destroying themselves. The available land for agriculture was no longer sufficient to feed the growing population, the islanders cut down all the trees on the island for fuel and to build their great *moais,* or totem statues, and without the means to build canoes and leave the island, they eventually resorted to war and cannibalism. Many theorists see what happened on Easter Island as a warning to us all.[11] They call it the Rapa Nui Syndrome, and ask whether it is possible that our society is going the same way. When we look at the building industry today such fears may be well founded. Only time will tell.

The good news is that it is not too late. We still have a generation to adapt our lifestyles to survive the rapid changes occurring around us resulting from climate change, and to radically reduce the damage done by those lifestyles driving climate change. There are many positive signs: it looks increasingly as if Russia will ratify the Kyoto Agreement; people are taking very seriously the need for Contraction and Convergence of carbon dioxide emissions; building regulations are tightening and people are being put back into the heart of the design process; major players such as the insurance and energy industries are now understanding the need to act fast to avoid the catastrophic changing of circumstances around us; new technologies are emerging that offer great hope for the future, particularly in the fields of renewable energy and fuels; governments are now gearing up to address the global scale of the war being waged around us, and the days of global excess are numbered as we face up to the fact that in the very nature of our own species lie the problems and their solution. But urgent action is necessary *now,* for what is at stake is

15.5.
A great Moais, on Rapa Nui Island, a totem to the potential for a society to exceed the carrying capacity of its land. (*Source:* Cliff Wassman)

not the hubris of a long lost culture or king but the very survival of all the species on this small, green planet, Earth.

> In Egypt's sandy silence, all alone,
> Stands a gigantic Leg, which far off throws
> The only shadow that the desert knows.
> 'I am great Ozymandias' saith the stone,
> 'The King of Kings this mighty city shows
> The wonders of my hand.' The city's gone,
> Nought but the leg remaining to disclose
> The site of that forgotten Babylon.
>
> We wonder, and some hunter may express
> Wonder like ours, when through that wilderness
> Where London stood, holding the wolf in chase
> He meets some fragment huge, and stops to guess
> What wonderful, but unrecorded, race
> Once dwelt in that annihilated place.
> 'Ozymandias' Horace Smith (1779–1849)

NOTES AND REFERENCES

1 Look at the differences between the American and British versions of Brand, S. (1997) *How Buildings Learn*. London and New York: Weidenfeld & Nicolson.

2 For a fuller text with reference on both the issues of infrastructure and scenario planning see the companion website http://books.elsevier.com/companions/0750659114.

3   Roaf, S., Fuentes, M. and Thomas, S. (2003) *Ecohouse 2: A Design Guide*. Oxford: Architectural Press.

4   Roaf, S., Horsley, A. and Gupta, R. (2004) *Closing the Loop: Benchmarks for Sustainable Buildings*. London: RIBA Publications.

5   The Insurance Industry is now entering a phase where it will no longer insure high-risk buildings. In the long run, the price of insurance should reflect the degree of risk. If the industry does not successfully manage such risks there will be social and political pressures and the ultimate threat of nationalization. For further discussion of these issues see our companion website http://books.elsevier.com/companions/0750659114 and the following websites: ww.aag.org/HDGC/www/hazards/supporting/supmat2–4.doc and http://www.munichre.com. And see: Dlugolecki, A. (ed.), Agnew, M., Cooper, M., Crichton, D., Kelly, N., Loster, T., Radevsky, R., Salt, J., Viner, D., Walden, J. and Walker, T. (2001) *Climate Change and Insurance*. Chartered Insurance Institute Research Report, London, 2001 (available on www.cii.co.uk).

6   See the section on infrastructure on the companion website http://books.elsevier.com/companions/0750659114.

7   Klinenberg, E. (2002) *Heat Wave: A Social Autopsy of Disaster in Chicago*. Chicago: The University of Chicago Press.

8   http://www.corenetglobal.org/pdf/learning/9_11_impact.pdf. See also the business continuity section PAS 56 on www.thebci.org.

9   John Kennedy, of the Churches Together in Britain, points out that the cost of ecologizing new build houses in the UK is soon lost in general inflation. Think back to the first house that was completed under New Labour – say to mid-1998. The cost of ecologizng such a new-build house would have been around £3000. It would have been likely to expect that house to have appreciated by some 50% in 5 years, thus losing that initial £3000. The cost of more stringent building regulations would simply have been eclipsed by house-price inflation. In fact, the average house price cost has increased by 80–100% over that time.

10 Meir, I. and Roaf, S. (2003) Between Scylla and Charibdis: In search for the sustainable design paradigm between vernacular and hi-tech. *Proceedings of the PLEA Conference*, Santiago, Chile, November (with apologies to Professor Bordass).

11 There are many books and websites available on the history of Easter Island and for a short introduction and link see: www.netaxs.com/~trance/linklist.html.

INDEX

Italic page numbers refer to illustrations

" Of course I'm worried about climate change, but what can I do? **"**

If you're worried about energy use and climate change, you're certainly not alone. There are millions of us around the world – and together we can make a powerful difference. We can make the world's governments turn their promises into action. We can campaign for serious investment in wind, wave and solar power. We can persuade the UK Government to reject the dangerous alternative of expanding nuclear power.

Join Friends of the Earth and be part of the solution. All it takes is to pick up the phone or visit our website now.

020 7490 1555
www.foe.co.uk/join

Friends of the Earth

Friends of the Earth inspires solutions to environmental problems, which make life better for people.